Information Sciences Series

Editors

ROBERT M. HAYES
University of California
Los Angeles, California

JOSEPH BECKER
President
Becker and Hayes, Inc.

Consultant

CHARLES P. BOURNE
University of California
Berkeley, California

Joseph Becker and Robert M. Hayes:
INFORMATION STORAGE AND RETRIEVAL

Charles P. Bourne:
METHODS OF INFORMATION HANDLING

Harold Borko:
AUTOMATED LANGUAGE PROCESSING

Russell D. Archibald and Richard L. Villoria:
NETWORK-BASED MANAGEMENT SYSTEMS (PERT/CPM)

Launor F. Carter:
NATIONAL DOCUMENT-HANDLING SYSTEMS FOR SCIENCE AND TECHNOLOGY

Perry E. Rosove:
DEVELOPING COMPUTER-BASED INFORMATION SYSTEMS

F. W. Lancaster:
INFORMATION RETRIEVAL SYSTEMS

Ralph L. Bisco:
DATA BASES, COMPUTERS, AND THE SOCIAL SCIENCES

Charles T. Meadow:
MAN-MACHINE COMMUNICATION

Gerald Jahoda:
INFORMATION STORAGE AND RETRIEVAL SYSTEMS FOR INDIVIDUAL RESEARCHERS

Information Sciences Series

Allen Kent:
INFORMATION ANALYSIS AND RETRIEVAL

Robert S. Taylor:
THE MAKING OF A LIBRARY

Herman M. Weisman:
INFORMATION SYSTEMS, SERVICES, AND CENTERS

Jesse H. Shera:
THE FOUNDATIONS OF EDUCATION FOR LIBRARIANSHIP

Charles T. Meadow:
THE ANALYSIS OF INFORMATION SYSTEMS, Second Edition

Stanley J. Swithart and Beryl F. Hefley:
COMPUTER SYSTEMS IN THE LIBRARY

F. W. Lancaster and E. G. Fayen:
INFORMATION RETRIEVAL ON-LINE

Richard A. Kaimann:
STRUCTURED INFORMATION FILES

Thelma Freides:
LITERATURE AND BIBLIOGRAPHY OF THE SOCIAL SCIENCES

Manfred Kochen:
PRINCIPLES OF INFORMATION RETRIEVAL

Dagobert Soergel:
INDEXING LANGUAGES AND THESAURI: CONSTRUCTION AND MAINTENANCE

Robert M. Hayes and Joseph Becker:
HANDBOOK OF DATA PROCESSING FOR LIBRARIES, Second Edition

Information Retrieval and Processing

Lauren B. Doyle

Consultant,
Becker & Hayes, Inc.

A WILEY-BECKER & HAYES SERIES BOOK

MELVILLE PUBLISHING COMPANY
Los Angeles, California

Copyright © 1975, by John Wiley & Sons, Inc.

Published by Melville Publishing Company,
a Division of John Wiley & Sons, Inc.

All rights reserved. Published simultaneously in Canada.
No part of this book may be reproduced by any means,
nor transmitted, nor translated into a machine language
without the written permission of the publisher.

Library of Congress Cataloging in Publication Data:

Doyle, Lauren B   1926–
  Information retrieval and processing.

  (Information sciences series)
  An up-to-date version of Information storage and retrieval by J. Becker and R. M. Hayes.
  "A Wiley-Becker & Hayes series book."
  Includes bibliographies and indexes.
  1. Information storage and retrieval systems. 2. Electronic data processing. 3. Information science. I. Becker, Joseph. Information storage and retrieval. II. Title.

Z699.D67   1975   029.7   75-1179
ISBN 0-471-22151-1

Printed in the United States of America

10 9 8 7 6 5 4 3 2 1

Information Sciences Series

Information is the essential ingredient in decision making. The need for improved information systems in recent years has been made critical by the steady growth in size and complexity of organizations and data.

This series is designed to include books that are concerned with various aspects of communicating, utilizing, and storing digital and graphic information. It will embrace a broad spectrum of topics, such as information system theory and design, man-machine relationships, language data processing, artificial intelligence, mechanization of library processes, nonnumerical applications of digital computers, storage and retrieval, automatic publishing, command and control, information display, and so on.

Information science may someday be a profession in its own right. The aim of this series is to bring together the interdisciplinary core of knowledge that is apt to form its foundation. Through this consolidation, it is expected that the series will grow to become the focal point for professional education in this field.

Preface

It was in 1959 that Joseph Becker compared the data gathered during his travels to various U.S. centers of documentation activity with the syllabus of a course then being taught at the University of California by Robert M. Hayes. The evident mutual interest was so great that it led to an agreement and the development of the manuscript for the book, INFORMATION STORAGE AND RETRIEVAL: TOOLS, ELEMENTS, THEORIES. Published in 1963, this book was the first to interrelate broadly the expanding new technologies of the late 1950s (including computers and microfilm) with systems for storing and retrieving documented information. Because of its broad coverage of this realm it has become a classic and the cornerstone of the resulting Wiley series on the Information Sciences.

Since 1963 the information landscape surveyed by Becker and Hayes has taken on completely new appearances, as well as a new significance in civilized society. Computers have become faster, more economical, more powerful, and more numerous by many orders of magnitude. Entirely new information technologies have been developed. The revolution of time-shared computers, interconnected by telecommunications, has taken place—with the most profound ramifications for the information retrieval art. The field that was once known as "documentation" has broadened its scope and is now thought of as a domain of "information science."

Several years ago when Becker and Hayes contemplated updating their book, they realized how hopeless "revision," in the traditional sense of the word, would be. Major sections of the book would have to be rewritten from the ground up. New chapters would have to be introduced (such as the one describing the subdiscipline "evaluation of information retrieval systems," a barely nascent activity at the time the 1963 book was being written). In short, a totally new book was required. Unfortunately, both Becker and Hayes were committed to an extent that would prevent their carrying forward the time-consuming activity needed to produce such a book. It is within this context that I volunteered to prepare an up-to-date version, based on the original book and borrowing from it whatever text material continued to be valid, but researching and rewriting across the broad spectrum encompassed by the contents of the original book as necessary.

During the period of manuscript preparation, Joe Becker and Bob Hayes have made themselves available as technical consultants, and also have participated in most major decisions about the new book. In that sense, this book is theirs as well as mine. One of our joint decisions was to change the title to INFORMATION RETRIEVAL AND PROCESSING, which reflects what the present book covers, as well as suggests what has happened in the last decade to the subject area covered by the original book. Thus, though the "storage" aspect has changed much between 1963 and now, the real dynamism has been in relation to the man–machine interface of information retrieval systems, in other words, the processes of input/output. The term "processing" not only nicely subsumes the important input-storage-output triad, it also alludes to necessary computer-programmed operations that are not directly connected with retrieval, and to numerous other essential noncomputer technologies such as reprography and communications.

Another major decision in which the three of us concurred was the omission of the theoretical part of the 1963 book. The mathematical treatment of information retrieval provided by Manfred Kochen's recent PRINCIPLES OF INFORMATION RETRIEVAL suffices well, in this regard, for the Wiley Information Sciences Series.

The present book embodies a change in structure and focus to reflect the fact that the reader of today's book is much more likely to be an interested college student with a great awareness of the current information revolution than was the case ten years ago. Thus, hardware, materials, and processes used in connection with information systems are discussed first, in Chapters Two through Four. The subject of information retrieval *per se* begins with Chapters Five and Six, which have to do with librarianship and documentation. Because of their somewhat historical slant, these chapters (along with Seven) are the only ones taken from the 1963 book which adhere to their original character. Chapter Seven presents a simplified concept of an information system and its components, and paves the way for discussion of computerized retrieval in the chapters to follow, especially for data retrieval in Chapter Eight and document retrieval in Chapter Nine. Chapters Ten through Twelve, on language processing, evaluation, and user studies, describe important facets of the information retrieval field that have developed strongly since 1963.

Numerous colleagues have been of generous assistance as sources of information and critical enlightenment. I wish to acknowledge the help of Katherine Block, Steve Silver, Vladimir Almendinger, Jim Paris, and Marion Rice. Two of my former associates at System Development

Corporation, Charles Kellogg and Donald V. Black, have assisted me on numerous occasions, as has Harold Borko of UCLA. As always, the preparation of a book means a monumental typing job, and in this connection I wish to thank Antoinette Ziegler, Carole Bailey, and Nancy Culver.

LAUREN B. DOYLE
Santa Monica, California

Table of Contents

Chapter One

The Expanding Information Environment   1

    Doubling Times: A Snapshot of Information Flux
Growth and Information Finding   5
    The Information Center Phenomenon
    Some Social Effects of Information Growth
The Changing Technology of Information   12

Chapter Two

Information Processing—Publishing and Reprography   16

Primary Publishing   17
    Letterpress
    Offset
    Photocomposition
Reprography and Micrographics   27
    Duplication Processes
    Micrographics
    Roll Microfilm
    Microfiche
    Ultramicrofiche
    Updatable Microfiche

Chapter Three

Information Processing—Digital Storage and Transmission   53

Binary Number Coding   53
    The Bit as a Measure of Information

xii   Contents

    Input to Digital Storage   59
        Keyboard Input
        Key-to-Tape and Key-to-Disk Input
        Cassettes, Cartridges, and Floppy Disks
        Re-Entry Records
        Optical Character Recognition
        Online Input
        Keyboard/Display Terminals
        "Smart" and "Intelligent" Terminals

    Digital Storage   89
        Magnetic Recording
        Magnetic Drums
        Magnetic Tape
        Magnetic Disks
        Magnetic Strips
        Laser Memories

    Output from Digital Storage   103
        Printers
        Enter CRT

    Data Communications   109
        Channels of Communication
        Communication Systems
        Facsimile Transmission

Chapter Four

Concepts of Programming and the Nature of Digital Computers   116

    Concepts of Programming   117
        The Use of Storage in Computer Programming
        High-Level Languages

    Physical Nature of the Computer   132
        Patterns of Computer Use

Chapter Five

The Librarian and Recorded Knowledge   142

    History of Recording Media   142
    History of the Library Profession   144

Library Functions	146
Library Tools	149
The Problem Areas	162
Specialization in Libraries and Information Services	164
Library Automation	166
Subsystems for which Automation is Being Contemplated	

Chapter Six

To Meet the Information Crisis: New Methods of Indexing and Subject Analysis — 170

Coordination of Subjects	173
Efficient Mechanized Coding	177
Formalized Abstracts	179
Analysis of Subject Relationships	184

Chapter Seven

The Information Framework — 189

Chapter Eight

Information Retrieval Systems—Data — 196

Information Structure—Utilization and Consequences	197
Complexity and Data Structure	
Storage Programming	207
Sequential Organization	
Indexed Sequential	
Direct Access	
List Structure	
Organization of Data by Linkages	
Data Management Systems and Languages	219
Data Management Packages—Some Examples	
Evolution of Languages	

xiv   Contents

Chapter Nine

Information Retrieval Systems—Documents   238

Systems for Processing Documented Information—General Characteristics   239
- *Acquisition*
- *Initial Processing*
- *Cataloging/Analysis*
- *Immediate Distribution*
- *Storage/Preservation*

The Last Twenty Years in Information Retrieval   261
- *Use of General Purpose Computers*
- *Use of Special Purpose Devices*
- *Use of Word Cooccurrence in Searching*
- *Online Retrieval Systems and Iterative Searching*

Chapter Ten

The Processing of Language Data   285

Language and Computers

Processing by Simple Matching   290
- *Automatic Indexing*
- *Word Frequency Methods in Automatic Indexing and Abstracting*

Processing by Structural Analysis of Sentences   316
- *Syntactic Analysis*
- *Syntax as an Aid to Noncognitive Question-Answering Systems*

Processing by Means of Semantic or Conceptual Schemes   324

Chapter Eleven

Evaluation of Information Retrieval Systems   334

Evaluation Parameters   337

Some Landmarks in the Evaluation Era   339

Relevance and Other Issues   350
- *Relevance*

> *Precision*
> *Recall*

Evaluation of Components 359
> *Interindexer Consistency*
> *Use of Surrogates in Determining Relevance*
> *Evaluation of Extracts*
> *Other Directions*

The Value of Information 366
> *The Resurgent Interest in Cost*
> *An Old/New Approach to Evaluation*

Chapter Twelve

The User of Information 375

Scientific and Technical Information Use 376

Methods of Conducting User Studies 377
> *Diaries*
> *Questionnaires*
> *Interviews*
> *Direct Observation*
> *Analysis of Existing Data*

Relating Typical Users to "Ideal" Informations Systems 380
> *Impediments of Time and Space Minimized*
> *Finding and Summarizing Aids Provided*
> *Responsivity to Individual Preferences*

The User and Existing New Information Systems 385

The Scientist-User as an Information Processor 386
> *The Invisible College*
> *Modeling the Scientist*

Overview of the User 392

Index 395

Chapter One

The Expanding Information Environment

"Environment" is commonly thought of in terms of physical or social surroundings. But there is another kind of environment that engulfs us almost as totally as the material world: We live in an environment of symbols. Civilized people are immersed in a sea of words, numbers, diagrams, pictures, musical sounds, and other meaningful codes, in transient and recorded forms. Symbolic information is everywhere—in homes, offices, schools, and shops; one cannot escape it and still be a part of modern life.

Information is recorded, is stored, and after a time accumulates. Any large-scale sustained endeavor is likely to have associated with it a growing collection of paper. There are hospitals having stores of records more voluminous than their total storage of medicine. Some city police departments in the world operate without firearms—but none operates without files. The law itself is a mass of paper, and in lawyers' offices the books are likely to cost more—and occasionally even weigh more—than the furniture.

Much information is essentially current; it is brought into being to serve definite, imminent purposes. A great deal of it, however, is of temporary value—discussions, telephone calls, memoranda, etc.—and no trouble is taken to preserve it. Information is ordinarily recorded and stored only when it is judged to have continuing potential importance. As time goes on, of course, the potential importance of an item of information is likely to decline; nevertheless, it will often be kept for whatever possible worth it may have. Even an item having little or no value may be easier to retain than to throw out. Thus, stores of information are generated and grow, and at maturity contain items of all shades of importance. But the distribution tends to be heavily skewed toward the accumulated and less important items.

The king-sized example of the growth of an information store is the Library of Congress, which doubles in size every 15 years. In 1970, it possessed more than 61 million items, including 15 million books and pamphlets, 30 million manuscripts, over 1 million Braille books, 750 thousand microfilm reels, and millions more items in various media (Bowker, 1971). One would think that the justification for such mammoth collections would be that every item has a purpose, but experience suggests otherwise. In Moscow's huge Lenin Library, half of the books have never been requested, even by a single reader (Bershadskii, 1962). The New York Public Library contains 3½ million books classified as "brittle," and the pages of many of these have decayed to the point that they are unusable (Micrographics, 1970).

All this is perhaps a necessary negative consequence of the nature of information, and is the price we pay for having as many units of information as possible in a state of availability and readiness for use. After all, who can say what book or document, even the most archaic or obscure, might not turn out to have decisive importance for some one information seeker? More than that, as Olney (1963) observes: ". . . The history of cataloging suggests that intellectual pre-eminence among nations goes hand in hand with possession of the largest and best indexed collections of written material. . . ."

Doubling Times: A Snapshot of Information Flux. The study of information retrieval might be satisfyingly straightforward if only the world of information would remain static. But expansion and change rule the scene, not only in relation to the many problems of dealing with large amounts of information, but in relation to the technically and economically available solutions to these problems. The expansion is also chaotic, varying strongly from one information medium to another, from one sphere of activity to another, and from one time to another. As one highly relevant example of the extent of the changes in the landscape, a book like the present one cannot be merely revised after the passing of a few years; it must be almost completely rewritten. This very consideration makes it advisable for us to begin the book with a fairly vivid discussion of the growth patterns of information. Then the reader is in a position to extrapolate, from whatever he reads in the chapters to follow, toward some sensible view of the world of information that may apply one, two, or three years from now.

Figure 1.1 illustrates some major facets of the information explosion in terms of *doubling time*, the period of time it will take a given information parameter to double in amount or in rate. Not all the doubling times presented pertain to information. Some are included because they are generally familiar, and create perspective in relation to some of the not-so-familiar information parameters. It is notable that world population growth, so worrisome to many contemporary thinkers, is at the slow extreme of the doubling-time scale. Thus, almost every significant information growth parameter, in the United States and the rest of the world, is greater by one or more orders of magnitude than the world's rate of population increase. Where this is not so, as in the case of the world output of books since the fifteenth century, it is usually for growth rates that have been measured over a long span of time—decades or centuries. Most growth rates increase steeply the closer one comes to the present. Martin and Norman (1970) point out that: ". . . The sum total of human knowledge changed very slowly prior to the relatively recent beginnings of scientific thought. It has been estimated that by 1800 it was doubling every fifty years; by 1950, doubling every ten years; and that presently it is doubling every five years. . . ." Such changes necessarily apply to rates of production of new information as well as to the total accumulation. Brown (1971) states: ". . . It has been estimated despite the absence of reliable data that the doubling time of . . . the rate of scientific publication from 1800 to 1966 has been reduced from one hundred years to fifty, ten, and six years. . . ."

Several binary comparisons are shown in Figure 1.1, indicated by vertical arrows relating pairs of dashed lines. One, for new book titles in the United States, depicts a sevenfold change in doubling time from the first half of the century to the second. It is interesting to note that most of the speedup in new titles took place during the age of television.

Not all doubling times become shorter toward the present. Some growth rates are intrinsically subject to saturation. Television ownership maintained its less-than-a-year doubling time for only a few years. By now, almost all U.S. homes have television (98.7 percent in 1971), and the rate of increase in ownership is more or less proportional to the nation's population growth. This could change. For example, the growth curve for radio ownership (not shown) did not saturate entirely, because of the increase in two-, three-, and four-radio families after the introduction of cheap, transistorized receivers.

The most arresting feature of Figure 1.1 is that a number of the most rapidly increasing parameters are associated with potential solutions to problems in coping with information. The two doubling times bracketing the one-year mark pertain to computer capacity. Unlike the television

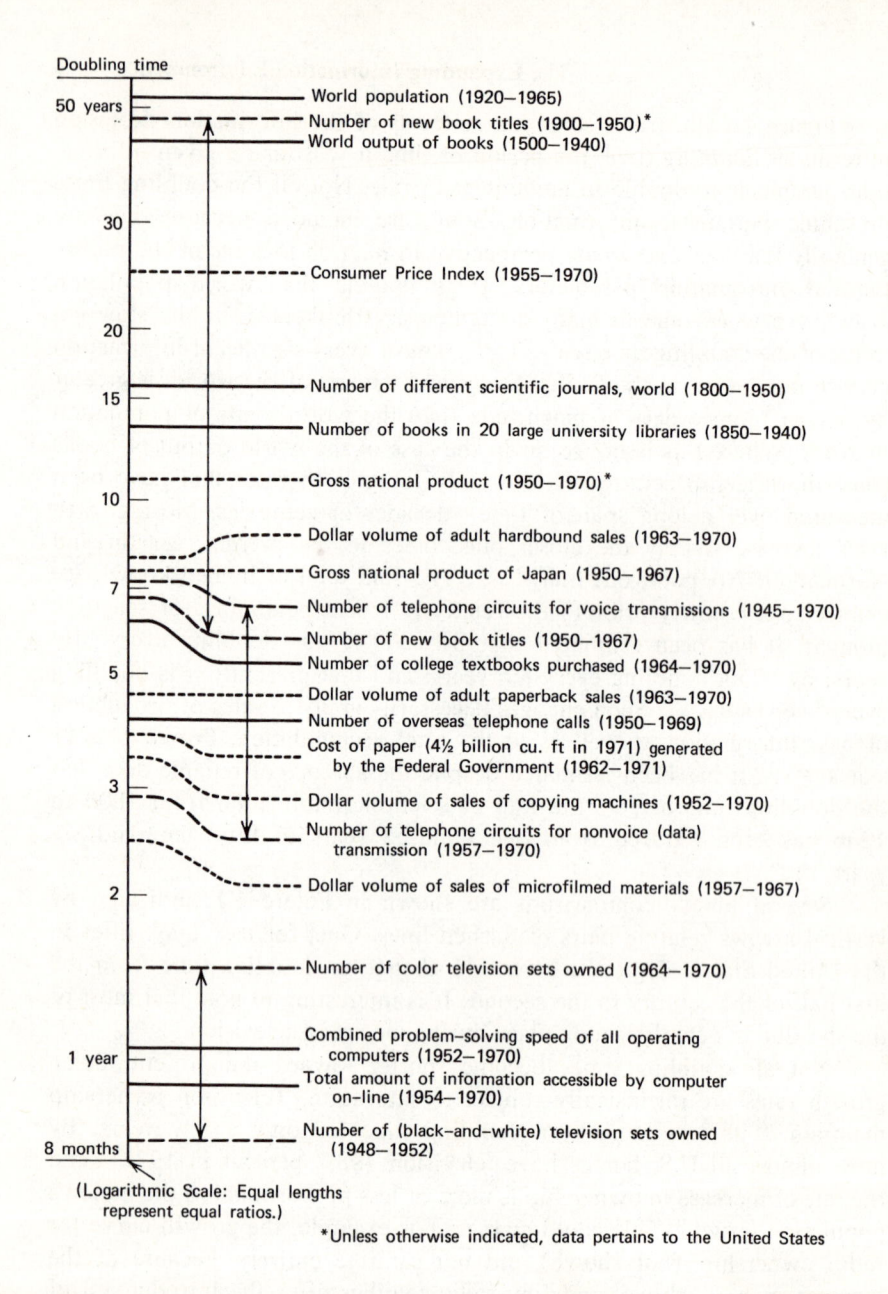

```
Doubling time
50 years  ─── World population (1920–1965)
          ─ ─ Number of new book titles (1900–1950)*
          ─── World output of books (1500–1940)

30

          ─ ─ ─ Consumer Price Index (1955–1970)
20

15        ─── Number of different scientific journals, world (1800–1950)
          ─── Number of books in 20 large university libraries (1850–1940)

10        ─ · ─ Gross national product (1950–1970)*
          ─ ─ Dollar volume of adult hardbound sales (1963–1970)
          ─── Gross national product of Japan (1950–1967)
 7        ─── Number of telephone circuits for voice transmissions (1945–1970)
          ─── Number of new book titles (1950–1967)
 5        ─── Number of college textbooks purchased (1964–1970)
          ─ ─ Dollar volume of adult paperback sales (1963–1970)
          ─── Number of overseas telephone calls (1950–1969)
          ─ · ─ Cost of paper (4½ billion cu. ft in 1971) generated
                by the Federal Government (1962–1971)
 3        ─ · ─ Dollar volume of sales of copying machines (1952–1970)
          ─ ─ Number of telephone circuits for nonvoice (data)
                transmission (1957–1970)
          ─ · ─ Dollar volume of sales of microfilmed materials (1957–1967)
 2

          ─ ─ Number of color television sets owned (1964–1970)
              Combined problem-solving speed of all operating
 1 year       computers (1952–1970)
              Total amount of information accessible by computer
              on-line (1954–1970)
          ─ ─ Number of (black-and-white) television sets owned
 8 months     (1948–1952)
```

(Logarithmic Scale: Equal lengths represent equal ratios.)

*Unless otherwise indicated, data pertains to the United States

Figure 1.1 Doubling times of some growth parameters. Horizontal lines are differentiated to aid comparison. Dotted lines pertain to cost or dollar parameters. Dashed lines pertain to pairs of parameters that are linked, for comparison purposes, by vertical arrows. Most of the data on this page are from four sources: 1.) The 1971 Statistical Abstract of the United States; 2.) The Bowker Annual (1971); 3.) Martin and Norman (1970); 4.) and Bagdikian (1970. (See references at the end of chapter.

growth rates, they manifest little or no hint of the possibility of reaching saturation. Regarding computers, Gruenberger (1970) generalizes that: "... Just about everything about computing that can be quantified changes by a factor of two every three to four years, and this rate of change has been maintained now for twenty years. If there is a knee to any of the growth curves, it has not made itself evident. . . ."

The growth curves for television ownership and for nonvoice transmission are reflective of the expanding pressures to transmit large quantities of information at electronic speeds over geographically large distances. Television forced the development of coaxial cable and microwave wideband transmission channels, without which national network broadcasting would be unfeasible. Later, communications satellites brought us into the era of international television. Paralleling all this is the rapid growth of the transmission of computer data over telephone lines. Because of the low capacity and high error rate of telephone lines, and the growing popularity of remote-location computing, it is probably inevitable that computers will soon make use of the same broadband facilities available to television.

If the second-to-fastest doubling time, that for amount of information stored on-line, continues for just a few more years, it will become economically feasible to store library-sized amounts of information in computer-accessible locations. These amounts of information would also be in readiness, via the broadband transmission facilities just mentioned, to be sent anywhere in the world on request. The consequences of this in relation, for example, to the rapid international sharing of scientific and technical information are being actively discussed and investigated (Samuelson, 1971).

GROWTH AND INFORMATION FINDING

Information has a "poverty in the midst of plenty" aspect that arises from its extreme diversity and its high specificity in relation to the tasks or needs of an information user. Such a user, confronted by a store of information, is somewhat like the bearer of a lock in the presence of several million keys—a few of which *almost* fit.

Keepers of large stores of information, since before the Alexandrian Library in the third century BC, have made information user's plight tolerable through organization, usually through some meaningful grouping of topics. As a result, no one ever has to look through several million items in a large library, but can generally confine his searching to a hundred or so. Furthermore, indirect organization—in the form of indexes and catalogs—permits almost immediate pinpointing of any volume whose identity is known. Some information, such as that in business files, can be structured in detail down to the smallest item, and it is for such formatted records that organization best assists information finding. These traditional methods have sufficed throughout most of history, including the first five centuries after the invention of printing.

Unfortunately, the increasing rates in the production of information that have so affected the last several decades are, in case after case, upsetting previously orderly ways of doing things. In 1945, in words that never become stale, no matter how often they are repeated in discussions such as this, Vannevar Bush said:

> ... There is a growing mountain of research. ... The investigator is staggered by the findings and conclusions of thousands of other workers—conclusions which he cannot find time to grasp, much less to remember as they appear. ...
>
> The difficulty seems to be not so much that we publish unduly in view of the extent and variety of present-day interest, but rather that publication has been extended far beyond our present ability to make real use of the record. The summation of human experience is being expanded at a prodigious rate and the means we use for threading through the consequent maze to the momentarily important item is the same as was used in the days of square rigged ships. ...

It seems only a short time ago that Bush wrote these words, but in the meantime things have so changed that his words are at least twice as applicable as they first were. A vignette that illustrates one manner in which the information flood has intensified pertains to the K-meson, a subatomic particle that had not yet been discovered at the time of Bush's words, and is told of, appropriately, in Toffler's (1970) *Future Shock*: "... Dr. Emilio Segre, a Nobel Prize winner in physics, declares: 'On K-mesons alone, to wade through all the papers is an impossibility.' ..."

Thus, a branch of physics that was literally nonexistent 25 years ago had, by 1970, swollen to the point that even the leading physicists found they could not keep up with the literature in detail. It is this tendency of rapid growth of new specialties, rather than of any mere uniform multiplication across the whole span of knowledge, that defeats traditional methods of organizing recorded information.

Efforts to impose a hierarchical topical structure (such as one would find in a public library) on new and unpredictably expanding areas of knowledge encounter *at least* two sources of frustration:

1. If a domain of knowledge is growing at a rapid rate, it is overwhelmingly probable that some of the parts of that domain are growing at a vastly greater rate than is the whole body. Therefore, any attempt to

establish a system of equally emphasized subdivisions (i.e., categories, subcategories) will fail, after a time, as a result of the disproportionate growth of some of the subdivisions.

2. Hierarchies tend to have a one-dimensional basis even where—as in the Dewey Decimal System—provisions are made to encode second and third dimensions. In laying out a hierarchy, one hopes to have adjacent subdivisions more closely related than are the separated subdivisions. Unfortunately, the growth of knowledge too often imparts unanticipated close relationships to widely separated subdivisions, and the original logical basis for the hierarchy is eroded. (Later on, especially in Chapter Five on Librarianship and Chapter Six on Documentation, details will be given on such problems and on historical attempts to meet them.)

The Information Center Phenomenon. The areas of greatest chaos in the growth of knowledge have been in science and technology since the 1940s as a result of large investments in research and development by a number of advanced nations. Of course, the advantages that should have come from having an abundance of scientific and technical information were (and still are) seriously compromised by the inadequacy of facilities for handling, disseminating and retrieving the documented knowledge gained through these investments. In the United States, according to Price (1963), roughly one-tenth of the total research and development budget is wasted on unsuspected duplication of effort.

Partial solutions to the problem of growth of scientific and technical literature have come through *information centers*, and a more recently designated variant, *information analysis centers*. Kertesz (1968) speaks of the general concept of information centers as follows:

> Information centers are formally organized groups of technical men for handling technical information in great depth, in a narrow, well-defined field, and in a timely and efficient manner, primarily for their peers. This definition emphasizes timeliness, thus eliminating monographs which usually take several years to prepare....
>
> The novel feature of the concept lies in the formalized structure. The people involved in this activity are experts in their field; in many cases they established their own reputation by their own research. Quite often, the information activity is carried out on a part-time basis to ensure that the staff retains its technical competence....

The distinction between information centers and information analysis centers arose when it was realized that the centers appeared to be evolving along two major paths:

   1. Some centers put emphasis on document-handling activities, or, at least, document-oriented activities, including such functions as

abstracting, indexing, announcing, etc. They were often large institutions serving major branches of government, such as the Atomic Energy Commission or the National Aeronautics and Space Administration. They appeared to veer away from the characteristics (defined above) of high dependence on participation of experts in the field, becoming, in effect, current awareness factories. The term information center became restricted to such organizations.

2. Other centers evolved more strongly toward involvement of professional experts, and were often more interested in the processing of raw informtaion, rather than documents. Simpson (1962) defined this kind of center (which has come to be called an information analysis center) as: ". . . an organization which exists for the primary purpose of preparing authoritative, timely, and specialized reports of the evaluative and analytic, monographic, or state-of-the-art type. It is an organization staffed in part with scientists and engineers and, to provide a basis for its primary function, it conducts a selective data and information acquisition and processing program. . . ." Examples of information analysis centers are the National Oceanographic Data Center, the National Clearinghouse for Mental Health Information, and the Defense Metals and Ceramics Information Center at Battelle Memorial Institute.

Figure 1.2 indicates the diversity of scientific, technical, and other fields having information analysis centers in the United States. Many of these are supported by federal or state governments, and the number of such centers has increased from a dozen in the nineteenth century to the three hundred supported by the federal government alone in recent years (Carter, 1967).

What we are seeing in information centers—and even more in information analysis centers—is a flight away from organization in the classificatory sense toward another mechanism for making information available: synthesis and condensation. Abstracts, bibliographies, annual reviews, state-of-the-art reports, and other such condensed summarizations serve the same weeding-out and narrowing-down functions for the new and expanding fields as do classification and subject cataloging for the older, relatively stable fields, and for knowledge in general. The methodology of the information center avoids the intractable structure-of-knowledge problem by enlisting specialists in a field to construct ad hoc groupings of references. In monographs, review chapters, and state-of-the-art reports, the outline of the specialist-author's discussion serves as a momentary (and presumably appropriate to the times) basis of organization of the topic.

PHYSICISTS
GEOPHYSICISTS
METALLURGISTS
SCIENTISTS
COMPUTER PROGRAMMERS
INFORMATION SPECIALISTS
TECHNICAL WRITERS
DOCUMENTALISTS
NUCLEAR PHYSICISTS
MATHEMATICIANS
MACHINING CONSULTANTS
SYSTEMS ANALYSTS
CHEMISTS
BIOLOGISTS
ENGINEERS; ELECTRICAL, CIVIL, MECHANICAL, CHEMICAL, NUCLEAR, INDUSTRIAL
DENTISTS
LIBRARY SCIENTISTS
MEDICAL PRACTITIONERS
MANAGEMENT SPECIALISTS
REFERENCE LIBRARIANS
BIBLIOGRAPHERS
TECHNICAL CONSULTANTS
CYTOLOGISTS
ONCOLOGISTS
ENDOCRINOLOGISTS
CLINICIANS
COMMUNICATION SPECIALISTS
PHOTOGRAPHERS
DRAFTSMEN
METEOROLOGISTS
SOCIAL WORKERS
OCEANOGRAPHERS
TOXICOLOGISTS
PHARMACISTS
HYDROLOGISTS
EPIDEMIOLOGISTS
VETERINARIANS

BIOCHEMISTS
PATHOLOGISTS
DEMOGRAPHERS
STATISTICIANS
ECONOMISTS
ADMINISTRATION SPECIALISTS
ENTOMOLOGISTS
HEMATOLOGISTS
CARTOGRAPHIC TECHNICIANS
GEODESISTS
EDITORS
SCIENCE EDUCATION SPECIALISTS
ACQUISITIONS SPECIALISTS
LANGUAGE SPECIALISTS
DOCUMENT ANALYSTS
RESEARCH ASSISTANTS
ABSTRACTORS–INDEXERS
CRYSTALLOGRAPHERS
INTERNATIONAL RELATIONS SPECIALISTS
POLITICAL SCIENTISTS
MILITARY SCIENCE SPECIALISTS
AFRICAN STUDIES SPECIALISTS
MIDDLE EASTERN SPECIALISTS
PSYCHOLOGISTS
HISTORY SPECIALISTS
LATIN AMERICAN SPECIALISTS
READING SPECIALISTS
PHYSICIANS
SURGEONS, PLASTIC
ARCHITECTS
DEMOGRAPHERS
MINERALOGISTS
TEACHERS
PSYCHIATRISTS
LINGUISTS
SOCIOLOGISTS
GEOLOGISTS

Figure 1.2 Fields having information analysis centers. Weisman (1972).

Such specialists are also in a position to deal directly with content rather than merely with documents.

Information centers and information analysis centers are, of course, only two of the most important manifestations of response to accelerating supplies of information. They are given prominence here because they are "hard core" formal responses, at one end of a spectrum running from spontaneous information-seeking strategies by individual users to the carefully planned institutional measures just discussed. It is well recognized, moreover, that the initiatives taken by individual users of information to bypass institutions (information centers, libraries) are an increasingly powerful supplement to those institutions, as a result of the increased efficiency of travel and communications. In the jet age, scientists and other specialists can telephone, visit, and meet together over great distances; more information is exchanged more quickly in this manner than could possibly be dealt with economically by information centers. These user initiatives, in aggregate, are termed "the invisible college" (Allen, 1969), and though the phenomenon has operated for centuries, its significance today appears to increase as rapidly as some of the curves in Figure 1.1.

Some Social Effects of Information Growth. The availability of unprecedented amounts of information, and especially of *new* information, affects not merely our methods of organizing and retrieving it, but often our very way of conducting enterprises involving the use of information.

How we educate people is one example. Predicting what a college graduate will need to know in a given field is no longer as straightforward a matter as it once might have been. Obviously one cannot teach new knowledge before it comes into existence, yet such knowledge will surely come into being, and somehow will have to be assimilated by students who have graduated and left school. More broadly, one cannot know in what way *old* bodies of knowledge will interact in the solution of problems 5 or 10 years hence. Ecological problems, for example, repeatedly cause relatively unrelated subdivisions of knowledge to be brought together. Solution of an air pollution problem might require information in automotive engineering, photochemistry, and meteorology. The study of water pollution by pesticides can interrelate marine biology, agricultural economics, entomology, and chemistry.

Professional obsolescence is one of the unfortunate side effects of education's inability to prepare people for the deluge of new knowledge. It has been a common experience for engineers to find themselves unemployable, displaced by younger people who have had well-timed opportunities to absorb the new knowledge in a rapidly changing field. More often the professional person retains his job but functions with much less effectiveness than he might have, given the new knowledge. The American Medical Association (1966) reports:

. . . Medical knowledge has been growing so rapidly that no practitioner can safely rely on what he learned as a student, or consider his own resources as adequate for optimal patient care. It is now widely agreed that for a physician to remain highly competent his education must not terminate at the end of a formal residency, but must continue as long as he practices. . . .

Despite this opinion, the process of keeping up with new knowledge is likely to be, for most people, an increasingly futile proposition. It is, therefore, probable that educational processes will be restructured, to some degree, along the lines envisaged by Adelson (1972):

. . . The changeability of the environment and the . . . growing mass of knowledge are leading to a shift in emphasis away from attempting to learn what is known in anticipation of its possible later value, toward learning the means of finding out what one has to know when the need arises. . . . The design of an educational process to suit objectives such as these could be very different from what educators are used to. . . .

A corollary to this is that education, particularly at the university level, may increasingly stress acquiring the basic understanding necessary to *assimilate* new facts more than it will stress the facts themselves.

Another example of a social activity strongly affected by information growth is government. Surely in no other area is the need for information so critical as it is in governmental decision making. Also, no other organization has had quite the problem of dealing with huge amounts of information as has the U.S. Government since World War II. Bourne (1963) reported: ". . . the Federal Government produces 25 billion pieces of paper per year and has accumulated enough records to fill 7.5 pentagons, at a total cost of 4,000,000,000 dollars a year. . . ."

The very existence and availability of large amounts of information puts a kind of responsibility on political and governmental leaders that they didn't have in an earlier era. In the nineteenth century, when today's information resources and communication facilities were almost nonexistent, diplomats in isolated outposts often had to deal with border crises personally and on their own authority. Timely reference of the problem to their national governments was often impossible. Wheeler (1972) makes this point, and adds:

. . . All this changed when information became copious and instantaneous. Every crisis, no matter how small and no matter how remote, was referred immediately to the highest executive echelon for resolution. No one at any lower level had a sufficient quantity or breadth of information. Minor executives were converted into the telemetering components of an automated decision-making process even before the advent of the information machine. . . .

Indeed, a governmental leader today can suffer political loss if he acts or makes decisions without recourse to information known to be available to him. Accordingly, governmental executives (and in particular, the President of the United States) are obliged to employ large staffs whose major purpose is to gather and filter the information that is needed to make top-level decisions. Legislators, for a variety of reasons, are usually more leanly supplied with highly processed information than are executives, and one former congressional aide (Twohey, 1973) attributes the evident decline of the U.S. Congress as a coequal branch of government (vis-à-vis the President) to a poor diet of information. Congressional staffs are limited (either by law or by budget), and most congressmen do not have the manpower to collate, digest, and adequately summarize the large amounts of information obtainable from such sources as lobbyists, constituents, committee witnesses, government bureaus, other congressmen, and so on.

THE CHANGING TECHNOLOGY OF INFORMATION

To complete the overview presented in this chapter (and depicted diagrammatically in Figure 1.1), it is necessary to consider briefly the magnitude of recent developments in information technology, some of which were not heard of 10 years ago. During the last decade, the parameters associated with computer capacity and on-line storage capacity have been doubling every year, and thus the world of information handling is undergoing monumental change. In addition, other impressive technologies (some peripheral to the computer and others relatively unrelated) are making their own large contributions to the changing horizon.

Peripheral instruments such as photoelectric character readers and cathode-ray tubes are now in fairly common use; 10 years ago most of what we see today was either under development or used exclusively in military systems. Although image-handling peripheral units such as these have not yet revolutionized input and output of information to and from computers, in the coming 10 years they are very likely to do so.

Information technologies not directly related to the computer have also progressed rapidly. In Figure 1.1 two of the strongest growth areas are in reprography, specifically in full-size copying and in microfilm. Copying has expanded to the point that reproducing machines throughout the world produce more than a billion copies a day. Microfilm is rapidly being transformed from an archival storage medium to an active publishing/reading medium.

The changing picture of information technology consists not only of the advent of new media and machines, but also of increased use of the old. As Figure 1.1 relates, the use of the ancient medium of books is increasing (and, typically, faster towards the present). Likewise, the mails and the telephone are increasingly used. The number of overseas telephone calls per year has increased tenfold since 1960 (Pierce, 1972).

A very significant element of today's information picture is the increasing number of media choices available to an information system planner. These choices include not only those of individual media such as microfilm or magnetic tape, or of modes of transmission such as cable or microwave, but of many working combinations of these. Certain large corporations now rarely print computer output to yield cubic yards of paper, as they once had to do; they now photograph cathode-ray tubes with microfilm cameras, so that what were once cubic yards of output now become cubic inches. Many books are now published via the following bizarre route: keyboard to magnetic tape to computer to cathode-ray tube to camera to offset printing. This methodology of publishing is almost pure twentieth century; only the camera and the paper are fixtures of earlier times.

Information technology is one sphere of contemporary activity for which declining costs are more characteristic than rising costs. The declining cost of computing is perhaps the most spectacular example; a typical computation which cost \$200,000 to perform on a 1955 digital computer can be done today for one dollar (Bagdikian, 1972). Quite apart from the computer, the general cost of handling data electronically—encoding, storing, and transmitting—is declining. In regard to data transmission by telecommunications, Dittberner (1971) states that costs are likely to drop by a factor of five by 1980.

The ever-decreasing cost of handling information electronically may not seem altogether beneficial, for, in a way, it aggravates the deluge-of-information problems we have been discussing. Thus, not only are there to be larger amounts of information generated and stored in the future, but the ease of access to any part of the world's supply of information should become steadily greater. And so, whatever importance all the various processes of information organization and location (classification, cataloging, indexing, abstracting, outlining, referencing, and so on) may have had in the past, or may have in the present, can be expected to intensify—like nearly everything else connected with information—in the future.

With all the thoughts of this introductory chapter in mind, we may regard this book's purpose as not merely presenting the subject of information retrieval and processing, but also as an invitation to the reader to look upon our information environment and its great problems with a degree of concern commensurate with the idea that information, after all, is our basic resource in solving most of the other problems of this complex civilization.

REFERENCES

ADELSON, MARVIN (1972), Education: At the Crossroads of Decision, *Information Technology: Some Critical Implications for Decision Makers*, The Conference Board, New York, pp. 107–129.

ALLEN, THOMAS J. (1969), Information Needs and Uses, in Cuadra, C. A., ed., *Annual Review of Information Science and Technology*, Vol. 4, Encyclopaedia Britannica, Chicago, pp. 3–29.

AMERICAN MEDICAL ASSOCIATION (1966), *The Graduate Education of Physicians* (Report of the Citizens Commission on Graduate Medical Education, Commissioned by the American Medical Association, Chicago).

BAGDIKIAN, BEN H. (1971), *The Information Machines*, Harper & Row, New York.

BAGDIKIAN, BEN H. (1972), Mass Communications, in Sackman, H., and Borko, H., eds., *Computers and the Problems of Society*, AFIPS Press, Montvale, N.J., pp. 231–261.

BERSHADSKII, R. (1962), *The Scientist Who Knows Everything*, STL Document 9990-6138-KU-000 (translated by Z. Jakubski from the Moscow publication "New World"), Space Technology Laboratories, Redondo Beach, Calif.

BOURNE, CHARLES (1963), *Methods of Information Handling*, John Wiley & Sons, New York.

The Bowker Annual (1971), R. R. Bowker, New York.

BROWN, HARRISON (1971), UNISIST: Growing Interest in a Worldwide Science Information System, *Journal of the American Society for Information Science*, 22:4, pp. 288–289.

BUSH, VANNEVAR (1945), As We May Think, *Atlantic Monthly*, 176:1, pp. 101–108.

CARTER, L. F., et al. (1967), *National Document-Handling Systems for Science and Technology*, John Wiley & Sons, New York.

DITTBERNER, DONALD L. (1971), Telecommunications Costs, in Becker,

Joseph, ed., *Interlibrary Communications and Information Networks*, American Library Association, Chicago, pp. 160–162.

GRUENBERGER, FRED (1970), The Shakedown Decade, *Datamation*, 16:1, pp. 69–72.

KERTESZ, FRANCOIS (1968), The Information Center Concept, in Elias, A. W., ed., *Key Papers in Information Science* (1971), American Society for Information Science, Washington, D.C., pp. 67–86.

MARTIN, JAMES, and NORMAN, ADRIAN R. D. (1970), *The Computerized Society*, Prentice-Hall, Inc., Englewood Cliffs, N.J.

Micrographics News & Views (August 14, 1970), 1:3, p. 5.

OLNEY, JOHN C. (1963), *Library Cataloging and Classification*, System Development Corporation Technical Memo TM-1192, Santa Monica, Calif.

PIERCE, JOHN R. (1972), Communication, *Scientific American*, 227:3, pp. 30–41.

PRICE, D. J. DE SOLLA (1963), *Little Science, Big Science*, Columbia University Press, New York.

SAMUELSON, KJELL (1971), International Information Transfer and Network Communication, in Cuadra, C.A., ed., *Annual Review of Information Science and Technology*, Vol. 6, Encyclopaedia Britannica, Chicago, pp. 277–324.

SIMPSON, G. S., Jr. (1962), Scientific Information Centers in the United States, *American Documentation*, 13:1, pp. 43–57.

TOFFLER, ALVIN (1970). *Future Shock*, Random House, New York.

TWOHEY, JOHN C. (1973), Information Everywhere—But Little of Help to Congress, *Los Angeles Times*, April 22, Part 11, p. 6.

WEISMAN, HERMAN M. (1972), *Information Systems, Services, and Centers*, Wiley-Becker & Hayes, New York.

WHEELER, HARVEY (1972), Artificial Reasoning Machines and Politics, in Sackman, H., and Borko, H., eds., *Computers and the Problems of Society*, AFIPS Press, Montvale, N.J., pp. 231–261.

Chapter Two

Information Processing– Publishing and Reprography

This chapter and the chapter to follow describe such processes as composing, printing, copying, storing, input/output, displaying, and microphotography, which handle information in bulk, in contrast to the more discriminatory kinds of processes, such as indexing, abstracting, and retrieval. Bulk processes operate in relative independence of the content represented by the symbols being processed. These processes, when functioning perfectly, would operate just as successfully on complete gibberish as on the works of Shakespeare.

The very title of this book, *Information Retrieval and Processing*, suggests the foregoing distinction. "Processing" can be thought of as a family of operations, each of which acts uniformly on every item of information presented, and includes the idea of having the items in a place available and in a form available for ultimate use. "Retrieval," also in a broad sense, suggests all processes that are selective in nature; this—the case can be made—would even include the process of reading, for the mind is very selective indeed in extracting information from the printed page.

For more than a century, librarians have made a distinction between the physical book and its information content. Prior to 130 years ago, there was considerable debate about which of these should be the responsibility of librarians, and it appears to have been resolved when Sir Anthony Panizzi, the Librarian of the British Museum, convinced a Royal Commission that librarians should be the keepers of physical books, rather than retrievers of content. Since then, the economic constraints under which libraries so often find themselves have stabilized this point of view, which is that if a book itself cannot be preserved and made accessible, no index or catalog entry to it will be worth much.

And so we begin, in these two chapters, by looking at what we are characterizing as the bulk processing aspects of information handling, and we start with those processes connected with the generation of information in the first place.

PRIMARY PUBLISHING

The two basic bulk processes of publishing are composition and printing. They have both undergone near-revolutionary changes in the last two decades. To understand these changes, we first examine *letterpress*, the mode of typesetting/printing that has been predominant thus far in publishing.

Letterpress. Most books, magazines, journals, and newspapers have been produced through letterpress printing, which prints from ink applied to a raised surface that can consist of type, plates made from type, or engraved illustrations. Anyone who has seen a rotary press in operation knows that pages—many of them per second—are produced by pulling continuous strips of paper over inked metal rollers that contain replications of entire pages of raised type, each page-image having been cast as a hemicylindrical metal surface.

Preceding the printing process is typesetting or, more broadly, composition. Most of the text in books and magazines is set on line-casting machines such as linotypes. In order to grasp better the new relationship between composition and computers, it is well to take a close look at how linotypes work.

The output of a linotype is a slab of typemetal, an alloy of lead (85 percent), tin (10 percent), and antimony (5 percent). (Copper is a constituent in hand-set type, to give durability, but not in the typemetal of line-casting machines.) The thickness of this metal strip varies with the size of the type, and the length is equivalent to a column width; a page or a single column set in type is an assemblage of many such strips, stacked together like slices of bacon. The width of the strip (or "height" when positioned in galleys for printing) is 0.918 inches (Woods, 1963), and must be absolutely constant, so that the raised surface of the type can be flush over a whole page, producing an even, black impression on the paper.

A linotype machine has, among other things, a keyboard and a pot of molten typemetal. When a linotype operator fingers a key, an ingeniously

18 Information Processing—Publishing and Reprography

designed brass wafer called a *matrix*, or *mat*, drops into a holder adjacent to the pot of typemetal. Each mat has the inverse image of a raised type character on the edge facing the pot. (A mat is pictured at the right of the cross section blowup in Figure 2.1.) At the top edge are studs and grooves from which the mat hangs as it is mechanically conducted from place to place on the machine. Each character has a unique set of grooves, which allows the machine to sort the mats automatically for re-use.

When an entire line of mats is assembled, the holder presses the mats firmly against a slot that forms an outlet for the molten metal, which is forced into the slot and solidifies. The antimony in the typemetal alloy causes the metal to expand somewhat on cooling, so that every crevice presented by the row of mats is filled, thus producing sharp images of each character and punctuation mark.

The process of making all lines of type equal in length is known as *justification*, and is achieved by uniformly varying the widths of the spaces between words to compensate for the varying total extent of all the words in a line. The manner of doing this is simple yet clever. When an operator keys a space between words, a thin steel wedge called a *spaceband* falls into place among the mats. When the operator completes as many words

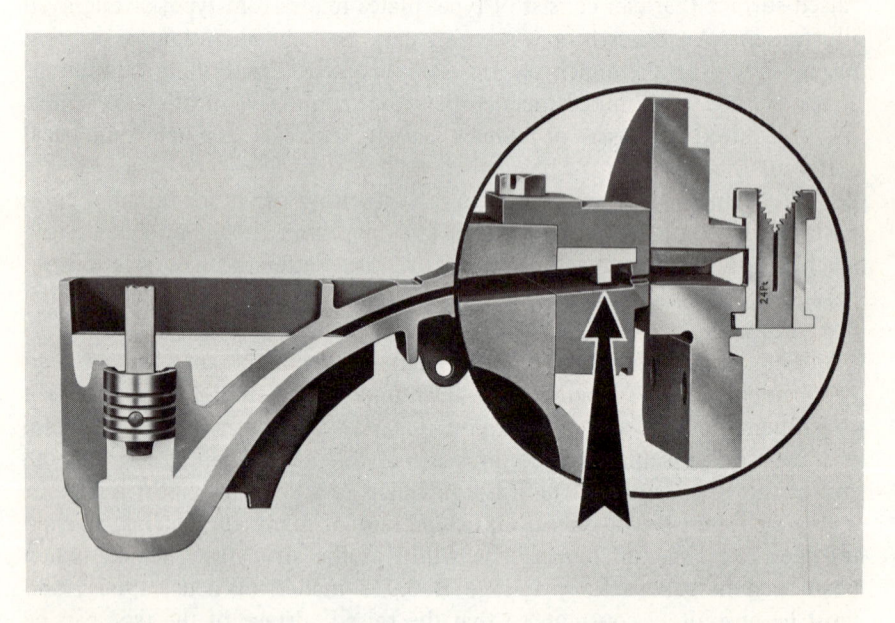

Figure 2.1. Cross section blowup of slug-casting mechanism of line-casting machine. Plunger in pot at left forces molten metal through throat and mouthpiece into mold and against line of brass matrices where metal immediately hardens to form the type slug. (Courtesy Intertype Co.)

as will fit on that line, all of the spacebands are simultaneously pushed into the row of mats, each enlarging its own space in wedge-like fashion. The pushing stops when the row of mats is exactly the length of a standard line (Figure 2.2).

Offset. Line-length justification was one of the first applications of computers in typesetting. It did not arise in connection with letterpress printing, however, but in a newer kind: *offset printing.*

The purpose of the raised surface in letterpress is to enable the printing press to implant ink where it is supposed to go. However, there are chemical as well as mechanical methods of distributing ink on paper. Chemical methods in bulk information processes characteristically have much greater diversity than the mechanical. In reprography, as we learn later, chemical or physicochemical methods (e.g. photography) are used practically to the exclusion of all others. It is therefore not surprising that chemical methods have also had an impact on printing.

Offset printing is the most prevelant such physicochemical process. The theory of offset is based on the mutual antipathy of water and grease and the disposition of greasy substances to adhere to each other. Preliminary steps in the preparation of the plate are taken to ensure that the image will receive greasy ink. Generally a grease-base ribbon is used on typewriters preparing paper plates. When camera negatives are involved, metal and paper plates can have a grease-receptive image burned into them.

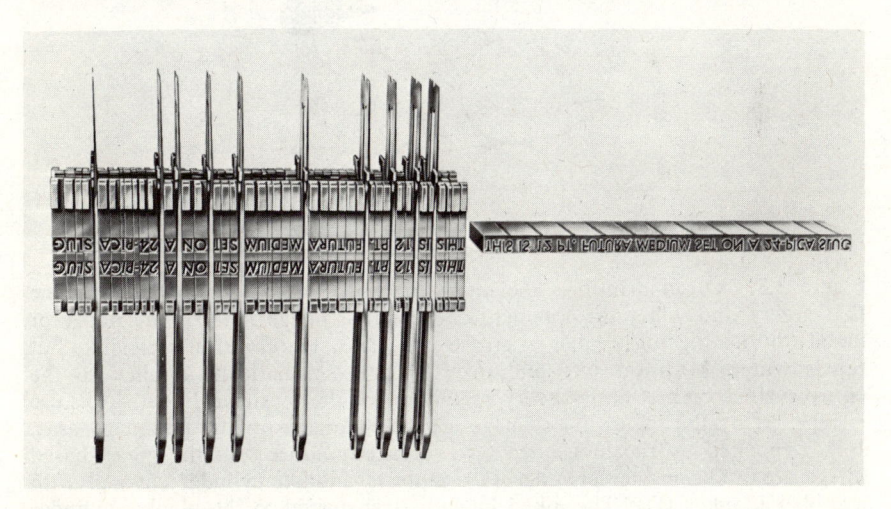

Figure 2.2. Line of brass matrices with spacebands between each word and the type slug (right) which would be cast from the line of mats. (Courtesy Intertype Co.)

20 Information Processing—Publishing and Reprography

In the latter case, the negative is placed over plates which have been treated with a photosensitive, grease-attracting chemical. Arc lights expose the negative; light passing through the transparent areas of the film fixes the grease receptive chemical on the plate. After washing, the plate is left with an image that will repel water and attract oily ink. This plate, whether paper or metal, is flexible and can be wound around a press roller (note roller C in Figure 2.3) to begin the print cycle.

Equipment which implements the printing process is constructed basically with five features: an ink fountain, a water source, a plate cylinder, a cylinder covered with a rubber blanket, and an impression cylinder. These are so synchronized that, as the plate cylinder turns, the plate is first washed with water which aheres to the nonprinting areas only. Then it passes the grease-base ink fountain, where the ink is repelled by the water except in the image area, where it is attracted. As the cylinder revolves further, the inked image is transferred to the rubber blanket, which in turn deposits the impression on paper. The plate never comes in contact with the paper but is offset by the rubber blanket; hence the origin of the name "offset duplication." For each new plate, the rubber blanket must be wiped clean.

The fact that the master is a direct (not mirrored) image of the final

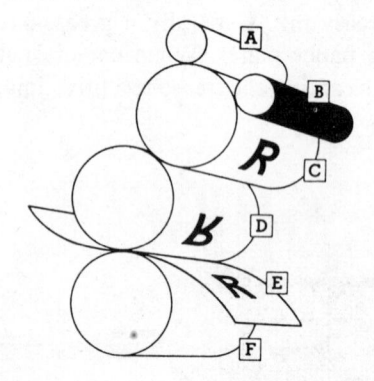

Figure 2.3. Offset printing. The multilith process is based on the principle that grease and water do not mix. The positive image area of the paper or metal duplicating master has a grease base and, therefore, attracts ink, but repels water. Moisture (A) and ink (B) are automatically applied to the entire surface of the master every revolution of the master cylinder. Moisture is repelled by the grease base image area but adheres to the nonimage area. Ink is repelled by the moistened open area but adheres to the grease-based image area. The master cylinder (C) contacts another cylinder covered with a rubber blanket (D). The inked image is transferred to the blanket cylinder in negative or reverse form. The inked image is then "offset" or transferred to a sheet of paper (E) in positive form as it passes between the rubber blanket cylinder (D) and an impression cylinder (F).

copy in offset printing allows the use of a wide range of techniques, from the simplest to rather sophisticated, in composition and offset master preparation. Printing on small presses or duplicating machines is most often done by use of a paper master, usually prepared on a typewriter. It may even be handwritten or drawn. When quality or volume is an important consideration, the offset master is more likely to be made on a metal plate and the printed copies on large presses. The metal plates are made from a negative obtained by photographing the original. This type of printing is frequently referred to as photo-offset.

Photocomposition. As mundane as the process of offset printing may seem, it has been an avenue by which the printing industry is being transfigured. The time-honored technology of hot metal is yielding to a strange new set of composing tools, including punched paper tapes, magnetic tapes, cathode-ray tubes, cameras, and computers. This new technology, in addition to being swift and relatively error-free, seems certain to streamline the publishing cycle (Figure 2.4).

The new technology is termed *photocomposition*, for the camera is usually at the nodal point of any left-to-right flow diagram of the whole process. To the right, following the photographing of a page image, will occur all of the steps of offset printing that we have just described. To the left, preceding the photographic step, are the numerous steps of copy preparation, typesetting, and page makeup, all done with the help of various computer-age instruments.

There are a number of reasons the new technology arose with offset printing rather than with letterpress. The initial reason was the fact that offset printing permits page makeup to be completely independent of the actual printing process, because practically anything can be photographed. One can use a typewriter, a teletype or line printer, a cathode-ray tube, or even letterpress typesetting.

The second factor was the realization, quite gradual, that many things could be done to a page image in computer storage. The very earliest task contemplated was justification, which was found of necessity to entail computerized hyphenation. Kolb (1970) explains:

> ... Justification requires the adding up of the width of all characters in a line, determining just where the line break will occur by calculating the number of characters which will print on the line, and then distributing the space left over between words (or letters).... The justification process may require hyphenation to eliminate abnormal amounts of white space between words. It was found, in the early 1960's, that computers could perform these calculations and, as well, logically break words at their hyphenable points. A number of special-purpose computers were designed for hyphenation and justification and to prepare paper tape to run hot metal or photocomposition

machines. As the performance/cost ratio of new model computers became more favorable, it was decided that this work could be handled by general purpose computers. These now comprise the bulk of industry installations. Hyphenation and justification programs have been written for a number of systems, including Honeywell, IBM, RCA, Univac, General Electric, and DEC. . . .

It was realized that general purpose computers could do other useful things besides hyphenate and justify. They could format, i.e., determine space between paragraphs and subsections, position headings, footnotes, illustrations, etc. They could make corrections and alterations, insert and delete index entries, and sort and alphabetize. Indeed, it is now fairly widely understood that the number of editing and composition tasks that can be computerized is practically unlimited. When a computer is given a cathode-ray tube, an entire class of new possibilities emerges. Kuney (1968) reports:

> But of more importance from the view of information processing was the appearance of the first character-generator devices. From data stored in the memory of the computer, these machines produce characters by a series of off-on signals that enable a beam . . . to construct a character on the face of a cathode-ray tube (CRT). They are capable of speeds of several thousand characters per second, and they can also be used to produce graphics, including chemical structures. One such system has been developed by Chemical Abstracts Service using a modified IBM 2280 CRT. On the 2280, the characters are generated by electronically "painting" characters on the face of the CRT. . . .

The greatest contribution of the new technology to publishing may come because it permits error-correcting operations to become cleanly separated from composition itself, which was not practicable with hot metal composition. One can now visualize the typesetting/printing process as consisting of three separate, successive steps:

1. Typesetting and error correcting. The input to this step is a final draft manuscript. The output is an error free typeset version on magnetic or paper tape.

2. Photocomposition. The tape is input to a computer-driven photocompositor, which justifies, hyphenates, formats, paginates, and so on. The output is a number of photographs of pages displayed on CRT.

3. Offset printing. As previously described.

The separation of error correction from composition may vastly reduce the necessity for authors to participate in the error-correcting process by allowing a methodology of *verification* to take the place of conventional proofreading. Proofreading and author involvement in it was impossible to sidestep in hot metal composition because of an innate tendency of linotypes and their operators to produce numerous errors. In photocomposition, however, once an error-free tape is delivered to the computer installation, there is no reason to expect the introduction of errors of a type that must be uncovered by proofreading; computer errors, which of course do occur, have a tendency to be either gross or highly repetitious, and detectable by the most casual of inspections. Note that through electronic/photographic technology, composition has truly become a bulk process.

The problem of author alterations has long been a drag on the publishing industry. Shatzkin (1969) estimates that the McGraw-Hill Book Company spends $465,000 in one year for the aggregate costs of author alterations. Moreover, the penalty in terms of publication delay time is substantial. As Shatzkin explains:

Predicting the precise time that proof will be returned is impossible.... [No] intelligent compositor attempts to schedule composition corrections in advance. In place of scheduling, he (and the publisher for that matter) resorts to queuing. When the work comes in, it takes its place in line—and the more work in line, the better the assurance of even flow and lower cost. That's where the book spends most of its manufacturing months—on a series of waiting lines at the publisher, the author, and the printer.

Actual production time in a manufacturing schedule is probably less than one month, which may indicate how costly in time is our verification through proof. In the case of cathode-ray tube composition, if the magnetic tape is right—the result will be right.... If the time that the tape will be ready can be predicted, the succeeding steps can be scheduled very precisely —and they are fast. With a production department of average competence ..., modest quantities of books—like 2,000 to 25,000 copies—can be delivered three to four weeks after the tape is released....

Figure 2.4 contrasts the tangled relationships between author, publisher, and printer that occur in conventional publishing with the cleanly separated functions feasible in publishing built around photocomposition. Verification, a process long used in the computer field in preparation of input, involves machine comparison of two copies keyboarded by different people; superficially the process may appear wasteful. However, one saving ensues immediately: no human eye has to scan a proof. Typographical errors are detected by machine and are corrected by keyboard personnel. If the draft is perfect, from the author's viewpoint, then in most cases the magnetic tape should be. As is evident in Figure 2.4, even bigger savings result at later stages, in the shortening of the composition process and in the elimination of the queuing and the cross-traffic of repeated dispatching

24

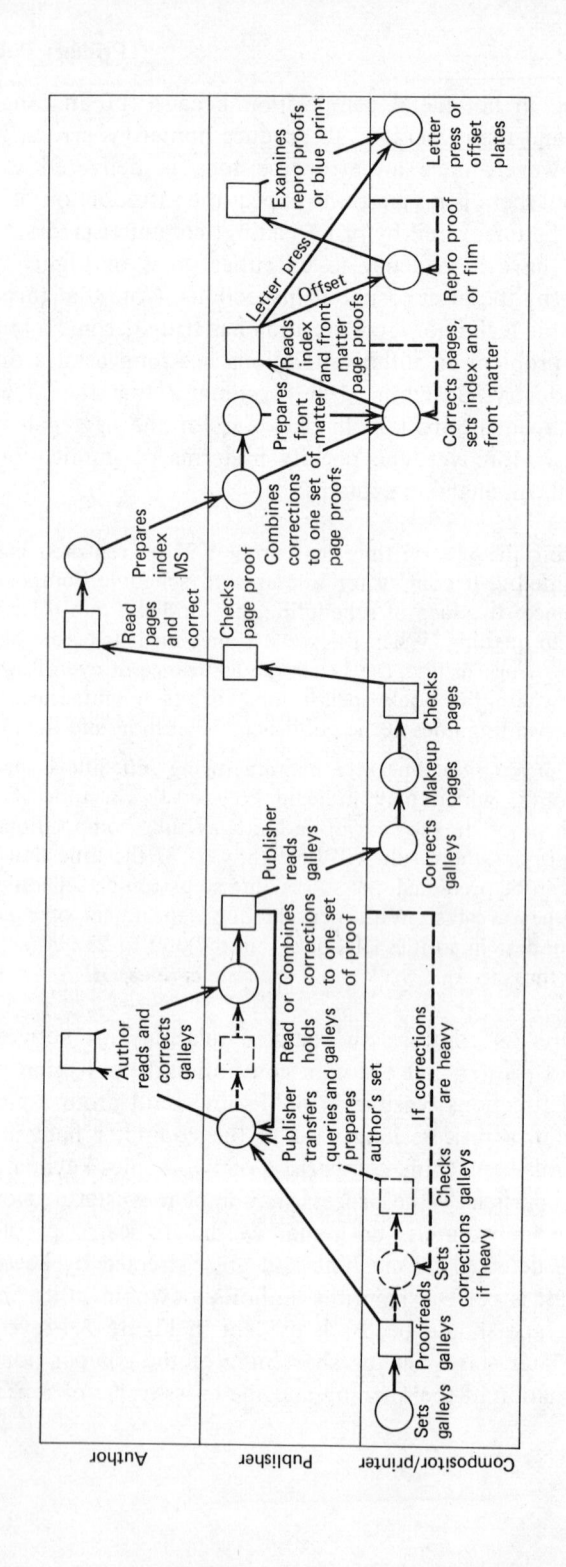

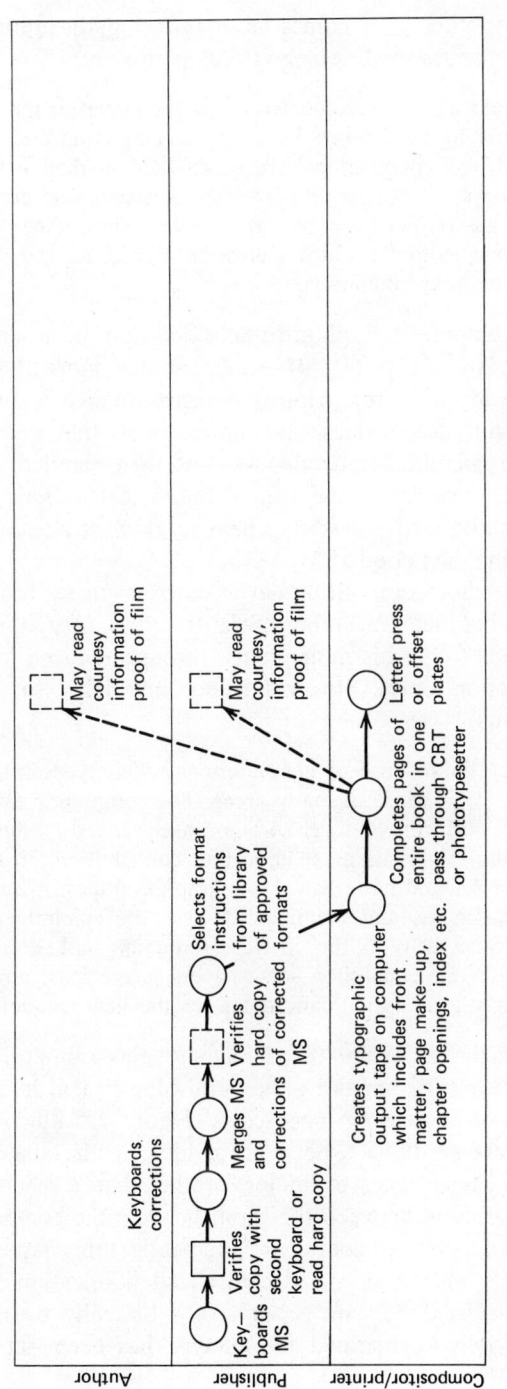

Figure 2.4. Manuscript work flow with computer composition. (Courtesy *Publishers Weekly*.)

and reading of proofs. Another gain comes from reducing the author's need to make last-minute changes. As Doebler (1970) points out:

> Something that . . . should also be recognized . . . is the effect on the content of the manuscript of long time delays between its completion and final publication. (People) in book publishing have noted that, in their experience, most revising (as opposed to straight correction of mechanical errors) is done to update statements that have become obsolete since they were written, or to clarify passages that could not have been so conceived prior to the deadline for completing the manuscript.

The revolution in computerized photocomposition has been under way for about a decade. Andersson (1970) estimated that more than a thousand computers were in use in the printing industry, though many of these were small special-purpose devices. As impressive as that number may seem, however, such computer-controlled systems then handled only about 3 percent of all the type set in the United States. *Computerworld* (1972) expected the computerized typesetting field to grow at an annual rate of 30–35 percent during the period 1971–1975.

One inhibition is that photocomposition devices are expensive, costing 10 or 12 times as much as hot metal machines (Strauss, 1969). A publisher using them, however, tends to get his money back through reduced labor costs and shorter production times. But this is not invariably so, and Sedgwick (1970) comments:

> The . . . main reason for limited use of computer-controlled typesetting is that it doesn't make economic sense in many areas. The computer's ability to create a file, update it, perform whatever sorts are needed, and . . . finally paginating and composing . . . is its most important contribution. In fact, for such publications as price and parts lists, bibliographies, indexes, library book catalogs, telephone books, and membership lists, the computer has become a near economic necessity as the central production tool. Publications that do not require this capability—newspapers, magazines, novels, brochures, etc.—are currently marginal candidates for the new technology.

For books and magazines, despite the foregoing, photocomposition offers impressive opportunities for remaking the publishing system in such a way as to pare down ever-increasing labor costs. Figure 2.4 illustrates one aspect of this, but there are other aspects not evident in the diagram. For one, photocomposition is an *office* technology, rather than a machine-shop technology. The interaction between the publisher and the composer can be direct, rather than between floors via pneumatic tube. Another aspect—very important for magazines—is decentralized publication. For years, newspapers have utilized the wire services in a basically wasteful way. Material that is initially keyboarded for teletype has been—at the receiving end—re-keyboarded by linotype operators. This expensive mode of rapid dissemination for decentralized publication is not necessary with photocomposition. At the first keyboarding a tape is produced, the contents of which may be either wired or physically transported, depending on the need for speed; the content of the tape is then used as direct input to the photocompositor.

Metropolitan-type daily newspapers were probably the last important arm of publishing to benefit from photocomposition, because over the years they had developed such a highly efficient production method based on hot-metal technology. Nevertheless by 1973 at least 1000 smaller-sized newspapers in the U.S. had adopted photocomposition, and now the larger ones are changing over. *The Los Angeles Times*, the nation's largest standard-size newspaper, in both circulation and advertising volume, is in the midst of a five-year plan to implement photocomposition and will, in effect, replace linecasting machine operators with typists (*Business Week*, 1973). The changeover is costly and difficult, and has required the *Times* to run two systems side-by-side, one based on the old hot-metal technology and the other on the new, until the transition becomes complete in 1975.

REPROGRAPHY AND MICROGRAPHICS

Reprography is a term that was intended to subsume all aspects of document reproduction, such as printing, office duplication, or the production of microfilm. In this book we classify printing under publishing rather than under reprography, not only because this appears to be customary, but because many people now feel it is important to make a distinction between the initial run of a document and any duplication of it that might come later, i.e., retrospective duplication. This distinction now extends into the realm of microfilm, which until recently has been associated almost exclusively with retrospective duplication. But in the last few years a trend toward first-time publication in microfilm has set in; accordingly, such activities are termed *micropublishing*. (Microfilm is a generic term that includes roll microfilm, microfiche, and various other micrographic media.)

Retrospective duplication, especially in microform, has been looked upon as a threat to the publishing industry because of the potential it has for diminishing hardcopy sales and defeating the purpose of copyright, which is to ensure that authors are compensated for the use of their work. When the contents of an entire book can be photoreduced and placed on a pocket-sized strip of film, the danger of widespread copying is very real. Contact duplicating of microforms is a cheap and available process, as we discuss later in the chapter. Full-size copying is also seen as a threat to copyright, even though it is expensive to copy an entire book on a Xerox machine; partial copying in libraries is so widespread that hardcopy sales must be affected in some degree.

Quite apart from cheap microform reproduction, the media are evolving in still other ways to aggravate the concern about copyright. Newer forms of reproduction are coming along, e.g., magnetic tape storage and facsimile transmission (Chapter Three). When libraries begin to share resources and distribute materials via telecommunications, they will naturally have to purchase fewer books to render a given level of service. (This, of course, is the idea behind resource sharing.) Where should the line be drawn between the right of the public to have access to information and the rights of publishers and authors? Nelson (1971) observes:

> As is known, technology has made obsolete many parts of the copyright law, which dates back to the first decade of this century. The real problem is that no one has found a good way to do something better that will satisfy all of the interests involved.
>
> Dissemination of microfilm has been feared by the publishing industry as something that would encroach upon its domain and decrease its revenues.

Figure 2.5. "Yes, George, it does say, 'No part of this may be reproduced, stored in a retrieval system, or transmitted, in any form or by any means . . . without prior written permission.'" (Courtesy *American Libraries*.)

This may have some validity, but adequate cooperation may result in something akin to what happened in the paperback market. At first, paperbacks were opposed, but later they were accepted, and they have added greatly to the publishing industry.

Sophar (1970) reports on the copyright infringement case of Williams & Wilkins versus the United States Government. The suit concerns the principle of "fair use." It is hoped by some that out of this suit will come some beneficial precedents regarding the copying of literature.

By 1973 the Williams and Wilkins suit was being appealed and was well on its way to the U.S. Supreme Court, but it is not likely that any court decision will lead to true settlement of the issue, which is loaded with technical/economic problems that have never been faced before. There is, for example, no agreement on whether a suitable method exists for the collection and distribution of royalties that accrue from duplicating copyrighted materials (Gannett, 1973). The very idea of the bookkeeping, to record which users copy how many pages of which publications, introduces seemingly insoluble difficulties. As of now, the traditional system for compensating authors still floats. Henry (1974) surveys the situation and states that the financial incentive to write has not yet been affected measurably by copying machines or microfilm. On the other hand, the general profitability of book publishing (quite apart from any encroachment of copying) is declining, especially for books on scientific and technical specialties (Benjamin, 1974). Clearly, the decreasing cost of copying and the increasing costliness of books are trends that have to clash soon, one way or another.

Before discussing the individual processes and products of reprography (first those of full-size duplication and then those of micrographics), we note that full-size duplication and microduplication have somewhat different purposes and uses. Most full-size duplication processes do not require trained personnel to carry them out; office copying is practically a do-it-yourself operation, varying from informal publishing of circulars, leaflets and mail-outs to individual page copying. (Copying machines are now so widely available to the public that it would be difficult to ascertain all of the purposes for which they are actually used.)

At some time in the next decade, probably, what has been true for full-size copying will become more true for microforms, especially for such tasks as printing out full-sized hard copy from microforms. To date, however, this has not been common. The accent, rather, has been on reduced-volume storage, on preservation, and on dissemination processes where small size and weight are economically advantageous, such as nationwide distribution of documents by science information centers. This situation can be expected to change, however, as microfilm processes and products begin more and more to work themselves into our information culture.

Duplication Processes. The duplication of printed documents is technically simpler than that of continuous-tone or multicolored items (e.g., photographs, illustrations, x-rays, maps) because one must deal with only two conditions in reproducing an image: black and white. The number of ways of transferring such elemental images is very large, given today's technological resources, and it is not surprising to find a large number of document duplication processes available. Thirty such processes are systematically discussed in William Hawken's *Copying Methods Manual* (1966), most of which have exotic names such as Ektalith, Diaversal, Electrofax, autopositive, and of course, xerography.

It would be confusing to describe the realm of full-size copying in its utmost detail, and also inappropriate, in view of the dominance of electrostatic duplication (of which Xerox is the foremost example) over all other copying methods. (Eye-legible copying might be a more significant term than full-size, for it includes macro-size reproductions that are enlargements or miniatures of the original—in other words, any duplication which is not in the realm of microfilm.) Instead, we describe the major distinctions among the various processes and the chief physicochemical categories, giving brief examples of specific processes, and then present a detailed description of the Xerox process.

The first distinction among duplication processes pertains to the method of forming the duplicate image. The most uncomplicated method, geometrically at least, is *contact copying*, in which a sheet of sensitized paper is placed firmly against the document to be duplicated, and light or pressure is used to transfer the image. The "document" can be a press plate or a stencil. In the case of the former, we have ordinary printing (see letterpress or offset, described previously). In the case of the latter, a stencil—a waxy sheet that is perforated by typewriter keys so that ink from a roller may be forced through the perforations to generate duplicates—is used in the Mimeograph process, which, before Xerox, was the most common method of office duplication.

Where an original document, rather than a plate or master, is the model for contact copying, white light is most often the agent by which the image is transferred. There are two ways of using light in contact copying, the direct method and the reflex method. In the direct method, light is actually passed through the page being copied, after which it impinges on sensitized paper or film. Wherever the page contains printed characters, the ink will not transmit the light, and the corresponding part of the sensitized paper will remain unexposed. One drawback of the direct method, and the reason it is not extensively used for full-size copying, is that character images on *both* sides of a page intercept light; accordingly only pages with material on one side can be successfully copied. This method, however, is widely used in microfilm copying—for example, in either the Kalvar or diazo methods of microfilm duplication.

More satisfactory for full-size copying is the reflex method, in which light, having first passed *through* sensitized paper or film, is reflected off the page to pass back through the sensitized paper in the opposite direction. The strength of the light is so adjusted that the combined effect of the transmitted and reflected light is needed to produce "white." Light striking a printed character will be absorbed, and the sensitized paper at that location will remain "black." An interesting variation of the reflex method uses infrared radiation rather than visible light. An example of this is 3M's Thermo-Fax process, in which infrared rays are passed through the copy paper to the original. Wherever a printed character is, the absorption of the infrared rays will generate extra heat, which is sufficient to blacken the copy paper at that location. A disadvantage of the reflex method is that light and heat radiation are reflected at angles as well as straight back through the copy paper; thus occurs the fuzziness of the print that characterizes methods such as Thermo-Fax.

Any duplication method that employs a lens to form an image on light-sensitive material is in the category of *optical copying*; in a way similar to contact copying, such methods divide up into *direct methods* and *indirect methods*. In a direct method, the lens focuses an image directly on the surface of a sensitized material, which in turn becomes the copy. An example is the Electrofax process, in which a lens focuses a page-image on an electrically charged zinc-oxide-coated piece of paper. The photoconductive oxide allows the charge to drain off wherever light impinges. Subsequently powder particles having an opposite charge adhere to the dark portion of the image. Varian Associates has adapted this process to the production of full-size hard copy from microfilm (*Micrographics News & Views*, October, 1971).

An indirect method of optical copying requires an intermediate image, from which the final copy is made. The most notable such method is silver halide photography, in which a *negative* serves as the intermediate image, from which a final copy is made. A lens is used to form the intermediate image, but is not necessarily required to transfer that image to the final copy. In that step either contact copying or projection printing (enlargement) is used. Silver halide photography, incidentally, is practically unsurpassed as a duplicating method in producing durable and high-quality copies. The process is capable of reproducing, with high fidelity, images that most other duplication processes are totally unable to handle, including delicately toned x-rays, multicolored images, and high-reduction microfiche. Unfortunately, as is well known, the method is lacking in convenience and cheapness—the qualities that go far to explain the success of xerography as a duplicating process (which, as we shall see, also uses an indirect method of optical copying).

Veaner (1969) lists five basic physicochemical processes on which the most successful commercial methods of full-size copying are based: silver halide photography, electrolysis, diazotypy, thermography, and electrophotography (also called electrostatic). The last category includes xerography. The first four of these processes, having largely lost out in the vast arena of office copying, have tended to relegate themselves to specialized, albeit often important, roles in reprography. All the processes involve the use of surfaces that are sensitive in various ways to light or infrared radiation. Most often the surface is that of the copy paper; sometimes the surface is that of a roller or master, from which the image is transferred to unsensitized paper. Light-activated chemical change, in which some element or compound in the sensitive medium reacts (thereby changing its color or degree of darkness), is the most typical physicochemical process. This takes place in silver halide photography, diazotypy, and thermography. Electrophotography and electrolysis both involve some light-induced change in the electrical properties of the sensitive medium, which leads subsequently to a change in color or degree of darkness. In electrophotography, light causes the dissipation of a previously formed electric charge; later, the dark spaces—which still have a charge—attract tiny dark-hued particles. In electrolysis, light causes a change in electrical conductivity in the sensitized medium; later, an electric current flowing through the light-affected portions (but not through the dark portions) causes a chemical change and (hence) a color change.

The largest number of separate processes listed by Hawken (1966) fall under silver halide photography, which is probably the most versatile of the five basic processes. All silver halide processes (including everyday black-and-white photography) involve the behavior of the element silver on exposure to light: it changes from the "invisible" silver ion (in its compound with chlorine or bromine) to metallic silver, which becomes visible as a result of the formation of a cloud of microscopic metallic particles wherever light impinges. The cloud is denser where the light illumination is greater, and this is the basis for the great fidelity to tone of silver halide processes.

We have already discussed the most well-known specific silver halide process, under indirect methods of optical copying. However, there are also direct methods of optical copying for silver halide, i.e., methods that produce positive prints directly, rather than from a negative. One is the autopositive process, which was discovered by the astronomer Sir John Herschel in 1839. The process is based on the fact that the reduction from silver ion to the metallic form, just described, does not proceed "in one fell swoop," but in steps, some of which are reversible. Suppose a film coated with silver halide emulsion is exposed to light over its entirety but is not placed in a developing solution (which is required in the standard process to convert the light-activated silver to the metallic form). At this point, yellow light of suitable frequency will deactivate the silver; if the yellow light is that of a positive image, all the light areas will be deactivated and will not be turned dark by the developing solution. Thus, the lighter parts of an image are made to do the reverse of what they do in the usual silver halide process, and a positive, rather than a negative, is the result.

The autopositive process lacks the tonal fidelity of the standard process. However, it is adequate for any copying process dealing with simple black and white, such as engineering drawings. The fact that autopositive is a direct optical method makes it convenient in certain routine clerical operations. The Photoclerk, known widely in library circles, is perhaps the best example of this.

Most silver halide processes are *wet*. They require solutions to be applied for developing the silver and for removing the underdeveloped silver (the well-known "hypo" of all photography). This is a part of the inconvenience of the overall silver halide method. There is, however, a *dry silver* process, in which heat (rather than an action of a developer) is used to bring out the image. But here again, fidelity to tone is not good, and the unremoved silver tends to darken with age. But, because of its convenience (5 seconds per print), dry silver is good enough for the production of full-size hard copy from microfilm (which is usually wanted on a temporary basis only). The 3M Company has long specialized in dry silver printers, and in its Model 201 embodies a 35mm roll film reader along with the printer (Spreitzer, 1973).

In the last few decades, the search for convenient and low-cost methods of copying has meant getting away from silver halide, and getting away from wet processing in general. The essence of a dry process is not necessarily the total absence of liquids in the process, but the absence of the need for chemical baths or other cumbersome liquid-handling systems (such as characterized the now obsolete spirit duplication, or "ditto" process). Thus, the electrolytic process (the next of the five basic processes we are discussing) qualifies as dry, even though a liquid solution is involved in forming the image.

The electrolytic process depends on the behavior of a layer of resin-bound zinc oxide in response to light. The zinc oxide, which is white, forms a coating on a paper base, and sandwiched between the paper and the oxide is a thin metallic layer which acts as a conductor. Light renders the zinc oxide layer conductive. Subsequently, a sponge containing an electrolytic solution is drawn over the oxide surface while an electric current is applied. Wherever the white oxide layer is conducting, a darkish metal plates out; the result of this process, as can readily be seen, is a negative image. This process is most commonly used for printing full-size hard copy from microfilm, and the 3M Company (already mentioned in connection with dry silver) was a pioneer of the process, and specializes in various microform reproduction processes, including one that will reproduce color (Revill, 1970).

The diazo process, or diazotypy, is sometimes referred to by the descriptive name *whiteprinting*. Unlike standard silver halide photography, the impingement of light brings about whitening rather than darkening, thus giving positive copies; whereas silver's tendency to darken is promoted by light exposure, that of diazonium salts (the active agent in diazotypy) is destroyed by light. Though the diazo process is among the cheapest (1¢ per copy) it has limitations as a convenient method. The original must have printing on one side only and must have opaque images on translucent paper capable of passing ultraviolet light. The original is placed under pressure on the paper with the image side up. Ultraviolet light is played across the original. The light passing through the translucent portions of the original disintegrate the diazo compounds, making them incapable of acting as a coloring agent. By passing the dry paper through gaseous ammonia, the dye remaining in the image area is brought out and a readable, dry positive results. The Ozalid process uses the diazo technique. We are to meet the diazo process again later under the topic of microform duplication, which is perhaps one of the most significant present uses of diazotypy.

Thermography, the fourth of the processes we consider, has already been introduced in our discussion of reflex contact copying. Hawken (1966) lists three such processes, Thermo-Fax, Eichner, and Ektafax, and characterizes them as poor in dealing with continuous tone (as, indeed, most reprographic processes are), and fair to poor in reproduction of fine detail. In spite of this, Thermo-Fax had become quite a common copying process before Xerox really got rolling, for it had a fair measure of convenience. However, anyone who has ever put a Thermo-Fax copy and a Xerox side-by-side can readily understand why the latter has won out.

Electrophotography is the most successful of the basic duplication processes. We have already mentioned Electrofax. Far more well-known is the Xerox process (sometimes referred to as *xerography*, a word derived from Greek, meaning "dry printing"). Xerox derives part of its advantage over other methods from the fact that plain, untreated bond-weight paper can be used to hold the duplicate image. As with Electrofax, the white part of an image dissipates an electric charge, but that charge is spread over a selenium-coated drum which, rotating, transfers the image to the paper (Figure 2.6). To do this, it rotates through a developing station where a toning powder is cascaded on the surface. The powder adheres only to the charged areas. As the drum continues to rotate, the powder image on the surface is rolled into contact with the paper, which has also received an electrical charge that is spread over its entire surface. The charge causes the toner powder to be transferred to the paper, which is then subjected to heat in order to fuse the powder to the paper. The drum is then cleaned off while continuing to rotate, and the cycle is repeated for the next print or offset master. This is a most versatile and convenient method of office copying.

An interesting new development on the Xerox front is a dry copier, the Xerox 6500, that will reproduce up to seven different colors in one image on ordinary paper (Free, 1973). This is not the first color copier; the 3M Company has marketed one for several years—but like many other marginally successful methods we've described, it requires specially treated paper. Various methods of duplicating through color photography have existed for many years, but as a class they suffer from the cumbersomeness and/or expense that afflicts photography generally.

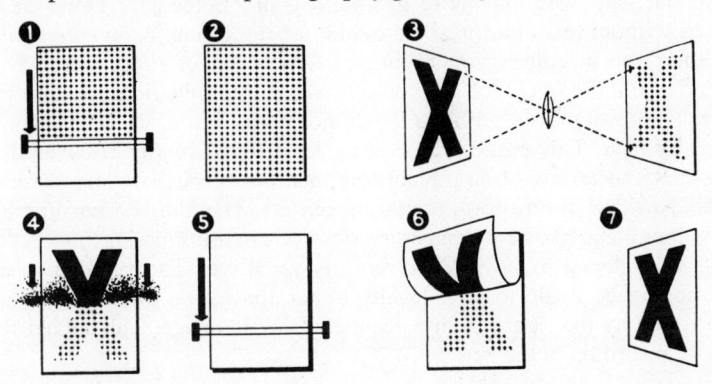

Figure 2.6. Steps in the Xerographic process: 1.) Selenium-coated plate receives positive electric charge as it passes under wires. 2.) Plate has full positive charge (plus marks). 3.) Image of document is projected through lens. Charge is dissipated in white areas by exposure to light, leaving "dark" areas still charged. 4.) Plate is dusted by negatively charged dark powder, which converts remaining positively charged areas to a visibly black image. 5.) Sheet of paper is placed over the plate and receives positive charge. 6.) Positive charge attracts negatively charged powder from plate to paper. 7.) Powder is fused by heat for permanent adherence to paper.

As in black-and-white xerography, the 6500's color process makes use of a rotating selenium-coated drum. Three different toners are used, to apply the colors magenta (a deep purplish red), yellow, and cyan (a shade of blue), but three rotations of the drum are required—one for each toner—to generate one duplicate image. The seven possible colors are the three basic ones and their combinations; two at a time yield red-orange, green, and indigo; all three yield black. The image to be copied is placed face-down on glass, and reflected light from it is passed through color filters in the proper sequence to match the three toners.

Micrographics. The term *micrographics* apparently is replacing the more cumbersome term *microphotography*, which pertains to the production and use of miniaturized records. "Micrographics" has the correct implication that processes other than strictly photographic are subsumed; in particular, the diazo process already described for full-size duplication is also applicable to the copying of microforms. Indeed, a great variety of methods have been available for many years to the processors of micro-images, as summarized by Heilprin (July, 1961):

> In their early stages microfilms were confined almost exclusively to silver halide storage. A new medium with different properties entered with the discovery of photosensitive dyes such as diazo and Dr. Chalkley's dicyanide. Since they have molecular units smaller than most silver grains, perhaps the principal gain was that more generations of photocopies could be reproduced without loss of a threshold quality of resolution. A potential gain may be their use in copying microimages. A new set of properties was introduced with discovery of photoelectrostatic reproduction, or xerography. Here the developer is neither a liquid nor a gas, but a dry powder or toner, fixed by heat. This reduces processing time. Then it was discovered that a plastic (Kalvar) could be a recording medium through photorelease of gas bubbles which in turn form scattering centers. The film is insensitive to daylight handling, has complementary density on transmission and reflection, and is developed by heat. More recently yet it was discovered that another plastic can be made to melt locally under the action of an electron beam controlled by the signal from a scanned graphic image. This added thermoplastic recording to the list.
>
> All of these media fit within the gross structural pattern of the microforms. The engineer now has a variety of choice for storage media, with a wide spectrum of physical properties.

Though the term "micrographics" may be recent, the history of the field goes back to 1839 when J. B. Dancer, an English optical manufacturer, is said to have made the first microphotograph, using Daguerre's newly invented photographic process. Some years later, microphotographs became commercially available as novelties, mounted in small magnifying tubes as souvenir messages. More serious uses were not long in coming. According to Kish (1966):

> Microfilm had its first important application during the Franco-Prussian War. With Paris under siege, the surest way out of the French capital was by air. A surprising amount of traffic managed to move out of the city in free balloons. Unfortunately, it was not feasible for the balloons to return. The city was a tiny target for a drifting balloon, and the prevailing winds were not helpful.
>
> French photographic technicians attacked the problem and managed to institute an efficient airmail service between Paris and Bordeaux with the aid of carrier pigeons and microfilm. Their pigeons, carrying almost weightless rolls of thin film sheets in their tails, succeeded in flying out of range of Prussian shotguns and mostly evading the Prussian falcons sent up to stop them.

The recent history of micrographics began with the invention of the rotary camera in 1925 by George McCarthy, a bank employee, who wanted a convenient means of recording checks and other records. This invention, later improved by Eastman Kodak, became the familiar Recordak machine, and was widely used by American banks during the 1930s.

The use of microfilm expanded, in business and in libraries. Until World War II, the microform medium was regarded mainly as a means of storage and preservation of records, usually those that were seldom looked up, but that had to be available when needed. The war, which gave a boost to so many lines of technology, did so for microfilm in the form of V-mail, which made it possible to move mail efficiently and quickly to millions of service men overseas. Here was a true "microfilm system," in which a major advantage of the medium—compactness—was utilized in the performance of an otherwise near-impossible job. V-mail was probably the first instance of large-scale production of hard copy from microfilm.

During the 1950s, expanding defense efforts gave further impetus to microfilm, as new methods became needed to deal with the myriad of complex engineering drawings of aircraft and missiles. The accent was now on retrieval as well as storage, and the *aperture card* was devised, bringing together the technologies of microfilm and of electronic accounting machines (EAM). With this method, each photoreduced engineering drawing was mounted in a window (aperture) in an EAM card (Figure 2.7); a code was keypunched in each card, so that a file of drawings could be sorted, updated, and so on. Retrieval could also be done by machine, but usually it was most satisfactory to organize the file for simple manual

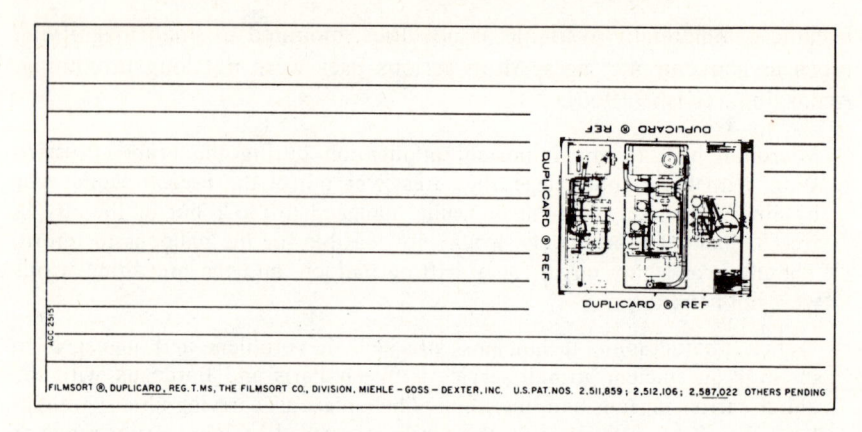

Figure 2.7. Microfilm aperature card.

access. The late 1940s and early 1950s saw a proliferation of devices in which a microform was combined with a macroscopic code element by which retrieval could take place through mechanical, magnetic, or optical search. Some of these are to be described later.

Engineering drawings comprised only one facet of the problem of dealing with scientific and technical information, and aperture cards did not prove to be the basis of a general solution for microstorage of documents. Slowly the concept of *unitized microfilms* gained ascendancy whereby photoreduced documents could be stored and retrieved in ways similar to full-sized documents. Today, anyone thinking of applications of micrographics to documentation in science and technology thinks in terms of *microfiche* rather than microfilm. A typical microfiche is a 4" by 6" sheet of film containing images of a document's pages, laid out in rows and columns. With microfiche, two levels of direct access are available: (a) a given microfiche can be picked out of a microfiche deck by scanning eye-readable titles; and (b) a given page can be accessed in a microfiche viewer by horizontal and vertical positioning.

Probably the most significant development in the last 10 years has been *ultramicrofiche* (UMF), where reduction ratios of greater than 150:1 are obtainable, as compared to the 24:1 microfiche standard for most U.S. Government documents. The 150:1 ratio—an achievement requiring several interrelated technological advances—makes it possible to store 3000 page images on a single 4" by 6" fiche, bringing the concept of a microfilm library to the threshold of feasibility. Because UMF may become a mainstream of use of microforms, we scrutinize it more closely later in the chapter. (Reduction ratios greater than 150:1—such as 600:1—are physically possible using visible light, but probably impractical. Unitized records at such ratios become too small to be handled conveniently.)

Roll Microfilm. Though it is being displaced in many areas, roll microfilm is still widely used. In public libraries, for example, roll microfilm is still the number one form of the micrographic medium; it will probably continue to be, for librarians regard reels of film as more loss-proof and theft-proof than unitized film. In government and industry, however, the changeover to microfiche has been substantial. In general, many organizations that photoreduce records for safekeeping (and not for retrieval) will probably continue to use microfilm simply because there is no compelling reason for change.

Roll microfilm stores document images at reduction ratios typically around 15:1 to 20:1, on reels of film. At first documentation was recorded continuously on spools of film using special purpose microfilm cameras; the most common film sizes were 16mm and 35mm. Along with the camera, other equipment was evolved for viewing the film—first by hand with a magnifying glass and later by mechanical viewers. In early systems desired images were located by visual scanning of the set of stored images, assisted, perhaps, by an indication of their linear positions, in inches, along the film. The *Lodestar* microfilm viewer manufactured by the Eastman Kodak Company is a more advanced viewer, which provides a visual frame index. It uses spool film but in cartridge form to simplify film loading and unloading. More recently, several developments have appeared which automate the location of particular frames by their linear position on the reel.

However, although microfilm satisfies the basic requirements for achieving more compact storage of the printed information, its access time is slow even when the difficulty of locating a specific image on the spool is overcome (by organizing the original material in a logical manner before filming, by providing visual index marks recognizable at viewing time, or by automatic linear indexing). These technical considerations of access time and display may not be too important in routine library operations which involve microfilming sets of material like newspapers and periodicals. But when continuous film is used as the primary recording medium for storing a heterogenous collection of documents keyed to a subject or named object index, the questions of rapid access and display become very serious.

The basic principles of an electronic microfilm searching system were advanced by Vannevar Bush of MIT in the early 1940s as a means for overcoming these deficiencies. A prototype model called the Rapid Selector was designed and built by Engineering Research Associates of St. Paul, Minnesota. The late Ralph R. Shaw supervised the development and performed most of the bibliographical experimentation. The machine handled microfilm with associated patterns which described the contents of documents. Code and document images were on large, 2000 foot reels of 35mm microfilm containing 72,000 image frames each, which went through the machine at 5 feet per second or 2400 identified pages per minute. Copies of the documents as selected by proper code recognition were copied, on the fly, photographically.

The code was in the form of black and clear dots which identified each document either by number, name, author, or contents. In this machine the code appeared on one half of a 35mm film and a photographic image of the document on the other half, as shown in Figure 2.8. As the film passed through the selector, the coded area was projected on a photocell. This photocell was masked by a cutout of the complement of the projected code being sought. Recognition occurred when no light struck the photocell. This initiated a signal which fired a photographic flash lamp when the selected microfilmed document was in the copying position. The light projected an image of the desired document onto unexposed microfilm which became the output of the Rapid Selector.

Numerous other microfilm searching devices patterned after the Rapid Selector were built throughout the 1950s and 1960s, most notably the Benson-Lehner Corporation's Flip (Film Library Instantaneous Presentation) and the File Search System of FMA, Inc. (Figure 2.9). The most prominent currently used is Eastman Kodak's Miracode which we discuss in Chapter Nine, as an example of a special purpose retrieval device.

The Rapid Selector, the Benson-Lehner Flip, the FMA File Search Machine, and Eastman's Miracode all utilize microfilm with binary coded data stored for automatic searching. Thus, each provides a means for mechanized document retrieval. However, none of them provides an answer to the basic operational disadvantages of continuous film files: it is awkward to interfile new material in an orderly sequence, and the search mechanism must examine the entire file to satisfy every search request. Unsurprisingly, such methods have generally given way to microfiche, and only Miracode is commercially available today.

Microfiche. Unitized film files are able to overcome many of the disadvantages just discussed. In fact, the considerations that led the data-processing industry to emphasize disk storage and to de-emphasize magnetic tape are quite similar to those applying to micrographic storage. Disk storage (Chapter Three) came into prominence because it could provide direct access, through an addressing system, to any requested file of data. Direct

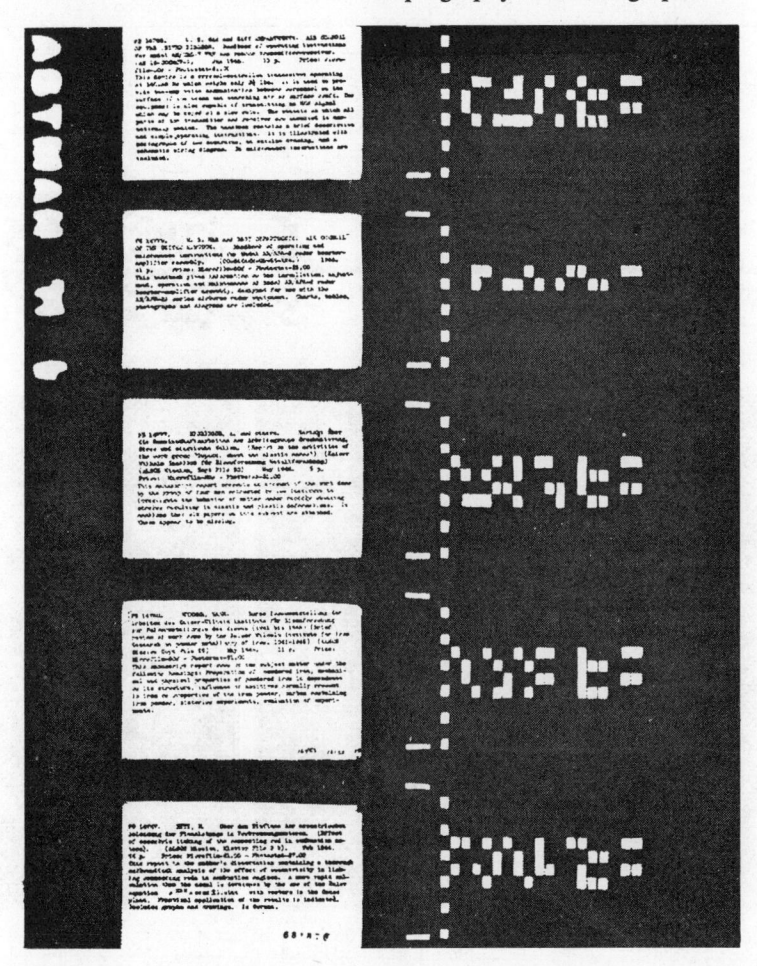

Figure 2.8. Rapid selector film format.

access is even a feature of libraries, where one can usually proceed directly —in minutes—to find a known page in a known book. The value of a comparable capability for microfilm is obvious, but it was not realized for many years because the medium was thought of mainly as a means of storage and preservation (or for easy transportability in the case of V-mail), and only gradually did the importance of accessibility emerge.

Microfiche today is the principal form of direct-access microfilm. A typical unit of microfiche is a rectangular sheet of film on which microimages are arranged like days of the month on a calendar. The number of squares is not limited to 31, of course, and some microfiche are being marketed containing 3000 images per fiche. A one-foot-long shoe box of micro-

Figure 2.9. FMA File-Search film format.

fiche could contain 5000 books having a total of more than 10 million pages, and one is able to have the entire contents of a moderately large library within arm's reach. Thus, what would be access in a minute or two in a book library becomes access in seconds in a microfiche library.

Microfiche is of French derivation, *fiche* meaning "slip of paper" or "sheet." (The term is said actually to have been coined by a Hollander, Dr. Van der Volk.) Other countries in Western Europe, especially Holland and Germany, contributed to the development and use of microfiche as early as the 1930s. The first in the United States to see the importance of microfiche were government agencies dealing with research and development, such as the Atomic Energy Commission and NASA. Their problem was the storage, retrieval, and handling of scientific and technical documents. A unitized approach, in which each document could be associated with a separate unit of film, was perceived to meet their needs far better than roll microfilm (where many documents would be present on each film unit) or aperture cards (where each document's contents would have to be spread over several cards). This philosophy of unitization, i.e., one book per unit of film, applies as well to books as to research documents, and, as we are to see shortly, it is being applied in the realm of high-reduction microfiche. Unitization is a *system concept* that affects efficiency in many basic operations of documentation—reproduction, dissemination, ordering, retrieval, and so on.

There are people who claim, with some justification, that a microfiche will never take the place of a book or a document in convenience, meaning ease of reading and handling. Nevertheless, microfiche appears to offer the closest approach, among all microforms, to the convenience of hard copy. Given a microfiche reader of acceptable quality (an important requirement), there are three ways the convenience of a user is abetted by the microfiche format.

1. Fiche are generally stored in ordered decks (e.g., by LC number, alphabetically by author, etc.), enabling one to pick out units quickly, as from a library shelf, even though more in the manner of thumbing through a card catalog.
2. Accessing individual pages by horizontally and vertically stepping a fiche positioned in the reader should, in principle, be as easy as turning pages in a book. Only the ingrained habits of the populace are likely to make it not so in fact.
3. Eye-legible descriptive information at the top of each fiche can provide browsability in a microfiche deck.

Somewhat ironically, the very format that makes microfiche easy to use compared to other microforms, makes it harder to manufacture initially. The rotary camera, which for so long has photographed checks and other business records, is the essence in simplicity of operation. Documents to be photographed are merely placed on a conveyor belt, and are sensed mechanically, triggering an automatic photographic process. The process is simple because one cares nothing about the position or angle of the document's image on file—only that it is recorded. Images on microfiche, however, must be precisely arrayed in a gridiron fashion. How can one do this, photographically? It is quite impractical, of course, to lay individual documents out on a large flat table, and photograph them in one exposure. Another approach would be to photograph pages in separate exposures and paste the microimages into a grid pattern on a sheet of blank film of the proper size. This procedure has been used, although it is cumbersome, and, as it turns out, unnecessary, because the paste-up can be accomplished photographically by means of a step-and-repeat camera. The step-and-repeat camera can be moved so that as each page is positioned to be photographed, its image is focussed at the precise position it should occupy on the film—thus a *microfiche master* is created. A disadvantage here is that a mistake in photographing any one page is capable of ruining the entire master; but the state of the art has evolved so that this is no longer a serious problem.

Microfiche, in addition to being nearly ideal from the standpoint of accessability, can be a powerful basis for an information *system*, in which many users are served in diverse ways through processes of microform duplication, hard copy generation, and information transfer, storage, and retrieval. At the root of the information flow diagram for such a system would be the microfiche master. The master can be the point of departure for numerous modes of information dissemination, among which are:

1. Exact microform duplicates may be produced, via the diazo or Kalvar process of contact printing. Such duplicates may be either disseminated to the readers or used as submasters.
2. Hard copy may be produced by magnifying the microimage to readable size (a process termed *blowback*) and printing by a suitable reprographic process.
3. The master's image may be scanned and transmitted *as an image* in a television-like process.
4. The letters of the words in the page context of each image may be digitized through an optical character recognition process.

Processes one and two are in common use in a number of scientific information centers in the United States. Process three can be expected to proliferate as soon as interlibrary networks for resource sharing are widely used, perhaps within a few years. Process four has attracted interest among users of COM (computer output microfilm, Chapter Three) as a way of getting old computer output read back in; predictably, the process is called CIM (computer input microfilm).

It does not follow from the above, though, that microfiche is the ideal master in all cases of reproduction or transmission. The Defense Documentation Center, in fact, uses a dual-camera setup (Gordon, 1972) to make both microfilm and microfiche masters, the former for hard copy and the latter for duplicates. It is to be noted that hard copy can be made just as readily from duplicates as from masters. This may become the predominant process eventually because it will be the *user*, generally, using a duplicate at a decentralized location, who will decide—based on his inspection of a number of microfiche—which documents or images he wants to take home as hard copy.

Many college students are now familiar with coin-operated duplicating machines, where book pages may be copied for as little as 5¢ each. Such facilities may soon be common for the micrographic media also. For example, Encyclopaedia Britannica, in connection with its Microbook Library program, is offering a reader/printer, for use by students in libraries, for about $2,000—a figure commensurate with copying machines in general (*Micrographics News and Views*, June, 1971). Coin-operated reader/printers are now on the market (Sawyer, 1970).

Offsetting the ease of access and use of microfiche is their vulnerability, individually and as a collection, to a variety of hazards. As librarians know so well, a book can meet many grim fates; this applies with even more force to microfiche, simply because they are small. Smallness brings with it brand new hazards, to which books are not ordinarily subject; for example, one can drop a fiche deck on the floor. (It would take a major earthquake to cause the corresponding fate for a shelf of books.) Smallness also guarantees that some kinds of damage will have an effect on microfiche hundreds of times greater than on books. A 20:1 reduction ratio, which applies to length measure, means a 400:1 reduction in area; therefore a cigarette burn which could wipe out a word or two on a book page can destroy an entire page on microfiche. On the other hand, it must be taken into account that microfiche, because of ease of duplication, are more replaceable than books, and at costs of only 5¢ to 25¢ per fiche.

File integrity is a problem with microfiche. Ease of physical access to individual fiche means also ease of getting them out of order. Fortunately, there is a simple solution to maintaining fiche deck order: paint diagonal lines of various colors across the top of a deck. With this process, called *diagonal striping*, one can not only spot out-of-order fiche, but can use the stripe pattern as a guide to refilling. A well-designed deck top pattern can also enable one to spot missing fiche in the file.

Ultramicrofiche. Prior to 1960 almost all microfilm production was in the range 10:1 through 25:1 in reduction ratio. This may seem strange in view of the fact that some of the first microimages made by Dancer in 1839 were at reduction ratios of greater than 100:1. The typical federal government reduction ratio of 24:1 permits no more than 98 document pages to be present on a 4" by 6" fiche; longer documents must spill over onto one or more trailer fiche. Why, then, were higher reduction ratios not made use of at the outset?

There are many differences in degree, between 24:1 and 100:1, which become in practice differences in kind. One example of such a difference is in the problem of guarding against the effects of dirt and dust in the manufacture of microfiche masters. What would be "careful film processing" at 24:1 becomes "cleanroom conditions" (rubber gloves, special clothes, air conditioning, etc.) at 100:1. Another such difference is the problem of error, which—being proportional to the number of images on a fiche, which in turn is roughly proportional to the page *area* represented on a fiche—is 16 times as much of a problem at 100:1 as at 24:1. As Tauber and Myers (1962) stated the problem:

> ... However, the practical limitations of straight photographic techniques have discouraged the development of devices capable of producing large quantities of microimages at these high reduction ratios. To accomplish this implies laying down multiple images on a common surface and exposing them individually by some form of step-and-repeat technique. The major difficulty ... results from the relatively high probability of an error occuring at some point in the process. An error might be, for example, an improperly focused image, or ... from a piece of dirt either in the optical system or upon the film emulsion itself. In many cases it is simply "human error." Basically, there exists no satisfactory inspection procedure to detect, as well as correct, errors before the final development of the master matrix. Therefore, correction of one or more imperfect images would require the rerecording of the entire matrix of images....

The National Cash Register Company (NCR) solved a number of the key technical problems connected with the production and use of ultramicrofiche (UMF), including the problem of dealing with error. According to *Advanced Technology/Libraries* (1972):

> ... A partial listing of NCR's contributions to UMF technology is impressive and includes the following: construction of the first successful large-area, step-and-repeat camera-recorder; solution of the problem of how to prepare as many as three thousand error-free microimages on a single substrate; the first demonstration of the feasibility of large-area, high-resolution contact printing; the invention of laminating UMF in plastic; and the design and construction of the first UMF reader (and reader/printer) to utilize 'low-cost' optics and a tungsten light source....

Because of these developments, all but the largest of books in libraries can be handled on unitized microfiche. The potential system conesquences for libraries are huge, and even the role of libraries may change as a result

Reprography and Micrographics   47

James, W.   PRINCIPLES OF PSYCHOLOGY v.1   LAC 20001

                                                                                                     LAC 20001

James, William, 1842-1910.
    The principles of psychology. London, Macmillan, 1891.

    2 v. illus.

    Originally published by H. Holt, 1890.
    "Several chapters have been published successively in Mind, the Journal of speculative philosophy, the Popular science monthly and Scribner's magazine."—Pref.

    1. Psychology.

Figure 2.10. Ultramicrofiche containing 701 page images (bottom); same ultramicrofiche in catalog-card style holder (top).

of the fact that in microform entire books may be easily duplicated. It is very probable that in time users will be willing to forego seeing the original material on loan from their library in favor of getting a duplicate, expendable print for personal use. Should the user wish to avoid building up a vast paper library of his own, the alternative would be to obtain a duplicate copy of the microform for desk viewing. L. B. Heilprin (January, 1961) makes just this point when he distinguishes between a D (duplicating) Library and a C (circulating) Library. He maintains that through increased microform usage, and advances in communications, we can expect to see the D-Library achieving considerable popularity and prominence in the future.

> Thus many problems of storing multiple copies; of loss through wear, mutilation and stealing; of cost and effort of charging out and charging in; of binding and rebinding, can be simplified or eliminated in a D-Library. The D-Library can combine photoreduction of scale; i.e., compact storage, high mobility through optical and electronic transmission of images, and great economy of operation. The D principle of dissemination by reproduction of expendable or vendable copies will almost certainly alleviate many present physical problems.

One of the greatest of the physical problems to which Heilprin alludes is the deterioration of books, which the largest and oldest of our libraries are now encountering in a massive way. Growing numbers of documents are being termed "brittle books." These books, most of which were published in the 50 years following the Civil War and the introduction of pulp paper, have actually undergone a degree of decomposition so that the paper breaks or crumbles when handled. The New York Public Library has an estimated 3.5 million brittle books, and the Library of Congress 2.5 million. As larger numbers of more modern books begin to enter the brittle category, more and more libraries will be affected, and it will become increasingly evident that a coordinated program of putting books on UMF (especially those 25 percent of brittle books for which only one copy is known to exist) is the only way that such book holdings can be saved.

Unfortunately, the cost of such a massive filming would probably be prohibitive; for most such books no market would exist. It, therefore, seems likely that no rescue attempts of the brittle-book population will be made. (There are important exceptions which we will discuss later.)

Of course, the question will be ever more frequently asked as to why there should be books at all. The potential that microfiche has (and UMF in particular) for the dissemination of information beyond what is possible for books has brought a new form of publishing activity into existence, called *micropublishing*. *Micrographics News and Views* (August, 1971) offers the following definition of micropublishing:

Micropublishing: Editorially controlling, promoting, and offering for public sale and distribution material which is in a microform format on film. The micropublisher may or may not have been directly involved in the production of the microform media for publication.

Original micropublishing: . . . Where the microform is either the only vehicle of publication or is offered more or less simultaneously with full-sized copy as an optional alternative. . . .

Retrospective micropublishing: Republishing in microform that material which has been published previously in another medium.

As an activity, micropublishing is said to be growing rapidly and, according to the source quoted above, out of the $400–$500 million overall micrographics industry revenues about $56 million comes under the category of micropublishing. It is predicted that by 1975 the revenue figure will be $200 million, which will probably amount to about 5 percent of the total revenues for the entire publishing industry.

An example (Figure 2.10) of a venture in *retrospective* micropublishing is that of Encyclopaedia Britannica, whose Library Resources division has developed integrated packages of books on UMF (reduction ratio varying from 55:1 to 90:1, as a consequence of varying page size and type size) for use in college libraries. The reduction ratio was chosen so that in nearly all cases it is possible to place all the contents of a book on one 3″ by 5″ fiche. The first such package, the *Library of American Civilization*, contains 20,000 titles of pre-1914 books, thus sidestepping copyright complications. If enough such packages could be made up, it would constitute a solution to the brittle-book problem we spoke of earlier. The package, also known as the Microbook Library, costs $21,500 and includes 5 sets of printed book catalogs (author, title, and subject) and 10 sets of catalogs in UMF form.

Such micropublished material is not intended merely to be stored for reference, especially in a college setting. One hopes that it will be used, on a daily and routine basis, by both faculty and students. In order for this to be realized, a *portable reader* is an essential. The Microbook Library has associated with it a lap reader, having a 7″ by 10″ screen, and costing about $150. Optionally battery powered and weighing less than 5 pounds, this reader enables students to use Microbook material at the study location of his choice (*Micrographics News and Views*, October, 1970). More recently, Microvision, Inc. (Newport Beach, California) reports a portable fiche reader selling for less than $100 and operating on regular battery or automobile battery via cigarette lighter.

An example of *original* micropublishing is the Sears, Roebuck and Company parts list catalog, for use in helping customers get replacement parts for mechanical items. The parts file has more than 70,000 pages covering four million parts, and the near impossibility of publishing and distributing (not to mention using) such a collection of information in the form of books is readily seen. The pages are contained on 4″ by 6″ microfiche transparencies, each of which contains 2079 images arranged in 33 rows and 63 columns. Sears and Roebuck had previously used 16mm microfilm as the basis for their catalog system, but were driven to UMF when they found that their catalog occupied nearly a mile of film length. The process of updating the catalog on UMF takes 2 or 3 days; the pre-microfilm process of updating required 4 weeks and 76 tons of paper!

Updatable Microfiche. The kinds of microfiche we have been discussing are "frozen in concrete" at the moment of their manufacture. Ways of updating microfiche do exist, but they are expensive and only the original manufacturer is equipped to do the job. However, a number of techniques do exist by which the user himself can add, delete, or replace images in fiche format. Without a methodology of this type, no system of office record keeping on microfilm would be viable unless the records are microfilmed merely for storage and preservation. (A computer-based methodology for updating microlm will be discussed in Chapter Three.) Any system in which records have to be looked up, consulted, and kept current, such as for a file of patient data in a hospital, needs a unit of storage which is at least as malleable as an office file jacket. Two examples of the products of firms marketing updatable microfiche are:

1. The microfolio process of the Arcata Microfilm Corporation. This process for making up a microfilm record begins with an optically clear acetate sheet, generally 3″ by 5″ or 4″ by 6″. Images are added to the sheet, individually or in rows, through the use of an adhesive applied to the non-image-bearing edges of the developed film. For proper positioning and actual mounting of the image on the sheet, or fiche, a small mounting machine (which may be placed on a desk top) is used.
2. The microjacket of the NB Jackets Corporation. A transparent array of fiche-holding channels, called a jacket, rather than an empty sheet, is used as a starting point in making up a record via the microjacket process. A jacket serves as a film holder, and the film is inserted in one of the several channels thereof as one would insert a credit card or driver's license in one of the celluloid holders in his wallet. A typical channel has a breadth slightly greater than the height of the image it is designed to contain. Thus a whole row of images, adjacent to each other on a filmstrip, can be inserted.

Channels run horizontally across the fiche and are open at both ends, so that film strips might be inserted both from the right and from the left; it is possible, in an updating operation, to insert a new film strip from one side and push out an old film strip on the other. A 4" by 6" fiche might have from six to more than a dozen such channels (depending on the size of the images), one above the other.

REFERENCES

Advanced Technology/Libraries (1972), High Reduction Microfiche, 1:2 (February).

ANDERSSON, P. L. (1970), Phototypesetting—A Quiet Revolution, *Datamation*, 16:16, pp. 22–27.

BENJAMIN, CURTIS G. (1974), Soaring Prices and Sinking Sales of Science Monographs, *Science*, 183:4122, pp. 282–284.

Business Week (July 28, 1973), An Automated L.A. Times, pp.50e–50g.

Computerworld (October 25, 1972), Computer Systems Spark Growth in Typesetting, p. 30.

DOEBLER, PAUL D. (1970), Publication and Distribution of Information, in Cuadra, C.A. ed., *Annual Review of Information Science and Technology*, Vol. 5, Encyclopaedia Britannica, Chicago, pp. 223–257.

FREE, JOHN R. (1973), Xerox 6500 Makes Color Copies on Any Paper, *Popular Science*, 203:4 (October), p. 107.

GANNETT, ELWOOD K. (1973), Primary Publication Systems and Services, in Cuadra, C.A., ed., *Annual Review of Information Science and Technology*, Vol. 8, American Society for Information Science, Washington, D.C., pp. 243–275.

GORDON, RONALD F. (1972), Microform Programs and Operations at DDC, *Journal of Micrographics*, 5:5, pp. 229–231.

HAWKEN, W. R. (1966), *Copying Methods Manual*, American Library Association, Chicago.

HEILPRIN, L. B. (January, 1961), On the Information Problem Ahead, *American Documentation*, 12:1, pp. 6–14.

HEILPRIN, L. B. (July, 1961), Communication Engineering Approach to Microform, *American Documentation*, 12:3, p. 217.

HENRY, NICHOLAS L. (1974), Copyright, Public Policy, and Information Technology, *Science*, 183:4123, pp. 384–391.

KISH, JOSEPH L., Jr., and MORRIS, JAMES (1966), *Microfilm in Business*, Ronald Press Company, New York.

KOLB, EDWIN R. (1970), Computer Printing Forecast for the '70's, *Datamation*, 16:16, pp. 28–31.

KUNEY, JOSEPH H. (1968), Publication and Distribution of Information, in Cuadra, C.A., ed., *Annual Review of Information Science and Technology*, vol. 3, Encyclopaedia Britannica, Chicago, pp. 31–59.

Micrographics News and Views (June 30, 1971), 12:2, p. 8.

Micrographics News and Views (August 15, 1971), 3:3, p. 5.

Micrographics News and Views (October 31, 1971), 3:8, p. 4.

NELSON, CARL E. (1971), Microform Technology, in Cuadra, C.A., ed., *Annual Review of Information Science and Technology*, Vol. 6, Encyclopaedia Britannica, Chicago, pp. 77–111.

REVILL, D. H. (1970), Recent Developments in Reprography, *The Library World*, 71:838, pp. 295–298.

SAWYER, TED (1970), Photocopying and Microform Production, *Business Graphics*, 4:9, p. 8.

SEDGWICK, HENRY D. (1970), Goodbye Hot Metal, Hello Cool Tape, *Datamation*, 16:16, pp. 32–35.

SHATZKIN, LEONARD (1968), In-House Composition: Effects on Publishing, *Publisher's Weekly*, 194:15, pp. 27–30.

SHATZKIN, LEONARD (1969), Some Effects of Computer Composition on the Editorial Process in Book Publishing, *Publisher's Weekly*, 195:14, pp. 28–31.

SOPHAR, GERALD J. (1970), Williams and Wilkins vs. U.S. Government, *Newsletter of the ASIS*, 9:5, pp. 1–4.

SPREITZER, F. F. (1973), Developments in Copying, Micrographics, and Graphic Communicaitons, 1972, *Library Resources and Techincal Services*, 17:2, pp. 144–167.

STRAUSS, VICTOR (1969), The New Composition Technology: Promises and Realities, *Publisher's Weekly*, 195:18, pp. 62–65.

TAUBER, A.S., and MYERS, W. C. (1962), Photochromic Micro-Images, a Key to Practical Microdocument Storage and Dissemination, *American Documentation*, 13:4, pp. 403–409.

VEANER, ALLEN B. (1969), Reprography and Microform Technology, in Cuadra, C.A., ed., *Annual Review of Information Science and Technology*, Vol. 4, Encyclopaedia Britannica, Chicago, pp. 175–201.

WOODS, ALLEN (1963), *Modern Newspaper Production*, Harper and Row, New York.

Chapter Three

Information Processing–Digital Storage and Transmission

The processes of Chapter Two all deal with information in terms of images, usually images of entire pages. An exception is found in the second step of photocomposition. Although the output of that step is a CRT-displayed page that is photographed, the input is not an image: it is on magnetic tape in *digital* form.

The digital mode of storage and transmission is becoming crucial in many kinds of information systems, and has special importance for information storage and retrieval. Along with microfilm, digital storage is one of two major ways of retaining information in greatly condensed form. Ten years ago it appeared that microfilming and digitizing would be alternative, perhaps competitive, methods of storing information. But with the development of computer output microfilm, to be discussed near the end of this chapter, it is apparent that microfilm and digital storage supplement each other remarkably well within the framework of a single information system.

BINARY NUMBER CODING

The word "digit" means both "number" and "finger," and both meanings are appropriate in the visualization of the digital form of information. The association goes back to primitive counting on the fingers, but in all forms of computational equipment, including the most complex of computers, there is the same association between physical events and numbers corresponding to them.

In much the way that counting on the fingers led to the decimal number system, counting with computers led inevitably to a system of *binary numbers*, specifically to a number system built exclusively on the digits 1 and 0. Computers, of course, do many things aside from ordinary computation, but all can be done in terms of binary numbers; likewise information of any kind—numerical, alphabetical, even pictorial—can be stored and processed in binary form.

Digital computers are able to manipulate items of information at speeds from 1 million to a 100 million times as fast as is possible for the human hand or brain. By what means does this rapid manipulation take place, and where—physically—are the "digits" of the computer? As we are to learn in Chapter Four, these great speeds are attainable through circuitry interrelating a large number of small units, each capable of being swiftly changed between two stable states, e.g., relays that are either open or closed, tiny magnetic fields that are oriented in either of two opposite directions, diodes that are either transmitting electric current or not transmitting. Changes between one state and another in such *bi-stable elements* are among the fastest processes under the control of man—and they have been getting faster by the year. In the 1950s processes took place in microseconds (millionths of a second), in the 1960s in hundreds of nanoseconds (billionths of a second), and in the 1970s—? Bi-stable elements are fast because they are simple and because—as a result of being simple—they can be made small. A foremost example of such a bi-stable element is the magnetic core, thousands of which make up a computer's high-speed memory. Huskey (1970) observes:

> During the fifteen years that cores have been in use, the materials have been improved, the size has decreased (increasing the speed), driving current requirements has been reduced, and cores have been made less temperature sensitive. For example, early memories were made from 80-mil (cores), with a memory cycle time of 5 microseconds. Now, 18-mil cores with cycle times of 500 nanoseconds . . . are standard. . . .

The earliest computers primarily did *arithmetic* in terms of the bi-stable units. Numerical representation of what was happening physically in the computer required the use of the binary number system. If a bi-stable unit can be either "off" or "on," this can correspond numerically to either "0" or "1." Numbers larger than "1" can be expressed by having sufficiently many bi-stable units in a row. To understand this, we must view the binary number system *as* a number system, apart from the computer.

The basis of a number system is the relationship between the process of counting and the symbols representing the count. Once again it is helpful to visualize counting with one's fingers in the decimal system. We employ the symbols 1 to 9 to correspond to each successive digit counted; at the tenth digit, however, we do not use some new symbol X to represent it, but write the old symbol 1 followed by the null symbol 0. This is a way of saying that a full count of the fingers has been made, and that the counter is being set back to zero in readiness for a second count. The symbol preceding the zero, 1 in this case, is used to keep track of how many full counts have been made.

Many people cannot quite accept the idea that number systems can be based on counts other than ten. If human beings had been endowed with 12 fingers instead of 10, doubtlessly the intellectual development of the race would have led to a duodecimal system; why would one want to count only to 10 when nature has given him 12 handy appendages? One can do arithmetic in the duodecimal system; arithmetic, after all, is a shorthand method of counting.*

A number system often used by computer programmers is based on counting to eight, rather than to ten; it is the *octal* number system. In the octal system one forgets that he has ever heard of the symbols 8 and 9, and steps his counter to 10 just after the count reaches 7. (Most programmers have in recent years shifted from the octal system to the hexadecimal, based on counting to 16. These systems will be discussed further in this chapter under *output*.)

Once one is accustomed to the idea that ten is not a magic number, and that number systems can be based on counting to 12, to 8, to 5, or any other whole number other than zero, the idea of having a number system with only the digits 1 and 0 no longer seems preposterous. In binary, instead of counting to ten and setting the counter back to zero, we count to two and set it back. Here are some familiar decimal numbers and their binary equivalents:

1 = 1	4 = 100	7 = 111	10 = 1010	99 = 1100011
2 = 10	5 = 101	8 = 1000	12 = 1100	100 = 1100100
3 = 11	6 = 110 **	9 = 1001	24 = 11000	1974 = 11110110110

---

*The story of the development of number systems in various civilizations is a complex one, and by no means a clean sweep for the decimal system. The topic is exhaustively treated by Knuth (1969).
**Note that doubling a number in binary involves merely adding 0; thus, all even numbers end in zero.

56 Information Processing—Digital Storage and Transmission

As soon as it is established that any decimal number can be faithfully represented as a binary number, then it follows that much else can be represented in binary—in particular, any information that can be expressed as decimal digits. As a most important example, the alphabet can be set in correspondence with decimal numbers: $A=1$, $B=2$, $C=3$, ..., $Z=26$. These numbers, of course, can be translated into binary and thereby stored in a computing machine made up of bi-stable elements.

There is, however, a slight catch: one has to have a method for avoiding the confusion of alphabetical and numerical information. A very straightforward means of doing this is to enlist an additional bi-stable unit as a distinguishing code. Thus if $Z=26$, and given the binary version of 26, 11010, one can precede this number with a binary digit such that a 1 designates the letter Z (111010) and a 0 designates the number 26 (011010). The convention actually used in most computers is somewhat different, but the principle is similar. The principle may be seen to operate in one of the most well-known schemes for coding of so-called alphanumeric data, used in connection with IBM's System/360 computer:

a = 10000001	n = 10010101	? = 11000000	L = 11010011	Y = 11101000
b = 10000010	o = 10010110	A = 11000001	M = 11010100	Z = 11101001
c = 10000011	p = 10010111	B = 11000010	N = 11010101	0 = 11110000
d = 10000100	q = 10011000	C = 11000011	O = 11010110	1 = 11110001
e = 10000101	r = 10011001	D = 11000100	P = 11010111	2 = 11110010
f = 10000110	s = 10100010	E = 11000101	Q = 11011000	3 = 11110011
g = 10000111	t = 10100011	F = 11000110	R = 11011001	4 = 11110100
h = 10001000	u = 10100100	G = 11000111	S = 11100010	5 = 11110101
i = 10001001	v = 10100101	H = 11001000	T = 11100011	6 = 11110110
j = 10010001	w = 10100110	I = 11001001	U = 11100100	7 = 11110111
k = 10010010	x = 10100111	! = 11010000	V = 11100101	8 = 11111000
l = 10010011	y = 10101000	J = 11010001	W = 11100110	9 = 11111001*
m = 10010100	z = 10101001	K = 11010010	X = 11100111	

*Where numerals are concerned, the eight-bit code here is used only for storage; for computation, the numbers are translated into straight binary.

This tabulation is only a subset of the coding scheme; not included is a whole family of codes standing for various punctuation marks and other special symbols. This tabulation does, however, give a complete picture of the systematic features of the binary coding scheme. Suppose we speak in terms of the commonly used word *bit*, which may be regarded as a contraction of the term binary digit. It can be seen that all of the symbol codes are eight bits in length; this bit-length is standard for IBM 360-series computers. Such a unit of bit-length is called a *byte*; if English text is being processed, the various letters, spaces, and punctuation marks are stored successively in bytes in the same order as they occur in the text.

Another interesting feature of the code is that alphabetical and numerical sorting can be done (which has not always been so easy on IBM computers earlier than the 360). Alphabetical sorting is a straightforward process because the numerical code for each letter increases with its position in the alphabet. If one uses all eight bits of the code in the sort process, the capital initial letters and lower case initial letters are separated from each other, and from numbers; if, however, only the final six bits are used, upper and lower case variants of an initial letter are brought together, while still being separated from numbers.

When the concept of a "byte" originated early in the 1960s, its standard length was six bits. The change to eight bits was motivated *partly* by the expectation that computers would be called upon with increasingly greater frequency to handle language materials and a great variety of special symbols, especially in the case of computers in publishing (Chapter Two). To visualize the problem with the six-bit code, we note that the bit-length of a code limits the number of distinguishable binary representations that can be stored therein. A one-bit code can handle only two representations, 0 and 1; a two-bit code can contain only four, 00, 01, 10, and 11. In general, the number of representations that can be stored is the nth power of 2, where n is the bit-length; thus a byte of six bits can accommodate 64 different characters. In the days of the six-bit byte, computers were constrained to dealing only with capital letters, or with lower case—but not with both. Consulting the above tabulation, one can count 52 upper and lower case letters plus 10 decimal numbers—62. But the capacity of a six-bit byte is 64, which leaves little room for necessary punctuation marks and special symbols. The eight-bit byte, however, accommodates 256 symbols, more than adequate space for all letters of both cases, numerals, punctuation marks, and even Greek letters.

The IBM eight-bit code is called EBCDIC, which is an acronym for extended binary-coded-decimal interchange code. As has been true of previous IBM alphanumeric codes, compatibility exists with respect to the 80-column IBM card. The relationship between the card-punch code and the eight-bit byte code can be easily seen by comparing the foregoing tabulation with Figure 3.1, below. Lower case letters, not shown in the figure, are indicated by the use of two-hole combinations in the top three rows of the card, rather than one hole, as used for capitals.

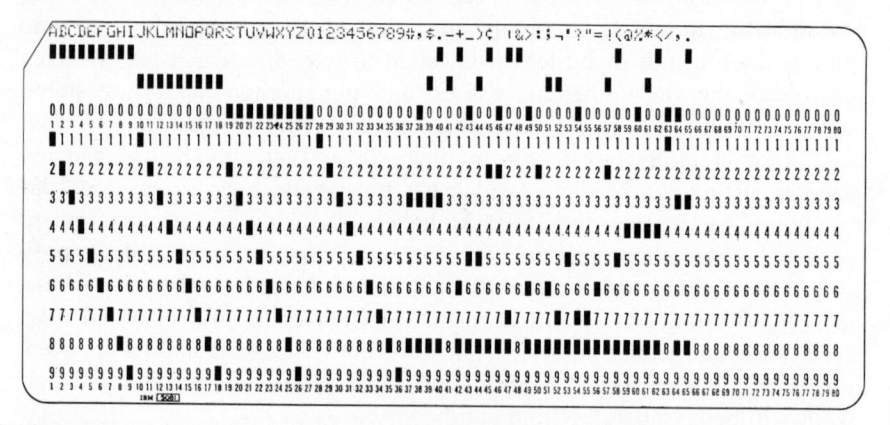

58   Information Processing—Digital Storage and Transmission

Figure 3.1. Punched card showing EBCDIC card coding system (Courtesy IBM Corp.)

The Bit as a Measure of Information. The image of a punched card in Figure 3.1 reminds us that the handling of information in digital form did not arise with the computer, but goes far back in time, even before the 1880s, when punched cards came into use. The first digital representation of information sprung from efficiency requirements in communication at a distance. Speaking and writing are arts so familiar and so facile that their efficiency, or lack of it, may seldom seem to be an issue. From time to time, however, the need to communicate beyond the range of the human voice has given rise to relatively cumbersome, unnatural methods, such as telegraphy, semaphore, or smoke signals. The fact that these methods are cumbersome forces attention on techniques of "making every move count" in the conveyance of information.

This is most evident in the case of a smoke signal: one cannot readily form an A-shaped or B-shaped cloud of smoke, and is limited to a series of puffs to express a message. Sender and receiver must carefully decide in advance what is important to communicate, to get the best out of a smoke signal—the maximum amount of information in the minimum number of puffs. A variant of the smoke-signal method was the communication by lantern flash at the outbreak of the American Revolutionary War. The message "one if by land and two if by sea," which informed Paul Revere of the coming of the British, is actually a two-bit binary code, where 00 (complete darkness) means "no news yet," 01 and 10 (which in this case cannot be distinguished from each other) means "by land," and 11 means "by sea."

Contrast the two-bit code with the number of bits that would have been needed to spell out "by land" or "by sea" using EBCDIC 8-bit code. Even a telegraph-like dot/dash method of flashing the lantern would have required in the neighborhood of a dozen flashes, a number that can be reduced by eliminating the redundant word "by." One begins to get an idea of the effort that can be saved through the design of an efficient communication code.

A binary digit, a bit, which, as we have seen, is an index of storage capacity, can also be used as a measure of communication efficiency and of information itself. One bit of information is that which is capable of reducing a receiver's uncertainty by 50 percent. Paul Revere had his uncertainty reduced by the lantern flashing. Before the signal he thought "it will either be by land or by sea"; after the signal he knew it would be "by sea." We also can see that the historic lantern was used inefficiently, since two flashes should not have been necessary in the coding arrangement; for example, the choice of either a red lantern or a green lantern could have been an appropriate one-bit signalling device. The idea of the bit of information has been extensively developed mathematically, so that—according to the well-known science of *information theory*—it is possible to compute minimum or optimum numbers of bits required in a great many coding and communications situations.

Though we now have telephone, radio, and microwave communications that can transmit, in a second, a thousand times as much information as Paul Revere received, the issue of efficient coding of information has not become less. On the contrary, it has increased, for our civilization behaves in such a way as to crowd whatever communication channel capacity is available to it. Becker (1968) observes:

> Regarding the computer's interface with communications, it should . . . be pointed out that the communications we enjoy in this country were originally designed for the telephone system some 42 years ago. They were initially intended to carry voice communications, not the data of the digital computer, nor the teletype, nor the output of a video camera. . . .Thus, there is inefficient use of a system . . . designed for some other purpose. . . .

Becker goes on to cite an AT&T prediction that during the 1970s the volume of data communications flowing over the telephone lines will exceed the volume of voice communications.

INPUT TO DIGITAL STORAGE

The familiar punched card (Figure 3.1) has been used as a system of digital storage since the 1880s, when Herman Hollerith developed it to permit the mechanical handling of census data. Complex machines to handle the punched cards—sorters, collators, tabulators, verifiers, automatic punches, and so on—formed a vast data processing empire well before the advent of computers, and International Business Machines became its giant self mainly through the marketing of these machines (now known as electronic accounting machines). Computers, of course, have so greatly outstripped the electronic accounting machines as data processors that the punched card is no longer so much a medium for information storage or processing as it is a means of input to the computer.

The input process is the crossover point between information storage as we are accustomed to it (books, papers, and other forms of printed data) and digital storage. It is at this point that the conversion must take place from the familiar letter and number shapes to the alien binary digits of *machine language*, as the digital representation is commonly termed. Two general routes exist for conversion to machine language, keyboarding and automatic character recognition. This statement, however, applies only to printed data, and not to the full range of data that computers handle. In scientific and engineering applications of computers, it is quite common to feed data from a variety of measuring instruments into computer storage, as for example in the performance of wind-tunnel testing.

Keyboard Input. Key depression was and still is the most widespread means of converting alphanumeric data to machine language. Probably the most common keyboard input is via IBM 026 or 029 keypunch machine, the output of which consists of cards such as the one in Figure 3.1. Error is the number one problem in any method of keyboarding. In the case of the IBM machine, errors are controlled by means of a *verifier*, a machine with a keyboard like that of the keypunch machine. The verifier operator feeds just-punched cards through while typing from the same data-sheet as did the keypunch operator. When the verifier detects a punch pattern discrepancy, an alarm is lighted as a sign that either the verifier operator or the keypunch operator has made a mistake. The verifier operator then rekeys the discrepant character; if it is the verifier's mistake, the keyboarding continues uninterrupted, but if the punch is actually in error, the machine fails to punch a certifying notch at the right-hand end of the card. Later the incorrect card can easily be seen and picked out of the deck for repunching. Verification is an expensive way of error checking, but it has repeatedly proven its worth, especially with regard to the input of computer programs and numerical data, which are inherently difficult to proofread, and for which a single error can prove very costly when a program is run.

As we are to see later in the chapter, keypunch machines are very primitive and cumbersome when compared to the semiautomatic or computer-assisted keyboards that have recently been coming into use. Nevertheless some degrees of automaticity are present in these early machines. Most commonly, a *program card* mounted on a rotating drum is used to provide automatic control of the fields to be punched on the cards —skipping fields when they are not needed, duplicating fields one card to the next when desired, or automatically shifting from numeric to alphabetic in a given field. (Note: a field is a fixed range of contiguous columns on a card, such as columns 1 through 10, 26 through 40, etc.; thus the program card acts as a complex version of the tab on a typewriter.)

A factor (aside from verification) that makes card punching among the more expensive methods of keyboarding is its intrinsic slowness, compared, for example, to typing. The mechanical nature of the 026 or 029 machines is a large part of the reason: the complex mechanism needed to pull the card past the punch station while keying is just naturally slower than corresponding mechanisms on a typewriter. Also, an operator must be constantly attentive that characters are being punched in the proper column. An error sensed by the operator cannot be corrected; an entire new card must be punched. For these and other reasons (including allowance for nonproductive operator time), a production rate of about 6000 keystrokes (characters) per hour is expectable, as compared to a production of 12,000 per hour by a typist.

Figures 3.2 and 3.3 illustrate another major input medium, punched paper tape. Such punched tape made up a larger percentage of input in the early days of computing than it does today, although it is still a common means of input. With such machines as the Flexowriter, punched tape can be produced as a by-product of typing for publication. As more than a note of interest, the production of such tapes in connection with publishing goes back to the nineteenth century, for they were used for the automatic control of monotype typesetting machines. H. P. Luhn, whose work we discuss at length in Chapter Ten, used monotype tapes as computer input in his famed automatic abstracting experiments in the late 1950s. Unfortunately for the development of the art of text processing by computers, the tape-driven monotype was long ago eased to the sidelines of publishing by linotype and similar typecasting machines (Chapter Two). If the monotype had prevailed, it could have led to a much earlier partnership between the world of publishing and that of data processing.

The astute reader has probably noticed the analogous relationship between punched cards and punched tape, on the one hand, and microfiche and roll microfilm, on the other (Chapter Two). The gradual loss of ground by paper tape to punched cards in data processing has occurred for many of the same reasons that roll film is losing out to fiche. Unlike

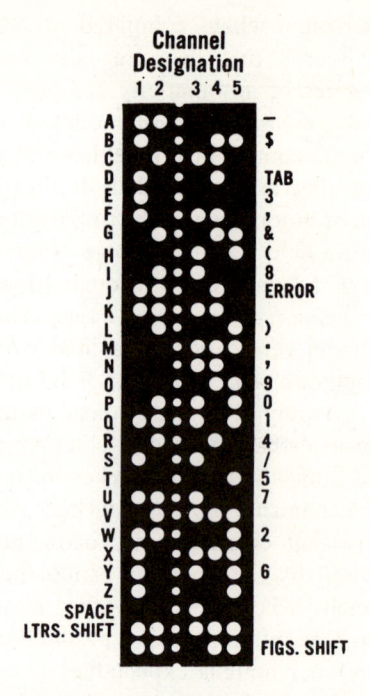

Figure 3.2. Standard 5-channel punched tape code system.

tape, cards can be sorted, interfiled, and otherwise rearranged, and the correction of errors on tape is a far less workable proposition than is the case for cards.

It is interesting to consider the nature of some of the chief uses of punched paper tape today. One use is, as it was in the beginning of computers, as an alternative to magnetic tape. As anyone knows who watches television or movie dramas involving computers, data is fed into the computer from magnetic tape. But in the 1950s, when the first computers were operated, it was quite common to use punched paper tape for this purpose. Punched tape quickly lost out to magnetic tape because the latter is faster and is erasable, and hence may be used again and again. Still, paper tape, and the apparatus that goes with it, has the virtue of cheapness, relative to magnetic tape. For this reason paper tape finds continuing use in minicomputer peripherals (where cheapness is the name of the game) both as input and as auxiliary storage.

Another prominent use of paper tape today is as a means of increasing the efficiency of data entry in on-line systems. A Teletype machine (which we shall talk about in greater length under "On-line Input") is the

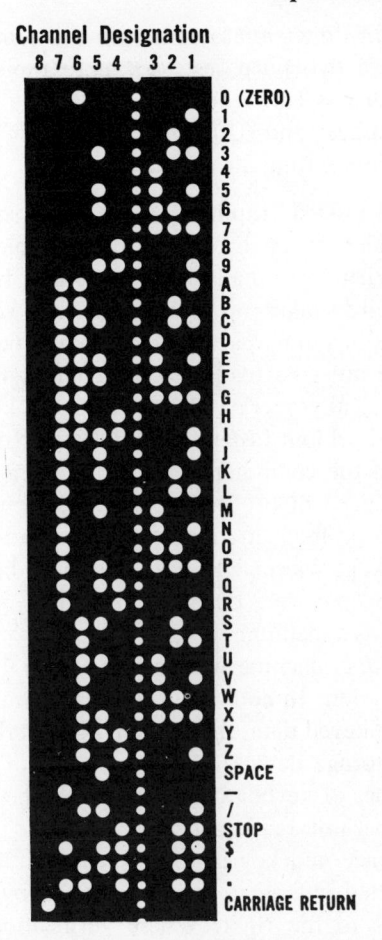

Figure 3.3. Standard 8-channel punched tape code system.

most common on-line input device, and often has a tape punch next to its keyboard. This punch permits the Teletype user a choice of input modes:

1. Direct entry, in which key depressions are immediately transmitted over telephone lines as coded audio signals (equivalent code shown in Figures 3.2 and 3.3).
2. Buffered entry, in which the code is punched on the tape while the Teletype is in an off-line status. At a later time the paper-tape reader is used in the transmission of the already-punched data over the telephone lines.

Alternative 2, which is used whenever a large amount of data has to be transmitted (and when direct interaction with the computer is not immediately needed), serves two purposes; (a) more rapid sending of audio signals (a human typist is slower than a paper tape reader) and hence reduction of line charges, and (b) the provision of an opportunity to correct errors before committing the data to the line.*

Key-to-Tape and Key-to-Disk Input. As we have seen, punched cards and paper are deficient as media, being nonerasable and nonreusable, without microfilm's virtue of small storage volume. Indeed, printed text stored on punched cards takes up many times the volume as the same material stored in files of typing paper. Then, having been keyboarded, the cards and paper tape must be read into the computer; card readers and paper tape readers typically operate at rates of several hundred characters per second (cps), and seldom faster than 2000 cps. In contrast, magnetic tape may be read into the computer at 300,000 cps, a rate commensurate with the computer's speed of processing. Clearly, for input purposes it is desirable to have data on magnetic tape or other rapid-input medium: the computer cannot be kept waiting. Hence, sooner or later in the development of computers, people were destined to wonder why punched paper had to be put up with as a medium of input.

The first *key-to-tape* machine was introduced in 1965** by Mohawk Data Sciences Corporation. In addition to the use of magnetic tape in lieu of cards to receive the keyed data, the concept of *buffering* was introduced. A buffer is a small storage device, often consisting of magnetic cores, in which one or more lines of keyboarded material can be temporarily stored. When a keyboard operator realizes he has made an error, the machine allows him to backspace and key in the correct character. On some keyboards, even an omitted character can be inserted by, in effect, shoving subsequent characters to the right. Where verification is practiced, the machine can act as its own verifier, because the contents of the buffer can be matched against re-keyed data. If the buffer-stored material is found to be correct, it is then released and written on magnetic tape (Carey, 1970). (Note the similarity—and the superiority—of this procedure to that already discussed for Teletype and paper tape.)

Key-to-tape machines are used either as "stand-alone" units or as groups of keyboards from which data are merged (Dorn, 1973). In the

---
*Corrections of paper tape are perforce limited in nature, since one cannot erase holes in paper; one can punch additional holes, however, and "all holes" is, in fact, an erase mechanism.
**Prior to 1965 the use of paper as direct input to the computer was often sidestepped through use of a card-to-tape converter, and the cards were then saved for backup storage.

latter case, opportunities for functional sharing are present. As a rudimentary example, there is a great deal of space on a single magnetic tape (enough for 20 to 30 million alphabetic characters), and therefore there is no intrinsic reason why each keyboard should be provided with a separate tape-writing mechanism when instead data from all keyboards can be written on one tape. This realization has led to a "central collection" arrangement, a multi-station key-to-tape system in which a central controller (often a minicomputer) is used to coordinate the actions and inputs from a number of keyboards. Some functions, including error detection, editing, formatting, and merging new and old data, can be carried out centrally, at a saving, rather than individually at each keyboard (Feidelman, 1973).

The fact that magnetic tape must be accessed serially (by winding it past a read-write head) imposes great limitations on an input system of this kind. However, any part of a magnetic disk memory can be accessed directly (as we shall further appreciate when disks are discussed in greater detail under Storage), and this makes disks even more appropriate than tape as a receptacle for input from numerous keyboards. This fact resulted in the *key-to-disk* or *shared processor* concept. (These two terms are often used interchangeably because a shared processor—often a minicomputer—is needed to take full advantage of this method of pooling input.) To understand what a disk (rather than a tape) will do for such a system, visualize a situation in which several keyboard operators are jointly updating the data on a single tape. The data to be updated are, of course, necessarily accessible in linear fashion on a tape. If there are five operators, A, B, C, D, and E, and if their updated data is entered in the same time order as they are listed here, magnetic tape would be entirely suitable for collecting their data—provided the old data to be updated is present on the tape in the same order, A, B, C, D, and E. In that case a new tape can be written, with each operator making his updating contribution in sequence.

Such a joint-updating system would work much better, however, if one did not have to worry about the sequence in which things are done. Not worrying about sequence in a straight key-to-tape system, however, implies the necessity to do a great deal of backspacing and jumping from here to there on the tape—a time-consuming and troublesome process. It is at this point that the value of a disk memory, with its direct access, can be seen.

Current semantics notwithstanding, most "key-to-disk" systems are still key-to-tape systems, in that the ultimate output is still a magnetic tape. The disk is used in much the same manner as a buffer in a straight key-to-tape device. But because it (*a*) is a vastly larger and more flexible buffer,

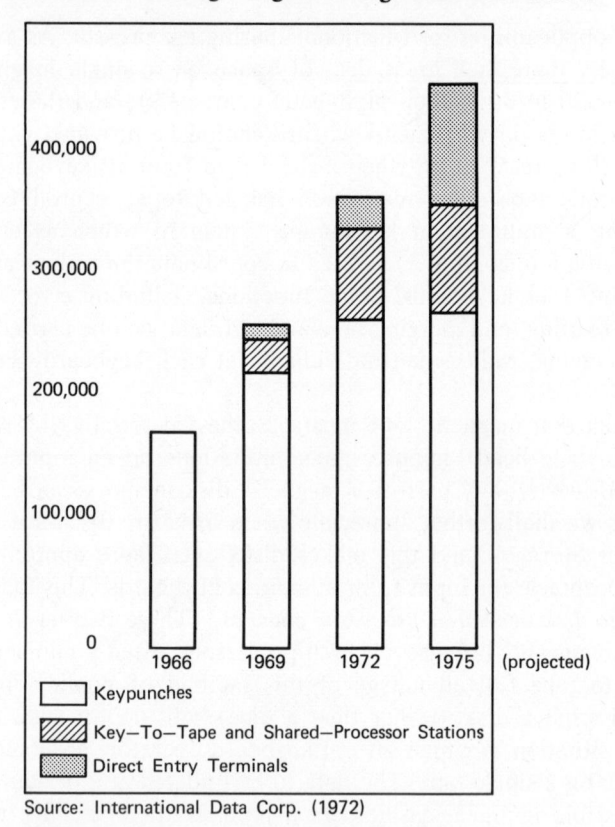

Figure 3.4. Entry keyboards used with U.S. computers.

Source: International Data Corp. (1972)

(*b*) is connected to many keyboards rather than one, and (*c*) is minicomputer-controlled, many more things are possible than with a simple buffer, especially in the province of arranging and rearranging data in desired formats. Positioning, generation of blank or skip fields, left zero filling, duplication, code conversion, and many other such operations needed, for example, to place data in a form for eventual summary output, are easy to carry out with such a disk/minicomputer entry system (Rosbury, 1970). The final output is a tape (rather than disk pack or some other medium) for reasons of economics and convenience: magnetic tape combines relative cheapness as a storage medium with ready availability for computer input (Reagan, 1973).

Key-to-disk, along with key-to-tape, systems have keyboarding rates from 40 to 50 percent higher than those of keypunch machines. In key-to-disk systems, productivity per man-hour has been known to increase by 20 percent over punched-card keyboarding even during the first year of operation of the new system (Mills, 1973).

Cassettes, Cartridges, and Floppy Disks. The trend of the times to minicomputers, and to minidevices of many kinds, has brought miniaturization of magnetic storage also, in the form of tape casettes and cartridges, and floppy disks. These storage devices function rather similarly to the disks we have just been discussing: they provide enlarged and flexible buffer capacity to a keyboard. Eventually their contents are transmitted to computer-compatible tapes; the contents of a cassette, for example, would be written on tape by a cassette-to-magnetic-tape converter.*

The significance of these ministorage units is that they provide great potential for cheap, off-line data capturing—in a way that keypunch machines have traditionally done in a bulky and cumbersome way. The output of a keyboard using a floppy disk, for example, might be the equivalent of 2000 punched cards—nicely compressed on a platter about the size of a 45 rpm record. Though the economics of this mode of keyboarding are not yet clear, costs are dropping so rapidly that the mode may one day prove to be the ultimate in cheapness for key data entry. These devices are in principle attachable to keyboards that are already used for other purposes, such as cash registers; the fact that some of the personnel cost is thus "already accounted for" has given much impetus to point-of-sale data collection in business.

Cassettes and cartridges, which look and operate somewhat alike, are an extension of the stand-alone key-to-tape, rather than the key-to-disk, principle, in that they evolve toward individual and uncoordinated keyboarding. The cassette device, commonly termed a *digital cassette recorder*, uses an upgraded version of the standard Philips-type cassette originally developed for audio recording. Cartridges differ from cassettes in a number of ways, such as having ¼" tape, whereas cassettes have the standard 120-mil (⅛") width. This and the other design differences supposedly give cartridges greater performance and reliability than cassettes; but basically their function is the same (Davis, 1973). Though usually used on a stand-alone basis, cassettes and cartridges can easily be used on a shared-processor basis.

The floppy disk (also called a *diskette*) is a storage unit which, unlike a cartridge or cassette, can be handled and transported independently of its mounting and drive mechanism. About 8" in diameter, the diskette is normally carried in an envelope, to prevent wear or damage; the envelope contains a small slot through recording at the keyboard or reading at the computer takes place. One diskette can hold 250 thousand characters, and may be conveniently mailed. The diskette, like cassettes and cartridges, is well suited for stand-alone keyboarding.

---
*Recently, however, equipment for direct reading of these units into computer storage has been introduced.

68   Information Processing—Digital Storage and Transmission

The keyboarding methods discussed thus far, including keypunch and paper tape, key-to-tape, key-to-disk, and those just discussed, are adapted to volume input or production-type environments, which require either no feedback from the computer or the minimal kind of computer-assistance that shared processors and minicomputers offer. This kind of input is ordinarily termed *off-line input*, whereas that requiring feedback or communication with a large computer is termed *on-line input*, which we shortly discuss. It is well to recognize, however, that the distinction between off-line and on-line is becoming increasingly blurred with the development of minicomputers, sophisticated keyboard electronics, and other advanced devices that provide all degrees of computer-like feedback, from the very rudimentary to the highly diverse. A two-level feedback arrangement, involving a minicomputer and a large central computer, is diagrammed in Figure 3.5. Businesses carrying on transactions with the public are increasingly likely to use this kind of input configuration. Many recent production keyboards, especially in the key-to-tape and key-to-disk area, are surmounted with small display scopes, making them ostensibly on-line devices; but in practice such devices may be used exclusively for

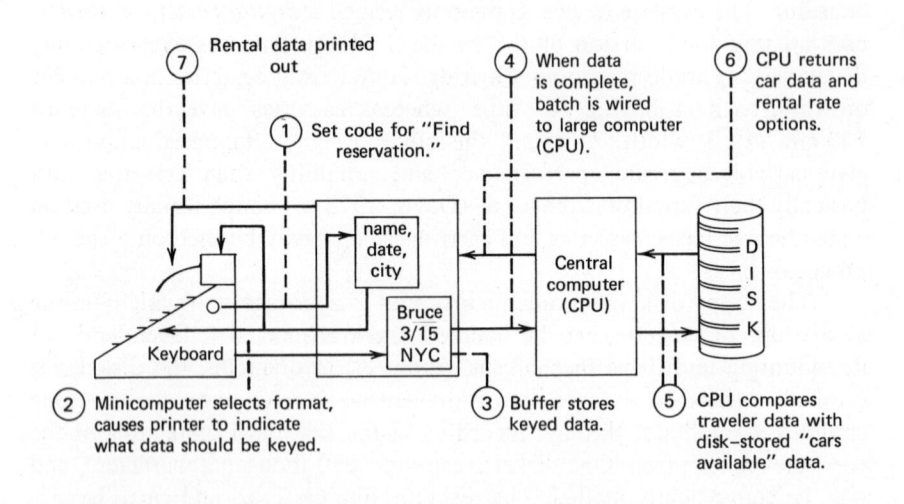

Figure 3.5. Sketch of a contemporary keyboarding arrangement using an "intelligent terminal" principle, part of a system operated by a well-known car rental agency (Haavind, 1972).

volume input and seldom if ever in the conversational mode, as a true on-line terminal would be used.

Re-entry Records. When a computer systems designer turns his attention to input components, he tries to avoid keyboarding, and its associated personnel costs, wherever possible. A simple way of bypassing keyboarding is the use of *re-entry records*—punched cards produced as output from a mechanized system and containing data in both printed and machine-readable form. Such records can serve to communicate data to people and then, subsequently, to re-enter the same data into the mechanized system without the need to keypunch it. They are perhaps most familiar in their use as utility bills, mailed to the customer with the request "Please return this part" imprinted on the re-entry portion. In libraries, they are especially useful in circulation control systems, in the form of prepunched book cards, transaction cards, and borrower cards.

Optical Character Recognition. As we have already appreciated, computers—composed of their many bi-stable elements—must do all their computing and processing, all their "thinking," in terms of digitized bits of information. But is it really necessary that a computer should receive its input in the form of bits? Why not in the form of images? The blind man reading Braille takes in data at a very slow rate in comparison to the man with acute vision, who can scan a book page at a glance, and even (if he has eidetic memory) retain its contents. Computers have been blind in the same sense, forced to finger the holes in punched cards, and thus capture information bit by bit, when much more should be physically possible, for computers can, without difficulty, bring new information into their high-speed core memories at rates exceeding 30 million bits per second. The fastest optical character readers can take in information at a thousandth of this rate, and punched card readers at about five ten-thousandths. Card readers, it must be noted, are at or near their practical upper limit in speed; but no one knows how high the upper limits might be for optical readers.

As seems to be true for so many other instruments allied with computers, the history of character-reading machines predates the computer era. Oddly but appropriately some of the first investigations were connected with helping the blind. In 1914 Fournier D'Albe invented the first known reading machine for the blind. He wanted to evolve a simple, hand-operated device which a blind person could move across the printed page and from which he could obtain meaningful aural output. With it a blind person would be able to read a wider range of printed material of his own choosing and do so unassisted.

D'Albe's machine produced five distinct tones, based on the scanning of five photosensitive elements. The machine was not quite portable, and scanning was accomplished mechanically by moving along one line of print at a time. The presence or absence of pieces of print in a letter resulted in a different set of tones being produced. In 1946 the Radio Corporation of America developed an electric pencil which could be moved across one line of print at a time and which emitted aural signals whose frequency was a function of the position of a beam of light in the pencil as it passed over segments of printed letters. Varying signals generated different sounds, and to the highly trained and sensitive ears of the blind one letter could be distinguished from another.

Later Mortimer Taube (1948) suggested that the signals emitted by the electric pencil be coupled to a facsimile device so that a copy of the printed page being scanned could be transmitted to a remote station. He said, however, in a note of caution:

... During the war the Radio Corporation of America (RCA) Laboratories worked on the development of a scanning device which could be held in the hand and which could activate a sound producing apparatus when passed over a printed text. This machine was intended as a device to enable blind people to read ordinary printed books. Unfortunately it has so far proved impossible to use the scanner on texts selected at random since the shapes of letters vary too much in different texts. For example, a letter "a" in one font may sound more like an "e" in the same font than like an "a" in a different type font. ...

Optical character readers (OCR) consist of three basic functional units: (*a*) document transport, (*b*) scanner, and (*c*) recognition unit.

The function of the *document transport* is to move each document to the reading station, position it properly, and move it into an *out* hopper. Transport mechanisms can be divided into two basic types, one for handling individual documents (paper sheets or cards) and the other for handling continuous rolls (cash register or adding machine tapes).

The function of the *scanner* is to convert the alphanumeric characters, symbols, codes, or marks on a document into analog or digital electronic signals that can be analyzed by the recognition unit. Scanning techniques include mechanical disc scanners (as employed in the pioneer Farrington machines) to flying spot scanners, image dissectors, and television pickup tubes. Optical scanning involves projecting an image of the character by reflected light to a lens system. The optical system sharpens the image and transmits it on through two intersecting slits to a photo-multiplier (a tube capable of converting light patterns into electrical signals). Since the white parts of the image reflect more light than the black portions of the image do, the photo-multiplier essentially receives a continuous stream of spots of light. Theoretically, if the combination of spots

Input to Digital Storage 71

of light for the image of each character is different, the converted electrical signals will be different. These differences are the basis of the ability to discriminate between characters.

The character recognition unit accepts the signals from the scanner and compares them with a signal library. This is a reference store and set of rules providing well-defined recognition criteria by which to decide which letter or character a given signal represents. Three methods are presently used for making this comparison: (*a*) *exact match*—requiring an absolute match with all or part of the character in the store; (*b*) *best fit*—a unique identification of the character but not necessarily absolute; and, (*c*) *threshold*—which allows for an acceptable degree of match between the character and the store. As might be expected, exact match is very accurate but will reject many characters as unidentifiable. The threshold method is least accurate and may produce a high rate of ambiguous identification.

An exact match character recognition technique is possible at low expense and with low requirement for sophisticated interpretation logic *if* one confines his scanning to specially designed characters. The earliest large-scale use of character readers was of this sort, and was pioneered by oil companies in the processing of credit cards.

The principle is viewed at its input end by most drivers, but they may not have any idea of what happens later in the process. Embossed on each customer's plastic credit card is his account number. (Type faces for the ten numerals were so chosen as to ensure maximum reliability by building in large differences between each of the characters.) When gasoline is purchased, the customer presents his card. It is used to imprint his name and account number on a tabulating card invoice. The gasoline attendant writes in the dollar amount by hand. At a central location, automatic character-reading machines scan the account number imprinted on the invoice and automatically punch it into a tabulating card. An operator proofreads each invoice and, as a by-product, keys in the dollar amount in an adding machine which is coupled with a card punch. Thus, the dollar amount also gets punched "automatically" into the tabulating card. Conventional electronic accounting machines then sort, collate, and merge the punched invoices and prepare monthly billing statements for the customer.

The basic operating speed of the reading equipment is 180 invoices per minute. It has built into it sufficient error-check devices to keep the reject rate low. Dirty thumb prints and handling smears have had only insignificant effects on the system. Experience in field installations, such as that of Standard Oil Company of California, has proven it to be very reliable.

Another inexpensive way to obtain exact match reading is by using a nonoptical principle which, like the gasoline credit card, employs special characters but which also provides a means of accurately interpreting symbols that have a high probability of being written on, stamped on, or otherwise defaced. We refer, of course, to the use of magnetic ink on bank checks (Figure 3.6).

The Bank of America has been a leader in the development and application of electronic systems to banking. During the cousre of its research efforts, it encouraged the Stanford Research Institute (SRI) to pursue automatic character recognition (Eldredge, 1955). The great bulk of banking business is done by check, and Bank of America appreciated the enormous benefits which would be derived if some automatic means were devised to sort and handle checks.* SRI developed a system for the magnetic reading of numerals which operates as follows.

1. Original numerals, in a prescribed type font, are imprinted on the check by using ink containing magnetic oxide.
2. The check is fed past a prereading station which essentially is a magnetic field, and the magnetically inked numerals are energized or charged.
3. Next, the numerals on the check are placed in almost direct contact with a conventional magnetic read-head of the kind normally used in magnetic tape systems.
4. The magnetic read-head senses the signals which are generated by the thin layer of magnetic ink. Since the type font of the numerals

---
*More recently Bank of America has shifted from magnetic ink to straight OCR.

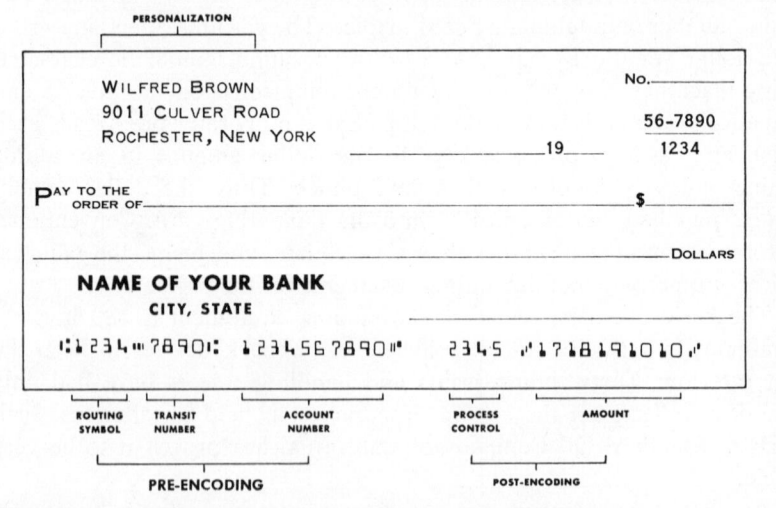

Figure 3.6. Magnetic ink character recognition. (MICR.)

was originally designed to produce ten (0–9) distinguishable signals, each numeral produces a distinctly different signal or waveform when passed under the read-head.
5. These signals are amplified, filtered, and transmitted to correlation networks. These electrical networks have the signal characteristics of each number stored for reference in circuitry.
6. When a given signal passes through the correlation network, it exists as an output signal for a particular numerical character. This output signal is used to punch cards, write on magnetic tape, print, etc.

The magnetic-ink character-reading system is secure against most of the common types of defacement. Overprinting, dirt, or writing across the numbers causes no trouble. Embossing, for example, by a ballpoint pen, causes no difficulty, nor does wrinkled or sharply creased paper. Even though during the reading process close contact with the read-head is desirable, a layer of transparent adhesive tape over the numbers does not prevent reliable results. This means that torn checks can be repaired without detriment to the reading system. Imprinting with magnetic ink is highly durable and can withstand thousands of transits across the read-head with no impairment of the signal.

The examples given are the earliest and, even now, most widely used character recognition techniques. They do not, of course, constitute any approach to a general solution of the problem of automatic optical input from the printed page. Some insight into the nature of this problem can be gained by comparing the recognition logics of Figures 3.7 and 3.8, both of which are special character recognition systems that, as shown, convert directly into a binary code, and Figure 3.9, which is one of the simplest of the more general techniques of character recognition. The General Electric code (Figure 3.7) converts characters into the same sort of binary code as shown earlier for the IBM System/360. It is identical to the last four bits of the IBM code, except for the number 7; correcting for this apparent incompatibility is, however, a trivial matter. Disregarding the odd special symbols of the National Cash Register code, one notes slightly more readable numerals with, however, a somewhat longer binary representation. Going from these codes to the Farrington recognition code, we make the jump from simple conversion to true recognition. For the former codes any tilting, change in size, or other significant variation would very probably lead to errors in coding. For the Farrington code, however, some variability is tolerable, and one may adjust parameters for such criteria as "vertical" or "middle" to accommodate variations that may be encountered.

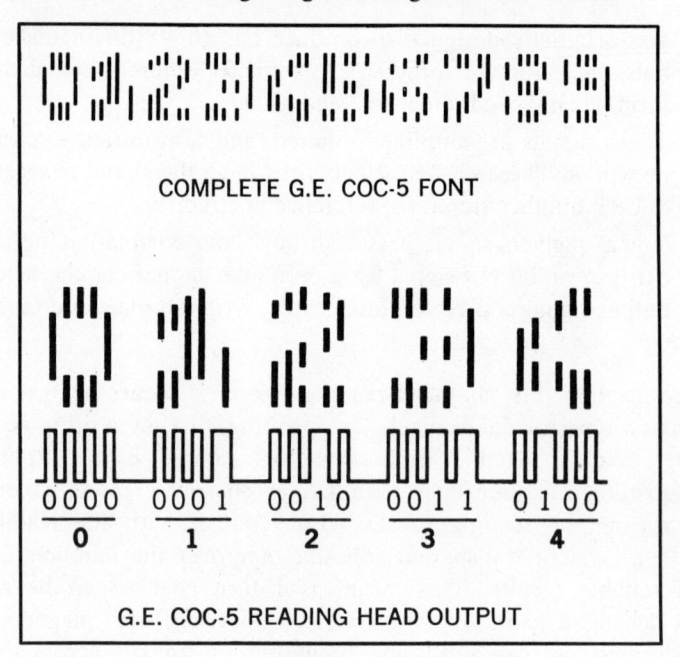

74   Information Processing—Digital Storage and Transmission

COMPLETE G.E. COC-5 FONT

0 0 0 0	0 0 0 1	0 0 1 0	0 0 1 1	0 1 0 0
0	1	2	3	4

G.E. COC-5 READING HEAD OUTPUT

Figure 3.7.

NATIONAL CASH REGISTER "NOF" FONT
(Lines show upper and lower reading tracks)

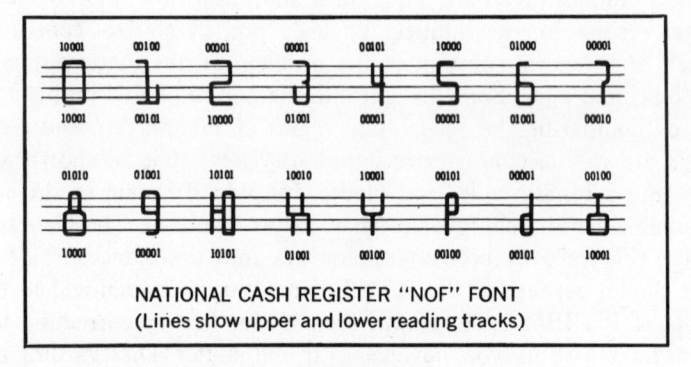

Figure 3.8

The most casual survey of a collection of printed matter will reveal a great diversity of type fonts. The road to developing multifont character readers has been a long one, and essentially a matter of extending principles like those in Figure 3.9 to cover the major kinds of variation from font to font—presence or absence of serifs, boldness, length-to-width ratios, italics, and so on. As a result machines now exist, such as the CDC 915, Farrington 3030, and Opscan 288, that will recognize four or five

Character Recognition Criteria *

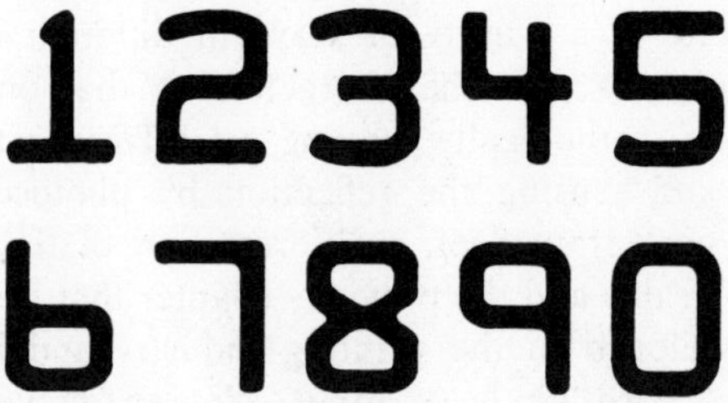

12345
67890

	0	1	2	3	4	5	6	7	8	9
LONG VERTICAL LEFT	+		−	−	−	−	+	−		−
LONG VERTICAL RIGHT	+	+	−	+	+	−	−	+		+
HORIZONTAL TOP	+	−	+	+	−	+	−	+	+	+
HORIZONTAL MIDDLE	−	−	+	+	+	+	+	−	+	+
HORIZONTAL BOTTOM	+	+	+	+	−	+	+	−	+	−
SHORT VERTICAL UPPER LEFT & LOWER RIGHT	+	−	−	−		+	+	−	+	+
SHORT VERTICAL UPPER RIGHT & LOWER LEFT	+	−	+	−	−	−	−	−	+	−
SHORT VERTICAL LEFT & RIGHT SIMULTANEOUSLY	+	−	−	−	−	+	−	+	+
SHORT VERTICAL UPPER LEFT					−	+				
LONG VERTICAL LEFT & RIGHT SIMULTANEOUSLY	+								−	
MIDDLE PROJECTING RIGHT					+					−

+ CONDITION MUST BE DETECTED

− CONDITION MUST NOT BE DETECTED

* Courtesy Farrington Manufacturing Co., Needham Heights, Mass.

Figure 3.9. (Reprinted with permission of *Datamation*, copyright Technical Publishing Co., Greenwich, Conn.)

different fonts and even hand-printed characters. The cost of an optical character reader varies according to its reading speed and its versatility in reading fonts and extends from $60,000 to more than $1 million (Andersson, 1971).

The process of optical reading, as already described, has two successive steps: scanning and recognition. Almost all contemporary optical readers scan, or sense, by means of a photocell or an array of photocells. Also, methods of chopping up each character are employed, so that the character's various components might be then matched against a library of stored criteria (such as in Figure 3.9) and identified. This segmenting of characters is done in a variety of ways in different readers, e.g., by moving a system of slits past the character, so that only part of it is sensed at a time; by methodically moving a CRT-generated spot of light over a character, and sensing the reflection by photocell; or by using several photocells, each trained on a different part of the same character.

We have seen in this and the previous chapter that the art of handling paper is highly developed in the printing industry and for the punched paper and punched card kinds of input. Not so, however, for optical character recognition (OCR). Rabinow (1969) explains:

> One of the surprising things . . . is that the problem of handling paper is every bit as difficult as the problem of recognizing characters. The reason for this is that the paper that OCR machines are expected to read has in some cases been handled or mishandled by human beings. . . . Because OCR machines are fast, the problem of handling such paper at very high speeds is extremely difficult. While the paper moving problem is gradually being solved, there are, at the present writing, no machines which can handle such documents without occasional, or perhaps, more truthfully speaking, frequent jams . . .and the quality of paper handlers can be categorized not by whether they have jams or not, but by how easy it is to unjam the machine when the jam occurs. . . .

The varied font problem and the paper handling problem are difficult enough so that it is still true, as it was 15 years ago when readers were first used with credit cards and bank checks, that those who get the greatest practical use out of the character-reading form of input are those who work with relatively standardized kinds of documents. EDP Analyzer (1969) describes a hospital medical records application in which a Control Data 3300 computer receives input from a CDC 915 optical scanner. The following statements characterize this application:

1. After studying a number of alternatives, the hospital concluded that use of optical scanners was the cheapest route to the use of a computer. The expense of either keypunching or on-line input led to their rejection by the hospital.
2. All documents which are used as input are those that would have been typed anyway, such as hospital admission forms or order forms for drugs and services. Thus OCR input is a by-product of regular operations.
3. Such documents are typed up on machines with standard OCR typing elements (Figure 3.10), thus avoiding the font problem.

Most input forms are freshly prepared, and with low diversity, minimizing the paper-handling problem.
4. *All* input, even that of computer programmers, is by OCR; the use of punched card input is unnecessary at any point in the system.

To the extent that a user of OCR technology is able to control the generation of his input documents, standardization of the kind just described is a far cheaper and more satisfactory route than dependence on some of the sophisticated omni-font machines now on the market. Many business and government organizations, which are often in control of the paper they have to deal with, are in a more fortunate position in this regard than are libraries and documentation centers.

Though the state of the art of OCR has developed to as fine a point as any other technology of input/output, its history up to the present has been one of continually lagging behind the expectations of its proponents, either as a partial or as an ultimate keypunch replacement method. A major impediment is that there are many kinds of information that do not exist in assembled machine-readable form, prior to input, and for which keyboarding by a human operator is an unavoidable first step. In other words, there are broad areas in which OCR may not be used as a means of bypassing keyboarding. This is true, for example, wherever data must be gathered by interview or handwriting, as in police crime reports or in job applications. In general it is true whenever information funneled through each input station must come from a variety of sources.

```
ABCDEFGHIJKLMNOPQRS
TUVWXYZ0123456789.,
'-{}%?♪⅄⊣:;=+/$*"&
```
USASC CHARACTER FONT

ÜÑÄØÖÆẞ£¥

ADDITIONAL CHARACTERS FOR INTERNATIONAL USE

Figure 3.10. USASC character font. (Reprinted with permission of *Datamation*, copyright Technical Publishing Co., Greenwich, Conn.)

On-line Input. Until about 1965 all keyboarding was off-line, meaning that the depression of the keys produced nothing but holes in cards, or paper tape that had no direct interaction with any computer system. In general, the computer programmer had no way of interaction with the computer except through punched cards, unless he were also the computer operator—which in most installations was very seldom the case. A strong factor that led to on-line use of time-shared computers was the awareness of how advantageous it would be for programmers to have direct interaction with the computer.

This could be done if a keyboard were wired to a buffer unit, so that typed characters could be stored in readiness for instant entry as input to an operating computer program. A programmer could, for example, type out several instructions to the computer and release them from the buffer simply by pressing the keyboard's carriage return button; a program (previously designated via keyboard) would, within milliseconds, execute the instructions and set up output that would be typed out at the same keyboard generating the input. Such a facility would look like a "typewriter that types back at you." A programmer, using a facility of this sort, could build up his programs, instruction by instruction and loop by loop, checking them out directly on the computer and correcting errors.* The program checkout process would then be speeded up by a factor of ten or greater, for no longer would the programmer have to wait 24 hours as his meticulously prepared coding sheet joined the queue of other programmers' coding sheets to go through keypunching, verifying, compiling, and other such batch processes of an essentially off-line nature.

On-line interactive terminals are now available to many kinds of users aside from programmers; on-line *retrieval* systems will be discussed in Chapter Nine and elsewhere in this book. On-line computer systems become economical by serving many users simultaneously, thus the phrase *time-shared computer.* Such simultaneous use is possible because of the great speed and capacity of contemporary computers. It is possible to accommodate as many as 100 users on one computer. This means that the programs to be used by each of the 100 are stored on magnetic disks, where they can be read into the computer's high-speed memory and executed in rotation. This rotated-use process takes place so swiftly that each user, seated at his remote Teletype or other in-out facility, may have the illusion that he alone is making use of the computer—unaware that 99 others are being served at the same time.

It is not practicable to discuss the input aspects of on-line terminals without also discussing their output, thereby getting somewhat ahead of

---
*The process of writing programs is discussed in Chapter Four.

ourselves in topical order. (Before on-line terminals became common, the input and output functions of a computer were generally completely separate, and embodied in physically separate machinery. Keypunches were keypunches and printers printers, and thus individual units of equipment could be neatly classified as either input or output; exceptions to this, such as magnetic tape drives and disks, having both input and output roles, were classifiable as auxiliary storage.)

The workhorse of remote input/output for the vast majority of on-line computer users has been the Teletype (Models 33, 35, and 37); according to a recent survey, 73 percent of the surveyed users communicated with the computer via Teletype (Hillegass, 1973). The simple, inexpensive (rent: $60–$75 per month) device combines input and output functions not merely in the same piece of equipment, but literally in the same set of typewriter keys.

When used for input, the keys are set in motion by the action of the user's fingers at the typewriter-style keyboard. As on a typewriter, characters are printed on paper rolled around a platen. But also electrical impulses corresponding to each character (in a code similar to those shown in Figures 3.2 and 3.3) are sent over the line to the computer; since, in most time-sharing systems, the line to the computer is apt to be a telephone line, these electrical impulses are first converted into audio signals (which telephone equipment, after all, is built to transmit). These signals must be converted back into digital pulses at the other end of the line. When output occurs, pulses from the computer activate the Teletype keys, which print the message or data on the paper encircling the platen. Since this paper is the same paper as used upon input, it constitutes a complete record of the dialogue between the user and the computer.

It should be made clear that "communicating with the computer" is but a convenient figure of speech, and the "dialogue" in reality is between the user and the programs being executed at his request by the computer. These programs are generally of two classes, (*a*) system programs available to all users of a given time-shared computer, and which enable the user to operate the computer during his portion of the shared time, and (*b*) the user's own programs, which, of course, can perform any data processing operation that the user selects. The user ordinarily has his own programs stored in a magnetic tape library at the computer site, and knows how to request them by appropriate labels; or, if the user happens to be a programmer, he can compose and check out programs of his own creation while seated at the terminal.

Aside from Teletype, the Univac DCT 500 and the IBM 2741 are among the frequently used terminals. The latter is more expensive ($125 per month) than Teletype, and has a higher line transmission rate (12–13 characters per second as compared to Teletype's 10 cps) and a longer print column (132 characters per line compared to Teletype's 72). The IBM machine also uses the Selectric typewriter ball, rather than individually actuated print faces for each key. We touched on Teletype's buffer capability in our above discussion of punched paper tape. The terminal IBM 2740, Model 2 (similar to the 2741), actually uses a magnetic core buffer that will hold up to 440 characters. This machine also has the interesting capability of time-sharing a telephone line with several like terminals, thus getting closer to the full transmission capacity that such a line can provide.

Keyboard/Display Terminals. There was once a time when cathode-ray-tube (CRT) displays were found exclusively at the output end of computer systems, and were customarily discussed as output equipment. However, though the nature of CRT displays is the same as before, and though they still function as output devices, computer systems themselves have changed so markedly in 10 years or so that CRT displays now function as much in connection with *input* devices (especially in on-line systems) as they do as pure output generators, and this conspicuous fact compels us to discuss them under input.

As has been the case with optical character recognition, high costs have held back the use of CRT displays for many years—until recently, when a point of genuine breakthrough appears to have occurred. From the 1950s, when some air-defense system display scopes were priced on a par with medium tanks, through the 1960s when many CRT's were in the $2500–$7000 price range, to the mid-1973 mark of $1500 (*Datamation*, 1973) these costs have declined and have brought the display scope close to its rightful place as widely available computer peripheral. Moreover, numerous non-CRT principles (such as are used in hand calculators) make certain somewhat limited displays "dirt cheap," and promise to do the same for all displays eventually.

There are two major categories of CRT displays, alphanumeric and graphic. Alphanumeric displays show only a preestablished set of characters, usually limited to a single font. One of the best known alphanumeric displays is the Charactron tube. As is typical of CRT displays, characters are generated on the face of the Charactron tube by transmission of a stream of electrons (Figure 3.11). Inside the tube, in front of the electron gun, is a small circular metallic mask. The mask has tiny holes in it shaped like the letters, numbers, and symbols to be displayed. The matrix on the mask acts like a stencil and allows only a tiny beam of electrons to pass through, which takes on in its cross section the shape of the character desired. (A magnified image of the matrix is shown in Figure 3.12.) Each

Input to Digital Storage 81

CHARACTRON® SHAPED BEAM TUBE

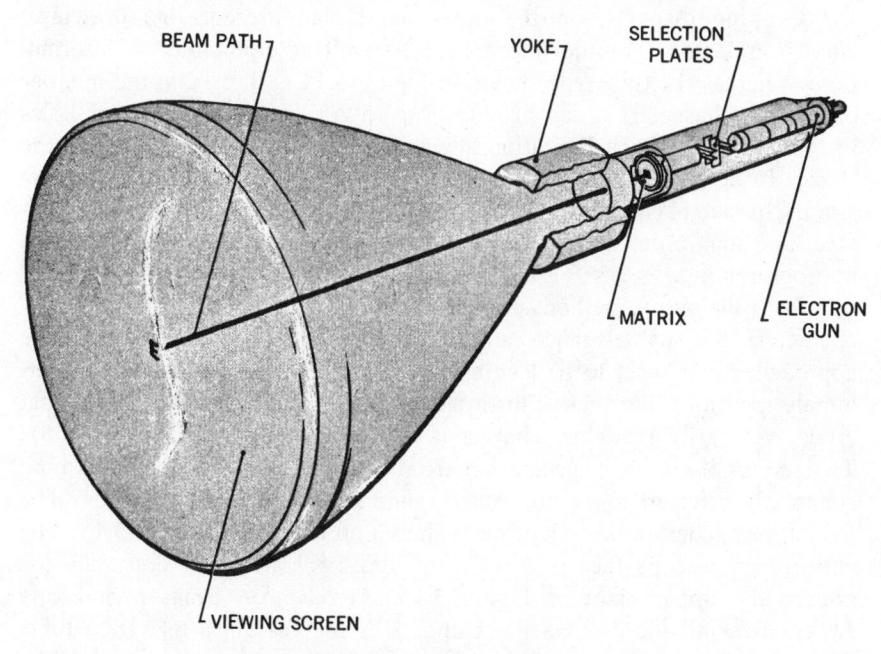

Figure 3.11. Cathode-ray tube character generation.

Figure 3.12. Etched matrix containing 96 characters and symbols.

character is projected to its proper position on the phosphor screen at the front of the tube. A typical display may provide enough such positions for 64 lines of text with up to 132 characters per line. The text to be displayed is initially stored in digital form in the computer, and it is an easy matter for a program to compute which of the characters should go where on the tube face, and the electron beam is directed accordingly. This beam, striking the phosphor screen, causes an area of its cross-sectional shape to glow, making that letter visible from the front of the tube.

Graphic displays, on the other hand, can present line drawings, curves, and other graphic information as well as alphanumeric information. Whereas the tube type shown in Figure 3.11 is limited in the number of distinct characters it can produce (up to 200) by the number of holes in the matrix, no such limitation affects graphic display tubes because the shapes to be projected are determined externally, i.e., by a computer program. Characters can be changed in size, slanted, rotated, converted to boldface, and manipulated in many other ways, due to the flexibility inherent in programming.

Both the above methods are capable of generating sharp, high quality characters, but such elegance can be expensive as well as unnecessary. The approaches that seem to be leading the way to really low-cost display terminals are more like those illustrated in Figure 3.13, in which somewhat crude, yet easily readable, characters are generated (Luxenberg, 1968). Two modes of character generation are shown, the dot pattern mode (more commonly referred to as *dot matrix*) and the stroke pattern mode. The dot-pattern generation mechanism is shown on the left of Figure 3.13. The entire display-scope face is divided up into 5×7 arrays of dots, like the one at the upper right of Figure 3.13. An electron beam periodically sweeps over all the dots on the scope, as is the case in a television tube. What any given character will be in a given 5×7 position is determined by code patterns similar to that in the bottom row left. How this code is transformed into a dot pattern can be seen with reference to the diagrams labelled *x deflection* and *y deflection* which are graphed in a time sequence running from left to right. Each "tooth" of the x deflection graph represents a sweep of the electron beam across a row of five dots in the pattern; for the first tooth, where the y deflection at the corresponding time is zero, the bottom row is swept; for subsequent teeth, the y deflection progressively changes, and the beam works upward from row to row. The lowest diagram (intensity control) consists in this case of on or off signals that determine whether a burst of electrons shall be fired at each dot whose "turn," governed by the x and y deflections, has come. The on-off sequence can be correlated, bit by bit, with the display scope's magnetic core array (upper left), where the information is stored, and with the scope-face dot matrix (upper right) that is swept by the beam.

The generation of the stroke pattern (lower right), like that of the dot pattern, is accomplished by changing the x and y deflections. The changes, however, are continuous rather than stepwise, and the bold arrows show the path swept over by the electron beam in generating the character R. The beam begins its sweep at (0,0) on the stroke pattern, and works its way up the lefthand side as a result of steady change in the y deflection, to form the shaft of the R. Then x is changed while y is held unchanged, moving the beam across the top of the pattern. Then y is changed, then x again. Finally, to generate the slanted member of R, x and y are changed simultaneously. The thin lines show the permissible path that the beam may sweep.

Thus, by restricting the forms of the characters, both in the stroke-pattern and in the dot-pattern approaches, the amount of information that has to be stored per character is minimized. Storage in a a display scope is required because of the need to refresh images on the phosphor from 30 to 70 times a second to maintain a flicker-free view, and the need for such storage is a good part of the cost of a display terminal; thus minimization of bits per character is a crucial matter. There exist some scopes designed so that the tube itself "remembers" (termed storage oscilloscopes), and do not require separate memories. These displays, however, may not be selectively erased (an important capability in interactive terminals), and have not prevailed vis à vis dot-matrix devices (Theis, 1968).

The fact that the market for electronic displays of all kinds is broadening so rapidly is likely to keep the technology and practice of character generation in a great state of flux, because there are so many parameters that govern which display system will be most satisfactory, while least expensive, in a given application. One such parameter is "maximum number of characters" required in a display field. In the swiftly growing field of display electronics for consumers, this maximum number is typically small, e.g., in such items as pocket calculators and electronic watches. Another important parameter, quite evident in such consumer items is miniaturization. With respect to both these parameters, the use of cathode-ray-tube generators becomes quite inappropriate at the small end of the scale because of the high power requirements and the high cost per displayed character (even if a suitably small CRT could be developed, which is doubtful).

The need for such small-scale displays is being met through a growing technology of self-illuminating characters. Most notable among these has been the light-emitting diode, in which the workhorse of modern electronics—the transistor—has been fashioned in a form that will glow when an electric current is passing through it (*Time*, 1972). For pocket calculators, seven such diodes arranged in the form of a figure 8 (Figure 3.14) will permit the generation and display of the digits 0 through 9, and one may generate a number of any size by having sufficiently many such diode configurations in a row. The cost of each digit is about $1.60, and can be

Typical dot-pattern character.

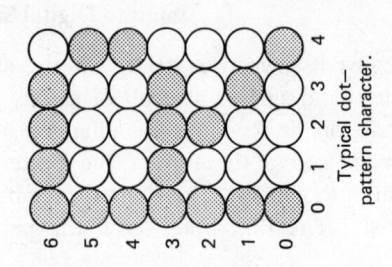

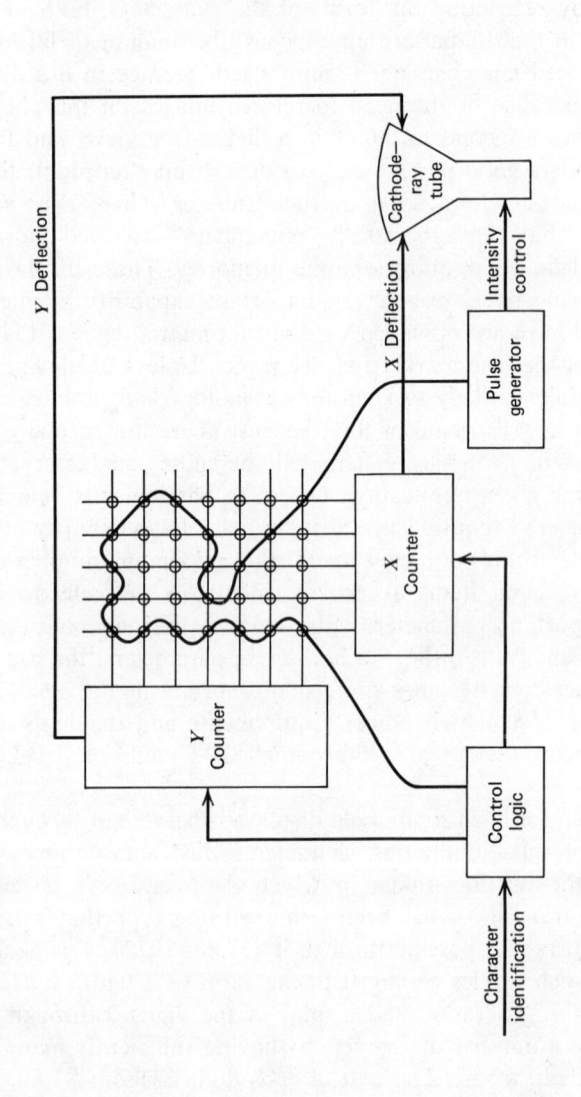

Fixed format dot generator (core storage).

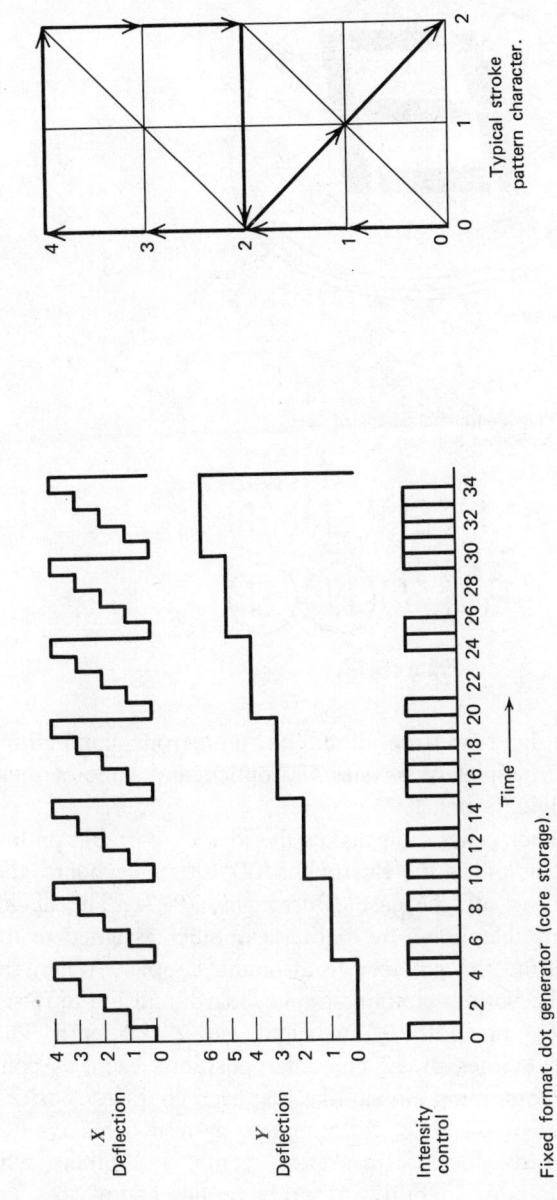

Figure 3.13. (Reprinted by permission from Luxenberg, H.R., and Kuehn, R.C., eds, *Display Systems Engineering*. New York: McGraw-Hill, 1968.)

85

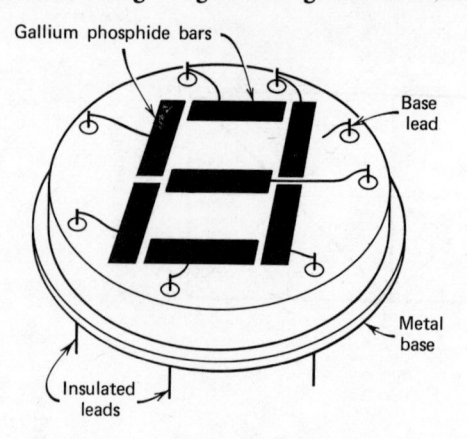

86   **Information Processing—Digital Storage and Transmission**

[Figure: Seven-segment LED display with labeled parts — Gallium phosphide bars, Base lead, Metal base, Insulated leads. Below: "Lighting combinations of bars produces numbers" showing digits 0 1 2 3 4 5 6 7 8 9.]

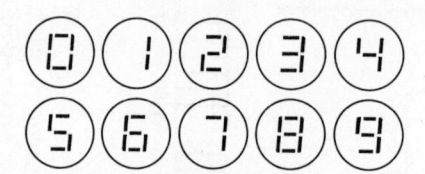

Figure 3.14.

expected to drop. The light-emitting diode has numerous competitors based on other bizarre principles of physics and optics, and some of these cost as little as 50¢ per digit (Sobel, 1973).

This mode of character generation makes the idea of portable on-line terminals feasible. An example is the Burroughs TD-700, a keyboard/display package that fits in an attaché case (Burroughs, 1972). The device may be put on-line at any telephone, by dialing a number assigned to the central computer and fitting the receiver to an audio coupler. When the attaché case is opened, the bottom contains the keyboard, and the upraised lid carries a display 14½" in width, 9" in height, and 2" in depth. This compact display, having 8 lines of 32 character positions each, is composed of numerous cells containing a neon-like gas; each character position has 35 of them arranged in the 5 × 7 dot-matrix pattern. This type of terminal is slanted towards doctors, insurance agents, and others who need a traveling information capability. Monthly rental, about $65, approximates that of a medium-priced Teletype (Anderson, 1973).

Despite the advent of such new technologies of character generation, and the miniaturized devices made possible thereby, the mainstream of display/keyboards is still CRT-centered and probably will remain so, for at least two reasons; (a) the great flexibility in generating all kinds of information in visual form, including graphs, charts, maps, etc., and diverse and precisely formed characters of varying size, font, and (even) color, and (b) the variety of ways a computer *user* can interact with displayed information.

The latter topic, interacting with displayed information, has already become too large to deal with justly herein. We can only give enough examples of this important aspect of keyboard/display terminals to illustrate the principles involved.

A rather basic mode of interaction, especially for terminals where the input is primarily text (letters and numbers arranged in horizontal sequences), is the use of the cursor, a small arrow or other symbol that permits the operator to know the position of the electron beam on the scope face. The cursor, in effect, couples the display scope and the keyboard, showing the operator where his keying action will take effect. The cursor may be manually moved, right and left, and up and down; this movement is the equivalent of moving the platen on an ordinary typewriter, so that an operator can skip lines, move back to make a correction, and so on. The cursor is generally manually controlled by buttons on the keyboard; the "cursor left key," for example, is, when flicked, a single backspace; when the key is held down, the cursor will move stepwise to the left until the key is released.

The cursor may also be computer controlled, and it is at this point that degrees of interactivity develop that are beyond those feasible to nondisplay terminals. If the keyboard operator is updating records, a computer-directed cursor can skip from place to place within the record format, based on a programmed determination of what new information is needed. Additionally, the computer may cause the cursor to skip format locations where the information can be updated by computation.

A menagerie of other interactive tools are available (many of them intended for graphic input, rather than text), and they are notable for having picturesque names: "light pen," "joystick," "mouse," and "tablet." The first and the last of these are probably the most general purpose, and the light pen may be one of the oldest, dating back to the SAGE Air Defense System. The light pen is a photocell device that can be pointed at any location on the CRT face; when the electron beam sweeps over the location, the photocell is activated at the precise time, and sends an impulse to the display scope's circuitry, where the x, y coordinates of the location are computed. In this manner, the operator may designate any character (or any element of the display whatsoever) for some special action. In the SAGE System, operators could thereby designate computer-processed radar blips as "suspicious," "hostile," "VIP," etc. In a more contemporary application, an electronic draftsman may key in a type of change (expand, erase, center, copy, etc.) and indicate by light pen where in a displayed blueprint the action is to take place (Schmedel, 1968).

The tablet (long known as the Rand tablet because of its invention at that facility) is a horizontal square of about 10 inches composed entirely of metallic dots, so closely spaced as to seem a smooth surface. Each dot corresponds to a point on a display scope, and an operator, by moving a stylus carefully from point to point on the tablet, may actually draw various figures which will immediately be CRT-displayed exactly as drawn on the tablet. It is the most expensive of the interactive devices we have named (Auerbach, 1971). Yet it is a device which is so general purpose and has so much ultimate potential as a means of easy interaction between human and computer that it is difficult to state with assurance where it might not eventually surface as an important computer-use tool.

"Smart" and "Intelligent" Terminals. One of the consequences of, and detractions from, on-line systems is communications—in particular the high cost and error proneness of sending and receiving data by telephone line. Also, time-shared on-line systems which must maximize the number of users in order to be dollar-effective, often suffer from near-overload conditions that result in a noticeable (to the user) slowdown in operations.* Both of these system flaws tend to cut down on the efficiency of on-line computer use, not only by raising per-user costs, but by cutting down in the interactive fluency that makes up much of the reason for using computers in an on-line mode. As it happens, both of these adversities can be met, to an extent, by building some data processing power into (or close to) the terminal itself.

Probably the concept of placing a portion of the computer's "brain" on the terminal's end of the telephone line led to the phrase *intelligent terminal*. The computer literature now speaks of "smart terminals" (somewhat less endowed than intelligent terminals), "dumb terminals", and even "sensible terminals." This development of phraseology is probably unfortunate in that it gives the impression that there is something decisively different about the "intelligent" terminals as compared to the kinds of terminals we have been talking about up to now. There is not, essentially, much difference, and the least misleading idea of intelligent terminals was probably given by Professor Andries van Dam (Brown University) in an article entitled "What is the IQ of Your Intelligent Terminal" when he defined intelligence as "the ability to do things locally" (Zientara, 1973).

---

*This is known as the "supermarket effect".

Sometimes the intelligence of a terminal is built into it in the form of keyboard and display electronics which allow an operator to do interactive work even when the terminal is off-line (an obvious advantage at times when the central system is down or when telephone service is interrupted). When the intelligence is embodied in a minicomputer at the terminal site, often several terminals are served in a way that we've already described under shared processors (Key-to-Disk). Probably the best way to think of terminal "intellectuality" is as akin to systems of distributing computing power in economical or practical ways, such as is determined to be most satisfactory in each individual computer system. Indeed, the system diagrams of some time-shared computing systems make one think of a living organism, with a central brain connected by nervous tissue (telephone lines) to outlying ganglia (minicomputers) in turn connected to receptor/effector organs (terminals).

DIGITAL STORAGE

A large digital computer can easily take in and process enough data to fill its expensive high-speed memory in a few milliseconds. Just as a professional man needs scratch pads, notebooks, and more formal publications to serve him as an auxiliary memory, so the computer needs nearby storage reservoirs in which to dump information that it has just finished processing, so that high-speed memory can be freed to process the next batch of data. Information thus placed in auxiliary storage can be recalled at a later time for further processing. Data processing is such a complex, many-staged activity that it could not be viably carried on without a variety of storage devices standing by, ready to give and receive data.

Magnetic Recording. To bring maximum efficiency to the use of auxiliary data storage, it is necessary to have a high-density storage medium, so that bits may be read in and out of computer memory at rates approaching the computer's own speed.* As we have noted, punched cards and even optical reading are far too slow to provide data at rates commensurate with the computer's processing speed. Fortunately, magnetic recording has been available from the beginning as a suitable basis for auxiliary storage. It has played a key role in the development of electronic data processing, and its own development has kept pace with that of the computer itself.

Magnetic recording is based on the fundamental relationship between

---

*Of the three media we are to discuss (tapes, disks, and drums), tapes are the slowest but some still manage to deliver up to 300,000 characters per second.

magnetism and electricity (Figure 3.15). Thus, if an electric current is passed through a wire wrapped around a small "u" shaped bar, called a *record head*, or *writing head*, a magnetic field will be created at the gap in the "u" which can be used to fix the magnetic state in a magnetizable surface. On the other hand, if a magnetized medium is passed by a similar (or the same) "u" shaped bar, now called a *reproduce head*, or *reading head*, an electric current will be generated in the wire. On this basic relationship the entire field of magnetic recording has developed, including that of audio signals, analog data, digital information, and video pictures.

To record digital information in this way, the appropriate binary codes are represented by a corresponding sequence of two different voltages in the electric current through the wire. The result is an identical sequence of magnetic fields and a resulting sequence of magnetically polarized spots on the storage medium as it moves under the recording head. In the reading operation, the process is reversed, and as the recording medium passes under the reading head, the succession of magnetic spots generates a corresponding succession of voltages in the wire. These are then interpreted by the logical circuitry to develop the binary coded representation of the information.

The density at which the binary coded data can be stored is described by the number of bits to the inch in the direction of recording and the number of channels to the inch across the recording medium. The densities possible in each case are determined by a number of considerations. The most fundamental of these is the basic geometry defined by the size of gap in the reading head and the distance from the gap to the recording surface. The smaller these two distances, the finer resolution and therefore the higher the density possible; in fact, contact recording, with essentially zero spacing between head and surface, is standard for magnetic tape, and densities of perhaps 1600 bits to the inch are not uncommon.

Another fundamental consideration is the speed at which the storage medium is moved past the reading head; the higher the speed, the stronger the signal generated and therefore the better the resolution possible. This results from the fact that the strength of the signal generated in a reading head is directly proportional to the rate at which the magnetic field on the storage medium passes by the head. In general, the signal level is on the order of perhaps $20/1000$ of a volt, and therefore the signal is at best difficult to distinguish from the background "noise" in the electrical circuit itself. At lower speeds and correspondingly lower voltages, dust particles. imperfections in the tape, and other sources of error could easily obscure the signal completely (Figures 3.16 and 3.17).

To record other than digital data, such as audio, video, and other analog information, the same techniques are involved, but different

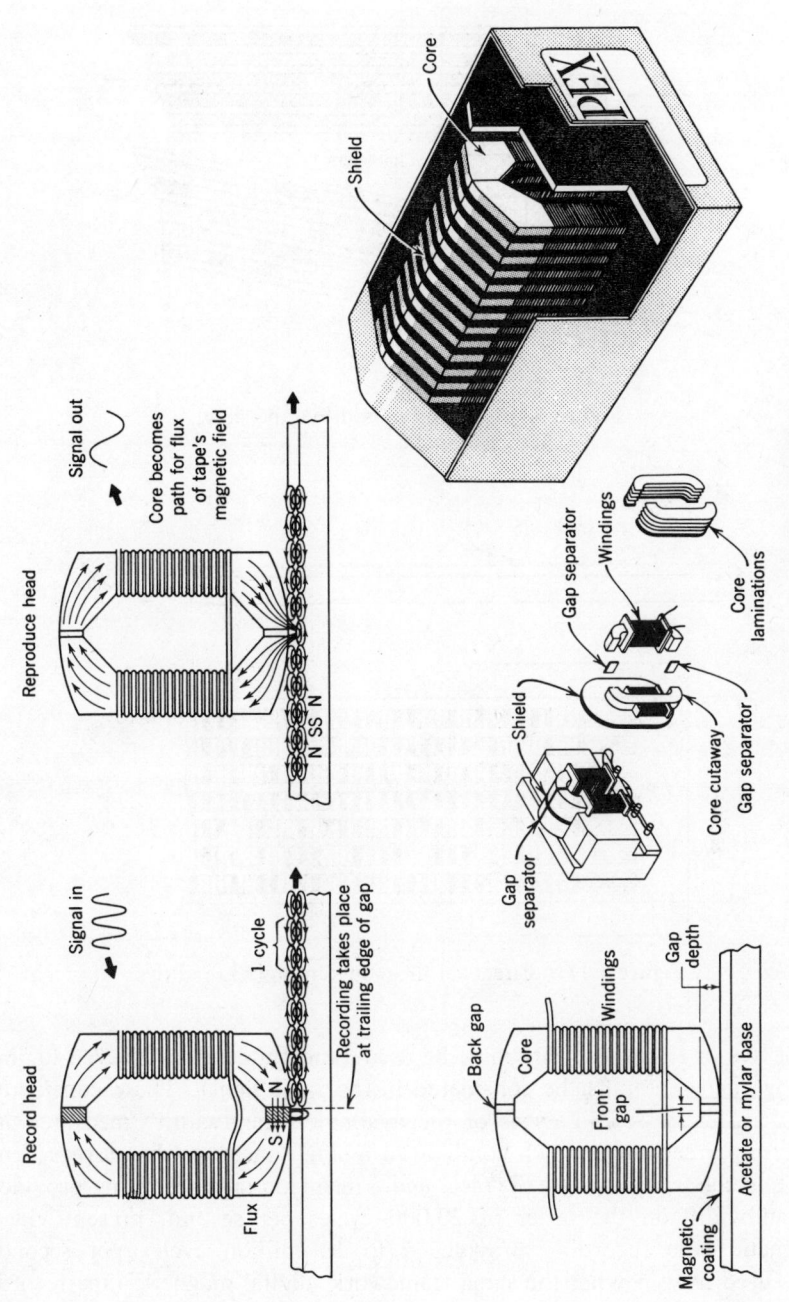

Figure 3.15. Principles of magnetic recording.

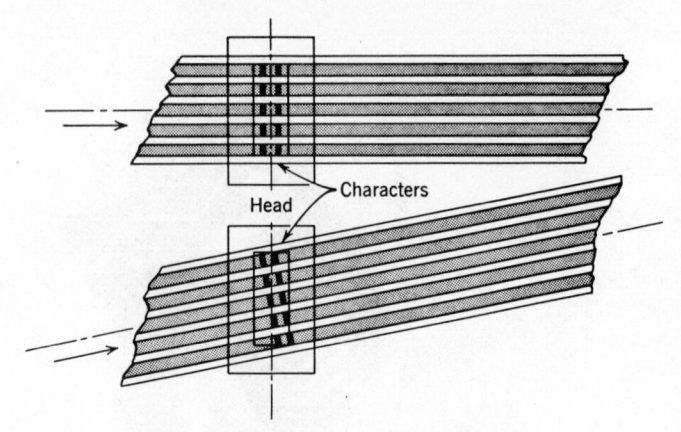

92 Information Processing—Digital Storage and Transmission

Figure 3.16. Error caused by tape skew.

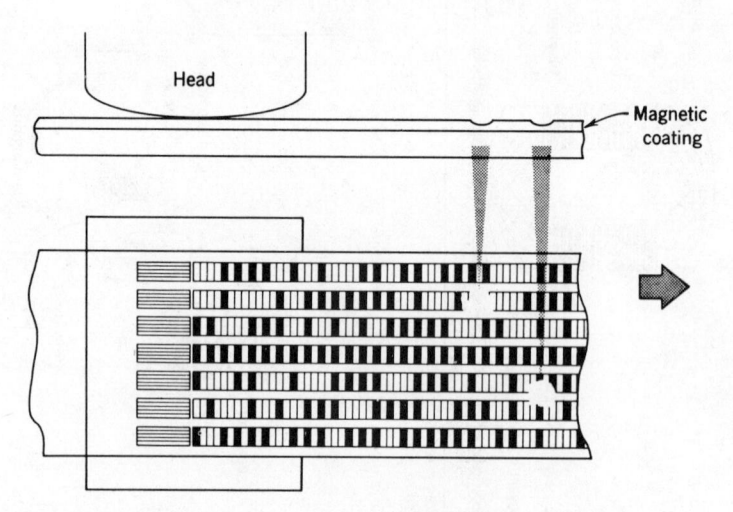

Figure 3.17. Effects of drop-outs in digital readings.

measures of storage density must be used (and fundamentally even digital storage densities must be considered in the same light). These considerations are expressed in terms of the available "bandwidth" measured in "cycles per second," which combine in a single measure the storage density and the transport rate. Typical audio magnetic tape recording provides a bandwidth on the order of 20,000 cycles per second, present video magnetic tape recording provides 5 to 10 million cycles per second. Measured in somewhat the same framework, digital magnetic tape recording presently provides up to 150,000 bits per second from each channel, which can be considered as the equivalent of perhaps 500,000 cycles per second.

Magnetic Drums. In certain respects the simplest physical medium for the recording of magnetic information is a cylindrical drum coated with material which will retain magnetic polarity. Such drums are rotated at extremely high speeds, limited only by the physical properties of the drum, so that the size of the signal will be correspondingly large. The reading and recording heads are placed in fixed positions close to the surface of the drum as it rotates under them. Each recording head will generate a "channel" of information (Figure 3.18). Most drum systems are limited by physical boundary conditions to a drum diameter of between 3 and 24 inches and to several hundred channels. As we have indicated, the density at which information can be recorded is a function of the distance between the reading head and the drum surface; the smaller this distance, the higher the density. Most drum systems utilize a mil (thousandth of an inch) spacing to provide typical densities on the order of 100 to 200 bits per inch.

Drums are relatively unsuitable for any large capacity storage, since they are limited to, generally speaking, less than five million bits (the equivalent of perhaps 750,000 alphabetic characters). Thus drums are not ideal for the storage of large files.

Magnetic Tape. Magnetic tape, on the other hand, represents an almost ideal sequential file storage medium. Information is stored on magnetic tape in channels, much as with punched tape, but in magnetic form so it can be erased and can be stored at much higher densities. Present magnetic tapes generally have 9 channels across a ½ inch tape and store at a density of 1000 or more bits to the inch per channel, utilizing contact recording (Figure 3.19). A typical reel of 2400 feet of magnetic tape may thus contain over 250 million bits of information, the equivalent of 20 to 30 million alphabetic characters. The tape handling devices transport the tape at high speed (200 to 300 inches per second) past the reading and recording head. The information transfer rate is fantastically high, in some cases over 300,000 characters per second.

One important issue concerning this method of recording is its "permanence." What is the life of magnetic tape and how permanent is the recorded data? In one sense, this has not been a significant issue. Methods for processing magnetic tape are usually designed to recopy files as they are updated. As a result, yesterday's tapes can provide the data needed if something happens to today's tapes. However, if one begins to store large amounts of essentially static, unchanging data in magnetic form, permanence will become a very significant issue. At this time, there is little

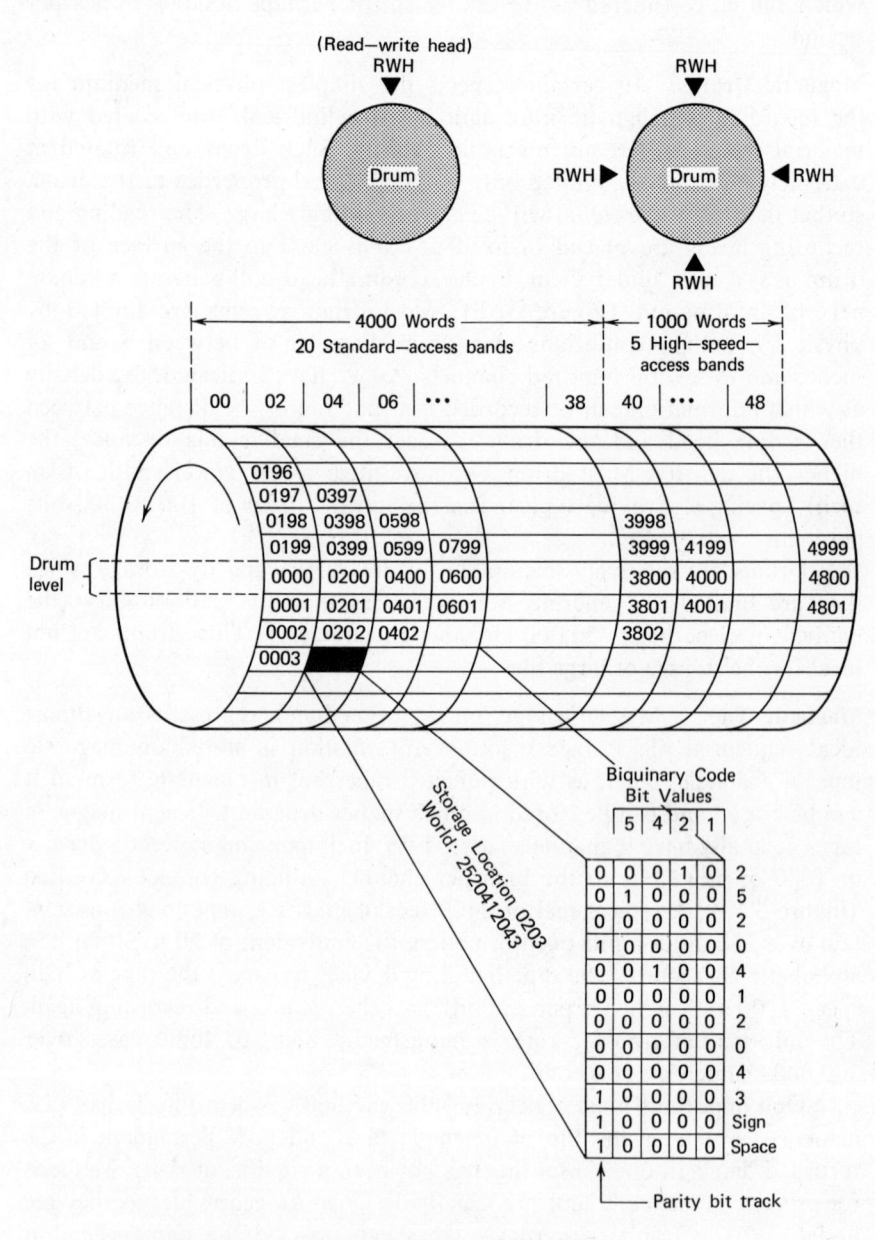

Figure 3.18. Magnetic drum addressing.

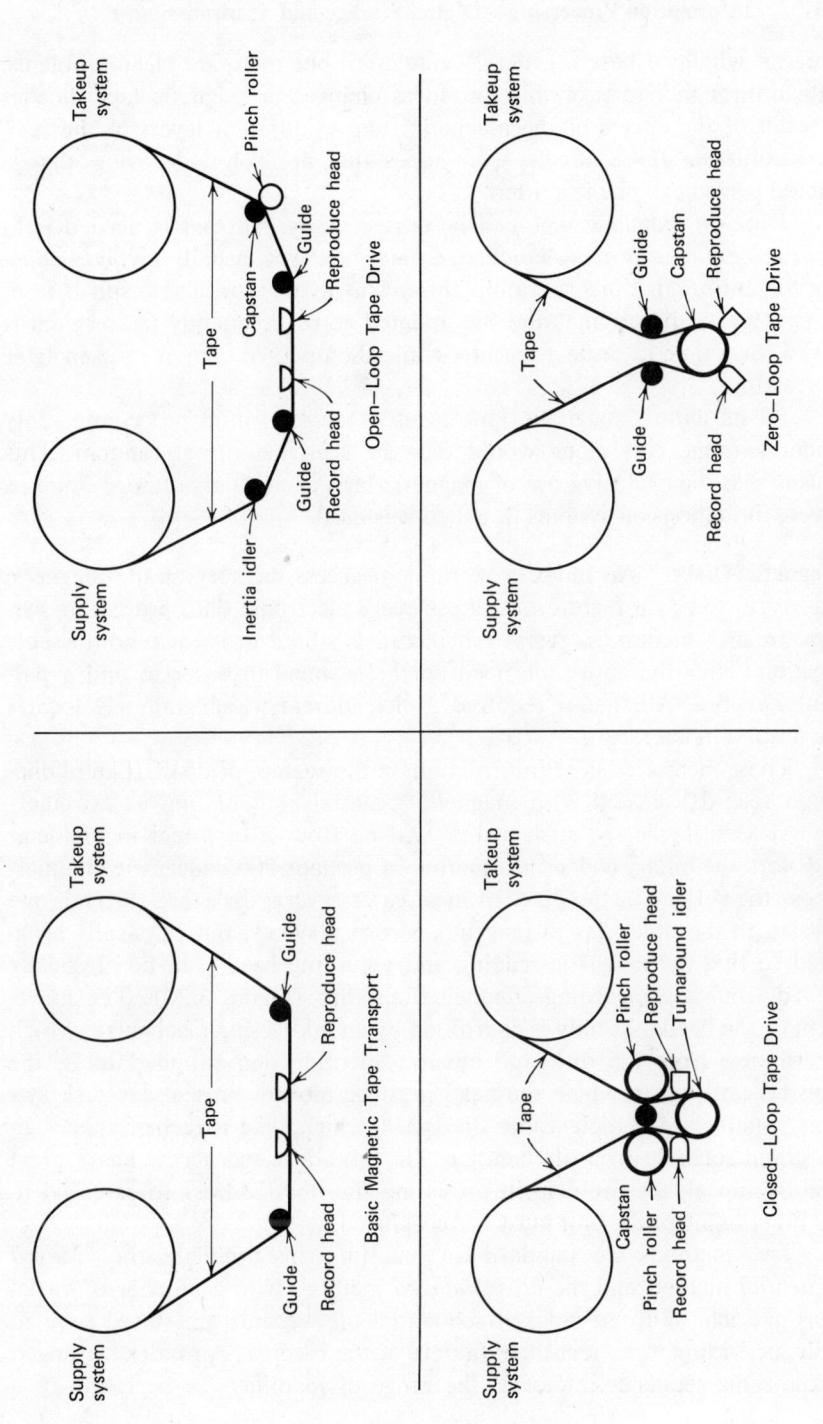

Figure 3.19. Magnetic tape. (Courtesy Ampex Corp.)

data on which to base a general evaluation, but there are clear problems. "Read-through," for example, produces changes in magnetic tape data as a result of the effects of the magnetic state in adjacent layers of the reel. To counteract those effects, even tapes that are not undergoing change should periodically be rewritten.

Data on magnetic tape can be erased easily. All that is needed is to rewrite new data over it. To change data, however, usually involves copying the entire tape, incorporating changes as they occur. The result is a set of two tapes: the original and the updated copy. Frequently the original is saved for a time to protect the file, while the updated copy is used in later processing.

By its nature, magnetic tape is used for sequential processing; only under extreme conditions would data be searched for at random. This means that the exclusive use of magnetic tape as auxiliary storage imposes severe limitations on systems in which it is used.

Magnetic Disks. An indexed or random access memory of the magnetic disk type now is a feature of almost every electronic data processing system. In such memories, every unit record is stored in its own addressable location. Thus the entire file need not be scanned in order to find a particular record. All that is required is the address which uniquely locates the desired index record.

These memories store information on the surface of disks (like phonograph records) coated with magnetic material and rotating at extremely high speeds. Typically, such a disk will be from 2 to 4 feet in diameter and store the binary coded information in perhaps 200 concentric channels across the surface of the disk. In most cases several disks are stacked, one parallel to the other (as in juke box record players), but physically separated so that the magnetic reading and recording heads can be physically moved from one recording channel to another (Figure 3.20). The movement of the head assembly is controlled by an addressing mechanism which determines, from the disk and channel identification supplied to it, the physical position to which the head must be moved. Present-day disk systems usually use a replaceable disk-pack which, like a reel of tape, can be stored separate from its handler. Though addressed access has a great deal of appeal, the problem in providing the item address so essential to the functioning of the unit must be recognized.

Two methods are standard for handling this problem: the *indexed sequential* method and the *cross-indexed* method, with a number of variations of each. With an indexed sequential file, records are stored sequentially, according to an identifier (a field of the record). An index, arranged in the same sequence, indicates the range of identifiers to be found in a

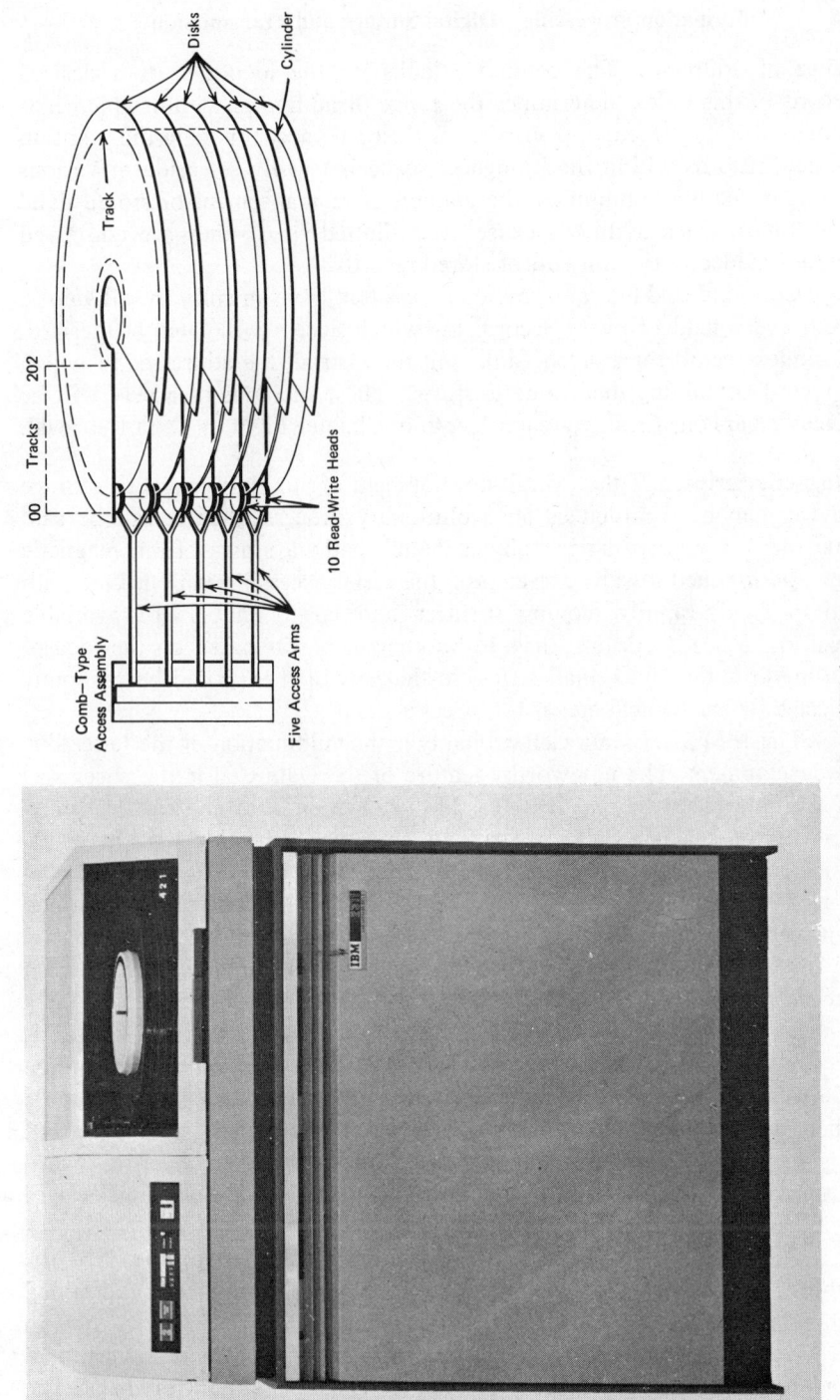

Figure 3.20. Disk memory.

range of addresses. The computer looks up the identifier of a desired record in this index, determines the range of addresses within which it is supposed to be stored, and then reads them. To accommodate the addition of new records within the sequence, space is usually set aside at various points in the file to minimize the amount of rearrangement of stored data. Sometimes, when additions exceed the allotted space, they are addressed by *link*s added to the contents of stored records.

Cross-indexed files are simple indexes that have an entry for all values, from every field of every record, on which access will later be desired. An index record for a given value will then list all the addresses in which a record containing that value is stored. These methods of access will be discussed at considerably greater length in Chapter Eight on Data Retrieval.

Magnetic Strips. If the overall development of auxiliary magnetic storage devices can be regarded as an evolutionary process, then it can be said that there were two major "phylogenetic" pathways away from magnetic tape, both aimed toward overcoming the serial access limitation. One path led to rigid, rapidly moving surfaces and large numbers of available read/write heads (drums, disks). Another path was based on the idea of cutting up a tape into small strips, so that any of them could be randomly selected by mechanical means for direct access.

The IBM 2321 Data Cell probably is the culmination of the latter line of development. The noteworthy feature of the Data Cell is the sheer size of the data reservoir that it is feasible to have on-line. The smallest movable unit of the Data Cell is a *Strip*, which is made of tape with a magnetic oxide coating on one side. Each strip is 2¼" wide and 13" long, and contains 100 parallel tracks running the length of the strip, and each track can accommodate 2000 characters; in other words, one strip has a capacity of 200,000 characters. Ten of these strips are held in a case, designated a *subcell*, and 20 subcells are grouped together in a larger holder called a *cell* (Figure 3.21). Each cell is a segment of a cylinder, and ten such cells fit together to make up the Data Cell Drive, which makes available on-line 2000 strips containing a maximum of 400 million characters (IBM, 1966). There are now disks that will hold this much information, and more, but this was not the case originally. (Because of enormous engineering investments and mass-production economies, it seems likely that disks will eventually eclipse the Data Cell principle.)

The read/write process entails successive selection of the cell, the subcell, and the strip, which is thereupon removed from its case and pulled around a drum to pass over a read/write head (Figure 3.22), which in turn must be positioned to read the proper tracks. Both access times and read-in speeds are considerably greater for Data Cells than for disks. The maximum time needed to obtain, read (or write), and return a strip is

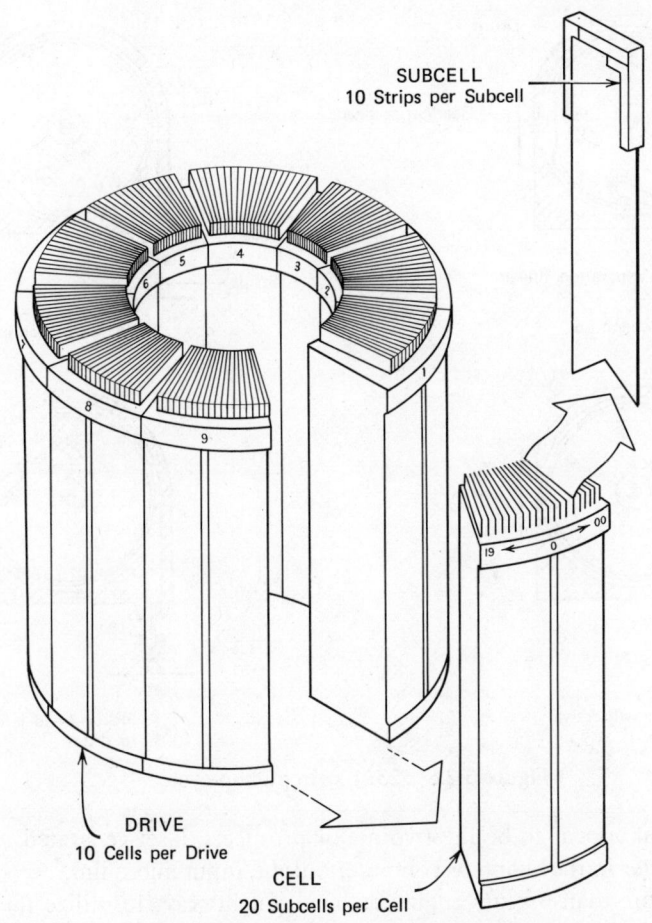

Figure 3.21. 2321 drive, cell, and subcell.

about 600 milliseconds. About two-thirds of this time is needed to move the individual strip out of its holder to the read/write head and back again, and another third in rotating the drive to the proper subcell location. As with disks, this time can be cut to much smaller amounts by careful access planning. Actual read-in speed is 55,000 cps.

The individual cells can be removed and stored, enclosed in protective covers. One might note that 15 million characters (10,000 typewritten pages) occupy three-eights of the volume of a cell. This storage density, in all the media discussed so far, is exceeded only by that of magnetic tape.

Laser Memories. Magnetic media have long dominated the scene in digital memories. Now, however, other media are coming onstage which are capable of outdoing magnetic storage in cheapness and reliability. We shall

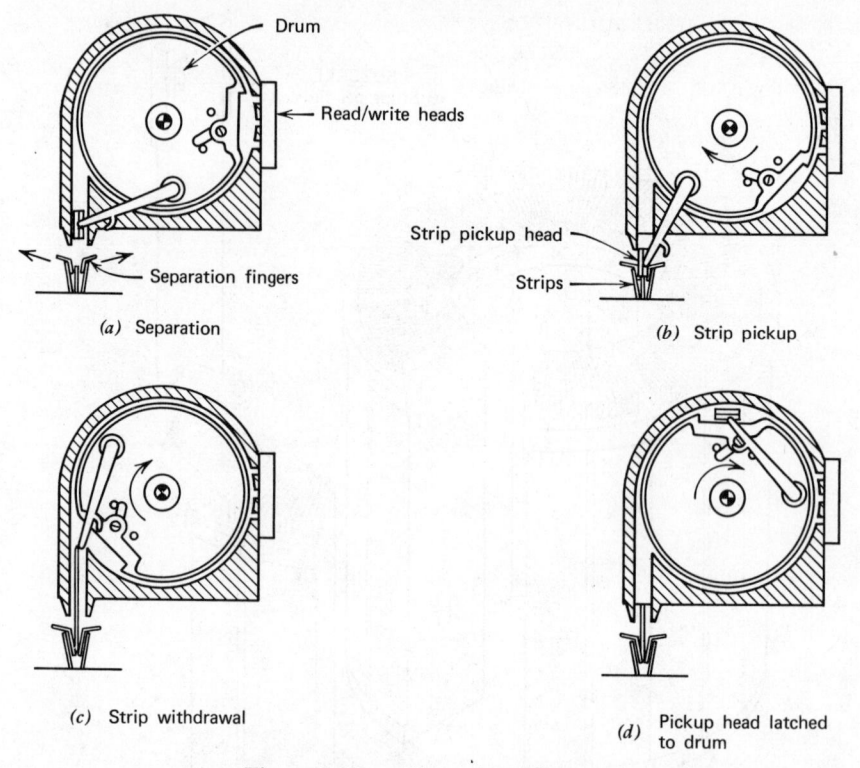

100   Information Processing—Digital Storage and Transmission

(a) Separation

(b) Strip pickup

(c) Strip withdrawal

(d) Pickup head latched to drum

Figure 3.22. 2321 strip pickup cycle.

discuss what appear to be the two major prospects, laser-generated memories and (later in the chapter) computer output/input microfilm.

For more than 5 years engineers have sought ways to utilize the laser beam as a means of conveying information, both in and out of the computer field. This search has been occasioned because the laser principle represents a degree of control over visible and infrared radiation that is as profound as that achieved earlier over electrons and the longer-wavelength forms of electromagnetic radiation. Lasers, potentially, can bring enormous change to information technology across a broad front, including high capacity transmission of data over a distance (Nelson, 1971), the storage of images through holography (Becker, 1973), and the storage of digital data in the trillions of bits.

The word *laser* began as an acronym, Light Amplification by Stimulated Emission of Radiation. Ordinary light, such as that from the sun or from a light bulb, is composed of a chatotic distribution of waves of all energies, wavelengths, and directions (one would not be amiss to visualize the wave pattern as similar to that of a storm-tossed sea). Lasers discipline light, so that wave energies are all precisely the same, and the waves are all in phase and traveling in utterly parallel fashion, like soldiers in ranks. From the standpoint of laser-generated storage, it is the quality of being utterly parallel that is applicable, for it is possible to focus such light precisely down to microscopic dimensions. Such light can act (in a variety of ways) to form bit patterns as dense as 10 million bits per square inch. Compare this to the 14,000 bits customarily stored in a half square inch on magnetic tape, and the potential of laser-generated storage becomes evident.

Light is a form of energy, and there are many ways of using a highly focused laser beam to generate a bit pattern. One method, for example, combines the principles of magnetic and laser-generated storage by using laser beams to demagnetize (by heat) spots on a thin film, which may then be remagnetized, on cooling, in one direction or another to form ones and zeros (Meetham, 1970).

The simplest approach, perhaps, is simply to burn holes in a medium using a focused laser beam. This is the principle used in one of the largest contemporary digital memories in operation, the Unicon Model 690, manufactured by Precision Instruments, Inc., of Palo Alto, California, and used as an archival storage for the ARPA network of computers (which includes several dozen major universities and other installations throughout the United States). The Unicon is physically located at the NASA Ames Research Center at Moffett Field, California, in support of the ultra-large ILLIAC IV computer there, but it is available to all other ARPANET computers as well (Brown, 1973).

The Unicon's ultimate capacity is a trillion bits; its manner of use, however, utilizes many bit-positions for nondata purposes (such as alignment and error checking), and thus the feasible upper limit for data storage is about 700 billion bits. The storage medium itself is 450 strips of Mylar coated on one surface with a thin layer of highly reflective rhodium metal; the strips are stored together in a carousel, and each is 30" long, 4¼" wide, and of the order of 10 mils thick (note the resemblance to the already discussed Data Cell). Each strip is capable of containing 1½ billion bits, where a hole burned in the rhodium coating represents a 1 and an unburned location represents a 0.

When a storage strip is selected for processing, it is pushed upward mechanically so that it can be grappled and pulled around a drum (again, like the Data Cell, and Figure 3.22 offers a good visualization of the process). Next to the drum is a read/write head which, however, has no resemblance to a magnetic read/write head. It consists of a mirror and lens arrangement whose purpose is to direct and focus the laser beam to the proper spot on the Mylar-rhodium strip. As with many other drum devices, the rotation of the drum serves to establish a linear track for bit storage, while movement of the mirror-lens unit parallel to the drum axis permits progression from one track to another.

The Unicon is called *archival storage* in part because of its large capacity, but also because it is a "write once" memory; as such it is akin to printed paper and punched paper tape: information is stored initially and therefore only reading may take place. Both writing and reading are achieved through control of the laser beam which, before reaching the mirror-lens unit, must pass through a *demodulator*, a device that can reduce the strength of the beam through polarization filtering. In the write mode, when the full strength of the beam (300 milliwatts) is allowed to pass, a hole is burned in the bit-position on which the mirror-lens unit is trained, creating a 1. The Mylar, being transparent to the beam, is unaffected. Creating a 0 entails simply cutting off the beam with the demodulator. Since the write rate (and also the read rate) is 2.8 million bits per second, the demodulator must act extremely rapidly. Indeed, it has a dark-light-dark cycle of 200 nanoseconds (billionths of a second), and at present the speed of the demodulator is the limiting factor on the Unicon's storage speed.

In the read mode, the demodulator reduces the beam strength to 15 milliwatts, at which intensity it does not burn holes but may be sensed. Here the reflective nature of the rhodium comes into play: where a 0 is indicated, the beam is reflected to photocell (a silicon photo-diode) and recorded as such for read-out; where a 1 is indicated, the beam passes through the hole in the rhodium, is not reflected or sensed, and this lack is recorded as a 1.

The Model 690 is in the nature of a prototype and its cost data may not be characteristic of the medium. A smaller version, the Model 190, is being made available, having ten of the Mylar strips and storing 15 billion bits, and is estimated to cost between $100 and $200 thousand. If these figures become typical, it would make the medium roughly 1 percent as expensive as on-line disk storage.

(A very recent advance in mass storage devices employs more conventional technology. The IBM 3850 system, which can store more than twice as many bits (i.e., 2 trillion) as the Unicon, is based on a magnetic tape cartridge of unusual geometry: a tape spool is only 2 inches in diameter and 4 inches in width. One cartridge can hold as much data as two or three reels of standard tape. A 3850 system contains several thousand of these cartridges arrayed in honeycomb-like cells, such that they may be selected mechanically for read/write operations. Thus is banished one of the chief disadvantages of tape systems up to now: the need for personnel to locate reels in the tape library and mount them on tape drives. The 3850 system, on command from a remote location, can select a cartridge and load its 50 million characters on a disk in less than a minute.)

OUTPUT FROM DIGITAL STORAGE

At the end of every data-processing job is its end result, and the reason for the computer's existence: output. At the point of output, instruments exist to convert relatively incomprehensible binary data into a form more interpretable by the human eye. Until the last few years, this conversion job was almost exclusively that of the output printer, usually referred to as a *line printer*. At first such output equipment as CRTs and computer-driven plotters remained in the realm of the exotic, used by only a few, whereas the line printer was universal and indispensible. Now, though the CRT revolution (described above) is well under way, the great bulk of final computer output is still yielded via printer.

Printed output is in alphanumeric (letters, numbers, punctuation, and special symbols) for most uses. A major exception to this is in programming or in computer systems checkout, where it is often advantageous to have an exact representation, in binary, of the contents of all or part of core memory. But with binary there is a major human factors problem: even the brightest programmers have trouble dealing with pages filled with ones and zeroes. The solution to this problem has been simple: if each item of core-stored information (character, quantity, or other small unit item) were to have its binary digits grouped in threes, starting with the right-hand digit, it will be found that each triad of digits can be set in correspondence with a digit in the *octal* number system, i.e.,

000 = 0	010 = 2	100 = 4	110 = 6
001 = 1	011 = 3	101 = 5	111 = 7

Accordingly, it has been common in programming to have core-dump printouts in octal. Familiarity with the octal number system (not difficult) permits the programmer to recognize numbers, even large ones, a task that would be almost unfeasible with binary. Moreover, if necessary, the programmer can easily convert the octal digits back into binary in order to trace the behavior of his program on a bit-by-bit basis. The latter capability is the reason octal numbers are used rather than decimal, from which the conversion to binary cannot be done in a simple digit-by-digit fashion.

As a result of the transition from 6-bit bytes, (whose contents can be smoothly represented by two octal digits) to 8-bit bytes, much of the programming field has shifted from octal numbers to *hexadecimal* numbers, in terms of which each 8-bit byte can be expressed as two digits. In order to count in the hexadecimal system, one needs fifteen symbols and zero; the practice is to supplement the numbers 1 through 9 with *A, B, C, D, E,* and *F*.

The use of letters to stand for integer quantities may seem alien even to mathematicians (who are not strangers to the use of letters as quantity symbols), but like any other such symbol-manipulating system it is valid when applied consistently, though it may take some getting used to. For the curiosity satisfaction of any reader who would like to play around with hexadecimal numbers, here is a table:

+	1	2	3	4	5	6	7	8	9	A	B	C	D	E	F	10
1	02	03	04	05	06	07	08	09	0A	0B	0C	0D	0E	0F	10	11
2	03	04	05	06	07	08	09	0A	0B	0C	0D	0E	0F	10	11	12
3	04	05	06	07	08	09	0A	0B	0C	0D	0E	0F	10	11	12	13
4	05	06	07	08	09	0A	0B	0C	0D	0E	0F	10	11	12	13	14
5	06	07	08	09	0A	0B	0C	0D	0E	0F	10	11	12	13	14	15
6	07	08	09	0A	0B	0C	0D	0E	0F	10	11	12	13	14	15	16
7	08	09	0A	0B	0C	0D	0E	0F	10	11	12	13	14	15	16	17
8	09	0A	0B	0C	0D	0E	0F	10	11	12	13	14	15	16	17	18
9	0A	0B	0C	0D	0E	0F	10	11	12	13	14	15	16	17	18	19
A	0B	0C	0D	0E	0F	10	11	12	13	14	15	16	17	18	19	1A
B	0C	0D	0E	0F	10	11	12	13	14	15	16	17	18	19	1A	1B
C	0D	0E	0F	10	11	12	13	14	15	16	17	18	19	1A	1B	1C
D	0E	0F	10	11	12	13	14	15	16	17	18	19	1A	1B	1C	1D
E	0F	10	11	12	13	14	15	16	17	18	19	1A	1B	1C	1D	1E
F	10	11	12	13	14	15	16	17	18	19	1A	1B	1C	1D	1E	1F
10	11	12	13	14	15	16	17	18	19	1A	1B	1C	1D	1E	1F	20

The sums given in this table are the same as those in the decimal system up to the value 09; but, as the table clearly shows, the count of 10 does not occur at the decimal value of 10, but at decimal 16, and thus the alien symbols must be brought in to keep the digits count going up past 09.

Printers. There is a great deal of variability among printers—in speed, in print quality, and in principle of operation. In general it may be stated about this family of equipment that higher speed and better print quality both mean greater expense; there is also a tendency for the higher speeds to be attained at a sacrifice of quality (a tradeoff which, however, does not hold for CRT output). Printers are divisible into two broad classes, impact and nonimpact printers. Impact printers use the typewriter principle, in which ink or carbon is caused by pressure to adhere to paper. For the slowest output devices, such as the Teletype (already discussed), the printing mechanism is literally a typewriter, the keys of which can be operated both manually and by the computer. The very earliest computers also used typewriters to generate output, but this means was very quickly realized to be a bottleneck, for even computers of the mid-fifties could generate output far faster than the 10 to 15 characters per second (cps) feasible with typewriter keys.

Thereupon began the era of electromechanical marvels that printed, more or less simultaneously, entire lines of characters, and capable of speeds hundreds of times greater (presently up to about 5000 cps) than a typewriter. Perhaps the most elementary way of achieving line-at-a-time speeds is illustrated in Figure 3.23, in which are shown two independently movable print wheels, and there are, of course, as many print wheels in a row as there are characters and spaces in a line. If the character *e* is signalled by the computer to a given wheel, the printer waits until the wheel has been rotated to the *e* position, as shown. Then the wheel must be brought forward in a movement such that *e* is moving at the same rate as the paper rolling across the platen, so that the *e* image can be impressed without smearing or tearing the paper (Canning, 1956). As can be appreciated from Figure 3.23, a multiwheeled impact printer would have a great many moving parts, and for this reason a repairman is likely to be seen more often working on the printer than on any other device in a computing installation. Development of impact printers has been aimed, in large measure, toward reducing the number of parts. A common principle seen today is in the "chain printer," in which a chain or belt containing all possible characters is pulled past every character position in a line (Lettieri, 1973). Opposite each character position is a hammer, which need only be struck at the proper time to print the correct character at that position. Thus, selection is achieved by precise timing rather than by the positioning of a print wheel, and only one revolving element (the chain) is required rather than as many as there are character positions. The "drum printer" operates very similarly (see Figure 3.24).

Impact printers, which are necessarily mechanical, are practically

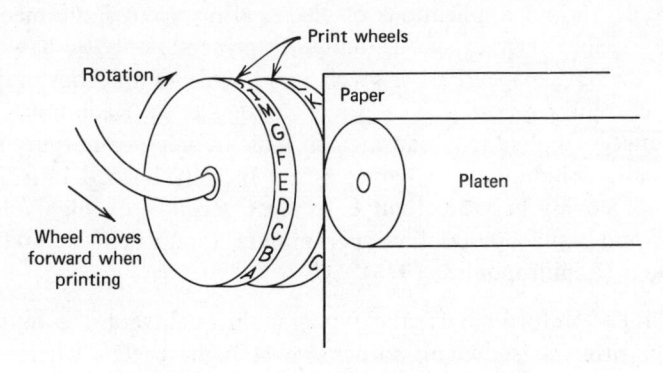

Figure 3.23. Principle of wheel printer.

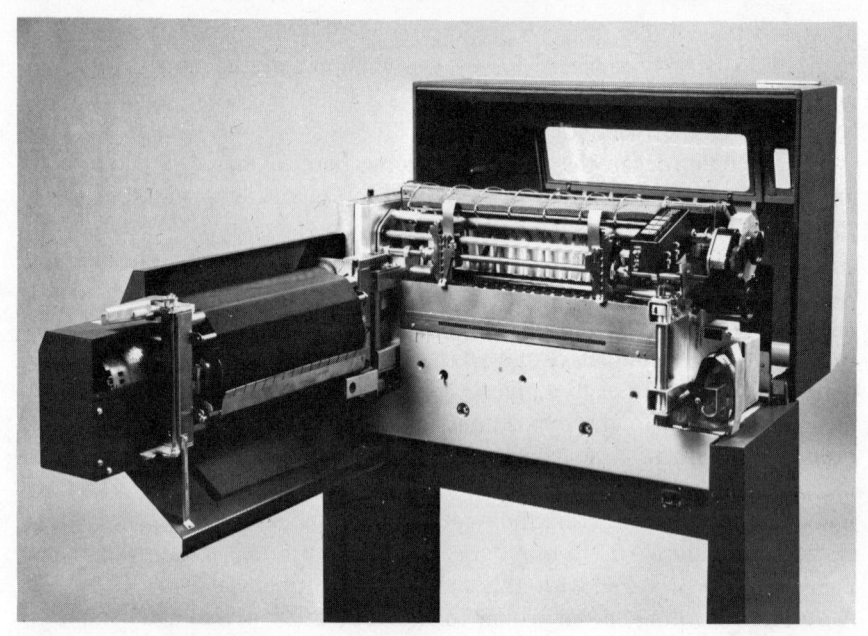

Figure 3.24. Dataproducts Model 2260 drum printer, opened for maintenance. Swivelled-out portion at left contains character drum, hidden behind inked ribbon except for left end. The drum rotates at a consistent rate and character selection depends on exact timing of the print hammers, which are assembled in the right-hand part of the equipment shown. (Courtesy Dataproducts Corp., Woodland Hills, Calif.)

limited in speed to a few thousand cps. In addition they are complicated, subject to breakdown, noisy, and limited to a hundred or so characters of one font. These limitations have inspired the development of printers working on other than the typewriter principle, and have led to a class of devices called, logically, *nonimpact printers*. Because most nonimpact printers use various applications of electrical or electrostatic mechanisms, they are capable of great speed, limited in principle only by how fast it is possible to move paper past a given point. One of the most rapid such devices currently reported is a printer designed by Radiation, Inc., for atomic energy applications (an area in which computer outputs are characteristically voluminous). Characters are literally burned into the paper (which is moving at more than 6 feet per second) by high-voltage discharges, and some 30,000 lines per minute (equivalent to 60,000 cps) are printed (Zaphiropoulos, 1973).

Enter CRT. Unfortunately, the typographic quality of the output from computer printers is difficult to achieve at high speeds; where sufficient quality may be obtained (as by the use of a printer with an executive-type Selectric typewriter ball), printing speeds are inadequate to generate anything as large as, for example, a library book catalog in a reasonable amount of time. The cathode-ray tube has presented a more than adequate answer to this dilemma, and this has been a large part of the impetus behind photocomposition (covered at length in Chapter Two), which is so rapidly changing the nature of printing/publishing technology.

But there is another way in which output printers have been less than satisfactory, and that is in the sheer bulk they must generate in paper in order to make available *all* of the potentially interesting output that a computer is capable of generating. The attribute of bulk turned equipment designers' thoughts to microfilm as a medium for computer output, and—as was the case for photocomposition—here also the cathode-ray tube has proved to be an ideal intermediate device between the digital information of the computer and a final medium that was preferable in many cases to the output of the line printer. A device for generating what is known as *computer output microfilm* (COM), consists of a CRT coupled with a microfilm or microfiche camera, and is termed a COM recorder. An appreciation of the speed of COM recorders may be gained from the equation by Avedon (1971):

One COM recorder = 30 impact printers = 5000 electric typewriters

The COM recorder principle was developed by Stromberg Datagraphix of San Diego, California, as an application of their own Charactron tube (Figure 3.11), which can generate an entire page, containing thousands of characters, in less than a tenth of a second; because the image is photographed during that time interval, there is no need to continue refreshing it, as in display for the human eye. The resolution power of the Charactron tube is more than 5000 lines per screen diameter, or sufficient resolution to display, unmagnified, the full detail of a human fingerprint.

A COM recorder does not necessarily have to be on-line to produce page images, even though the recorder's great speed makes this practicable. All that is necessary is for the proper coded information to be on magnetic tape, and the circuitry of the recorder is adequate to select and position the characters.

There are ways other than CRT to generate microfilm output. The 3M Company (St. Paul, Minnesota) aims an electron beam directly at the film in vacuum, thus bypassing the need for photographing a CRT face. The Memorex Corporation (Santa Clara, California) uses matrices of light-emitting diodes which can be selectively activated to form characters,

108 Information Processing—Digital Storage and Transmission

which in turn can be photographed (Advanced Technology/Libraries. 1972).

The *system* advantages of COM are hard to overestimate, reducing as it does both the bottleneck effect and the output bulk of line printers. (Reduction of output bulk is illustrated in Figure 3.25.) In such applications as the production of commercial catalogs, output times have been reduced twentyfold; in the case of J. C. Penney, total output time shrunk from 90 hours to 4 (Avedon, 1971). Another dimension of COM is in relation to duplication—and in most business applications, duplicates are the rule rather than the exception. Printout carbon copies are of the same order of expense as the original paper, and the bottom copies are often of questionable quality. Microfiche duplicates, however, are from one tenth to one hundredth as expensive as the masters.

Figure 3.25. The CalComp Microfiche Management System provides computer users with a high-speed technique or recording alphanumeric computer output on either 105mm microfiche or 16mm roll film. The girl standing by the equipment is holding the microfiche equivalent of the stack of printout paper on which her foot is placed. (Courtesy California Computer Products, Inc., Anaheim, Calif.)

Already, in the wake of COM, a coordinate sphere of activity called CIM (computer input microfilm) has come into being. CIM machines are being built and marketed, and though they work on principles similar to optical character readers, they must deal with images much smaller than those of OCR; such a machine has a scan line resolution of two microns (millionths of a meter). Microfilm's durability has increasing relevance to data processors, who now recognize the unsuitability of magnetic tape for long-term storage. Menkus (1971), in fact, lists four advantages of microfilm over tape storage; (*a*) stability as a medium, (*b*) storage in both human readable and computer readable form, (*c*) release of the tape reels for other processing, and (*d*) low storage space requirements.

DATA COMMUNICATION

Ten years ago a joke was circulating among computer people about the possible effects of linking a large number of computers together by cable. As the joke goes, one day it was decided to combine all the computers in the nation in the hope that the resulting supercomputer would have more data-processing skill than all the computers each acting alone. When the hookup was finally complete, the chief engineer whimsically asked a test question: Is there a God? There was considerable suspense as the newly created entity chewed away at the problem, with tapes spinning nationwide. Finally, after five full minutes came the answer: Q. Is there a God? A. Yes. There is *now*.

As many of the programmers who appreciated the joke must since have realized, the physical capability now exists for performing the above experiment. We have already noted, under the section Input to Digital Storage, the significance of remote interaction with computers via on-line Teletype. This is only one of many possible modes of data communication over long distances. Indeed, there are as many *possible* modes as there are permutations of the in/out units and storage units we have been discussing and the major kinds of telecommunications which we therefore now discuss.

Channels of Communication. The concept of a *channel* of communication is basic in thinking about telecommunications processes. A channel may or may not be a visible physical entity. In the case of a primitive telegraph line, the wire *is* the channel—but this simple state of affairs is not characteristic of modern telecommunications. A more typical channel situation is found in radio communications, in which many parties are sending and receiving through the same physical medium, in this case the atmosphere.

Individual communications channels are kept distinct through control of frequency, and a radio receiver has a frequency selector (dial, pushbuttons) by which any desired channel might be chosen. Sometimes the principle breaks down and one has the phenomenon of two broadcasting stations being received over the same frequency. A similar phenomenon occurs in the telephone system, called "crosstalk." Keeping channels from interfering with each other is a matter both of engineering and of observance of regulations such as those of the Federal Communications Commission (*EDP Analyzer*, 1969).

Along with the concept of a channel comes the notion of channel capacity or, as it is frequently termed, *bandwidth*. For purposes of data communications, capacity can be thought of as number of bits per second, although—as can be seen from Table 3.1—there is not necessarily a proportionality between bandwidth and bits per second. As also can be seen from Table 3.1, there is a large difference in capacity between the channel capabilities of the telephone system (voice grade channel and the various Telpak multichannel facilities) and those of microwave, coaxial cable, and satellite communications. Part of the limitation of the telephone system is that, as we noted at the beginning of the chapter, it was built for voice communication and works at audio frequencies. It is a general rule that the higher the frequency of a communications medium, the more data per second a channel can carry. Microwave channels, which have frequencies in megacycles, are capable of carrying megabits per second. *Computer Decisions* (1973) names eleven companies that are each planning microwave (or similar) networks linking a dozen or more U.S. cities by 1975. In the future even higher frequencies will be used. Dittberner (1971) states:

> . . . Millimeter wave transmission systems utilizing wave guides and optical systems using lasers are expected to be placed into service in the late 1970s or 1980s. These systems are expected to have data transmission capacities in the neighborhood of 25,000 megabits per second. . . .

Communication Systems. Figure 3.26 shows the gross elements of a typical communication system and their interrelations. Terminals are points of sending and receiving, and can in principle include any of the in/out or storage equipment we have been discussing, including, of course, the computer (Hayes and Becker, 1974). The buffer and control units convert the language of the terminals into signals compatible with the communications medium, and also keep the terminals and the communications channels in synchronization. For the on-line terminals discussed earlier, this unit is called a *modem* (modulator/demodulator); it converts input pulses from the terminals into audio signals for transmission over phone lines,

TABLE 3.1. Available communications services.

Service	Bandwidth	Bit Rate	Equivalent Voice Channels	Time (Seconds) to Transmit a Typed Page (Digital)
Low speed digital (Teletype)		75 bits/sec to 150 bits/sec (15 char/sec)	1/12	80
Voice grade	4 kc	Up to 2000 bits/sec on usual dial network	1	6
Series 8000	48 kc	Up to 40.8 kbits/sec with model 301 data set	12	.5
Telpak B (withdrawn)	96 kc	Up to 80 kbits/sec	24	.25
Telpak C	240 kc	Approximately 100 kbits/sec	60	.1
Telpak D	1 mc	Approximately 500 kbits/sec	240	.03
"Half video"	2 mc	Approximately 1 mbits/sec	480	.015
Video	4–5 mc	Approximately 2 mbits/sec	1000	.007
Microwave	8 mc	Approximately 4 mbits/sec	2000	.003
Coaxial cable	8 mc	Approximately 4 mbits/sec	2000	.003
Satellite	8 mc	Approximately 4 mbits/sec	2000	.003
T-2 carrier		6 mbits/sec	3000	.002
T-4 carrier		220 mbits/sec —sometime in the future	100,000	—

and converts these signals back into digital data at the output end. In the center of Figure 3.26 is represented the switching network, the function of which we are well familiar in the telephone system. Such a network is not always needed in a data communications system, for in many systems there is only one logical pathway for data from any given terminal.

Facsimile Transmission. A process in which documents and other images can be transmitted over communication lines is known as *facsimile transmission*. At a sending station, documents are scanned (in a process similar to OCR) and converted into a pulse pattern that can be sent by wire. At a receiving station, the pulse pattern can be reassembled into a copy, or

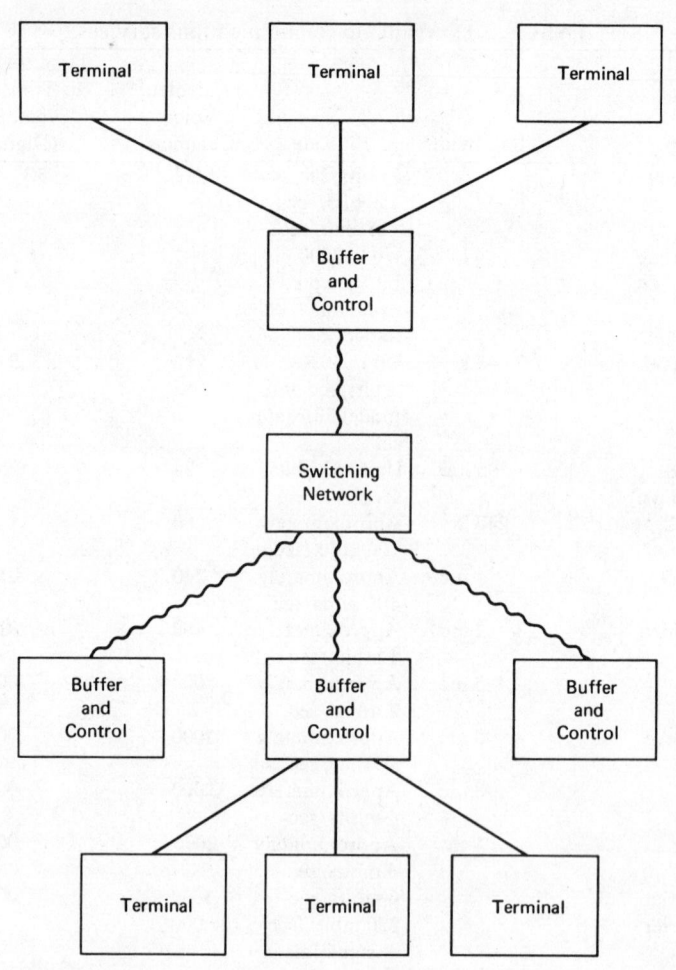

112   Information Processing—Digital Storage and Transmission

Figure 3.26. Schematic of communications flow.

facsimile, of the original and printed out, either as an array of tiny dots or as a reprographic image.

Copy quality, of course, depends on how many pulses per unit area of image are sent. In a high resolution system, such as that used to send proofs of newspaper pages, the pulse density is so great that a million or more bits per second must be communicated. Only microwave or a special telephone line can handle so much traffic. On the other hand, office facsimile systems are feasible at rates of two to four thousand bits per second, which is near the upper limit of capacity of the ordinary, voice-grade telephone line. At this rate a legible copy of an 8 ½"×11" typewritten page would take about 5 minutes to transmit.

It is to be noted: in digital form a character requires a maximum of only 8 bits to represent it in transmission by wire, whereas the crudest of images of a printed character (say, a 5×7 dot-matrix pattern) would require 35 bits. A fully legible, type-quality character requires hundreds of bits. Thus, ordinary printed matter having no pictures and stored in digital form would not be an appropriate subject for facsimile transmission.

REFERENCES

Advanced Technology/Libraries (1972), Computer Output Microfilm, 1:5 (May).

ANDERSON, L. H. (1973), telephone conversation, Burroughs Corp., Los Angeles, Calif.

ANDERSSON, P. L. (1969), Optical Character Recognition—A Survey, *Datamation*, 15:7, pp. 43–48.

ANDERSSON, P. L. (1971), OCR Enters the Practical Stage, *Datamation*, 17:23, pp. 22–27.

AUERBACH TASK FORCE (1971), *Latest Developments in Electronic Data Processing*, Auerbach, Princeton, N.J., pp. 223–237.

AVEDON, DON M. (1971), *Computer Output Microfilm*, NMA Monograph No. 4, National Microfilm Association, Silver Spring, Md.

BECKER, JOSEPH (1968), Address, "Tomorrow's Library Services Today," *News Notes of California Libraries*, 63:4, pp. 429–440.

BECKER, JOSEPH, and PULSIFER, JOSEPHINE (1973), *Application of Computer Technology to Library Processes*, Scarecrow Press, Metuchen, N.J.

BROOKS, F. P., Jr., and IVERSON, K. E. (1969), *Automatic Data Processing, System/360 Edition*, John Wiley & Sons, New York.

BROWN, RICHARD M. (1973), telephone conversation, NASA Ames Research Center, Moffett Field, Calif.

Burroughs Readout (1972), 1:5.

CANNING, RICHARD G. (1956), *Electronic Data Processing for Business and Industry*, John Wiley & Sons, New York.

CAREY, ROBERT F. (1970), A History of Keyed Data Entry, *Datamation*, 16:6, pp. 73–76.

Computer Decisions (1973), Alternatives to The Phone System (Staff Report), 5:12, pp. 28–33.

Datamation (1973), Product Spotlight, 19:6, pp. 163.

DAVIS, SIDNEY (1973), Digital Cassette and Cartridge Recorders Today. *Computer Design*, 12:1, pp. 59–71.

DITTBERNER, DONALD L. (1971), Telecommunications Costs, in Becker, J., ed., *Proceedings of the Conference on Interlibrary Communications and Information Networks*, American Library Association, pp. 160–162.

DORN, PHILIP H. (1973), Whither Data Entry?, *Datamation*, 19:3, pp. 49–51.

EDP Analyzer (1969), Current Status in Data Communications, 7:3.

EDP Analyzer (1969), Optical Scanning: It's on the Move, 7:6.

ELDREDGE, K. R., KAMPHOEFNER, F. J., and WENDT, P. H. (1955), Automatic Input for Business Data Processing Systems, *Proceedings of the Eastern Joint Computer Conference*, p. 94.

FEIDELMAN, L., and BERNSTEIN, C. B. (1973), Advances in Data Entry. *Datamation*, 19:3, pp. 44–48.

HAYES, R. M., and BECKER, J. (1974), *Handbook of Data Processing for Libraries*, 2nd ed., Melville Publishing Company, Los Angeles.

HILLEGASS, JOHN R. (1973), Piecing Out the Timesharing Puzzle, *Computer Decisions*, 5:2, pp. 24–32.

HUSKEY, HARRY D. (1970), Computer Technology, in Cuadra, C. A., ed., *Annual Review of Information Science and Technology*, Vol. 5, Encyclopaedia Britannica, Chicago, pp. 73–85.

IBM (1966), *Introduction to System/360—Direct Access Storage Devices and Organizational Methods*, International Business Machines Corp., Endicott, N.Y.

INTERNATIONAL DATA CORPORATION (1972), A Report to Management: Independent Computer Peripheral Equipment, *Business Week*, June 24, pp. 45–77.

KNUTH, D. E. (1969), *The Art of Computer Programming, Vol. 2: Seminumerical Algorithms*, Addison-Wesley, Reading, Mass.

LETTIERI, LARRY (1973), Which Printer When?, *Computer Decisions*, 5:8, pp. 15–19.

LUXENBERG, H. R., and KUEHN, RUDOLPH L. (1968), *Display Systems Engineering*, McGraw-Hill, New York.

MEETHAM, ROGER (1970), *Information Retrieval*, Doubleday, Garden City, N.Y.

MENKUS, BELDEN (1971), Retention of Data—for the Long Term, *Datamation*, 17:18, pp. 30–32.

NELSON, CARL E. (1971), Microform Technology, in Cuadra, C. A., ed., *Annual Review of Information Science and Technology*, Vol. 6, Encyclopaedia Britannica, Chicago, pp. 77–111.

RABINOW, JACOB C. (1969), Whither OCR?, *Datamation*, 15:7, pp. 38–42.

REAGAN, FONNIE H., Jr. (1973), Is the Keypunch Really Obsolete? *Computer Decisions*, 5:4, pp. 12–17.

ROSBURY, A. H. (1970), Shared Processor Keyboard Data Entry, *Datamation*, 16:6, pp. 101–104.

SCHMEDEL, SCOTT R. (1968), Electronic Sketching, in Orr, William, ed., *Conversational Computers*, John Wiley & Sons, New York.

SOBEL, ALAN (1973), Electronic Numbers, *Scientific American*, 228:6, pp. 64–73.

TAUBE, MORTIMER (1948), *New Tools for the Control and Use of Research Materials*, Documentation, Bethesda, Md.

THEIS, D. J., and HOBBS, L. C. (1968), Low-Cost Remote Terminals, *Datamation*, 14:6, pp. 22–29.

Time (April 3, 1972), Science, p. 72.

ZAPHIROPOULOS, RENN (1973), Nonimpact Printers, *Datamation*, 19:5, pp. 71–76.

Zientara, Peggy (1973), What is the IQ of Your Intelligent Terminal?, *Computerworld* (June 13), p. 10.

Chapter Four

Concepts of Programming and the Nature of Digital Computers

Many, and perhaps most, of the readers of this book will have been grounded in the fundamentals of digital computers at some point in their educations or careers, in contrast to typical readers of a book similar to this 10 years ago. To these readers nothing in the present chapter will be new, and they can best skip on to the information retrieval chapters that make up the latter portion of this book. To readers who have not yet been introduced to computers, a chapter on the subject is essential, because a study of information retrieval encounters computers at almost every turn in the road—as both Chapters Two and Three have already made clear.

This chapter departs from a customary practice by discussing concepts of programming first, delaying the presentation of the physical facts of computers. Ideas of programming can and should be understood independently of the nature of any computer by means of which programming might be implemented. Many of the ideas concerning information retrieval to be presented in later chapters can then be discussed in the abstract, with reference to these programming concepts, and thus independently of any actual hardware that might be used in a live situation.

CONCEPTS OF PROGRAMMING

A *program* in its general meaning, is a "plan for the sequencing of events." In computer programming this translates into "plan for the sequencing of tasks", or in an original more limited sense, "plan for the sequencing of steps in a computation."

Even rudimentary pencil-and-paper computation requires programming. Unless one is doing something as simple as adding two one-digit numbers, one has to decide in what sequence he will perform his penciled operations. A good example, which we shall continue to use in subsequent discussions, is that of a teacher adding up test scores to determine grades. As a rule, scores are arranged in vertical columns, with one column for each member of the class. A typical sequence of steps might be:

1. Select a column of scores.
2. Add up the numbers in the digits column.
3. Record the right-hand digit of the sum at bottom of column.
4. Add up the carry from the digits column together with all the numbers in the tens column.
5. Record the right-hand digit of the sum at bottom of column.
6. Add the carry to the numbers, if any, in the hundreds column.
7. Record the digits of this sum at bottom of column to complete the total of the scores of this pupil.
8. Select another pupil's score column and repeat steps 2 through 7; when all columns are totaled, continue to step 9.
9. Arrange the score totals in numerical order, with the largest at the top.
10. Assign grades.

People who carry out such hand computations may not be aware of the fact that they are executing a program of their own design. There are numerous ways to carry out the above procedure, each equally correct; deciding on which procedure shall be used is equivalent to designing a program. For instance, one can start with any pupil's column, and can continue with the rest of the pupils in any sequence. The choice of sequence makes no difference in the outcome, and yet the choice has to be made. The choice is usually made in an almost unthinking manner when done by pencil-and-paper methods, but it must be dealt with consciously by a programmer who is attempting to do the entire score totaling job on a machine.

Not only are there different ways of carrying out the above procedure, but there are also *other* procedures that will work. One need not, for example, separate the addition process into the summing of three columns of single digits. Some people are capable of adding number by number, i.e., 86+72=158; add 75 to that=233; add 62 to that=295; (and so on until the bottom of the column is reached). For most people this is a hard way to add, but the result is just as valid as that for the "easy" procedure. It is also possible for a machine to do the computation either way, and a choice must often be made.

When a desk calculator is used to perform the above computations, a person is freed from strictly arithmetical drudgery, but he still must decide on the sequence of carrying out the computations. Many people, when their minds are not tied down by the constant need to add, become aware for the first time that different addition sequences are possible, and that it may be better to do it one way than another. Some may invent auxiliary procedures, such as adding up the scores horizontally (as well as vertically by column), in order to sum and compare the horizontal and vertical totals as a check against possible mistakes in fingering the calculator keys. The extra labor of doing this in manual computation would be unthinkable in most situations.

However, as anyone realizes who has used a desk calculator, there is still much rote work involved. Stroking the calculator keys does not eliminate the bore of the continuing interrogation, "What is the next number? . . . the next number? . . . the next? . . . ? . . . (and so on)?" But this is the very sort of drudgery that machines are cut out for. All that is required to allow machines the privilege of selecting the next number is a machine-sensible medium containing the proper sequence of numerical values, interspersed with machine-interpretable instructions as to what to do with the numerical values.

Such a methodology was used as long ago as 1801, but not in application to adding machines. One of the first instances of the use of a program to direct a machine in the performance of banal, repetitive tasks was the invention of a textile loom that could be controlled by punched cards, by the Frenchman J. M. Jacquard. No doubt there was more concern, in those times, about the monotony of weaving than about that of addition. The use of punched cards in arithmetic, and in data processing generally, did not come for 80 years after Jacquard. The circumstances that gave rise to the development of machine data processing are described by Abrams and Corvins (1971):

> . . . The United States Constitution provides that a census be taken every 10 years, and by 1880 census reporting was beginning to become a major problem. The 1880 census took about seven years to process fully, and

someone in the Census Bureau became aware that the 1890 census might take well over 10 years to tabulate. Clearly, something had to be done. Hermann Hollerith, an employee of the Census Bureau, became interested in the problem of data tabulation, and . . . developed machines that could record, compile, and tabulate. . . . [The] Census Bureau completed and reported the 1890 census by 1893. . . .

Hollerith soon left the Census Bureau to found a tabulating machine company that eventually (in 1924) became International Business Machines. Hollerith developed the well-known IBM card, also known as the Hollerith card; but we shall refer to it by its generic label "punched card." An entire family of different machines was eventually developed to perform various kinds of operations on punched cards.

Considering once again the problem of totaling scores, at least five kinds of punched card machines would be required: (*a*) keypunch machines, to convert the score data to a machine-readable medium; (*b*) machines that add (such as the IBM 602 Calculator), to carry out steps 2 through 7 of the procedure described earlier; (*c*) machines that punch, to record the totals in machine-readable form for further processing; (*d*) machines that sort, to arrange the pupils' totals in numerical order for grading; (*e*) machines that print, for generating a record of the input (the pupils' names and scores) and the output (the names ranked by score total). The IBM line of punched card equipment contains all the machines required to do the job.

Though someone—the keypunch operator—still has to read numbers and tap keys, card punch machines minimize this form of human effort, since once a card is punched it can be involved in dozens or hundreds of subsequent machine operations. On the other hand, with a desk calculator each and every machine operation must be accompanied by rote use of human skills—often those of a professionally trained person who should be otherwise occupied.

All data in punched card operations can be put into machine-readable form, but the programming (or sequencing of the machine operations) is *not* handled via punched card input—although "card programmed calculators" were used for a short time in the late 1940s. As a rule, all programming is done by the punched card machine operator, in two ways:

1. By transporting cards from one machine to another in proper sequence.
2. By changing the wiring on any one machine. This is ordinarily done by rewiring a *plugboard*, a rectangular plate full of small electric sockets arranged in rows, and having the appearance of a cribbage board. The operator knows how to interconnect these

holes so as to cause the machine to do different things—most commonly to operate selectively on different regions of a punched card.

The Use of Storage in Computer Programming. The key feature that gives a computer its great power to process data automatically is its capacious magnetic memory. We shall describe the physical nature of this memory later in this chapter. It suffices for now, however, think of the memory as a huge slate on which may be written thousands of numbers in a fraction of a second by the computer; the computer can just as quickly read these numbers from the slate in order to process them. The computer's memory is usually so large that the classroom scores of which we have been talking, assuming 25 pupils having 20 scores each, would hardly occupy one percent of it.

A computer memory, containing data, can be visualized as a large rectangle of numbers (digits), having a horizontal dimension of from 6 to 12 digits and a vertical dimension of from two thousand to more than one hundred thousand, depending on the type of computer. Each short horizontal row of digits is termed a *memory register*; when a memory register is empty, all of the digits are, in effect, zero. The memory registers are addressable, so that if the memory has a vertical dimension of 30,000 (a common size), it therefore has 30,000 memory registers which are numbered sequentially from 1 to 30,000. Whenever a datum is stored, provision is made to have its address available for future reference. As we shall see, this provision is made directly or indirectly by the person who programs the computer.

We are now going to imagine what steps would have to take place in the use of computer memory in connection with the adding up of the classroom score data. We first visualize each pupil's scores laid out in consecutive memory registers, one score to a register. (A memory register can hold more than 2 or 3 digits, but we are allowing such inefficient use of memory for the sake of ease of explanation.) We store the data beginning at, say, memory address 1000. If each pupil is assigned 20 registers, the memory allocation will appear as follows:

Pupil #1	Memory Addresses 1000–1019*
#2	1020–1039
#3	1040–1059
#4	1060–1079

---

* Ordinarily memory addresses are expressed in octal (Chapter Three); we use decimal numbers here for the convenience of those unfamiliar with computer methods.

The score data for all 25 pupils, thus stored, will occupy 500 memory registers.

In an important respect, a computer operates much like a desk calculator: its circuitry is organized to correspond to actions that the machine can perform, actions that can be named and described to a machine user. For the desk calculator these actions may be merely add, subtract, multiply, and divide. For the computer the number of actions is much greater, often in the hundreds. Though each brand of computer may have a different family of actions from other brands, there are certain actions that practically all computers have in common, and these include, as might be expected, add, subtract, multiply, and divide. As also might be expected, we are going to use the "add" in processing the pupil score data.

What does add really do in the computer? Once again one can find a parallel in a desk calculator, which has a place (called a *register*) to contain the most recent number that has been either typed in or computed by the calculator. This number, whatever it is, is either displayed on a panel (mechanically or electrically) or else printed on the output paper.

A computer also carries such a "most recent number", and it lodges in a special register called an *accumulator*. In the process of addition, one of the numbers to be added is present in an accumulator, either because it was put there directly or because it was the result of a previous computation—again, just as in the case of a desk calculator. "Add" operates by taking a specified number and adding it to the contents of the accumulator. That "specified number" is specified by writing a designation *after* the word "add", and because data to be processed are in memory, this designation is generally the *address* of the number to be added. The total produced is placed in the accumulator, and we are ready for the next operation, whatever it may be.

The word "add" and the address (or other) designation that follows it are termed, collectively, "an instruction." Computer programmers write long lists of such instructions on coding sheets, indicating the order in which they would like to have steps carried out by the computer. These coding sheets are given to a keypunch operator, who punches instruction cards, thereby converting the instructions into a form that can be sensed by the computer. By means of a punched card reader, the instructions are fed into the computer, where they are placed in memory along with the data. The computer has circuitry that enables it to refer to these instructions in memory and to execute them *in the sequence indicated by the programmer*. This, then, is the means by which a programmer, starting with pencil and paper, is able to have the computer carry out a sequence of steps in a computation.

The manner of doing programming presented here is a primitive one, dating back to the first 10 years or so of stored program computers. It is also oversimplified but it will do for purposes of explaining programming, and we therefore save any remarks about how programming is presently done for later—after the basic concepts of programming have been absorbed.

We are now ready to look at what a program for processing the classroom score data will be like. Other instructions are required. For example, an instruction is needed to keep changing the address of the "add" instruction so that it works its way methodically through each pupil's data, stored in memory as already indicated. A common way of doing this is by means of an *index register*, which like the accumulator is a register having a special function. Computers commonly have from 4 to 16 index registers, and it is possible to use all of them more or less simultaneously in a data processing operation; we are going to put two of them to use.

At least three instructions are brought into play in the use of an index register:

1. A loading instruction initially sets the contents of the register to a number that is one less than the number of memory registers to be processed. (In the case of the test scores, this number would be 19.)
2. The processing instruction, in order to avail itself of the indexing capability, is preceded by a number that designates the register. If index register number 2 is used, the instruction would be written as 2ADD 1000. When the register is set to 19, the number 19 is automatically added to the specified address, the effect of which is that the contents of memory address 1019 are selected for processing.
3. There must be a way of methodically changing the index register contents, so that the instruction 2ADD 1000 operates on *all* the data for pupil #1, which is stored between addresses 1000 and 1019 (see foregoing pupil/address table). This is done by means of a "branch and decrement index" instruction. The best way of describing its function is to write (and execute) a five-instruction program which adds up the scores of one pupil:

2A	2LIX	19
	2LDA	1000
	BRU	3B
3A	2ADD	1000
3B	2BIX	3A

A word or two about programming notation is necessary at this point. The second and third columns, here, make up the actual program, with the instruction in the second column, and the instruction's object (called the *operand*) in the third column. The operand is usually a memory address, but not always. The first column is only a reference column for the programmer's convenience; using it, he can write his program without any concern for where the program will be actually stored in memory. The *address tags* are 2A, 3A, and 3B, which are later converted by a special program called a *compiler* (a program which operates on programs) into actual memory addresses. We have more to say about compilers later.

Ordinarily, the computer's circuitry compels it to execute the instructions in the same sequence they are listed on the coding sheet. In the five-instruction program shown, 2LIX 19 is executed first, i.e., index register number 2 is loaded with 19 as stated above. Then 2LDA 1000 is executed. LDA means *load accumulator*; since it is 2LDA, the number 19 from index register number 2 is automatically added to 1000, and the contents of memory register 1019 are placed in the accumulator (and, it is important to say, those contents are also retained unaltered in memory register 1019, which is generally the case when a memory register is referred to).

The exception to the "execute in sequence" rule comes with so-called *branching* instructions, which make it possible for programs to change their sequences according to conditions. Branching instructions give stored program computers much of their power because, as we shall soon see, they enable the same individual instructions (or groups of instructions) to be used over and over again. The third instruction shown above is an "unconditional branch," BRU 3B. Its function is to cause the computer to skip over the 2ADD instruction to the instruction at 3B.

The reason this skip is necessary is that we must change the setting of index register #2 before the first add; if we do not, we will be adding the contents of 1019 to 1019, and the score total will be grossly in error. We want to add 1018 to 1019, followed by 1017, then by 1016, and so on. The final instruction, 2BIX 3A, both decreases index register #2 by one and branches backwards to the instruction at 3A. In this way, the 2ADD instruction keeps adding fresh scores to the score total being maintained in the accumulator until index register #2 is decreased to zero. When a zero setting is reached, 2BIX is not allowed to branch, and the computer proceeds onward to the sixth (not shown) instruction. Notice that the 2ADD instruction was used 19 times. For the fastest computers now in common use, the procedure just described would take about one and a half microseconds (millionths of a second). The repertoire of instructions for the IBM System/360 computer is shown in Figure 4.1.

IBM System/360 Reference Data

STANDARD INSTRUCTION SET

NAME	MNEMONIC	TYPE	CODE	OPERAND
Add	AR	RR	1A	R1, R2
Add	A	RX	5A	R1, D2 (X2, B2)
Add Halfword	AH	RX	4A	R1, D2 (X2, B2)
Add Logical	ALR	RR	1E	R1, R2
Add Logical	AL	RX	5E	R1, D2 (X2, B2)
AND	NR	RR	14	R1, R2
AND	N	RX	54	R1, D2 (X2, B2)
AND	NI	SI	94	D1 (B1), I2
AND	NC	SS	D4	D1 (L, B1), D2 (B2)
Branch and Link	BALR	RR	05	R1, R2
Branch and Link	BAL	RX	45	R1, D2 (X2, B2)
Branch on Condition	BCR	RR	07	M1, R2
Branch on Condition	BC	RX	47	M1, D2 (X2, B2)
Branch on Count	BCTR	RR	06	R1, R2
Branch on Count	BCT	RX	46	R1, D2 (X2, B2)
Branch on Index High	BXH	RS	86	R1, R3, D2 (B2)
Branch on Index Low or Equal	BXLE	RS	87	R1, R3, D2 (B2)
Compare	CR	RR	19	R1, R2
Compare	C	RX	59	R1, D2 (X2, B2)
Compare Halfword	CH	RX	49	R1, D2 (X2, B2)
Compare Logical	CLR	RR	15	R1, R2
Compare Logical	CL	RX	55	R1, D2 (X2, B2)
Compare Logical	CLC	SS	D5	D1 (L, B1), D2 (B2)
Compare Logical	CLI	SI	95	D1 (B1), I2
Convert to Binary	CVB	RX	4F	R1, D2 (X2, B2)
Convert to Decimal	CVD	RX	4E	R1, D2 (X2, B2)
Diagnose			83	
Divide	DR	RR	1D	R1, R2
Divide	D	RX	5D	R1, D2 (X2, B2)
Exclusive OR	XR	RR	17	R1, R2
Exclusive OR	X	RX	57	R1, D2 (X2, B2)
Exclusive OR	XI	SI	97	D1 (B1), I2
Exclusive OR	XC	SS	D7	D1 (L, B1), D2 (B2)
Execute	EX	RX	44	R1, D2 (X2, B2)
Halt I/O	HIO	SI	9E	D1 (B1)
Insert Character	IC	RX	43	R1, D2 (X2, B2)
Load	LR	RR	18	R1, R2
Load	L	RX	58	R1, D2 (X2, B2)
Load Address	LA	RX	41	R1, D2 (X2, B2)
Load and Test	LTR	RR	12	R1, R2
Load Complement	LCR	RR	13	R1, R2
Load Halfword	LH	RX	48	R1, D2 (X2, B2)
Load Multiple	LM	RS	98	R1, R3, D2 (B2)
Load Negative	LNR	RR	11	R1, R2
Load Positive	LPR	RR	10	R1, R2
Load PSW	LPSW	SI	82	D1 (B1)
Move	MVI	SI	92	D1 (B1), I2
Move	MVC	SS	D2	D1 (L, B1), D2 (B2)
Move Numerics	MVN	SS	D1	D1 (L, B1), D2 (B2)
Move with Offset	MVO	SS	F1	D1 (L1, B1), D2 (L2, B2)
Move Zones	MVZ	SS	D3	D1 (L, B1), D2 (B2)
Multiply	MR	RR	1C	R1, R2
Multiply	M	RX	5C	R1, D2 (X2, B2)
Multiply Halfword	MH	RX	4C	R1, D2 (X2, B2)
OR	OR	RR	16	R1, R2
OR	O	RX	56	R1, D2 (X2, B2)
OR	OI	SI	96	D1 (B1), I2
OR	OC	SS	D6	D1 (L, B1), D2 (B2)
Pack	PACK	SS	F2	D1 (L1, B1), D2 (L2, B2)
Set Program Mask	SPM	RR	04	R1
Set System Mask	SSM	SI	80	D1 (B1)
Shift Left Double	SLDA	RS	8F	R1, D2 (B2)
Shift Left Single	SLA	RS	8B	R1, D2 (B2)
Shift Left Double Logical	SLDL	RS	8D	R1, D2 (B2)
Shift Left Single Logical	SLL	RS	89	R1, D2 (B2)
Shift Right Double	SRDA	RS	8E	R1, D2 (B2)

STANDARD INSTRUCTION SET (Continued)

Shift Right Single	SRA	RS	8A	R1, D2 (B2)
Shift Right Double Logical	SRDL	RS	8C	R1, D2 (B2)
Shift Right Single Logical	SRL	RS	88	R1, D2 (B2)
Start I/O	SIO	SI	9C	D1 (B1)
Store	ST	RX	50	R1, D2 (X2, B2)
Store Character	STC	RX	42	R1, D2 (X2, B2)
Store Halfword	STH	RX	40	R1, D2 (X2, B2)
Store Multiple	STM	RS	90	R1, R3, D2 (B2)
Subtract	SR	RR	1B	R1, R2
Subtract	S	RX	5B	R1, D2 (X2, B2)
Subtract Halfword	SH	RX	4B	R1, D2 (X2, B2)
Subtract Logical	SLR	RR	1F	R1, R2
Subtract Logical	SL	RX	5F	R1, D2 (X2, B2)
Supervisor Call	SVC	RR	0A	I
Test and Set	TS	SI	93	D1 (B1)
Test Channel	TCH	SI	9F	D1 (B1)
Test I/O	TIO	SI	9D	D1 (B1)
Test Under Mask	TM	SI	91	D1 (B1), I2
Translate	TR	SS	DC	D1 (L, B1), D2 (B2)
Translate and Test	TRT	SS	DD	D1 (L, B1), D2 (B2)
Unpack	UNPK	SS	F3	D1 (L1, B1), D2 (L2, B2)

DECIMAL FEATURE INSTRUCTIONS

Add Decimal	AP	SS	FA	D1 (L1, B1), D2 (L2, B2)
Compare Decimal	CP	SS	F9	D1 (L1, B1), D2 (L2, B2)
Divide Decimal	DP	SS	FD	D1 (L1, B1), D2 (L2, B2)
Edit	ED	SS	DE	D1 (L, B1), D2 (B2)
Edit and Mark	EDMK	SS	DF	D1 (L, B1), D2 (B2)
Multiply Decimal	MP	SS	FC	D1 (L1, B1), D2 (L2, B2)
Subtract Decimal	SP	SS	FB	D1 (L1, B1), D2 (L2, B2)
Zero and Add	ZAP	SS	F8	D1 (L1, B1), D2 (L2, B2)

DIRECT CONTROL FEATURE INSTRUCTIONS

Read Direct	RDD	SI	85	D1 (B1), I2
Write Direct	WRD	SI	84	D1 (B1), I2

PROTECTION FEATURE INSTRUCTIONS

Insert Storage Key	ISK	RR	09	R1, R2
Set Storage Key	SSK	RR	08	R1, R2

Figure 4.1. Set of instructions for the IBM 360 computer.

The program for processing all the scores of the 25 pupils could be written as follows:

1A	1LIX	24
2A	2LIX	19
2B	2LDA	1000
	BRU	3B
2C	0	20
3A	2ADD	1000
3B	2BIX	3A
	1FST	1500
	LDA	2B
	ARH	2C
	RST	2B
	RST	3A
	1BIX	2A

The instructions already explained are those from 2A to 3B; 2C, inserted, is not an instruction—it is only a number we need, and the skip area following BRU 3B is a convenient place to store it.*

The program begins at 1A, and we load index register #1 with one less than the number of pupils. The run-through from 2A to 3B processes the first pupil's scores, and then 1FST 1500 stores the contents of the accumulator (that pupil's total) in memory register 1524 (because of the influence of index register #1). The next four instructions have the purpose of setting up the section 2A–3B for use on the second pupil's scores, stored in the region 1020–1039. Now we can see why 2C was inserted:

---

* Thus the unconditional branch is one of the major conveniences of the working programmer. Not only can one insert constants after it, but one can make use of it in modifying programs, especially when adding new routines. A programmer is spared the labor of inserting the freshly added instruction in the midst of his program listings. All such patches are placed at the end of the listing and unconditionally branched to, then unconditionally branched away from after execution.

Strange as it seems, this way of constructing programs causes almost no loss in computer time, for the transition to distant parts of a program caused by a branch takes practically the same time as to proceed to the adjacent instruction (execution of the branch itself can take less than a microsecond in most computers). Where difficulties *are* caused, however, is in the complexity of the program listings, and the troubles that ensue when an old programmer quits his job and his programs must be figured out by his replacement. Very recently in the world of programming, significant spokesmen (Miller, 1973) have argued rather persuasively that unconditional branches are not really necessary in *any* program, and that the convenience of their use is heavily outweighed by the chaos they cause in program maintenance.

126 Programming and Digital Computers

we need the number 20 to add to the addresses at 2B and 3A. This is done as follows:

1. LDA 2B loads the accumulator with whatever address is at 2B, which is 1000 the first pass.
2. ARH 2C (add right half of 2C) selects the right half of the memory register, containing our number 20, and adds it to the contents of the accumulator. (In this case, the instruction ADD 2C would work as well, because the left half, being zero, would have no effect when added; nevertheless a habit-bound programmer would probably still use ARH).
3. RST 2B and RST 3A, both of which store only in the right half of a memory register, update the instructions to be involved in the addition of the next pupil's scores. Use of a FST (full register store) instruction would be wrong, because the accumulator contains 2LDA 1020, and 2LDA would be stored at 3A as well as at 2B. Such errors are often made by programmers, though, and explains why programmers must *debug* their programs.

Now that the add instructions have been suitably modified, register #1 is decremented so that the next total score is stored adjacent to (rather than on top of) the first total score. The branch carries the operation of the computer back to instruction 2A, which loads up index register #2 for the next 20-score add. Forty microseconds after this program is initiated, all 25 of score sets are added up and their totals placed in sequence in the 25 registers in memory locations 1500 through 1524. Notice, however that the total scores have not been ranked in order of their numerical values. We are not ignoring that issue—merely saving it to illustrate another tool of programming: the flow diagram.

Figure 4.2 is a type of diagram many programmers draw before they ever commit a computer instruction to a coding sheet. By means of flowcharting, the programmer can abstract his task, and the components thereof, from any considerations of what the computer and its peripheral equipment are able to do. This can be helpful in thinking, but even if not, can serve as documentation for what the programmer intended his program to do.

Figure 4.2 is congruent to the first 9 steps of the 10-step manual score adding procedure given earlier in the chapter; that is, the program when written on the basis of the flowchart will do everything except actually assign grades (we would suspect that most teachers would still rather have that last step left up to them).

It is common (though not strictly necessary) to draw different-

Concepts of Programming 127

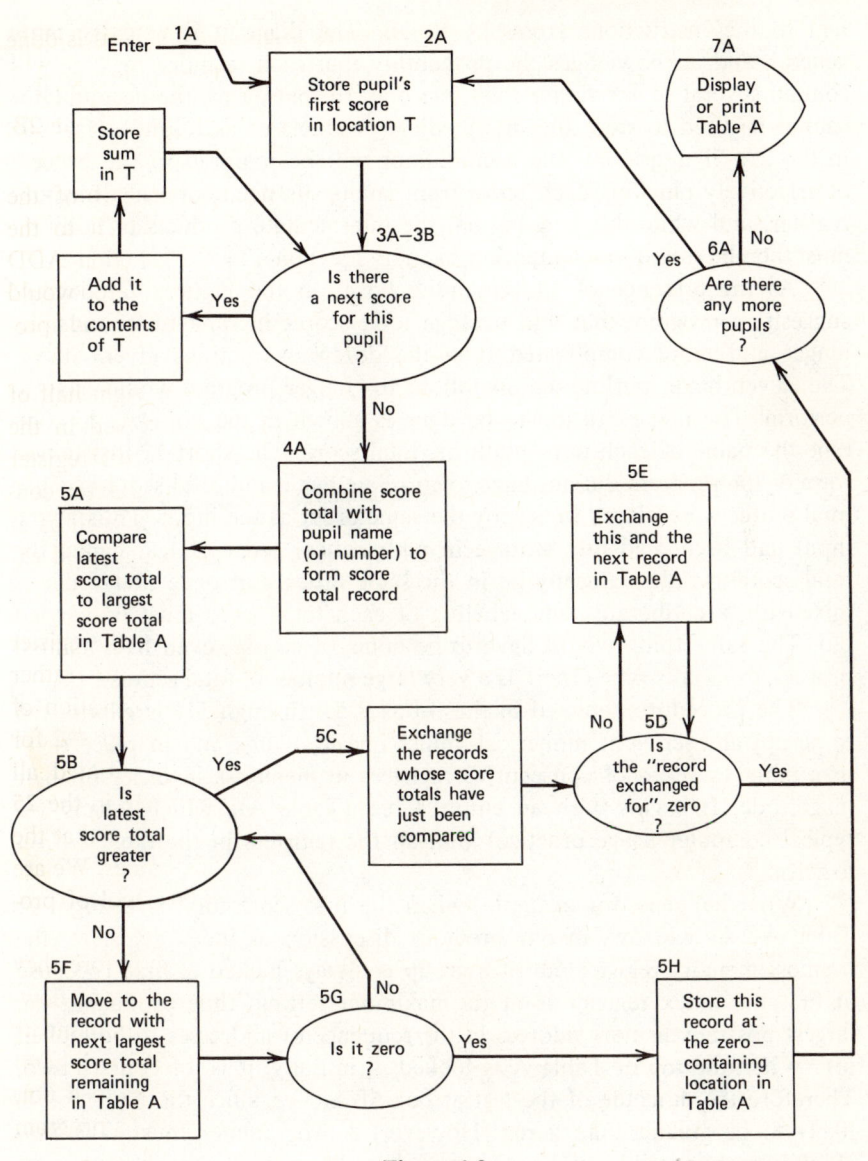

```
                    1A                    2A                      7A
    Enter ──────────►┌─────────────┐                         ┌─────────────┐
                     │ Store pupil's│◄────────────            │  Display    │
    ┌────────┐       │ first score  │                        │  or print   │
    │ Store  │       │ in location T│                        │  Table A    │
    │ sum    │       └──────┬───────┘                        └──────▲──────┘
    │ in T   │              │                                       │
    └────▲───┘              │                                Yes    │ No
         │               3A-3B                                 6A
    ┌────┴───┐        ┌─────────┐                         ┌─────────┐
    │ Add it │        │ Is there│                         │Are there│
    │ to the │◄──Yes──│a next   │                         │any more │
    │contents│        │score for│                         │ pupils  │
    │ of T   │        │this pupil│                        │    ?    │
    └────────┘        └────┬────┘                         └────▲────┘
                           │                                   │
                           No                                  │
                           ▼
                   4A                      5E
                  ┌──────────┐           ┌─────────────┐
   5A             │ Combine  │           │  Exchange   │
  ┌──────────┐    │ score    │           │ this and the│
  │ Compare  │    │ total    │           │ next record │
  │ latest   │◄───│ with     │           │ in Table A  │
  │ score    │    │ pupil    │           └──────▲──────┘
  │ total to │    │ name     │                  │
  │ largest  │    │ (or      │                  │
  │ score    │    │ number)  │                  │
  │ total in │    │ to form  │           No   5D▼
  │ Table A  │    │ score    │      ┌───────┐
  └────┬─────┘    │ total    │      │  Is   │
       │          │ record   │      │ the   │
       ▼          └──────────┘      │"record│
   5B                 5C            │ex-    │
  ┌──────┐       ┌──────────┐       │changed│
  │  Is  │──Yes─►│ Exchange │──────►│  for" │──Yes──┐
  │latest│       │ the      │       │ zero  │       │
  │score │       │ records  │       │   ?   │       │
  │total │       │ whose    │       └───────┘       │
  │greater?      │ score    │                       │
  └──┬───┘       │ totals   │                       │
     │           │ have just│                       │
     No          │ been     │                       │
     ▼           │ compared │                       │
  5F             └─────▲────┘                       │
 ┌────────┐            │                            │
 │Move to │            │                     5H     │
 │the     │       5G   │                  ┌────────┐│
 │record  │    ┌──────┐│                  │Store   ││
 │with next──►│Is it │─┘   Yes            │this    ││
 │largest │    │zero? │───────────────────►│record  ││
 │score   │    └──┬───┘                   │at the  ││
 │total   │       │                       │zero-   ││
 │remain- │       No                      │contain-││
 │ing in  │                               │ing loc-││
 │Table A │                               │ation in││
 └────────┘                               │Table A │◄
                                          └────────┘
```

Figure 4.2.

shaped boxes to correspond to various *types* of diagrammed functions. In Figure 4.2, straightforward operations involving memory registers are described in square or rectangular boxes. Elliptical boxes are for branches or decision points. The projectile-shaped box indicates an output function.

The first four boxes (upper left) in the sequence are roughly equivalent to the instructions from 2A to 3B. The diagram is actually more general, and acknowledges the probability that each memory register will contain several scores rather than just one. In that event, the accumulator cannot be used to store the intermediate products of addition, as is done in the 2A–3B sequence; the accumulator will be required in the process of selectively plucking each score from among its neighbors in a memory register, and while this is going on, the intermediate products of addition must then be stored in a temporary memory location (T).

As the presence of 11 remaining boxes in the Figure 4.2 diagram suggests, a program that will arrange total scores in rank order must be longer and more complicated than the dozen instructions given above. The eleven boxes outline the operations the longer program would have to perform. The first extra job to be done is shown in the box 4A; to combine the name of each pupil with his total score. The short 12-instruction form of the program did not have to correlate name and total score because total scores were placed in exactly the same order as the input. Thus, if the input had been read into storage in alphabetical order of last name, the total scores would naturally be in the same order. But once that order is mixed up, a deliberate name-labeling of each total score must be carried out. The same thing would have to be done, of course, even in a manual process, especially when there is a very large number of total scores.

The procedure depicted in the 8 boxes 5A through 5H is guaranteed to accept any series of numerical values one at a time and to place them in a table (a series of consecutive registers in memory) in order of their magnitude. It begins with an empty table (Table A), which means (in typical computer usage practice) that all the registers in the table are set to zero.

What happens, for example, when the first score total is brought to Table A? As we saw, in our previous discussion of index registers, the topmost memory register out of a group is always looked at first (because at first the index register is at its maximum setting, thus producing the largest possible memory address in the sequence of addresses to be looked at). When the top of Table A is looked at initially, it is, of course, zero. Therefore the outcome of the test at box 5B is *Yes*, since the first total is likely to be greater than zero. (However, a programmer must take into account every possible configuration of data that his program may process, including, in this case the unlikely chance that some student will score nothing but zeros on his tests. A trivial solution to this problem would be for the programmer to arbitrarily add 1 to every score total.)

A *Yes* answer at 5B leads to box 5C. The first total (actually the *record,* which includes a pupil name and a total) is stored by exchanging its contents for the zero contents of the top register of Table A, which are placed in the accumulator. In 5D a check is made to see if the exchanged record is really zero (later on it will frequently not be, but in the first exchange it is). A *Yes* answer sends the program back to box 2A to compute the total for the next pupil.

Let us suppose that the second score total is greater than the first one. Again the *Yes* route at 5B is taken, and again the contents of two registers are exchanged, but now, of course, what is brought into the accumulator is not zero—it is the first record that we have just stored. A test at 5D reveals it is not zero, and the *No* route leads to box 5E, where an exchange is made between the accumulator and the next-to-top register of the Table. Notice that as long as the contents of a register pulled into the accumulator are *not* zero, the program keeps shuffling back and forth between 5D and 5E, exchanging the accumulator and successively lower and lower registers in Table A. These registers will always be in the correct order, running from large to small. (The action of the routine can be simulated manually with playing cards, and the reader is invited to try it out.)

Now suppose that the second score total turns out to be *less* than the first. In this case the *No* route from 5B to 5F will be taken. We shift to the next largest total in the Table, which in this case is the empty next-to-top register. A zero test reveals that the next-to-top register is the proper place to store the second total. Here again, whenever nonzero values are encountered, the loop 5B–5F–5C cycles, moving the focus of the program to successively lower addresses in Table A until either a zero value is found, in which case storage is effected, or (!) until a *Yes* path is taken at 5B. The latter result occurs whenever a total somewhat intermediate in amount is successively compared at first to totals that are larger and then comes to a point in the Table where totals are smaller. In other words, the record having the total is inserted *at that point* in the Table, and records with lower totals are pushed downward in the Table by successive exchanges.

As in the case of the simple 12-instruction program we previously considered, the processing is complete when the index register that is loaded with "number of pupils" falls to zero. Table A is now arranged in the proper order for display to the teacher. An interesting question is: What order will result if, by chance, everyone has the same score total? This is an unlikely event, and yet, as before, one the programmer must prepare for (in general, *some* equal values are to be expected from time to time, and the behavior of the program when they are *all* equal is simply a way of investigating this facet to the nth degree). If the scores are all equal, the *Yes* route at 5B will never be taken. Each incoming score will be moved down the Table until a zero value is encountered and stored there. The order of the score total records will then be the same as the order of the input, presumably alphabetical by name.

High-Level Languages. The kind of programming described to this point is the primitive, step-by-step instruction of the computer that was universally used during the first 10 years of stored-program computing; it has since given way to more powerful programming methods. Yet such a primitive method is still used by a few programmers who believe that the use of *assembly language*, as it is commonly termed, is the best means of obtaining efficient computer performance. This efficiency stems from the fact that in assembly language one tells computers not only *what* to do, but also *how* to do it.

But this "leading the computer by the hand," though it may lead to efficient use of the machine, is somewhat inefficient in the use of the programmer's time. Moreover, use of assembly language requires a degree of training, aptitude, and experience that is not really necessary in the effective use of computers. In the last half of the 1950s, people in the computer field realized this, and soon many of them were at work developing easier-to-use *high-level languages*.

To see what "high level" means, think of an organization chart in a company. Such a chart looks a bit like an inverted tree, with the trunk at the top and the branches heading downwards. At the bottom, the twigs and leaves are the individual workers; the smaller branches are their immediate supervisors; going up, the larger branches become, successively department, branch, and division heads; finally, the trunk is top management. On an organization chart, the higher the level, the larger the number of employees are subsumed in the group charted at that level. "High level" has an analogous meaning in relation to programming: in a high-level language, each instruction corresponds to many primitive machine instructions. In some present-day high-level languages it is possible for a person to write three or four instructions that actually correspond to more than a hundred of the kinds of elementary instructions we have become acquainted with in this chapter.

How is this possible? Already we have touched on the notion of a compiler, a program that processes other programs. Early compilers simply freed programmers from certain intellectual labors that the computer itself could easily perform, such as converting the symbolic addresses used by a programmer (2A, 2B, 3A, etc.) into absolute memory locations; they also translated the programmer's mnemonic instructions (LDA, ADD, LIX, etc.) into number codes interpretable by the computer. But these compilers almost always replaced one program-written instruction with only one

Concepts of Programming 131

machine-interpretable instruction, and—as per our organization chart analogy—this would *not* be a high-level language (in fact, it is the very basement in programming languages). Many programmers would not use the term compiler for a program that converts instructions on a one-to-one basis, but prefer the term *assembler*. It is the practice, then, for the instructions a programmer writes on his coding sheet, i.e., the *assembly language,* to be translated—by an assembler—to corresponding machine-interpretable language.

An idea of how a true compiler operates is shown in Figure 4.3, wherein we set the 12-instruction program considered earlier in correspondence with a much smaller number of instructions. For example, the instruction on the left that reads ADD 20 corresponds to the assembly language instructions (right) 2A through 3B. Because, in the Figure 4.3 case, three or four assembly language instructions are needed for each instruction like ADD 20, the language at left qualifies as a high-level language, although a fairly rudimentary one.

The more complicated program represented in the Figure 4.2 flow diagram would probably require about 50 instructions in assembly language and as few as 10 high-level instructions such as those shown at left in Figure 4.3. To develop a high-level language, programmers put their heads together and decide what kinds of computer operations are most commonly used by programmers in a given area of computer applications. The list of operations would be long, and in an area such as engineering would undoubtedly include such processes as subtraction, multiplication,

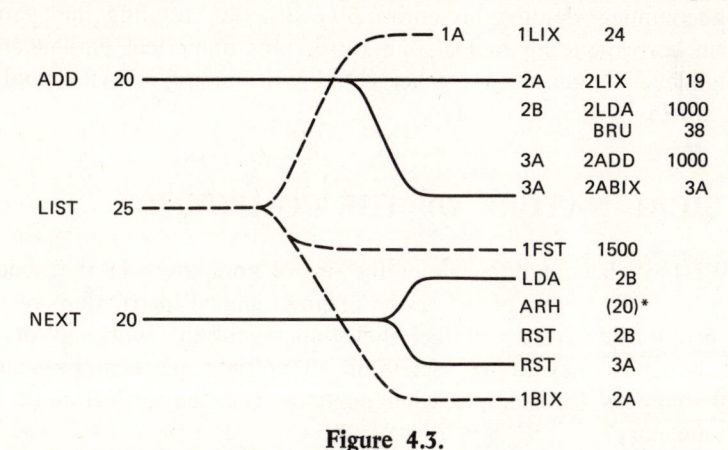

			1A	1LIX	24
ADD	20		2A	2LIX	19
			2B	2LDA	1000
				BRU	38
			3A	2ADD	1000
			3A	2ABIX	3A
LIST	25				
			1FST	1500	
			LDA	2B	
			ARH	(20)*	
NEXT	20		RST	2B	
			RST	3A	
			1BIX	2A	

Figure 4.3.

*Compilers typically place all constants needed by a program such as the number 20, in one storage area. A programmer can simply refer to whatever value he wants in simple fashion, and on compilation the value will be stored and its address inserted in the pertinent instruction.

division, square root, trigonometric operations, determination of logarithms, and so on. (These kinds of operations are typical of Fortran, a high-level language which has been in use for 15 years.) The programmers then write assembly-language instructions corresponding to each operation, and the number of such instructions would vary between 4 (or less) to as much as 50. Each of these groups of instructions would generally correspond to just *one word* (ADD, NEXT, etc.) of the high-level language. Then a compiler would be written to translate the words of a program written in the high-level language into the correct groups of assembly language instructions, or—to be more exact—translate it directly into machine language, for translation into assembly language would be an unnecessary intermediate step.

The jump from a high-level language to still higher levels of language is, as we have said, a matter of developing compilers that produce more and more machine instructions for each single word of the language. Because much programming effort has to go into the writing and checking out of these compilers, the more so as the level becomes higher, only broad usage of a given class of operations could justify the effort involved. As a convenient example of this, suppose we continue to belabor the test score totaling case, and assume that a day arrives when teachers all over the nation use computers to process test data. Then it would be the task of programmers to determine what kinds of processing teachers typically need. It is safe to say that the score addition and ranking of totals we have considered would be so common that it would be quite justifiable to provide a compiler yielding an entire 50-instruction totaling and ranking program corresponding to just one word, plus numerical parameters, in the high-level language. A teacher could write simply: TAR (total and rank) 20, 25.

PHYSICAL NATURE OF THE COMPUTER

We have been talking about the use of computers in the concrete, though symbolic, terms of the action of programmed instructions on data. Most people, however, will feel they understand the workings of computers better if they know something about their physical basis: what actually happens, for example, when a number is called forth from the computer's memory?

It is well to begin by looking at the structure of a computer system from the top down. Figure 4.4 is a computer system block diagram. As shown, a computer system involves an arithmetic and control unit (frequently called the *main frame*), an internal memory, and peripheral units. The latter, as discussed in Chapter Three, include files (magnetic tapes,

Physical Nature of the Computer 133

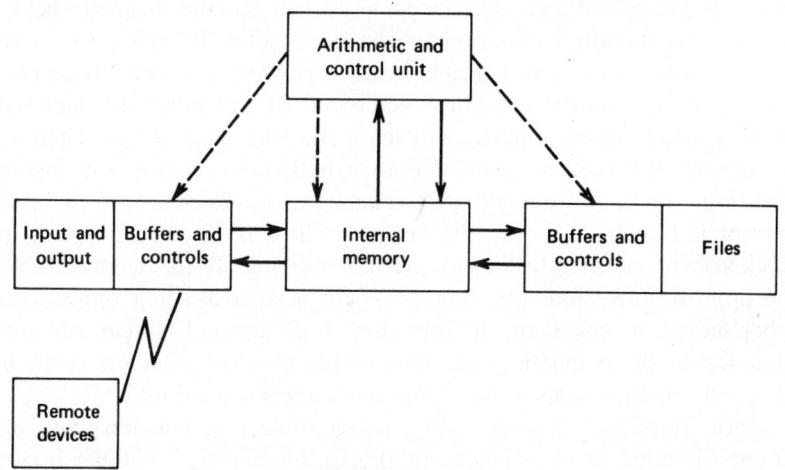

```
                    ┌─────────────────┐
                    │  Arithmetic and │
                    │  control unit   │
                    └─────────────────┘
┌──────────┬──────────┐  ┌──────────┐  ┌──────────┬──────────┐
│Input and │Buffers and│→│ Internal │→│Buffers and│          │
│ output   │ controls  │←│  memory  │←│ controls  │  Files   │
└──────────┴──────────┘  └──────────┘  └──────────┴──────────┘
     │
┌──────────┐
│ Remote   │
│ devices  │
└──────────┘
```

Figure 4.4.

drums, and disks) to which a computer has access, input/output equipment (punched card readers, printers, display scopes), and remote devices (Teletype units, data collection devices).

The major task of the arithmetic and control unit is the interpretation and execution of the instructions of whatever program is stored and operating in internal memory (note dashed arrow pointing to internal memory). Also, the arithmetic and control unit synchronizes program operation with use of the various in/out and auxiliary storage units (other dashed arrows). Data flow (solid arrows) is usually to and from internal memory. We have already spoken of traffic between internal memory and the arithmetic and control unit—the accumulator, the index registers and other important registers present in the latter unit. Traffic between memory and the various peripheral units is handled through buffer and control units, which perform functions in regard to data flow that are similar to the function a depot performs for railroad passengers, i.e., routing and waiting functions.

Internal memory is the very center of a computer system, and the interplay between it and the arithmetic and control unit is the substance of data processing. The physical entity in terms of which we can describe what actually happens in operations involving memory is the *magnetic core*. This basic unit of memory is a tiny ring of ferromagnetic material, a few hundredths of an inch in diameter.*

A fact most people remember from high school physics is that a current-carrying wire is surrounded by a magnetic field whose lines of

---

* During 1973 the more potent semiconductor memory unit became cheaper (per bit) than the ferromagnetic core; such units can be exepected to supersede cores in must computers in future years (Farmer, 1974).

force are circular. When the current is turned off, the magnetic field disappears; no measuring instrument can detect that the space surrounding the wire once contained a magnetic field. However, if one surrounds the wire with ring-shaped structures composed of ferromagnetic material, a suitably strong direct current will leave the ring magnetized. Then when the current is turned off, part of the magnetic field remains—in the rings. The rings, then, can be said to "remember." Furthermore, if the electric current is flowing one way, the magnetic field is directed one way (i.e., clockwise or counterclockwise) around the ring. If the current flows in the opposite direction, the magnetic field is also directed oppositely. In other words, by reversing the direction of the current we can reverse the direction of the magnetic field. This simple physical principle is the basis of everything that happens in a computer's internal memory.

An individual magnetic core, being subject to magnetization either in one direction or its opposite, in effect, "remembers" whether a current strong enough to magnetize it last flowed in one direction or another; thus, it remembers only two things. It may seem odd that such a small memory capacity would be adequate as a structural unit for a computer memory. Likewise, it may once have seemed odd that long messages could be sent using nothing but dots and dashes, yet that is the basis of the Morse code; the trick is in using a sufficiently large number of dots and dashes. For the computer, the trick is in having a large enough number of magnetic cores. It does not take a very large number of them, either, to represent an impressive amount of information. Ten pennies, each of which can be heads or tails, can—when arranged in a row—be made to display more than 1000 distinct combinations of heads and tails (try it!), and so can magnetic cores, when "heads" means magnetization one way and "tails" magnetization the other way. This of course is the binary number system," discussed in Chapter Three.

In a computer's memory, cores magnetized one way are designated zero and those the opposite way are designated one. Ten cores in a row can represent numbers from zero to 1023, as follows:

$$
\begin{aligned}
0\ 0\ 0\ 0\ 0\ 0\ 0\ 0\ 0\ 1 &= 1 \\
0\ 0\ 0\ 0\ 0\ 0\ 0\ 0\ 1\ 0 &= 2 \\
0\ 0\ 0\ 0\ 0\ 0\ 0\ 0\ 1\ 1 &= 3 \\
0\ 0\ 0\ 0\ 0\ 0\ 0\ 1\ 0\ 0 &= 4 \\
0\ 0\ 0\ 0\ 0\ 0\ 0\ 1\ 0\ 1 &= 5 \\
&\vdots \\
1\ 1\ 1\ 1\ 1\ 1\ 1\ 1\ 1\ 1 &= 1{,}023
\end{aligned}
$$

A typical computer memory register contains 32 cores in a row, and this handful of cores, each able to stand for only 1 or 0, is sufficient to represent any of the numbers from zero to 4 billion.

So much for the statics of storage in memory. The dynamic aspect, getting data in and out of storage, is even more interesting. The various phenomena involved are shown in Figure 4.5. The parallelogram shaped curve in Figure 4.5a is a plot of a *hysteresis loop*, which shows the relationship between the current strength in a wire and the degree of magnetization of a magnetic core through which the wire passes. The horizontal arrow is the current-strength axis, and the current-strength values H_t and $-H_t$ are the currents required to produce a condition of magnetic saturation in a core. Saturation in one direction around the core, produced by current H_t, is equivalent to *one*, and saturation in the opposite direction, produced by the equal but opposite current $-H_t$, is equivalent to *zero*. However, and this is a crucial property of magnetic cores, current values of $\frac{1}{2} H_t$ and $-\frac{1}{2}H_t$ are not sufficient to produce a change in magnetization, regardless of what state the core is in. This is because ferromagnetic materials are composed of microscopic grain-like regions (called *domains*) that cannot be disturbed unless a certain threshold in magnetizing current strength is passed. As the diagram suggests, a value of about $\frac{3}{4}H_t$ is strong enough to produce a halfway degree of magnetization. However, a computer builder has little use for currents that will produce partial degrees of magnetization, but has much use for a situation in which *two equal currents* neither of which, by itself, could alter magnetization, but both of which, reinforcing each other, could produce fully saturated magnetization opposite to what existed for that core previously. This state of affairs opens the way to a clever wiring scheme which, as we shall see, makes it possible to do things with arrays of magnetic cores.

Figure 4.5b shows a core with two wires (x and y) passing through it at right angles to each other. Suppose each can carry a current of $\frac{1}{2}H_t$ or $-\frac{1}{2}H_t$, and suppose the core is in the zero state. From the plot in Figure 4.5a we can see that as long as either or both of the wires carry a current of $-\frac{1}{2}H_t$ nothing will happen to the core's state of magnetization. Only if both have the positive $\frac{1}{2}H_t$ current will there be a change of state, and then it will be all the way to the saturated *one* condition.

What is the significance of the wires being at right angles? It is this: If one wire holds a row of cores corresponding to a given memory address, it is then a memory register, such as we discussed under programming. If it is initially empty, then all the cores are in a *zero* state of magnetization. Each wire passing at right angles through each core in this register is capable of changing the value of its core to the *one* state, but *only* if it has the cooperation of the register wire. Suppose the register has 10

136

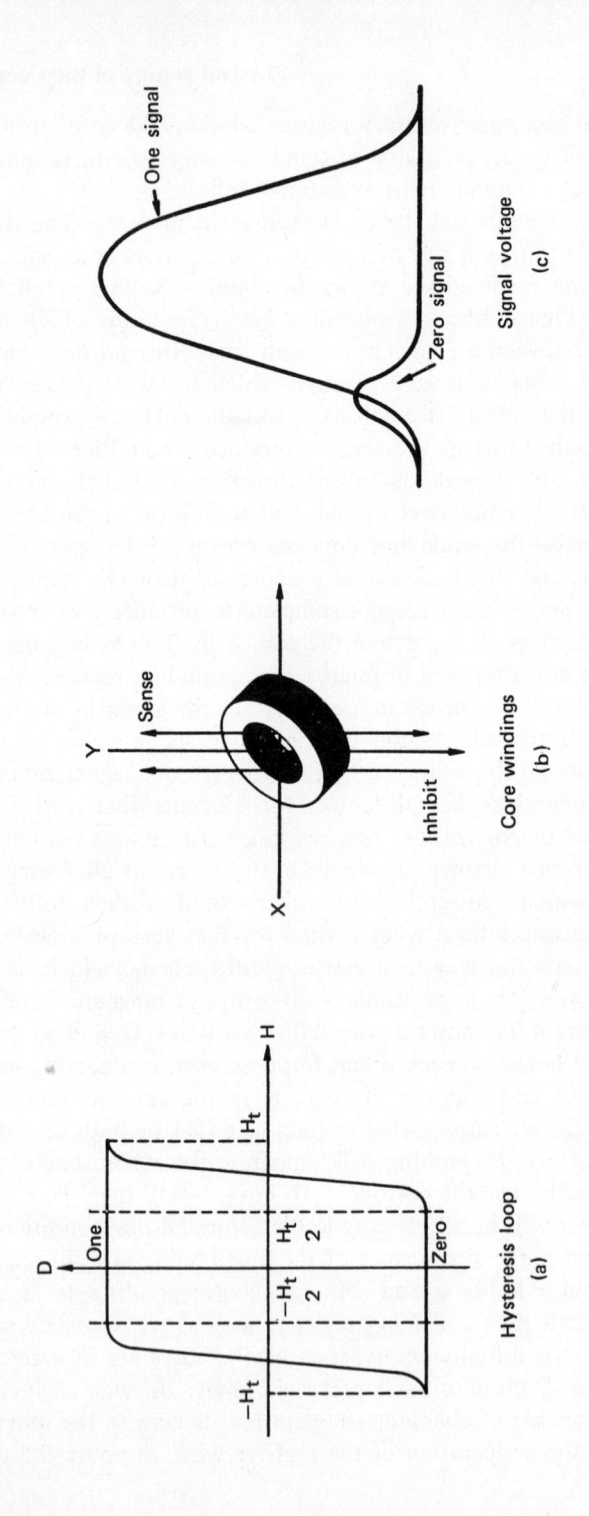

Hysteresis loop
(a)

Core windings
(b)

Signal voltage
(c)

Figure 4.5. Magnetic core memories.

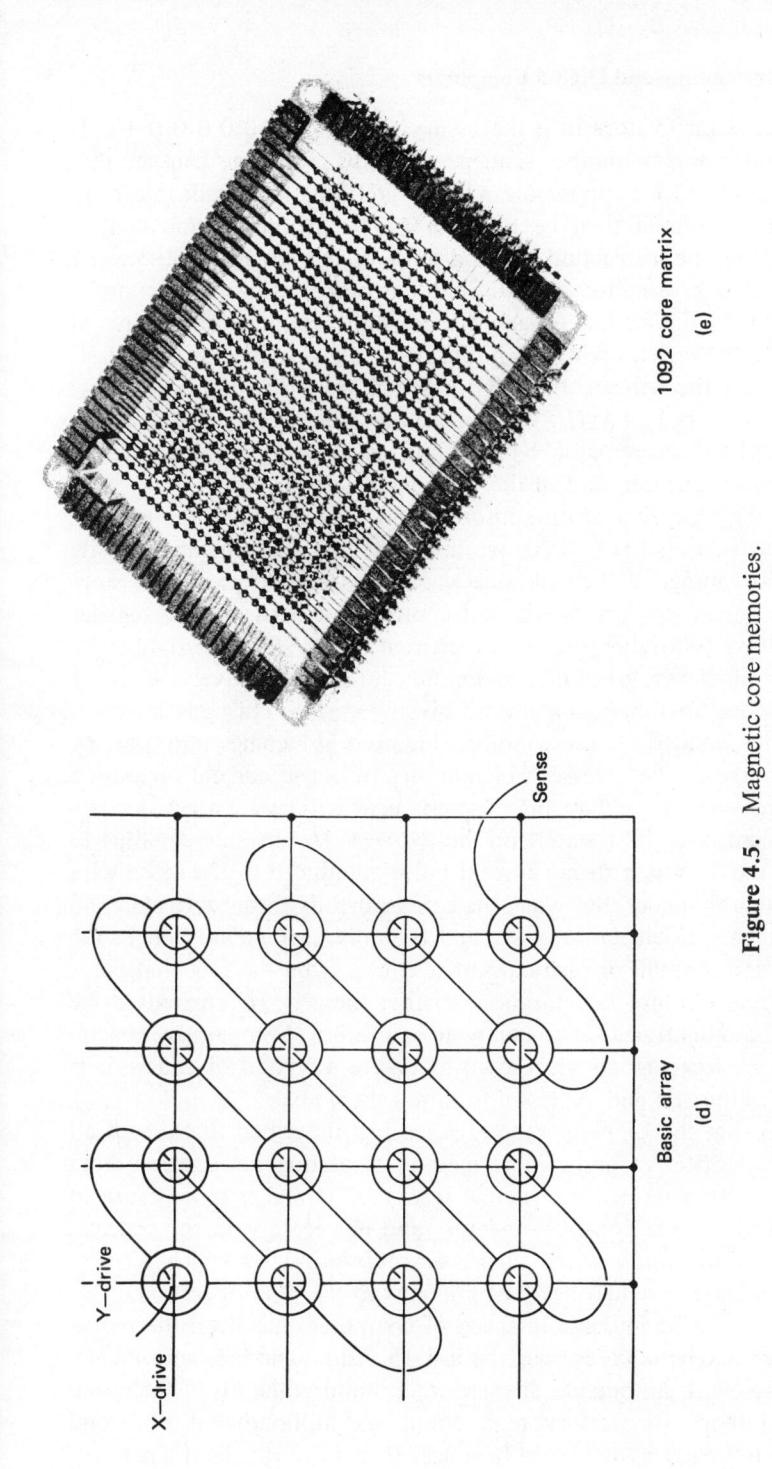

cores, and we want to store in it the binary number 0 0 0 0 0 0 1 0 1. (Looking at the binary number sequence already given, we can see that this is the number 5.) Suppose the address is 1000; the applicable computer instruction would then be FST 1000. The arithmetic and control unit, interpreting the instruction, sends a pulse of $+\frac{1}{2}H_t$ over the register wire corresponding to address 1000. Simultaneously, using the accumulator as a template, the arithmetic and control unit activates those wires at right angles to the register wires such that if the digit position is 0, $-\frac{1}{2}H_t$ will be sent over the wire for that digit position (i.e., that core in the row of cores), and if it is 1, $+\frac{1}{2}H_t$. We can see that reinforcement (the simultaneous flow of two currents of $+\frac{1}{2}H_t$) will occur only for those cores in the leftmost digit position and in the third from left position.

Such is the process of storing information. To accomplish the reverse, say in the instruction LDA 1000, we must use the cores in an opposite way, taking advantage of their physical capability to yield as well as store information. Again, the arithmetic and control unit activates the register wire for address 1000, this time with a current of $-\frac{1}{2}H_t$. The right-angle wires are not, however, given plus and minus currents selectively, as in the case of the store operation, but are all given $-\frac{1}{2}H_t$. This sets all cores to zero. At this point the sense winding (Figure 4.5b) comes into play, by taking advantage of the reverse principle of an electric current creating a magnetic field, namely: a changing magnetic field will create a current. So, wherever a core is in the 1 state, and the two $-\frac{1}{2}H_t$ currents combine to change it to the 0 state, a strong current pulse is induced in the sense wire passing through that core. But when the core is already in the zero state, no change in magnetic field takes place, and the only current induced in the sense winding is a small disturb current resulting from the fact that cores hardly ever reach complete saturation, so that the $-\frac{1}{2}H_t$ currents drive zero state cores slightly closer to complete saturation. Comparative magnitudes of the sensed currents are shown in Figure 4.5c and of course it is easy for the arithmetic and control unit to tell them apart.

The fact that the LDA operation, as we just described it, changes all cores back to zero is an undesirable method of getting information from memory (it is often termed *destructive readout*). It makes more sense to be able to read information from memory and not erase it in the process. For this reason an *inhibit* wire (Figure 4.5b) is provided which restores the cores to whatever value they had previous to the read operation.

One factor in the increase in speed of computers has been the reduction in size of magnetic cores over the last 15 years. The first core memories used cores with an outside diameter of 8 hundredths of an inch, and a typical reference to memory took about six millionths of a second (microseconds). Present-day cores have less than a fourth the diameter of an early core, and, being less massive, can be brought to saturation much more quickly, and access speeds of half a microsecond are common.

Because all the cores in a memory register can be changed simultaneously, the intrinsic speed of memory operations is obviously much faster than would be the case if cores had to be dealt with one at a time. It is possible in principle to fill an entire core memory, even one with a million machine registers, with data in less than a second. The point is somewhat academic, because peripheral equipment capable of providing the data to fill memory tend to lag behind the computer itself in speed; some magnetic drums, however, come fairly close to being able to provide data at the rate memory can accept it (Chapter Three). The fact that peripheral units have data transfer rates generally much lower than that of computers does not really matter in the gross scheme of data processing, because the bulk of the computer's operation, microsecond by microsecond, is in the interaction between the arithmetic and control unit and memory, and the basic limitation on computer speed resides therein.

Patterns of Computer Use. The fact that computers are steadily becoming faster, more capacious, more numerous, and therefore more available is causally related to changes, over the last decade, in the manner of their use. In the early 1960s most computer users were programmers whose offices were generally a geographical stone's throw from the computer itself. Any program usage by people who were not programmers tended to be highly institutionalized, i.e., by highly trained people in computer-based military systems or by workers in well-planned and regulated forms of business and industrial automation. When a nonprogrammer wanted to use the computer informally he would generally ask a programmer to set things up for him.

This programmer would be acquainted with the local program library, and would find, and prepare for use, the card decks for the required programs (most of which probably were written and checked out by other programmers long before). The programmer would write up a "job request" and submit it along with the program decks and data (which may have been previously stored on punched cards or magnetic tape) to computer operation personnel. This job would take its place in a queue of other jobs requested by other programmers; this way of using the computer predominated in the first 15 years of data processing, and is known as *batch processing*.

The time between submission of a job to the computer operator and the receipt of the printout containing the output of the program run was from several hours to a day. Such a delay could be irritating, but most computer users accepted it, as did the managements of organizations leasing computers. After all, computer time was then quite expensive, and the slowness of access to computers was a part of the overall atmosphere of deliberation and forethought regarding the correct use of these high-priced instruments.

As the cost of computer time plunged, computer users became more and more aware of the fact that personnel time wasted, by having to wait for computer runs, was a major expense, and perhaps a needless one. In 1964 and 1965 people began to plan computer systems in which jobs could be run and programs used on a minute-by-minute basis, directly by the user (rather than through such intermediaries as the programmer and the computer operator). The first experimental system was developed at Massachusetts Institute of Technology (Glasser and Corbato, 1964), and the first commercially available system was established by General Electric in July, 1965 (Jordain, 1969).

These systems had two basic characteristics. First, all manner of uses of the computer and its peripheral units could be controlled by a user from a single terminal (usually a Teletype or similar device) connected by cable to the computer. There need be no limit to the length of such a cable—it could be (and often today is) part of the telephone system. This meant that a user in Chicago could easily control computer operations at an installation in San Francisco. (This is the significance of the box marked "remote devices" in Figure 4.4.) This minute-by-minute control is aided by feedback from the computer via the same Teletype by which the user sends his instructions; this feedback, usually the output of programs just operated by the user, helps the user determine his subsequent procedures. Because of the back-and-forth communicative process between the user and the computer, systems built on this principle are often called *on-line interactive systems*, or simply *on-line systems*.

The second basic characteristic of the new systems is forced by the sheer economics of computer usage. Computers are so fast, and the reactions of users so slow, that to put the computer into the hands of a single on-line user would engender prodigious waste: a hundred programs could be run for a hundred other users in the time it takes a user to type out a command on a Teletype keyboard. And, indeed, there is no reason why a hundred users can't be simultaneously accommodated by a single computer. All that is required is a way of *time-sharing* the computer's capabilities between users, preferably in a manner such that no one user need be inconvenienced by the fact that 99 other users are also being served. This is, in fact, accomplished by having the computer shift its attention, from one millisecond (thousandth of a second) to the next, from user to user.

One would think that the computer would surely become "confused" by such rapid switching of attention. But such anthropomorphic visualizations are a poor guide to understanding this process. What one needs to visualize is a method of bringing into internal memory and operating many programs in a short interval of time. The methodology for this existed as long ago as 1955, when the first experimental SAGE Air Defense computer was built at Lexington, Massachusetts. (At that time, however, this kind of system was too expensive for any but military use.) Programs can be written so that they can be interrupted at millisecond intervals. A program, plus all the data it has produced up to the time of interruption, can be copied accurately into some peripheral storage unit, usually a magnetic disk. Then, a second or so later, this program and its data can be pulled back into internal memory again and executed. Since every core in memory is in the identical state it was at the time of the previous interruption, the program should then go on to operate as if no interruption had taken place.

If such an "interrupt and preserve" process takes place for 100 users, each in his turn, so few seconds will elapse between the time a user types *GO* (a typical signal for begininng a program run) until the output data the user desires comes clattering over the Teletype, that the user will have the illusion that he is being continuously and uniquely served by the computer. Because of this manner of splitting computer time up among users, systems having this characteristic are known as *time-sharing systems*. Also, because one seldom sees an on-line system which is not also a time-sharing system, the two terms have come to be used almost interchangeably.

The use of computers remotely in this manner is clearly a tool of of major significance for information storage and retrieval. Therefore we shall have a great deal to say about on-line time-shared systems in other chapters.

REFERENCES

ABRAMS, PETER, and CORVINS, WALTER (1971), *Basic Data Processing*, Rinehart Press, San Francisco.

FARMER, VIC (1974), A Look at 1985—Part IV, *Computerworld*, 8:13, pp. 17–20.

GLASSER, E. L., and CORBATO, F. J. (1964), Introduction to Time-Sharing, *Datamation*, 10:11, pp. 24–27.

JORDAIN, PHILIP B. (1969), *Condensed Computer Encyclopedia*, McGraw-Hill, New York.

MILLER, EDWARD F., Jr., and LINDAMOOD, GEORGE E. (1973), Structured Programming: Top-down Approach, *Datamation*, 19:12, pp. 55–57.

Chapter Five

The Librarian and Recorded Knowledge

HISTORY OF RECORDING MEDIA

From earliest time man has attempted to preserve his thoughts for posterity. A brief sketch of the history of early writing is useful in gaining an appreciation of the development of recorded knowledge (Johnson, 1955).

Archeaologists have unearthed many examples of various forms of writing chiseled into stone. Samples of Egyptian pictographic writing, known as hieroglyphics, were found cut into building stone dating back to 3 or 4000 B.C. They represent one way in which man devised a short hand method for conveying ideas and concepts to future generations. The translation of hieroglyphic characters on the Rosetta Stone in the early nineteenth century paved the way for increased understanding and knowledge of Egyptian civilization by modern scholars.

Clay was widely used for recording information during the Sumerian-Babylonian-Assyrian civilization. Writing on clay was less arduous than chipping away at stone because writing was done with a stylus of wood when the clay was soft; then the clay was baked for permanence. The writing is known as cuneiform (Latin for wedge shaped), which refers to the shape of the strokes made by the stylus. A vast amount of historical knowledge became available when cuneiform inscriptions were translated in the nineteenth century.

Clay tablets were awkward to transport and took considerable time to prepare for use. Consequently Egyptian papyrus, the forerunner of paper, evolved as a light-weight, convenient medium for both inscription and communication. However, the papyrus plant could only grow in certain geographical areas. Its source of supply was limited. Parchment, or dried animal skin, was plentiful and later replaced papyrus as the chief recording medium. Although the Chinese had already invented the art of paper making, its use had not yet spread westward during the Egyptian period.

The Romans sparked considerable writing activity. Cities were heavily populated, and government paperwork probably had its origin during that day. The needs of commerce and government made writing an essential ingredient to the culture of the time. Roman parchment books were rolled into scrolls and tied with a ribbon. When more than one copy was required, hundreds of scribes or slaves made the required duplication. Papyrus and parchment served as fixed media for recording. Once written, the record could not be erased and reused without considerable difficulty. The pressure of commerce and trade was probably responsible for the development of the *tabula* which consisted of a wooden board or metal sheet covered with wax. Writing was accomplished by using a metal pointed stylus, and a smooth blunt instrument served as an eraser. The *diptych* is the forerunner of our modern book. It consisted of two tabula hinged together at the center; when closed, the writing was protected. The diptych was a popular form of letter communication in its time. During this same period there evolved a book form known as the *codex*, which consisted of strips of papyrus or parchment folded into accordion pleats. Eventually one side of the pleats was sewn, and this, of course, was the beginning of our modern book form.

The Dark Ages which followed the fall of the Roman Empire witnessed very little writing activity. Churches maintained the best and only continuity in the field of historical recording. Church sermons, travel reports, exploration findings, and comments on human behavior were among the kinds of information recorded. Toward the latter half of the medieval period, church manuscripts, artfully styled and beautifully decorated, began appearing. Hand illumination enhanced the value of a book, and books were treasured as much for their artistic quality as for content.

In about 1440 A.D. Johannes Gutenberg invented the movable-type printing press. McMurtrie (1943) reported:

> In the cultural history of mankind there is no event even approaching in importance the invention of printing with movable types. It would require an extensive volume to set forth even in outline the far reaching effects of this invention in every field of human enterprise and experience, or to

describe its results in the liberation of the human spirit from the fetters of ignorance and superstition.

The combination of paper and the printing press has probably done more to preserve man's accomplishments than any other single human achievement. Without question it is largely responsible for the mountain of recorded information extant today.

HISTORY OF THE LIBRARY PROFESSION

Librarians have developed, over many years of operational experience, techniques for making this recorded material available. These techniques have weathered the storm of operation—they work. Libraries, generally speaking, are successful information systems; they provide their customers with information, and they do this with reasonable speed and at minimal cost; they excel at storing information and providing easy and often open, unlimited access to printed material. In fact, they are our main centers of recorded information, and librarians represent the only single source of professional experience on which we can draw to learn about the various kinds of activities normally associated with the organization of information files.

The library profession is a well-knit group, and the network of library activity in this country is highly organized, thriving on mutual interest and interlibrary cooperation. Standardized practices are common, so that a workable technical improvement in one library, for example, usually serves as a pattern for improvement in others. Therefore, while today's information storage and retrieval interests have machine overtones, it is well to understand established library structure, to study proven methods and techniques, and to become familiar with the tools which librarians have fashioned for the conduct of their work.

The American library system is an institution normally taken for granted. It is an active environment for self-education, recreation, and research having an immeasurable effect on our personal lives and educational development.

Present-day library tools—the card catalog, the subject classification scheme, periodical indexes, etc.—had their origin during a brief period of half a century, from about 1840 to 1900. It was during this time that subject cataloging rules were first formulated in Great Britain; the concept of a *union catalog* to cover the total listing of literature in the United States was proposed; subject heading lists were developed for periodical indexing, etc. The year 1876 was a particularly noteworthy one in American library history, for it was then that Melvil Dewey published the first edition of his now famous decimal classification scheme and the American Library Association was founded.

The most fertile period of library development took place shortly thereafter, from 1876 to 1900. This period is marked by the rise of the American university library, the wide adoption of card catalogs, the definition and introduction of the Library of Congress' subject classification scheme, and the initiation of a centralized distribution service by the Library of Congress for library catalog cards.

Since 1900 the library profession has seen a continual growth in the development of special library tools and in the area of documentation. At the turn of the century an international organization, Federation Internationale de Documentation (FID), was created. In 1909 John Cotton Dana founded the Special Libraries Association, and later in Great Britain the Association of Special Libraries and Information Bureaux (ASLIB) was organized. Another important professional organization founded in the United States several years later was the American Documentation Institute (renamed the American Society for Information Science in 1970).

In 1944, with the publication of Fremont Rider's *The Scholar and the Future of the Research Library* (Rider, 1944), the impact of modern research on the library was clearly described. Since 1950 the library profession has seen a mature and systematic attack on library problems and tremendous advances in the field of documentation and in the development of new techniques.

In September 1956, with the aid of a grant from the Ford Foundation, the Council on Library Resources was established. This is an independent, nonprofit corporation whose aim is to assist in the problems of libraries generally, and of research libraries in particular, and to aid in improving the resources and services of libraries. Its primary interests include the following:

1. Basic research in the processes of distribution, organization, storage, and communication (including transmission) of knowledge as these affect libraries.

2. Technological development looking to improvements in the physical-mechanical apparatus of library work (including the collections themselves) and to the application of mechanisms not yet utilized.

3. Methodological development looking to improvements of technique (as contrasted with improvement of apparatus, although frequently closely related thereto), including improvements effected

through coordination of effort as the result of cooperation, standardization, etc.

The Council works principally through grants or contracts to qualified individuals or institutions. It has been an important force in the library profession and responsible for considerable investigation and research in the areas of information retrieval and library technology.

An activity of the federal government which is of special interest to libraries, and to the entire field of information retrieval for that matter, is the Office of Science Information Service of the National Science Foundation. NSF has been very active in the field since 1958 at which time Congress established the Office of Science Information Service to give concentrated attention to ways and means by which the methods of storing, translating, abstracting, retrieving, and disseminating information could be improved.

LIBRARY FUNCTIONS

The aim of any library is to obtain, preserve, and make available the printed materials required for use by its patrons and in so doing to store recorded knowledge for future generations. In order to do this, libraries are generally divided into several key functions which, although performed separately, are interrelated.

Selection. The primary aim of this activity is to develop a usable collection of material, on a continuing basis, that will satisfy the information needs of the library's users. In a general library, for example public libraries, such needs are wide in scope because of the broad range of reading wants of the general public. In a special library, the collection will be built around a narrowly defined subject field and selection focused carefully to ensure adequate depth of coverage.

At the time a library is first established, the librarian will usually prepare an *acquisitions policy*, setting forth the selection criteria by delineating primary and secondary fields of interest. The policy statement is interpreted by the selection personnel in making their day-to-day judgment as to which items are to be acquired and added to the main collection. The procedure consists of regular screening of book announcements and book reviewing media which describe available material. Items considered pertinent to the library acquisition policy are ordered. The policy is normally broad enough to include publications in adjacent fields of interest and flexible enough to allow for modifications and adjustments as subject fields of new interest evolve.

The quantity of material ordered depends on the size of the budget. The process of selection is therefore vital and critical because the library's growth and development will largely depend on the results of efforts expended here. When selection is too broad, the library may be inundated with a flood of material of limited usefulness. Yet, if selection is too restrictive, it results in an incomplete collection, and this ultimately reduces the effectiveness of service to readers. Thus it is obvious that, quantitatively, the material selected for acquisition regulates how fast the library will grow in terms of the size of its collection and the number of people required to do processing work and, qualitatively, that the human judgment exercised in the selection process determines how worthwhile library service is likely to be.

The recommendations of the selection personnel are turned into action by the acquisition process. Libraries employ two main methods of procurement. One is by purchase and the other by gift and exchange. Most purchasing is done from book dealers and involves the routine operations of order preparation, fund allotment, payments, accounting, etc. Although purchase is the most important method, libraries also obtain printed material as gifts from benefactors or in exchange with other libraries. In addition to its ordering function, acquisition also includes responsibility for the receipt of the printed material, assignment of an *accession*, or sequence, number to each piece, and routing it on to the next processing stage.

Cataloging. Librarians distinguish between two kinds of cataloging—descriptive cataloging and subject cataloging. The former refers to the process of identifying the book and selecting the appropriate bibliographic elements for recording, whereas subject cataloging includes processes of classification and the assignment of subject headings. Essentially both processes provide the library with its main searching tools, and all subsequent use of the material will depend on the adequacy and accuracy of these tools.

Recording of bibliographic information is made on cards after the selection of pertinent elements from the title page of the book. Author's name, the title of the book, date, publisher and place of publication, number of pages, etc., represent the kinds of items selected. To ensure a consistent approach during this process, catalogers follow prescribed rules (e.g., American Library Association Cataloging Rules, Library of Congress' Rules for Descriptive Cataloging, etc.,) which fix the format of the recorded information (American Library Association, 1949). Cards are later prepared for filing by author and title into an alphabetical file known as a *dictionary catalog*.

No cataloging operation is complete until the book is classified. The process of classification is defined as the systematic placement of the books of a library into related subject groupings based on a prearranged subject plan or scheme. The classifier peruses the contents of the book and, after referring to the subject classification scheme, selects and assigns a symbol, known as a *class number*, which corresponds to the main subject theme of the book. This number is amplified by distinguishing symbols, usually for author, to form the *call number*, which is recorded on all catalog cards and serves as the book's permanent address. Before the book is actually placed on the shelves, the call number is recorded conspicuously on its spine to ensure that it will continue to be returned to that address. A library may use any classification scheme, but the Dewey Decimal Classification (Dewey, 1958) and the Library of Congress' Classification Schedule are the two most popular ones in the United States.

In addition to assigning the call number, the classifier also selects appropriate subject headings from a prescribed list (Library of Congress' List of Subject Headings, Sears' List of Subject Headings, etc.) in order to reflect in the catalog the main subjects treated by the book. Duplicate catalog cards are used, the subjects noted as words along the top of each card, and the cards filed in the dictionary catalog along with the title and author cards.

The Library of Congress prepares and sells catalog cards for most American books and for many foreign ones. Card sets provide full bibliographic information including suggested subject headings plus Dewey and Library of Congress call numbers.

Reference. Using the library's resources for the purpose of providing service is the function of the reference activity. Reference work was defined by Bishop (1915) as follows: [reference work is] the service rendered by a librarian in aid of some sort of study, the reference librarian as an interpreter of library resources, and reference literature as "dictionaries, almanacs, catalogs, cyclopedias, compendia," and other books held in the library for consultation.

The reference staff consists of a unit of trained librarians who give professional assistance to users in selecting and obtaining documentary source materials which are needed for research and other purposes. In some research and special libraries the reference staff plays a particularly active role in linking the information resources of the library to the needs of the requester. Reference librarians are constantly experiencing lessons in human communication as they work with requesters and attempt to express their information requirements in clear and meaningful terms. They soon discover, too, that each requester considers his own need for service not only justified but also important, and it becomes exceedingly difficult or impossible for the staff to distinguish between marginal and worthy service requests. Consequently the reference librarian normally tends to treat all requests with equal effort.

Staff services take many different forms. *Ready-reference* service is one. It consists of giving spot answers to questions. Reference librarians will also perform extensive searches for groups of facts. They compile lists of references to literature in various subject fields, called *bibliographies*. These are sometimes annotated as well. In fact, under certain circumstances (the work of the Legislative Reference Staff of the Library of Congress is a good example), the staff may even be asked to prepare articles for a requester which synthesize information on a given subject from many sources.

Not only does the experienced reference librarian have an intimate understanding of the library's own technical tools, but he also develops an overall personal appreciation for the general content of the library's collection and sometimes along with it an almost uncanny sense of knowing just where to go to get the desired information.

Circulation. When the exact reference to a piece of printed material is known, the circulation staff routinely provides it for library users. Circulation activity consists in getting the book from the shelf, charging it out to the reader, receiving it on return, and, finally, reshelving it. The greatest number of daily-user transactions in a library occur in the circulation department. Printed materials removed from the shelves in response to individual requests are either examined on the library premises, photoduplicated, or sent or taken elsewhere for use. An extensive interlibrary loan network exists in the United States, which makes the resources of every library more widely available. Established procedures and standardized forms are used for transmitting printed materials between libraries.

An important function associated with circulation work is record keeping. Statistical records are maintained on borrowers, overdue books, and the rate at which books are issued, returned, and shelved. These records are useful to management in planning, in personnel administration, and in analyzing the nature and amount of usage made of the collection.

LIBRARY TOOLS

Early libraries concentrated on the physical arrangement of books on shelves in prescribed order, sometimes according to size and color. As the number of books increased, however, additional organization was necessary to make the content of the library collection more accessible. To provide this organization, librarians developed subject classification schemes, the card catalog, and other tools. These bibliographic tools now constitute the keystone of the structure for control of the library collection and are the basic finding aids employed by librarians to assist scholars and researchers.

The Catalog. This is by far the most important tool available to the library in the management of its collection of printed material. It serves as the library's main index to the printed contents of its collection by indicating what material the library holds and where it may be found. The form of the catalog can either be card or book. Cards are generally the preferred form because of the interfiling advantage which they have when adding new material and making changes. Book catalogs, although more compact and thus more easily disseminated, do not possess this flexibility and are essentially outdated when printed. Library catalogs are placed in conspicuous locations to facilitate consultation. A union catalog is a special type of catalog which records the location of printed material on an interlibrary basis irrespective of geographic location.

The practice followed by most libraries in developing their *dictionary card catalog* is to include, in addition to an entry for author and one for title, an adequate number of entries for relevant subjects, filed under one or more visual headings. Such subjects are drawn from an established list so as to best represent the information content of the book.

A typical set of Library of Congress catalog cards which are used in its unit card system is shown in Figure 5.1.

The establishment of an appropriate list of subject headings and their organization and sequence in a catalog have been the subject of much discussion in the library literature. A subject heading system consists of the selection of words or phrases as main headings and the use of additional words and phrases as subdivisions. Subject headings are usually arranged in alphabetical order, and the subdivisions within each heading are also arranged alphabetically. Thus, for example, if one were to list all of the branches of chemistry, the subject heading would be CHEMISTRY, and five subdivisions might be Analytical, Inorganic, Organic, Physical, Physiological.

A subject heading system often referred to and one we are accustomed to using, is the yellow page section of the telephone directory. Here words and phrases are used as subject headings, and within each heading there is an alphabetical list of the commercial firms associated with the business or service listed.

One of the drawbacks of a subject heading system is the arbitrary or

① Author card

Malkevitch, Joseph, 1942- ⟶ Author
  Graphs, models, and finite mathematics ₍by₎ Joseph Malkevitch ₍and₎ Walter Meyer. Englewood Cliffs, N.J., Prentice-Hall ₍1973, c1974₎
    x, 515 p. illus. 24 cm.
    Bibliography: p. 567.
    Includes bibliographies.

② Title card

Graphs, models and finite mathematics
Malkevitch, Joseph, 1942-
  Graphs, models, and finite mathematics ₍by₎ Joseph Malkevitch ₍and₎ Walter Meyer. Englewood Cliffs, N.J., Prentice-Hall ₍1973, c1974₎ ⟶ Title
    x, 515 p. illus. 24 cm.
    Bibliography: p. 567.
    Includes bibliographies.

③ Subject heading
④ cards

Mathematics
Malkevitch, Joseph, 1942-
  Graphs, models, and finite mathematics ₍by₎ Joseph Malkevitch ₍and₎ Walter Meyer. Englewood Cliffs, N.J., Prentice-Hall ₍1973, c1974₎ ⟶ Imprint
    x, 515 p. illus. 24 cm. ⟶ Collation
    Bibliography: p. 567.
    Includes bibliographies. ⟶ Notes

Graph Theory
Malkevitch, Joseph, 1942-
  Graphs, models, and finite mathematics ₍by₎ Joseph Malkevitch ₍and₎ Walter Meyer. Englewood Cliffs, N.J., Prentice-Hall ₍1973, c1974₎
    x, 515 p. illus. 24 cm.
    Bibliography: p. 567.
    Includes bibliographies.

      1. Mathematics—1961-   2. Graph theory. 3. Mathematical models. ⟶ Subject heading recommended by LC
      I. Meyer, Walter, 1943-   joint author. II. Title.
    QA39.2.M335   1973   510   73-7580
    ISBN 0-13-368465-5   MARC

    Library of Congress   73

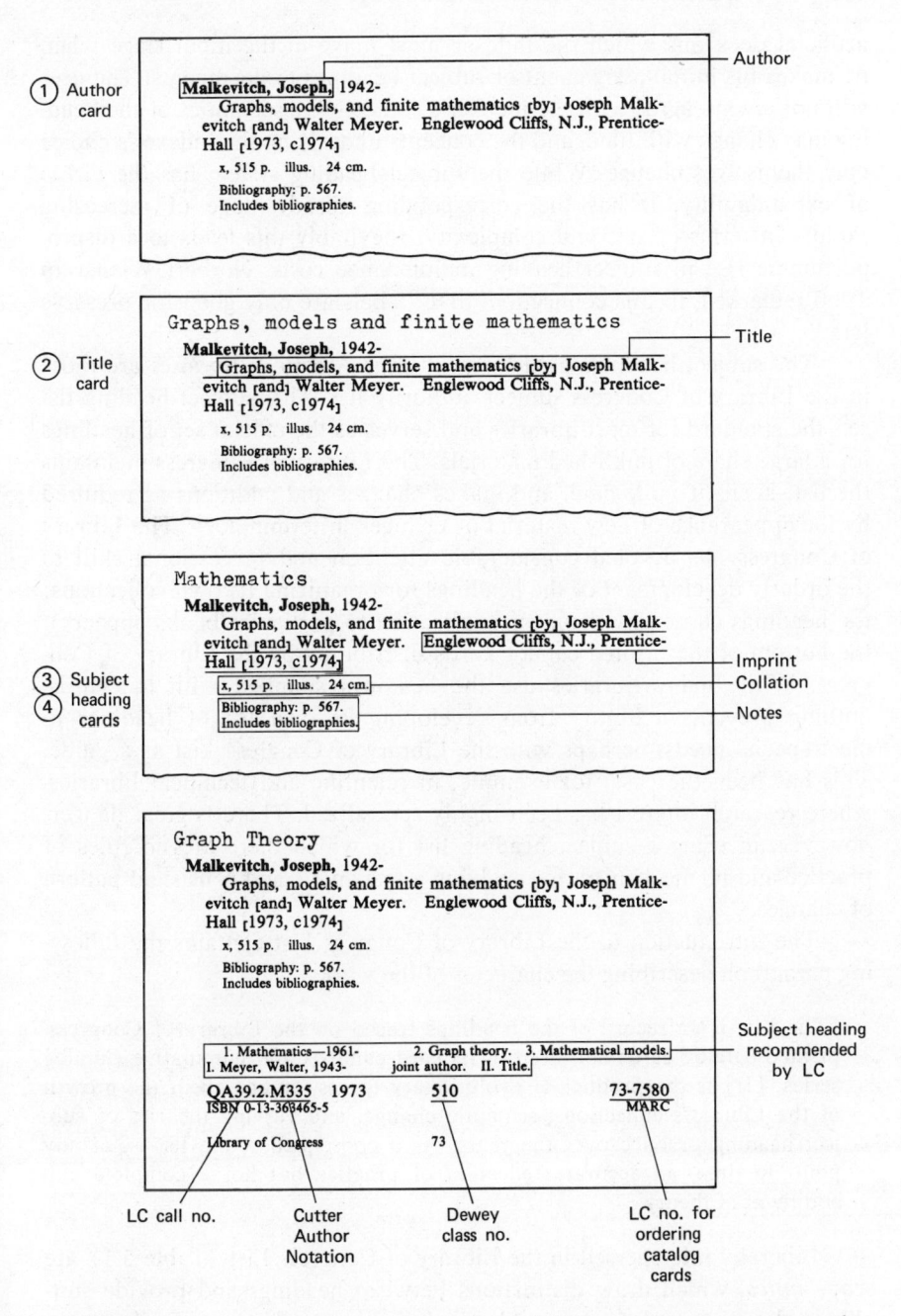

  LC call no.   Cutter   Dewey   LC no. for
                  Author   class no.   ordering
                  Notation   catalog
                                               cards

Figure 5.1   Contents of a set of Library of Congress printed catalog cards.

artificial decisions which the indexer must make at the input stage when he makes his initial assignment of subject headings to documents. The user will not always agree with the indexer's choice—the semantics of the heading may change with time, and the concepts underlying the indexer's choice may themselves change. While the subject heading system has the virtue of expandability, it has the corresponding disadvantage of increasing rapidly in terms of size and complexity. Inevitably this leads to a disproportionate rise in subject heading maintenance costs. Norbert Wiener in 1960 remarked, in this connection, that "labels are only good for preserve jars."

The subject headings used by most large American libraries are those in the Library of Congress subject authority list. This subject heading list sets the standard for most libraries and serves as the official set of headings for a large share of published materials. The Library of Congress maintains the list, keeps it up-to-date, and makes changes and additions as required by the appearance of new material or changes in terminology. The Library of Congress has devoted considerable attention and professional skill to the orderly development of the headings for organizing its own collections; the headings chosen by them for application to particular books appear at the bottom of the printed catalog cards distributed by the Library of Congress. While many libraries use the headings supplied with the cards, nothing prevents a library from developing its own list of headings to meet special needs, perhaps with the Library of Congress List as a guide. This has been the case, for example, in scientific and technical libraries, where research interest has been highly specialized. There is great danger, however, in using a subject heading list for which there are no rules of practice and no mechanism for evolving a systematic and consistent pattern of changes.

The introduction to the Library of Congress List contains the following paragraph describing the character of the work.

[The List is] a record of the headings traced on the Library of Congress' printed catalog cards and used in its card catalogs and cumulative Catalog series. [It] is the product of evolutionary forces, among them the growth of the Library's collections, semantic change, and varying theories of subject heading practice over the years. As a consequence, the list is, at any point in time, an accurate reflection of practice but not a complete embodiment of theory.

Liberally interspersed in the Library of Congress List (Table 5.1) are *scope notes*, which draw distinctions between headings and provide suitable explanation of their usage. Also included are many types of references. "See" references direct the reader to preferred synonymous terms, so that the user is led from his subject to the terms employed by the system (for example, Ex-serviceman *see* Veteran). The "see also" reference brings related headings together and directs the user to more specific subjects or topics and to applications of the subject; the aim of a "see also" reference is to coordinate subjects which are suggested as likely to be of interest to the user (for example, Transistors *see also* Tunnel Diodes). Reference may also be made to the Library of Congress Classification number when there is a close correspondence between a specific heading and the classification tables; the Library of Congress subject heading list in this way serves as a partial or limited index to the Library of Congress Classification. Three key symbols are used in the list: sa for see also; x to indicate which headings were referred from a "see" term; and xx to indicate which headings were referred from a "see also" heading. Thus, as shown in the entry below, a main subject heading carries with it all other associated terms or headings which may be used or found elsewhere in the system.

INCANTATIONS (BF 1558; GR540)

  sa Blessing and cursing
  x Spells
  xx Folklore
    Magic
    Occult sciences
    Superstition

The shelf list is an internal library catalog generally available only to librarians. It consists of one entry for every item in the collection and is arranged in a sequence which duplicates the order of the books on the shelves. For this reason librarians often refer to the shelf list as an *inventory catalog*.

To a limited extent the shelf list can also serve as a *class catalog*. Since cards in a class catalog are arranged by class number, a user is able to examine material in one general subject category just as he customarily does when he browses through a shelf of books in the library stacks.

The Classification Scheme. Classification is designed to organize books on shelves in a manner most conducive to their use. Many books and ideas are related either by subject or by some accidental property of the things beings classified. Thus books can be separated by such characteristics as language, alphabet, form, and date. Fiction in most libraries, for example, is arranged by author's name, and biography is also treated alphabetically by the name of the individual written about. Book collections have also been arranged by color, size, financial value, the language in which the material is written, etc.

TABLE 5.1 Library of Congress Subject Authority List (excerpt).*

Evolution (*Continued*)
  Statics and dynamics (Social Sciences)
  Teleology.
  Variation (Biology)
x Darwinism.
  Development.
  Epigenesis.
  Mutation (Biology)
xx Biology.
  Botany—Variation.
  Creation.
  Genetics.
  Heredity.
  Historical sociology.
  Man—Origin.
  Natural selection.
  Ontogeny.
  Philosophy, Modern.
  Phylogeny.
  Religion and science.
  Teleology.
  Transmutation of animals.
  Variation (Biology)
  Zoology.
  Zoology—Variation.
Evolutionary ethics. *See* Ethics, Evolutionary.
Ewe (African people) (*DT500; DT511; DT582*)
Ewe language. (*PL8161-4*)
  sa Fon dialect.
  Mina dialect.
Ewes.
  xx Sheep.
Ex libris. *See* Book-plates.
Ex post facto laws. (*Direct*)
  x Nulla poena sine lege doctrine.
  Nullum crimen sine lege doctrine.
  xx Criminal law.
  Due process of law.

SPECIAL TOPICS

1. Lower schools.—General works on examinations, whether for teachers or pupils, are entered under Examinations. Compilations of questions and answers for such examinations are entered under Examinations—Questions; when confined to a single country, state, or city, the subdivision Questions is added to the local subdivision, *e.g.* Examinations—Ohio—Questions. Compilations limited to a county are entered under state subdivision.

2. Universities and colleges.—Works on examinations in universities and colleges, as well as compilations of questions and answers for these examinations, are entered under Universities and colleges, with subdivisions Examinations. If limited to a single country, state, or city, the subdivision Examinations is added to the local subdivision, *e.g.* Universities and colleges—U.S.—Examinations. Works limited to a specific college or university are entered under that college or university, with subdivision Examinations. *e.g.* Harvard University—Examinations. If limited to a specific branch of study, that branch is added as a further subdivision, *e.g.* Universities and colleges—Wisconsin—Examinations—English; Harvard University—Examinations—Mathematics, and duplicate entry is made under the specific subject.

3. Universities and colleges.—Entrance requirements.—Works in which the requirements for admission to college or university are stated or discussed are entered

Examinations (*Continued*)
  sa Civil service—Examinations.
  Law examinations.
  also subdivision Examinations *under armies and navies, e.g.* France.
  Armée—Examinations.
  x Achievement tests.
  Competitive examinations.
  Teachers—Examinations.
  xx Education.
  Educational tests and measurements.
  Teaching.
  Notes under Examinations—Questions; Universities and colleges—Entrance requirements; Universities and colleges—Examinations.
  —Questions. (*LB3051-9*)
  Cf. note under Examinations.
  sa Mental tests.
  Note under Examinations.
  * * *
  —Ohio.
  —Questions.
  Note under Examinations.
Examinations, Medical. *See* Diagnosis; Insurance, Accident [Health, Life]—Medical examinations; Pensions, Medical examinations for; Premarital examinations.
Examinations in medicine are entered under Medicine—Examinations, questions, etc.
Examinations, Preparation for. *See* Study, Method of.
Examinations before trial. *See* Preliminary examinations (Criminal procedure)
Examiners (Administrative procedure) (*Direct*)

Retroactive laws.
Ex post facto laws (Canon law)
Ex-service men. *See* Veterans.
Ex-votes. *See* Votive offerings.
Exakta camera.
  Example under Cameras.
Examination of conscience. *See* Conscience, Examination of.
Examination of mines. *See* Mine examination.
Examination of the blood. *See* Blood—Analysis and chemistry; Blood—Examination.
Examination of witness. *See* Cross-examination.
Examinations. (*Direct*) (*College, LB2353, LB2367; Professional courses, LC1070-1071; School, LB3051–3060; Teachers, LB1763–5*)
  Here are entered works on examinations in general, *e.g.* discussions on the value of examinations, statistics, history, and similar general topics.
  under the heading Universities and colleges—Entrance requirements, subdivided in the same manner as Examinations, *e.g.* Universities and colleges—Entrance requirements; Universities and colleges—Austria—Entrance requirements; Pennsylvania. University—Entrance requirements; Smith College—Entrance requirements—Mathematics. Compilations of questions and answers for entrance examinations are entered under the subdivision Examinations.
4. Particular branches of study.—Compilations of questions and answers for examinations in a particular branch of study are entered under the specific subject, *e.g.* English language—Examinations, questions, etc.; Law—U. S.—Examinations, questions, etc.; Medicine—Examinations, questions, etc. General discussions, including the rules governing these examinations, are entered either under the appropriate phrase, *e.g.* Law examinations, or under the subject with subdivision Examinations, *e.g.* Accounting—Examinations.
  x Hearing examiners.
     Trial examiners.
  xx Administrative courts.
      Administrative procedure.
Example.
  sa Exempla.
     Ideals (Psychology)
     Influence (Psychology)
  x Model.
     Pattern.
  xx Authority.
      Ethics.
      Exempla.
      Ideals (Psychology)
      Imitation.
      Influence (Psychology)
Exanthemata. (*RC106*)
  sa Fever.
  also names of eruptive diseases, e.g. Erysipelas, Measles.
  x Eruptive fever.
     Fever, Eruptive.
  xx Fever.
Excardination (Canon law) (*BX1939.E*)
  sa Incardination (Canon law)
  xx Benefices, Ecclesiastical (Canon law)
      Clergy (Canon law)
      Incardination (Canon law)

---

* *Subject Headings Used in the Dictionary Catalogs of the Library of Congress*, 6th ed., Library of Congress, Washington, D.C., 1957

Subject classification concepts involve the use of a systematic plan for arranging subject matter according to some preconceived order. This generally requires the preparation of a subject plan known as a classification scheme, which organizes knowledge to a prescribed depth of detail. Plans of this kind vary from the ideal subject classification scheme, which embraces all knowledge in what has been referred to as the *tree of knowledge* structure, to more utilitarian arrangements, which attempt to organize knowledge according to patterns of user interest.

An examination of a typical classification scheme will reveal the following. The scheme will comprise those entries (words) which make up a given subject field. The entries will be arranged according to an organized structure which divides them into main classes and then into subdivisions of classes. The main class covers the more general concepts, whereas the subdivisions embrace areas of specificity. Each entry in the classification scheme carries with it a unique numerical or alphabetical notation. A *relative index* usually appears at the end of the scheme. Included in a relative index are the entries found in the scheme plus synonyms for the words used and related subject entries.

Classification schemes are used in libraries to place books acquired for the collection into an order which enables users to find books on the same subject in one place (Tauber, et al., 1954). The librarian, faced with the prospect of classifying a book, will have already been indoctrinated in the classification scheme employed by his library. The book is examined, its key subject noted, and the pertinent entry found in the schedule. The notation symbol given for the entry is assigned to the book as the basic part of its call number. The call number is then recorded on all catalog cards made for the book; it also appears on the book's spine to facilitate shelving and finding.

Several well-known and conventional classification schedules are in use in American libraries. A general understanding of their structure is a prerequisite to full appreciation of the nonconventional schemes described later.

Melvil Dewey prepared the first edition of his Dewey Decimal Classification in 1876. The oldest of the modern bibliographical schemes, it is in widespread use. The scheme has nine main classes with an additional one for General Works.

000	General Works	500	Pure Science
100	Philosophy	600	Technology
200	Religion	700	Fine Arts
300	Social Science	800	Literature
400	Language	900	History

The individual classes are represented by decimal integers from 000. to 999. Extensions, additions, and fine subdivisions are indicated by digits to the right of the decimal point. Most such use is limited to a 6-digit notation. However, the requirements of certain subject fields have extended the notation to as much as 9 digits to the right of the decimal point.

An interesting feature of the Dewey Decimal Classification is the recurring use of mnemonic aids. For example, the digit 5 is used in some portions of the schedule to refer to Italy, and thus 450 means Italian language and 850 Italian literature. Similarly, under languages a 3 stands for dictionaries, 4 for synonyms, 5 for grammar, etc. A book on synonyms of the Italian language would therefore be 454. Other classes also use special mnemonic aids. Librarians trained in the classification eventually learn to deduce considerable information about a book merely by examining its call number.

Form Divisions are still another technique used in the Dewey Decimal Classification to facilitate the like grouping of subject matter. The standard form divisions are

01 Philosophy and Theory
02 Handbooks and Outlines
03 Dictionaries and Encyclopedias
04 Essays and Lectures
05 Periodicals
06 Organizations and Societies
07 Study and Teaching
08 Collections and Polygraphy
09 History and Local Treatment

These numbers are used with any subject as appropriate. Thus 503 is a dictionary of science, and 850.09 means a history of Italian literature.

The Dewey Decimal Classification is divided into two main sections, the tables and the relative index. The tables are arranged in numerical sequence according to the main classes. By examining any section of the tables one can well determine the logic which caused a particular subject to be placed in a particular location. The tables are replete with helpful annotations to guide the classifier in making correct decisions and judgments. For example, certain terms are defined if for some reason there is doubt about the clarity of their meaning. Scope notes also appear to indicate to the classifier just which aspects of a given subject are intended to be embraced by a specific number. Other notes in the classification supply specific directions or instructions to the classifier. In addition to these instruction notes, the classification is generously supplied with cross reference notes which refer the classifier to other numbers where he should consider placing related material.

The second section, the relative index, is an alphabetical arrangement of subjects indicating their corresponding numerical location in the tables. The index performs two important functions: (*a*) It brings together various aspects of a subject to show their dispersion in the tables, and (*b*) it employs synonyms to assist the classifier in finding the main word used by the classification to describe a given subject.

Sixteen editions of the Dewey Decimal Classification have been published. Few libraries follow the classification precisely. Small libraries have no need for the detailed expansions, and the large or specified libraries have need for expansions in certain subjects beyond the standard ones. For the sake of consistency in the evolution of the classification, a Dewey editorial office was established in 1958 under the administration of the Library of Congress to coordinate expansions.

In 1889 Herbert Putnam, then Librarian of Congress, reorganized the Library and introduced a new classification scheme. This was done after careful and extensive review of the Dewey scheme and others. The formulation of the new scheme, known as the Library of Congress Classification, utilized the best features of existing subject classification plans and was designed to satisfy the classification needs of the *actual* contents of the Library of Congress' book collection rather than to meet a theoretical situation.

The classification is composed of several individual classes.* There is no special relationship among classes, each being chosen in a fairly arbitrary way. The Library of Congress is responsible for the consistent and continuing development of the classification, and through the U.S. Government Printing Office it distributes at low cost copies of each of the classes, separately bound, each with its own index. In this way libraries with special subject needs may use only those classes which apply to their particular interests.

Main classes are grouped as follows:
A   General Works, Polygraphy
B   Philosophy and Religion
C   History, Auxiliary Sciences
D   History and Topography (excluding America)
E–F   America

---

* U.S. Library of Congress, Subject Cataloging Division, Classification Schedules, Washington, D.C. (Classification Schedules have been published for Classes A-Z in various editions at various times.)

G	Geography, Anthropology
H	Social Science, Economics, Sociology
J	Political Science
K	Law
L	Education
M	Music
N	Fine Arts
P	Language and Literature
Q	Science
R	Medicine
S	Agriculture, Plant and Animal Industry
T	Technology
U	Military Science
V	Naval Science
Z	Bibliography and Library Science

As can be observed, the letters I, O, W, X, and Y are not used, these being reserved for future expansions. Actually K is not in being at the present time either, but it is under development. The notation followed is alphanumeric; thus Q means Science, QA Mathematics, QB Astronomy, QC Physics, QD Chemistry, etc., and QD181.C1 means Carbon. Although the form of notation employed has little mnemonic value, the notation is simple. The classification carries many forms of references, all designed to clarify intent, meaning, and usage for the classifier.

Because the Library of Congress classification was prepared by specialists and is patterned for the use and subject content of a very large initial collection, many large libraries in America and others throughout the world use it. Special libraries have found the separate, detailed classes to be complete in themselves, and consequently of great value, and all who use it are assured that it will be kept up-to-date and revised by professionally skilled persons.

The Universal Decimal (Brussels) Classification (UDC) is an adaptation of the Dewey Decimal Classification. UDC was originally developed by two Belgians, Paul Otlet and Henry La Fontaine. Their initial purpose was to design a universal classification scheme for bibliography and it was only later that the scheme came into use as a shelf location of books. At first the UDC flourished under the sponsorship of the International Institute of Bibliography, but in recent years it has been placed under the aegis of FID. An abridgement of the UDC describing its relationship to the Dewey Decimal Classification and providing the reader with a lucid introduction to its structure and principles was published in 1957 by the British Standards Institute in 1957. UDC uses general principles of classification similar to Dewey's but employs special symbols to permit detailed classification expansions. The notation can become exceedingly long and involved. However, libraries already utilizing the Dewey Decimal Classification have found UDC to be a logical way to achieve detailed expansion within their existing main structure. The classification has appeared in several languages and is controlled by FID.

Main classes include:

0   Generalities
1   Philosophy, Metaphysics, Psychology, Logic, Ethics and Morals
2   Religion, Theology
3   Social Sciences, Economics, Law, Government, Education
4   Philology, Linguistics, Languages
5   Pure Sciences
6   Applied Sciences, Medicine, Technology
7   The Arts, Entertainment, Sport
8   Literature, Belles Lettres
9   Geography, Biography, History

Although the UDC was based largely on the Dewey Decimal Classification, it has departed from the original work in terms of its comprehensiveness and the notation system employed. For example, it uses a plus sign (+) to unite two subjects contained in one book; thus 52+53 indicates that both Astronomy and Physics are described in the content. A slash sign (/) indicates that constituent subjects run in sequences; thus 52/58 is the same as 52+53+54···+58. The colon (:) is employed to show relationships, e.g., Lives of Astronomers would be 52:92. These are but a few of many signs used by the system. Together with the auxiliary tables, which increase the comprehensiveness of the main classification and aid in specifying subjects more precisely, they allow for many different combinations of notation and consequently more flexibility in the assignment of the final number, complex as it may appear. Table 5.2 shows a typical example.

Some libraries append an additional notation to the classification number of a book. This notation (e.g., Cutter author marks) represents a code for the author's name and facilitates the shelving and finding of a book in a large collection. In the biography sections of most public libraries, for example, books are arranged on the shelf according to the names of the individuals written about. Thus books from Adams to Washington are arranged in alphabetical sequence, and books about the life of a given individual can be found grouped together on the shelf. The Cutter

Table 5.2. Universal Decimal Classification (excerpt).*

626		Railway, highway engineering
625.1		Railway engineering track
625.2		Rolling stock, locomotives, etc.
625.3		Railways of special construction
	(23)	Mountain railways
	.31	Narrow gauge railways
	.32	Adhesion railways for steep gradients
	.33	Rack railways
	.35	Broad gauge railways (over 5 ft 6 in.)
	.36	Moving platforms
	.37	Railways with driverless trains
	.39	Other railways of special type

* International Federation for Documentation, Universal Decimal Classification, 2nd ed., revised 1957, London, British Standards Institution, 1957.

author marks also serve as a secondary filing mode to facilitate the physical arrangement of books on a shelf when many books by different authors are to be filed within the same subject classification number.

Cutter author marks are assigned from tables based on the statistics of distribution of names (Cutter). They are so constructed as to allow a two- or three-digit code number to represent a limited range of alphabetically allied surname spellings. The following portion of the tables is taken from the W section.

480 WEN
481 WENCKS
482 WENDELA
483 WENDLI
484 WENDS
485 WENGEN
486 WENI
487 WENL
488 WENR
489 WENY

In applying the code from the table, the classifier uses the first letter of the author's surname and then the number which covers the range within which the surname can be located. For example, an author named WENTHORP would be assigned a Cutter author mark of W488.

THE PROBLEM AREAS

As we have indicated, mainstays of the traditional library approach have been the subject catalog and the classification scheme. They establish the principles of use and set the rules for subject application to individual material. However, their use has some serious limitations. At best, content analysis, as a human process, is subject to a wide range of interpretation because of individual differences in the education, experience, and psychological orientation of the indexers. Despite the best training efforts, inconsistent application of subject headings or numbers invariably occurs among personnel using the same list. Consequently, information scattering that eventually affects the system's reliability results.

An even more critical limitation can be described as *impermanence*. Time has an adverse effect on the meaning of terms applied from a subject list. Knowledge and language are dynamic processes, and accurate labeling of information at one point in time may later be imprecise and out of context. The strictest form of administrative control and systematic review becomes essential in order to counteract a general wearing away or weakening of the meaning of terms as originally applied. Revision must take place continuously in order to define more precisely the limits of related subjects, to adjust to subject expansions and atrophy, and to clarify language ambiguities.

Librarians have not been unaware of these inadequacies in conventional tools nor of the difficulties encountered in applying them in practice. Kelley (1937) described the basic elements affecting the usefulness of conventional classification. Her description sums up what many others have been repeating many different ways in recent years. She pointed out that the changing order of knowledge makes the static perfection of any classification scheme impossible. The need, the interest, the material—all will change with time; any fixed classification scheme will be outdated almost from the moment of its creation. Any single hierarchical representation of subject matter is usually inadequate for expressing the great variety of relationships of interest, and the nature of systematic classification is to separate parts from whole. It thus breaks apart concepts when they do not need to be broken apart and, in fact, when it would be preferable that they were not.

Any classification or systematic order, in comparison with other more easily comprehended orders, such as the alphabetical or the chronological, has been artificially created, and, although to the creator it is the most natural classification, for the general user it may not be a natural way of viewing the world. Thus the tendency of any specialist is to organize a field of subject matter about his own special and immediate interest.

To develop a classification scheme that will meet the needs of all potential users in any given organization is exceedingly difficult if not impossible. Tough semantic questions enter into the problem, and they are inflamed by the belief of every specialist that he and he alone is competent to classify the field of his own specialty. It is noteworthy that no two such specialists, even when working together in precisely the same field, can come to 100 percent agreement on how their data should be categorized.

Furthermore, the content of books interferes with the satisfactory application of any system of classification, for typically they cut across a number of categories. It is impractical to reclassify old books on any wide scale, so expansions and reconstructions are difficult. The poor and faulty work of the classifier in applying a classification scheme produces almost insurmountable difficulties, particularly when complex and unfamiliar subject fields are involved. Too frequently the tendency is to determine the classification of a particular book by the use or purpose for which it was written rather than by the use which will be made of it. Finally, the long and confusing notation for very specific subjects in some of the classification schemes, involving some 15 to 20 decimal and alphabetic characters, makes communication difficult at best.

However, it must be emphasized that the aim of classification schemes, as used in libraries, is to place books acquired for the collection into an order which enables the user to find in one place books which treat the same subject. In this way books which the user is likely to want together he will find together. This is the basic and crucial question in the organization of any library system whether it is by classification or by any other scheme. Organization has the purpose of bringing physically together material likely to be wanted together.

Aside from these problem areas, which are a result of the basic characteristics of the material a library handles, there are other problem areas which are a result more of history and tradition. For example, the library traditionally has been regarded as a service organization. It has therefore never developed a significant degree of financial support, nor has it introduced normal cost accounting procedures. The result is that even today there are few accurate pictures of precisely what the costs of individual library operations are (Maybury, 1961; MacQuarrie, 1962). This lack of a cost accounting approach is perhaps not serious when the demands are limited and can be satisfied by the dedicated service of a limited number of people. But in the functioning of large information centers, particularly when equipment is involved, the question of costs and economic operation becomes a paramount one.

SPECIALIZATION IN LIBRARY AND INFORMATION SERVICES

Although the traditional library tools make location of a particular title from among miles and miles of shelving a routine and simple task in libraries today, by and large they are not designed to provide more than a rough-cut approach to the subjects covered by the printed material in their vast collections. In terms of the clientele served by general libraries, this may indeed be all that is needed, but when the same conventional general library techniques are applied to highly specialized collections of nonbook, technically detailed data, the weaknesses in precision of retrieval are keenly observed. Library techniques are serving as a springboard from which researchers are seeking more advanced techniques to cope with rapidly emerging requirements for more subtle and detailed access to information.

During the past quarter century, the library profession has therefore seen more and more specialization of information services. This development had its start in industry and government, where the need first existed to organize more minutely the recorded information of a narrowly defined subject field in support of intensive research demands.

As the areas of inquiry grow more specialized, research becomes more complex and the consequent library problems increase. The emergence of new ideas produces new facts together wtih new terminology, and the task of organizing them in proper relationship to each other poses a real challenge. There is an awareness among librarians that the selection and manipulation of fragments of information rather than entire documents will require unconventional tools. The traditional approach exemplified by the subject classification scheme and the card catalog and based on a preconceived arrangement of knowledge, is believed too confining.

Emphasis thus has been on finding new ways and means of codifying or indexing data so that they will lend themselves more to correlation than to group selection. The trend has been toward greater depth of content analysis. In addition to exploring new analytical methods, investigations have also been made of employing electronic machines for analysis, storage, and retrieval. It is reasoned that, because of the mass of data involved, storage and handling techniques may have to be of a more advanced character than those customarily used for manually shelving books and filing documents. Vannevar Bush (1945) said:

> A record, if it is to be useful in science, must be continuously extended, it must be stored, and above all it must be consulted. Today we make the record conventionally by writing and by photography, followed by printing;

but we also record in film, on wax discs, and on magnetic wires. Even if utterly new recording procedures do not appear, these present ones are certainly in the process of modification and extension.

The repetitive processes of thought are not confined, however, to matters of arithmetic and statistics. In fact, every time one combines and records facts in accordance with established logical processes, the creative aspect of thinking is concerned only with the selection of the data and the process to be employed and the manipulation thereafter is repetitive in nature and hence a fit matter to be relegated to the machines.

Some librarians have become particularly sensitive on the subject of the mechanization of information and library processes. They believe, and rightly so, that they have been retrieving information for years—and that it is basically a human process. In library terms they call it *reference work*, and most librarians trained in this field are very skillful information hunters. Their pride is therefore legitimately disturbed by suggestions made by some naive persons that a mechanical cure-all just over the horizon will place the Library of Congress in a small black box, increase efficiency a thousandfold, and do all this at less cost!

It is generally recognized, however, that during the next quarter century libraries will undergo changes comparable only to those that occurred in the years from 1875 to 1900, when a group of American pioneers changed the whole character of world librarianship. The basis of all modern library work was developed during that last quarter of the nineteenth century, but the pace then was leisurely and there was no noticeable outside pressure for rapid or drastic change. By contrast, the transformation of present-day librarianship is certain to be made under increasing pressures of output of publications as well as the urgently mounting needs of research workers.

Ridenour summed up the view of the library problem clearly when he said in his article in *Bibliography in an Age of Science.*

. . . What is needed is a re-evaluation of the whole fabric of the library, from the bottom to the top. In making this analysis, no prejudice should enter, nothing should be taken for granted.

To mention only one thing, a [research] library should no longer necessarily be regarded as a place where books are stored. Perhaps it is entirely something else. Possibly a library is a combination of study rooms, seminars, and a first-rate communication center of a specialized sort.

Machines are already playing an important role in many library and information situations. They are handling quantities of recorded knowledge and supplying necessary information, often more speedily and efficiently than the human librarian. Some organizations are using machines experimentally for indexing, abstracting, and translating. Unfortunately, most of the information concerning the present-day activities of electronic machines in the information field is highly technical and in some cases so evidently promotional that even those familiar with the work and intellectually sympathetic to it find it difficult to distinguish fact from fiction. All too typical is the type of advertising exemplified by

> The computer department is presently engaged in the design and development of an extremely high-volume, high-speed information storage and retrieval system. The ultimate system will not be bound by the present state of the equipment art. The problems involved cannot be stated in terms of the standard data handling system—nor is it expected that the solutions shall be.
>
> Exciting progress is being made. Already, under pressure of research, conceptual boundaries are disappearing and the limits of the possible are expanding. Further intensive research into new concepts—and effective translation of these concepts into equipment—promise major breakthroughs in this area.

Librarians, educators, engineers, manufacturers, documentalists—all those engaged in the information field—require a basic common source of knowledge which will enable them to develop workable solutions jointly. Professionals in each field particularly need a level of intellectual and technical briefing that will enable them to visualize themselves and their work in this new environment.

It would seem that today's aim in information storage and retrieval should not be to find a mechanical substitute for public or university or special libraries but to devise a complementary electronic organization which can keep pace with the expanding publishing rate in specific fields and provide means for automating technical library processing operations. There is every reason to believe that just as handwriting continued to flourish after the invention of the printing press, so general book libraries will remain a life necessity even though various forms of mechanization may be introduced.

LIBRARY AUTOMATION

In the decade 1960–1970 there arose a specific avenue of development toward the mechanization of libraries known as *library automation*. As presently conceived, library automation seeks to apply advanced equipment in three areas; (*a*) automation of the clerical functions of a library, (*b*) use of the computer as a management tool, subsuming planning, budgetary, and cost accounting functions, and (c) interlibrary communications.

Library automation, except in a long-range theoretical sense, does not address itself to automated retrieval of library content. Nearly all actual planning for library automation preserves intact the traditional schema for storing, retrieving, and keeping track of information, and none of the library methodology discussed in this chapter is destined for alteration (in the name of automation) in the near future. Because of its somewhat glancing relationship, even to conventional library storage and retrieval, library automation is slightly outside the scope of this book; accordingly, we describe only briefly its major compartments. We steer readers interested in the details of library automation to the *1974* Hayes and Becker book on the subject.

Subsystems for which Automation is being Contemplated. Library automation, like many areas of business automation, is built on the assumption that when new technology is introduced in an on-going activity, the safest path is a straightforward one. Generally this means that one does not aim for total automation of everything that can be conceivably automated, but only of those procedures which are most amenable, and preferably of those procedures that (a) can be computerized intact, and (b) have ample precedent for automation in other fields.

The library function which meets the foregoing criteria perfectly is administrative data processing. For such areas as administrative, financial, and personnel data processing, the ground has long since been broken for automation—in banking, in insurance, in commercial airlines, and in much of the rest of the business world. It is relatively easy to reckon the costs and the savings to be expected from this form of automation. However, because most universities now have computer centers, it is common practice for university libraries to have their administrative work pooled with other campus jobs and done centrally. This pattern may be extended to other kinds of libraries.

Where experience cannot be borrowed from business automation, the safest path is to automate subsystems that every library has, and that tend to be standard from one library to another. Such subsystems are circulation control, acquisition/ordering, catalog and index production, and serials records. Though specific precedents may not be easily found for these functions outside the library field, it should be relatively easy (once some libraries have taken the plunge into automation) to transfer experience from one library to another. Also most of the procedures of these subsystems need not be changed in order to allow their automation. Some changes, however, may come simply because computers make hitherto impractical procedures feasible; an example of such a procedure is the production of book catalogs, which the need for frequent updating made prohibitive when done manually.

Two areas whose automation may be more difficult, simply because the computer opens up so many new possibilities, are those of interlibrary communication and scientific management of libraries. The idea of a *library network*, which has been building up during the last decade, envisages a degree of resource sharing among libraries that would be impossible without computers and modern communications technology. One can guess that the resource sharing would have to be copious, and it would have to be efficient (especially in terms of time), in order to justify the large investments that would have to be made, in communications, for example. Such possibilities as direct access by readers to a remote library, however, make such investments seem attracitve in terms of ultimate payoff.

Scientific management, which subsumes systems analysis, cost accounting, long-range planning, and other such functions that are relatively neglected in contemporary libraries, will by this token require much developmental spadework. Since the payoff is increased efficiency of library service (a payoff that should be transferrable from one library to another), the investment appears very worthwhile.

REFERENCES

AMERICAN LIBRARY ASSOCIATION, Division of Cataloging and Classification (1949), A.L.A. Cataloging Rules of Author and Title Entries, 2nd ed., edited by Clara Beetle, Chicago, American Library Association.

BISHOP, WILLIAM WARNER, (June 1915), Theory of Reference Work, *Bulletin of the American Library Association*, Chicago, v. IX, pp. 134–134.

BUSH, VANNEVAR, (August 1945), As We May Think, *Atlantic Monthly*, v. 176, pp. 101–108.

CATALOGING RULES OF THE AMERICAN LIBRARY ASSOCIATION AND THE LIBRARY OF CONGRESS, editions and changes, 1949–1958, Washington, D.C., Library of Congress, 1959.

CUTTER, CHARLES A., *C.A. Cutter's Cutter-Sanborn Three Figure Author Table*, distributed by H. R. Hunting Co., Springfield, Ma.

DEWEY, MELVIL, (1958) *Dewey Decimal Classification and Relative Index*, 16th ed., Lake Placid Club, N.Y., Forest Press.

HAYES, ROBERT M. and BECKER, JOSEPH, (1974), *Handbook of Data Processing for Libraries*, 2nd ed., Melville Publishing Co., Los Angeles, Calif.

JOHNSON, ELMER D., (1955), *Communications: An Introduction to the History of the Alphabet, Writing, Printing, Books, & Libraries*, New York, Scarecrow Press.

KELLEY, GRACE OSGOOD, (1937), The Classification of Books, doctoral dissertation, New York, the H. W. Wilson Co.

MACQUARRIE, CATHERINE, (Fall 1962), Cost Survey: Cost of Ordering, Cataloging, and Preparations in Southern California Libraries, *Library Resources and Technical Services*, v. 6, No. 4.

MAYBURY, CATHERINE, (January 1961) Performance Budgeting for the Library, *ALA Bulletin*, pp. 46–53.

MCMURTRIE, DOUGLAS C., (1943), *The Book: The Story of Printing and Bookmaking*, New York, Oxford University Press, p. 136.

Nonconventional Technical Information Systems in Current Use, National Science Foundation, September 1959, and supplements.

RIDER, FREMONT, (1944), *The Scholar and the Future of the Research Library*, New York, Hadham Press.

THE STATE OF THE LIBRARY ART (1961), edited by Ralph R. Shaw, v. 4 [Retrieval Systems], New Brunswick, N.J., Graduate School of Library Services, Rutgers—The State University.

Subject Headings Used in the Dictionary Catalogs of the Library of Congress (1957), 6th ed., Library of Congress, Washington, D.C., p. iii.

TAUBER, MAURICE F., et al., (1954), *Technical Services in Libraries*, New York, Columbia University Press.

U.S. LIBRARY OF CONGRESS, Descriptive Cataloging Division (1949), Rules for Descriptive Cataloging in the Library of Congress (adapted by the American Library Association), Washington, D.S., U.S. Government Printing Office.

U.S. LIBRARY OF CONGRESS, Subject Cataloging Division, Classification Schedules, Washington, D.C. (Classification Schedules have been published for Classes A-Z in various editions at various times.)

Universal Decimal Classification (1957), abridged English edition, 2nd ed., British Standards Institute, London.

Chapter Six

To Meet the Information Crisis: New Methods of Indexing and Subject Analysis

A student of information science can easily get the impression that many of the profound changes in the processing and retrieval of information have followed squarely in the wake of the computer revolution. This could well be true in regard to data retrieval (Chapter Eight), but it is not the case for document retrieval. Great changes in methods of classification, indexing, and subject cataloging substantially preceded the advent and wide use of computers. These changes were primarily a response by information specialists to the information explosion of the last 30 years, and they have a strong effect on what is now done with computers in document retrieval. Thus, such techniques as *coordinate indexing, superimposed coding, semantic factors,* and *facet analysis,* which we discuss in this chapter, are not in the limbo of history (as they are sometimes represented to be), but are very much with us today, though usually in modified form. Therefore it is important to know about them in their precomputer versions, and the rationales behind them.

In previous chapters we have already glimpsed at ways in which information specialists have attempted to meet the increasingly rapid growth of knowledge. Chapter One indicated that the growth of knowledge has not been uniform, but has burgeoned selectively in the expansion of specialties. It described the phenomenon of the information center and the information *analysis* center. Chapter Five detailed the effects of the specialized-area growth pattern on librarianship, and, in particular, cited the rise of special libraries as a major effect.

The present chapter deals with a breed that has split off somewhat from traditional librarianship, in a small way during the 1920s and 1930s, and in a wholesale way after World War II, the documentalists, whose broad range of activities became known as *documentation*. As long ago as 1908, the Institute International de Bibliographie pictured the focus of documentation thus:

> Documents comprise all that which represents or expresses, by means of graphical signs (writings, pictures, diagrams, charts, figures, symbols), an object, a deed, an idea, or an impression. Printed texts (books, magazines, newspapers) today constitute the most numerous category of them. (Schultz, 1969)

With such a broad scope of interest, this field of study has become a rather amorphous one.

In fact, a great deal of confusion has existed as to just what constitutes the defining characteristics of the field of effort. Some of the attempts to define documentation have instead tended to increase the degree of confusion and obscure the boundaries between it and librarianship. Mortimer Taube (1953–1957) defined documentation as:

> ... the designation of the total complex of activities involved in the communication of ... specialized information ... including the activities which constitute special librarianship plus the prior activities of preparing and reproducing materials and the subsequent activity of distribution.

The implication is given that documentation is simply an extended form of traditional librarianship.

The use of the word "documentation" with this implication would be acceptable provided it truly represented the character of the work of the documentalists. However, careful examination of their work will show that the concern is rarely with the problems of operating libraries or even technical information centers. Instead it is concerned with the analysis of information systems and the development of techniques for new systems. Thus, documentalists seem to share the common purpose of creating new tools which can be meaningfully applied to the mass information problems of our times. The fact that such system design tends to be concerned with the entire range of information handling, from its initial creation to its final dissemination, is characteristic of the systems approach to any problem. The significant thing is that documentation is *not* best differentiated from normal library service by this concern with the complete cycle; rather, it is best differentiated from normal library service by the fact that it is primarily concerned with system analysis and design rather than system operation.

Another definition of documentation was given by James D. Mack and Robert S. Taylor (1956):

> The group of techniques necessary for the ordered presentation, organization, and communication of recorded specialized knowledge, in order to give maximum accessibility and utility to the information contained.

In this sense, Cutter, Putnam, Dewey, and other pioneers in developing tools for library organization were all functioning as information system designers when they established their techniques for library organization. On the other hand, many documentation centers are in no essential respect different from any library—they partake of the same operating problems.

In fact, looking at the sweep of history from Cutter *et al.* up to the present, it is apparent that the beginnings of documentation in the 1930s and the recent, more spectacular onset of *information science* is correlated with the numbers (and percentages) of all information specialists whose activities must be concerned with new methods, new systems, and new information realities rather than with routine management of a given information facility, i.e., people whose activities must be connected with *change*. In nineteenth century librarianship, the efforts of only a few scattered individuals (Cutter, Dewey, etc.) sufficed to bring forth necessary change. But by 1937 there were enough such individuals at work to justify the formation of a professional group, notably the American Documentation Institute.* By 1970 the scope of documentalists broadened to the point that collaboration with other professionals such as mathematicians, behavioral scientists, linguists, computer programmers, engineers, etc., was desirable, and the documentalists appropriately renamed their organization (which by that time had more than 1000 members) the American Society for Information Science.

As the basis for discussions to come, it seems desirable to present the work of some schools of documentation, schools usually identified with a particular organization and creative individual. Each has been concerned with the analysis of some critical aspects of organizing information; each has proposed a technique for answering the particular critical problems of concern to him. Frequently the resulting system has been presented as the final solution to the entire information retrieval problem, but it seems clear that such a panacea cannot be expected. The real contribution made by

---

* Note the much earlier formation of FID (Federation International de Documentation), as described in Chapter Five.

COORDINATION OF SUBJECTS

One of the consequences of the rapid growth of our information resources is that it has become more difficult to manage subject headings, especially in scientific and technical fields. New subjects spring up at a rapid rate, old subjects require greater subdivision, and still other subjects fade in importance. In the 1950s, Mortimer Taube observed that the great bulk of subjects were described by combinations of terms. Why, he wondered, strive to maintain a huge list of subjects when it was possible to create subjects by combining (at the occasion of search) a number of words culled from a much smaller list of subject components? Such a capability would be appealing both from the indexer's point of view and from the searcher's.

For example, suppose that a group of documents dealt with various processes (planting, harvesting, refining, etc.) in agriculture in various nations of the globe. A subject heading would normally consist of three elements, such as "planting," "red wheat," and "Afghanistan," and would be alphabetically listed under one of these elements, e.g., under "Afghanistan, red wheat, planting." Seldom would it be listed under all three (or four, if one counts the unmodified "wheat"); such a policy would lead to a very long list of headings because—as mathematics students understand —the number of permutations of a small number of elements is vastly larger than the number of elements. This is especially the case when one starts thinking of all the possible combinations of nations, processes, and products.

Thus, a list of all *potentially useful* subject headings in a realm such as worldwide agriculture could be astronomically long. Even a list of *actually applicable* headings for a given group of documents could be impractically long. Taube realized that a searcher could have the benefit of not only the applicable combinations of terms, but of the potentially useful ones also, provided a system was set up to let the *searcher* generate them as subject headings. Taube called this method "concept coordination," and the system by which it could be carried out became known as "coordinate indexing." A coordinate index can be set up in the following way:

Document content is to be represented by terms chosen from a prescribed list of subjects which are, to the maximum extent possible, in the form of single words or concepts, called uniterms. The terms are thus not subject headings in the sense used with a card catalog, since no effort is made to combine words into phrases covering complex concepts; in fact, a positive effort is made to avoid doing so. The coordinate index to documents is then based on assigning to each subject a card on which will be placed the identification number of every document to which that subject is relevant. For example, a new document, numbered 12345, might be concerned with subjects A, B, C, and D, such as the *growing* of *red wheat* in *Afghanistan*. For the subject A, which might be *grow,* there is a card to which will be added the particular document number 12345, etc. The set of documents which come in during a day, 12345, 12346, etc., will therefore be scanned by the indexer for those terms from the subject list which are significant in the documents. The cards for the set of terms related to the set of documents are pulled from the file of such cards; for 10 documents a day, each covering, say, 10 terms, one might have to pull as many as 50, 60, or even 100 cards from the files. On each of these cards will then be placed the particular document number for which that subject is relevant.

When a need arises—due to a request expressed as a combination of subjects—to recover relevant documents, the cards corresponding to the requested subjects are pulled from the file. Where a document originally involved each of them, the document number will be on each card. The search operation is therefore simply to scan through the sets of document numbers on each subject card, effectively correlating the numbers on each card with those on the other cards. Wherever a match occurs, it represents the number of a document for which these terms are simultaneously relevant. Hence it will presumably be a document significant to the request.

Certain factors must be considered in establishing a coordinate index system based on these principles. One relates to the choice of terms; another to the choice of format and representation on the term cards; a third relates to the operations required to post onto the cards and handle searches.

Early versions of coordinate indexing are not particularly easy to use. because one has to inspect and match visually a great many document numbers. From a typical searcher's point of view such a process might seem a backward step from the use of subject headings. Then came the idea to allow each concept, or uniterm, to be associated with a card, and each document number to which the concept might apply to be represented by a punch position on the card; when the indexer determines that the concept does apply to a document, he simply punches a hole in the punch position corresponding to that document. At search, concept coordination can be done by placing two such cards flush together. The concidence of any holes is readily visible, and indicates those documents to which both concepts apply. As Figure 6.1 illustrates, two, three, or any number of concept cards can be coordinated by this method. The feature of a light beam passing through holes has led to the usage of the name "Peek-a-boo" to describe this technique of storing coordinate index information. The origin of this somewhat undignified term is described as follows by Lawrence S. Thompson.

> Some American documentalists have used the rather ludicrous terms of "peek-a-boo," "peakable," or "peephole" for the type of punched card to be discussed in this essay. Other English-speaking documentalists have played with such other terms as "super-imposable," "optical" or "coincidentally" punched cards. Foreign terminology is less uncertain: "fitches superposables" (Fr.), "sichtlochkarten" (Ger.), "titthalkoft" (Sw.), or "onderwerpponska-arten" (Du.). They are also called Cordonnier or Batten cards after two of their leading exponents. The term "feature card" is advocated by J. L. Jolley and J. Edwin Holmstrom. Contrary to other punched card systems that use one card for one document or one item, the feature card system uses one card for one subject, characteristic, aspect, or feature.

J. Albert Sanford (1956) has written the results of his experience in using the techniques of a uniterm system. Referring to the problem of generating terms, he says:

> Let the documents themselves generate their own uniterms. Catalog one thousand documents. They will produce about one thousand uniterms. Weed this list carefully, combining synonyms. With this core, catalog another one

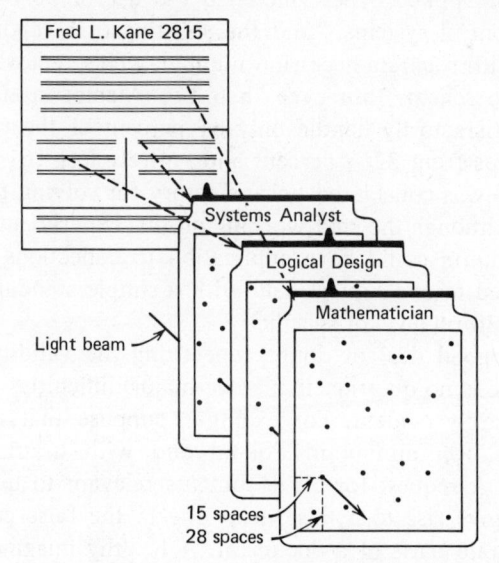

Figure 6.1. Termatrex cards.

thousand reports, using the *approved* basic list where possible, and then repeat the weeding operation.

In other words, do not start with a prescribed set of terms. Let the documents themselves generate the terms but control this generation by combining synonyms. Once some 8000 uniterms have been chosen, it has generally been found that addition falls off very rapidly even with highly varied subject matter. The curve for size of the term file begins to grow nearly flat when between 40 and 50,000 documents have been cataloged.

One particular criticism, which has been quite frequently quoted, is based on an experiment run by the Los Alamos Scientific Laboratory (Warheit, 1955). According to the report of their experiment, uniterm rules were followed as closely as possible. It was found that indexing was rapid but posting was slow and liable to errors which were not easily discovered.

The operational handling of requests has been particularly subject to considerable criticism from a number of places, including the Los Alamos experimenters. They found that a large number of irrelevant retrievals (then spoken of as *false drops*) were obtained. The test indicated that in spite of the use of an above-average number of uniterms, only 11 percent of the reports could be retrieved completely and without false drops. The reasons for failure in the remainder were analyzed and all suggested means for improvement applied. These included the use of *poly-terms*, such as "Aircraft fire control systems," and the splitting of a report into two or three sections with separate accession numbers. This removed most of the simplicity of the scheme, but even then Los Alamos statistics indicated that it could satisfactorily handle only 61 percent of the reports. It permitted false drops from 22½ percent and entirely lost 16½ percent. The system therefore was considered unsatisfactory for solving the problem of a large library, although the staff working on this experiment expressed the opinion that uniterm could have application to collections of reasonably small size, limited to one subject field with a simple standardized vocabulary, having a uniform level of specificity.

There is a good deal of doubt concerning the validity of such test results, but there is no question that some major difficulties in the uniterm system are certainly evident. For example, suppose that a document is concerned with iron mining in Poland and with uranium mining in Czechoslovakia. A request for all documents relevant to uranium mining in Poland will give rise to a false drop due to the false coordination of ideas from separate parts of a document. A healthy imagination can conjure up hundreds of ways in which unwanted coordinations of terms occur, and, of course, all of these ways would be capable of occurring in a coordinate indexing system.

Many of the schemes proposed by other workers on coordinate indexing, in recognition of this, have been concerned principally with the problems of reducing false coordinations. They are all based on an attempt to introduce into the basic uniterm system some means for representing the syntactical role played by the term. One way of doing this is to provide a separate term card for each possible syntactical role of a term, but it would seem that, in general, such an approach would result in a chaotic file. Another possible approach, one which has been explored in depth, is to introduce a *link* or *role indicator* as part of the document number recorded on the subject card, indicating the role played by the subject within a standard syntactical pattern (Montague, 1964). Such an approach requires the definition of the standard syntactical patterns of significance to the library and its usage. It must be recognized that this approach will enormously complicate the operation of the system; yet it does provide a mechanism for handling the syntax where the false drop problem makes it significant to do so.

Another area of major difficulty in the uniterm system is the handling of generic requests or, in general, any requests formulated in terms of a preconceived organization of the prescribed list of terms. The very character of the terms in the uniterm system is that they are treated as logically independent of each other. Thus, there is no degree of organization among terms explicitly stated. In order to handle generic requests, the specification of the particular terms covered must be provided externally, as part of the request, since the terms themselves will in no way exhibit the desired relationships to the generic concept. A possible approach would be to indicate a structural relationship among the terms. This would permit the handling of any type of question related to the prescribed structure. Such a structure would come, in time, to look "very like a classification," and this, of course, is the kind of constraint that uniterm was designed to get away from.

EFFICIENT MECHANIZED CODING

A second key documentalist is Calvin Mooers, president of the Zator Company (Cambridge, Mass.). Like Taube he was greatly concerned with the concept of coordinating terms. However, he considered the reverse approach of listing the subject terms for a single document on a single card and in doing so was concerned with the question of efficient storage of the subject information. The placement of these terms on the card was a basic problem because one cannot assign a fixed field or prededicated space to each possible subject, for this would in most cases use far too much space. On the other hand, it is extremely expensive to allow open fields with arbitrary location for a given subject. As Mooers (1951) pointed out: "... Scanning is a very powerful technique [but it requires] an elaborate and expensive sensing mechanism because of the need to search many alternative locations." These costs are substantially reduced if reading is restricted to invariant or fixed locations, and hence Mooers proposed the concept of storing the codes for all of the subjects related to a document in the same invariant place—one superimposed on top of the others—the concept of *superimposed coding*. The identification of each subject is thus recorded in the same field in exactly the same physical location.

To illustrate, let us say that most documents will cover five subjects. Normally, without the use of superimposed coding, each subject will be represented, depending on the size of vocabulary, by perhaps 4 characters. If a separate field were provided for each subject, at least 20 character positions—5 fields of 4 characters each—would be needed. To handle a request for subject A and subject B, it would be necessary to compare each of them with each of the subject fields, since there is no way of knowing in which of the positions either may actually have been placed. Mooers suggested storing all of the subject codes in the same field, essentially by providing a 20-character code for each subject. Then one need not worry about the fields in which particular subjects are coded but can merely match all desired subjects over the entire field.

It is immediately evident that this approach, although reducing the problems of comparison, substantially increases the probability of false drop due to the possible generation of the code of a nonrelevant subject from the superimposed codes of the actually relevant subjects. Thus, if the system is to be effective, the choice of codes must be made in such a way as to minimize the probability of producing such false subjects. That this is possible can be demonstrated by the following simple analysis of possible combintaions. If there are, say, 1000 possible subjects and any document will be represented by about, say, 5 subjects, the system will be concerned with at most the number of possible combinations of 1000 subjects taken 5 at a time. This number is less than 10^{13}, while with 20 decimal characters it would be possible to represent 10^{20} different such combinations with no possibility of introducing false subjects.

The problem lies in generating the codes for combinations of subjects from those for the individual subjects (Casey, et al., 1958). It can be shown—and Mooers has spent a great deal of investigation in demonstrating—that the most appropriate choice of subject codes for this purpose is a random one. This results, in principle, from the fact that random codes are the most efficient, for any organized coding is almost certain to dedicate some ranges of codes which will be overutilized and other ranges which will be underutilized. The classic example (Metcalfe, 1957) is the necessity, in the Dewey Decimal Classification, of representing subjects in engineering by extremely long (nine decimal digits in some cases)—and thus inefficient—codes, because three decimal digit numbers have been previously spent on subjects such as "Angels, Devils, and Satan." By introducing efficient random codes the available coding space will be better utilized, and the probability of generating identical codes from two combinations of subjects will be minimized.

Another, and independently useful, method for reducing the effects of this problem is to limit the number of terms very drastically. It has therefore been a part of Mooers' system to define very carefully the *descriptors* in terms of the subject field involved and in this way to limit their number substantially. In fact, whereas the uniterm system may well generate 5000 to 10,000 terms, a superimposed coding system will limit their number to perhaps 300.

The scheme of superimposed coding proposed by Mooers was subject to the same criticisms as that of coordinate indexing, that is, generic searches are difficult and false drops will occur because of improper coordination and the lack of syntax. The previously discussed approaches to answering these criticisms are probably not easy to use with superimposed coding. In fact, Mooers himself pointed out that random coding and classified coding probably cannot be reconciled. In addition, the possible generation of irrelevant subjects represents an additional source of false drops. Despite these difficulties, however, the technique of Mooers is a useful one, particularly applicable where coding space is at a premium, as is the situation with the use of edge-notched cards, such as the McBee-Key-Sort or those developed by the Zator Company itself.

FORMALIZED ABSTRACTS

The third documentation group to develop new approaches was the Center for Documentation and Communications Research of the Western Reserve University. The main participants in their program were James W. Perry and Allen Kent. They became particularly concerned with the problem of false drops and the difficulties with subject interrelationships which occur in the coordinate index or superimposed coding types of schemes. They therefore studied means of representing highly complex abstracts of documents in an effort to reduce these problems. In many respects the results were not abstracts but analytical studies in their own right in that information can actually be added to that of the document by the abstract description. The significant contribution was that they developed tools for description which could be utilized by virtually any system.

The Western Reserve system has perhaps best been described by Brian Vickery in a paper published in *American Documentation*, Vol. 10, 1959, entitled "The Structure of 'Semantic Coding,' A Review." The tables and examples presented in the following material are expected from his paper.

The structure of their so-called "telegraphic abstract" (Perry, 1956) is based on a number of elements for describing the information content of a document. The first is the *phrase*—a logical unit of thought within the document. Within a phrase, *subphrases* are individual words, or concepts, together with *role indicators* describing the particular role which th᠈ term plays in the phrase. The primary significance of the role indicators is that they provide a mechanism for handling syntax of the type required in particular subject matter. For the particular subject matter with which Western Reserve has been most concerned in their study for the American Society of Metals some twenty separate role indicators have been identified. (Table 6.1).

The individual terms are produced from *semantic factors* which are then particularized by *analytic infixes*, modifiers, and numerical suffices to pinpoint the particular term of interest within a group of terms. These semantic factors and analytic infixes thus represent a means of defining terms by their relationship to very general concepts. Western Reserve has defined some 214 semantic factors.

These semantic factors can be grouped as shown in Table 6.2 (the number of semantic factors and an example is added in each case).

Each semantic factor is represented by a code consisting of four alphabetical characters, the second of which is blank and will be filled by a letter representing the analytic relationship of a specific term to the semantic factor. Examples are given in Table 6.3.

The analytic relations and the corresponding alphabetic code for each are presented in Table 6.4.

Each term is represented by a semantic factor and the analytic relation which the term bears to it (or a set of these). Examples are given in

This method of producing terms, since it is based on a highly organized concept of the relationship among terms, allows for recovery in response to questions phrased within this structure of terms. Thus, generic questions within this framework will be handled without difficulty. However, it must also be recognized that relationships outside the structure defined by the chosen semantic relations will be as hard to handle in the

TABLE 6.1 Role Indicators for the Field of Metallurgy[a]

Representing an attendant condition:
1. KOV (*property given for*)
2. KEJ (*material processed*)
3. KAJ (*starting material*)
4. KUJ (*component*)
5. KWJ (*product*)
6. KQJ (*by means of*)
7. KAD (*machine or device*)
8. KAG (*subassembly*)
9. KAL (*influenced by*)

Applied to terms denoting material:
1. KWV (*given*)
2. KUP (*determined*)
3. KAP (*influenced*)
4. KAL (*influencing*)

Applied to processes:
1. KAM (*process*)
2. KXM (*negation*)
3. KAL (*influencing*)

Representing an attendant condition:
1. KAH (*attending condition*)

Miscellaneous indicators:
1. KIS (*location*)
2. KWB (*direction from*)
3. KWC (*direction to*)
4. KAB (*field*)
5. KIT (*time occurring*)
6. KIG (*geographic location*)
7. KIB (*organization involved*)
8. KEP (*person involved*)

[a] Note that each role indicator is represented by a code consisting of three alphabetic characters, the first of which is a K. *American Documentation*, July 1959, Vol. 10, No. 3.

Western Reserve system as they are in any other system and perhaps more so (Perry, 1958).

Western Reserve has used the term machine language to describe their particular coding of the terms as represented by semantic factors and infixes. It is somewhat difficult to understand the basis for such usage, but apparently it is due to the fact the codes are designed to be self-separating, so that it is obvious where one term ends and another begins without the need for space characters.

This approach has certain problems. Ambiguity is possible in the generation of term codes. In particular, how does one decide what semantic factor to use for a term and what particular analytic relation is involved? Two different analysts examining the concept as it appears in a document could well come up with two different representations. This is character-

TABLE 6.2 Classification of Semantic Factors[a]

General concepts:	*Ideas* (4, e.g. *Theory*)
	Relationships (10, e.g. *Agent*)
	Properties (4, e.g. *Chemical*)
	Fields (9, e.g. *Law*)
	Classifications (27, e.g. *Mineral*)
Relationships:	*Economics* (36, e.g. *Buying, Mining*)
	Physical (27, e.g. *Bones, Growth*)
	Social (32, e.g. *Security, Relgiion*)
States:	*Psychological* (4, e.g. *Emotion*)
	Action (16, e.g. *Disease*)
	Physical
	Sensible (12, e.g. *Color*)
	Conditional (12, e.g. *Weather*)
	Properties (11, e.g. *Fluid*)
Processes:	*Physical* (19, e.g. *Diffusion*)
	General (20, e.g. *Detection*)
	Material
	Change (33, e.g. *Concentration*)
	Constructive (41, e.g. *Building*)
	Destructive (29, e.g. *Cutting*)
	Industrial (15, e.g. *Printing*)
Substances:	*Generalized* (21, e.g. *Fuel*)
	Specific
	Organic (14, e.g. *Oil*)
	Inorganic (13, e.g. *Glass*)
	Preparations (9, e.g. *Paint*)
Objects:	*General*
	Natural (14, e.g. *Muscle*)
	Products (7, e.g. *Explosive*)
	Specific
	Natural (28, e.g. *Fiber*)
	Products (17, e.g. *Cosmetic*)

[a] *American Documentation,* July 1959, Vol. 10, No. 3.

TABLE 6.3 Sample Semantic Factors[a]

Body fluid, B-FL
Ground, G-RD
Electrolysis, L-TL
Device, M-CH
Motion, M-TN
Release, R-LS
Arrangement, R-NG
Iron, R-RN
Plastic, R-SN
Fish, F-SH

[a] *American Documentation,* July 1959, Vol. 10, No. 3.

TABLE 6.4 Analytic Relations[a]

A	*Categorical:*	the coded term is a species of the genus denoted by the factor.
E	*Intrinsic:*	the coded term is something of which the factor is a component.
I	*Inclusive:*	the coded term is a component of the factor.
O	*Comprehensive:*	the coded term is made up of several members of the class represented by the factor.
U	*Productive:*	the coded term helps to produce the factor.
Q	*Affective:*	the coded term makes use of, is determined, or is influenced by the factor.
W	*Instrumental:*	the coded term is produced by, acts on or is acted on by the factor.
X	*Negative:*	the coded term has a characteristic whose absence is denoted by the factor.
Y	*Attributive:*	the coded term is characterized by the factor.
Z	*Simulative:*	the coded term resembles, but is not, the factor.

[a] *American Documentation,* July 1959, Vol. 10, No. 3.

TABLE 6.5 Sample Term Codes[a]
(based on semantic factors of Table 6.4)

Term	Relation to Factor	Code	
Blood	Categorical	BAFL.	005
Soil	Intrinsic	GERD.	030
Electrolyte	Inclusive	LITL.	005
Machinery	Comprehensive	MOCH.	047
Propulsion	Productive	MUTN.	015
Extrusion	Affective	RQLS.	010
Spaced	Instrumental	RWNG.	023
Nonferrous	Negative	RXRN.	001
Copolymer	Attributive	RYSN.	011
Whale	Simulative	FZSH.	014

[a] *American Documentation,* July 1959, Vol. 10, No. 3.

istic of virtually all abstracting schemes, but perhaps this scheme is more subject to it than others, for determining the semantic factor and the analytic relation which are to represent the term is a process involving a substantial expenditure of intellectual effort. Another problem is the question of compromises in coding depth. One can represent a term by combining several factors which represent different aspects of this same concept. How many of these should be provided? The principal difficulty is the effort involved in creating the abstract. It is a substantial analytical process to create such an abstract from a document. In certain circumstances it may be well worth this effort. However, with any appreciable volume of documents, each with a fairly small probability of retrieval, it is probably not worth the effort.

In certain respects all these problems can be reduced by the use of a dictionary, and thus by standardizing the terms used, indexing or abstracting then becomes a matter of determining which among the possible standard terms is related to the given document, and the method of their generation is no longer significant in the indexing process. For the field of metallurgy, the Western Reserve group did develop such a dictionary of terms based on the specific semantic factors and analytic relations. However, if this approach is chosen, the process is as circumscribed as any other scheme and must be evaluated on these terms.

Even though these difficulties, and others, eventually defeated the method, the analysis made by the Western Reserve group helped to increase understanding of the syntactic problems in data representation. While the particular problem with which they were concerned was that of metallurgy, their results should make easy the development of similar analyses in other process-type industries.

A step-by-step outline of the procedure for the automatic encoding of telegraphic abstracts can be found in "Information Resources; a challenge to American science and industry," by Jesse H. Shera, Allen Kent, and James W. Perry, Western Reserve University Press, 1958. This monograph is based on the proceedings of a special meeting of the Council on Documentation Research in the same year.

ANALYSIS OF SUBJECT RELATIONSHIPS

The final school of study in organization of knowledge and representation of information was called *facet analysis*. Vickery (1959) probably presented the faceted classification approach in the clearest terms when he said:

> Traditional classification does not begin with individual terms as in Mooers, Taube, and Perry, but it starts from above, by division of an original universe of knowledge. The advocates of faceted classification, however, have begun to modify this pattern. Thus, terms can be stored into groups, each of which has been differentiated on the basis of a different characteristic. This sorting of terms into groups is called by Ranganathan "facet analysis." Instead of trying ot construct from the original universe one vast tree of knowledge, facet analysis first deals with the terms and groups them into categories [kinds, state, property—much related ot the "semantic factors" with which the Western Reserve group is concerned] and then arranges the terms within each category into the form of a classificatory map.

An explicit use of "fundamental" categories in classification was made by Ranganathan (1951). His colon classification exhibited, from the start, a division of classes into facets. The basis for this concept is the idea that one can describe the relationship among things in a universe in terms of their positions with respect to each of a set of fundamental facets. Within each facet, a set of specified values or terms is prescribed for representing the position of a given concept. To illustrate, consider literature on types of data processing storage media. It can be grouped in terms of one facet, the form of the medium, with possible characterizations as *card, strip, reel, drum,* etc. Similarly, it can be grouped on the basis of a second facet, the information rate, as low speed, medium speed, high speed. In effect, the combination of them is a classification of the storage media; one can describe a particular medium as being, for example, a low-speed card or a high-speed drum.

The main effort of the principal schools of facet analysis is to make evident the facets which will best characterize a field of interest. To illustrate the aims of such effort, consider the example given above. It may well become clear after a careful examination of the field of data processing storage media and of its literature that, say, some of the documents concerned with cards are about magnetic cards, some about punched cards, some about photographic cards. Initially these might well be treated as possible values within the facet *form*. But if it also became evident that similar terms were arising in the facet of *information rate,* an effort would be made to extract another facet—in this case obviously *recording* or something similar, with possible values of *magnetic, punched, photographic,* etc. The example is of course quite trivial, but the principle is essentially that of facet analysis—the extraction of basic criteria for differentiation. Ranganathan, in his quest for a categorization that would be explicit, exhaustive, and uniform, chose to establish five fundamental facets: time, space, energy, matter, and personality.

Once a facet schedule exists, a complex concept is represented by the particular combination of facet values which most adequately describes it. Document content is represented by the combination of such concepts—the coordination indicated, in the case of Ranganathan, as in Universal Decimal Classification (UDC), by a colon and other arbitrary signs between each two terms.

In order to store items in well-defined locations for later recovery by their faceted classification, it is necessary that the facet terms be put into a preferred indexing order. In other words, one must preestablish the order in which the facets for a given item are to be listed. Effectively this results in a hierarchical classification of the literature covered.

Recovery from such a classification leads to the concept in facet analysis of *chain indexing* or the production of subject index entries from the individual terms describing the item. It involves the production of a subject heading index or subject heading catalog by, in effect, a mechanical rearrangement of the facet classification codes assigned to the documents.

186   To Meet the Information Crisis

A discussion of this is given in "Classification Research Group Bulletin No. 5 on 54th meeting of CRG, ASLIB Research Project, College of Aeronautics, Cranfield," as follows:

> Since the object of faceted classification is to be able to express complex subjects by a single notation showing the terms involved in a preferred order (that which appears most logical and helpful to the user), it follows that provision must be made for finding the position of terms distributed in the subordinated positions. This is achieved by *chain indexing*. In the complementary alphabetical index the concepts in a given coded subject are cited (as words) in the reverse order of the code, together with the full code. Further entries are then made for each facet in turn, omitting one facet word on the left each time, whilst quoting the code number with one less facet code term on the right each time. The final card will thus be the first facet term (of the complete coded notation) alone, with its facet notation, and this is equivalent to the card appearing in a straightforward alphabetical index to all the terms in the classification. A complex example follows:
>
> Classified index entry: Ca (Cd-n-ea) Nbj-bk-vh   Ogb
>
> Facets: part   physical   parameters
>   properties
>
> Chain structure
>
> (1) C, structural part of aircraft; 2) a, combination; (3) Cd, wing; (4) -n, tail; (5) -ea, body; (6) N, aerodynamics; (7) Nb, aerodynamic entities; (8) Nbf, flow; (9) Nbj, transonic; (10) -bk supersonic; (11) Np, aerodynamic forces; (12) Nv, pressure on body; (13) h, center of pressure; (14) Og, aerodynamic reference parameters; (15) b, angle of attack
>
> It may also be decided that certain links in the chain (i.e., certain terms in the Schedules) should be omitted as "unsought." Steps 1, 6, 7, 11, 14 might perhaps be so designated. We are left with steps 2 to 5, 9, 10, 12, 13, and 15 to use in the chain index.
>
> Alphabetical index entries
>
> (1) Angle of attack: center of pressure: supersonic, transonic flow: body, tail, wing combination = Ca (Cd-n-ea) Nbj-bk-vh Ogb.
> (2) Center of pressure: supersonic . . . combination = Ca (Cd-n-ea) Nbj-bk-vh.
> (3) Pressure on body: supersonic . . . combination = Ca (Cd-n-ea) Nbj-bk-vh.
> (4) Supersonic, transonic . . . combination = Ca (Cd-n-ea) Nbj-bk.
> (5) Transonic flow . . . combination = CA (Cd-n-ea) Nbj.
> (6) Body, tail wing: combination = Ca (Cd-n-ea).
> (7) Tail, wing: combination = Ca (Cd-n).
> (8) Wing: combination = Ca (Cd).
> (9) Combination = Ca.

Many students find Ranganathan's vocabulary and writings very difficult to grasp, and his faceted classification is not widely understood. Easy reading on this subject, however, can be found in a book on *Faceted Classification* by Vickery (1960).

Although Ranganathan has said "the only sensible course is to confine ourselves to the fundamental constituent terms and leave the derived composite terms to individual classifiers" and "the same class number should be arrived at by anybody following the prescribed rules," the facts of life are that ambiguity is as likely in facet classification as it is with Western Reserve's semantic factors. It is almost certain that, in any operational system, a prescribed dictionary or schedule of terms must be used to ensure some uniformity of coding. This schedule may well have been created by a facet analysis, just as it might have been created from semantic factors or any other analytical technique, and to that extent will exhibit the interrelationships inherent in the particular analytical technique used. However, as soon as such a dictionary is introduced, it immediately limits the flexibility of representation.

In other words, none of the techniques for term specification can simultaneously eliminate ambiguity and retain flexibility. The choice must be made as to which is important for the particular informtaion system. Given that choice, each of the means for defining terms can be evaluated for the degree to which it represents the character of the field of knowledge covered by the information system.

REFERENCES

BULLETIN No. 5, Classification Research Group, *The Journal of Documentation*, v. 5, No. 1, pp. 39–57.

CASEY, R. S., PERRY, J. W., BERRY, M. M., KENT, A., (1958), *Punched Cards: Their Application to Science and Industry*, 2nd ed., New York, Reinhold.

JONKER, FREDERICK, (1958), The Descriptive Continuum: A "Generalized" Theory of Indexing, *Preprints of Papers for the International Conference on Scientific Information, 1958,* Washington, D.C., National Academy of Sciences, National Research Council.

MACK, JAMES D. and TAYLOR, ROBERT S., (1956), A System of Documentation Terminology, p. 20, in *Documentation in Action,* by Jesse H. Shera, Allen Kent, and James W. Perry, New York, Reinhold. Based on 1956 Conference on Documentation at Western Reserve University.

METCALFE, JOHN, (1957), *Information Indexing and Subject Cataloging*.

Alphabetical: Classified. Coordinate: Mechanical, New York, Scarecrow Press.

MOOERS, CALVIN N., (January 1951) Zatocoding Applied to Mechanical Organization of Knowledge, *American Documentation*, v. II, No. 1, pp. 20–32.

PERRY, J. W., KENT, A. and BERRY, M. M., (1956), *Machine Literature Searching*, New York, Interscience.

PERRY, J. W. and KENT, A., (1958), *Tools for Machine Literature Searching. Semantic Code Dictionary, Equipment, Procedures*, New York, Interscience. Library Science and Documentation, v. I.

RANGANATHAN, S. R., (1951), Colon Classification and Its Approach to Documentation in *Bibliographic Organization*, edited by Jesse H. Shera and Margaret E. Egan, University of Chicago Press, Chicago, Ill. (Papers presented before the 15th Annual Conference of the Graduate Library School, July 24–29, 1950.)

SANFORD, J. A. and THERIAULT, FREDERICK R., (January 1956), Problems in the Application of Uniterm Coordinate Indexing, *College and Research Libraries*, v. XVIII, pp. 19–23.

SCHULTZ, CLAIRE K. and GARWIG, PAUL L., (1969), History of the American Documentation Institute—A Sketch, *American Documentation*, v. 20, No. 2, pp. 152–160.

THE STATE OF THE LIBRARY ART (1961), edited by Ralph R. Shaw, v. 4, Part 2, Feature Cards by Lawrence S. Thompson, pp. 55–100, New Brunswick, N.J., Graduate School of Library Services, Rutgers-The State University.

TAUBE, MORTIMER, et al. (1953–1957), *Studies in Coordinate Indexing*, Documentation Incorporated, v. 1–4.

VICKERY, BRIAN C., (1959), Classification and Indexing in Science, 2nd ed., enlarged, London, Buttersworth Scientific Publications.

VICKERY, BRIAN C., (1961), *Faceted Classification—A Guide to Construction and Special Schemes*, ASLIB, London.

WARHEIT, I. A., (July, 1955), A Study of Coordinate Indexing as Applied to U.S. Atomic Energy Commission Reports, *College and Research Libraries*, v. XVI, No. 3, pp. 278–284.

Chapter Seven

The Information Framework

The previous chapter has given us a historical view of the development of the idea of "information systems," as seen from the eye of the documentalist. For a documentalist the abstraction of a "system" of handling information became necessary during the chaos of a period in which former methods (in particular those of the librarian) were not sufficing for many document storage and retrieval situations. The notion of a system or framework of information storage, flow, retrieval, and use was valuable in reminding the inventor-documentalist of his goals in reaching out for entirely new ways of dealing with information.

The spread of computer usage made system thinking still more important, for the computer provided a means of handling not just documented information, but also business data, scientific and technical data, and drawings and schematic data—all, potentially, in the same system.

Now that we have considered, in Chapters Two through Four, a plethora of techniques and machines for information handling (including storage, input, output, and transmission), and have later considered the precomputer approaches to total information systems, we are ready to entertain and ponder at least a rudimentary concept of an *information system*—a concept that will embody what *all* information systems are likely to have in common, regardless of the degree of mechanization or of the type of information handled.

It is important to note that a major flaw in the thinking of most documentalists and computer applicationists in earlier years was a tendency to overconcentrate on one component (i.e., device, machine, program) of a total system—and this (usually) in relation to some highly particular information problem. General purpose machines or systems were not ordinarily sought. The reason for this has been clear; it saves time to concentrate on solving a problem at hand, on developing a given device, or on formulating an elegant storage searching algorithm. The efforts of equipment manufacturers especially were too often specialized, based on the needs of a specific customer at a specific time. Curiously, though these piecemeal approaches often led to success in other areas of data processing and computer applications, they more often led to blind alleys and outright error in the realm of information storage and retrieval. It is with this in mind that we present this brief chapter to the discussion of an *information framework*—to encourage the student always to view individual problems or components in the context of a total information system.

A Simple System Diagram. What makes up an *information system* depends on what *information* is and what a *system* is. In classic information theory terms, information is comprised of symbols which, when broadcast by some sender, have the capability to reduce the uncertainty in the mind of some listener. Of chief interest to students of information retrieval is that information may be preserved as well as communicated. This can function as the basis of a distinction between an information system and a communication system. A mere communication system need provide only for the transmission of information (and not necessarily two-way transmission). It appears to be the custom, however, to require an information system to deal with both the preservation and transmission aspects of information, and we subscribe to that notion. In somewhat different words, an information system can be thought of as a communication system which provides for an unlimited amount of delay between receiver and sender, and which, therefore, must store the messages in some static medium, and which must also have the messages in a state of availability for whatever future receiver may present himself.

Figure 7.1 is a highly generalized diagram of an information system. As the brackets surmounting the diagram indicate, an information system can be conceived of as a front half (input) and a back half (output). Information units flow from left to right in the diagram (solid arrows), and these units, previously referred to as *messages*, are more aptly called documents when they are to be retained in store for potential future recipients, who, in their turn, are more commonly referred to as *users* of documents. Despite today's television, radio, and other information media, the most abundant form of stored information is still *printed data*, as reflected in the box at the beginning of the solid arrow path. Both for printed data and for material that is something other than printed data, it is very likely to be *characterized* (indexed) in terms of printed words, as well as *organized* (e.g., alphabetized, cross-referenced) in terms of these printed words.

The Information Framework 191

INPUT: Characterization and organization

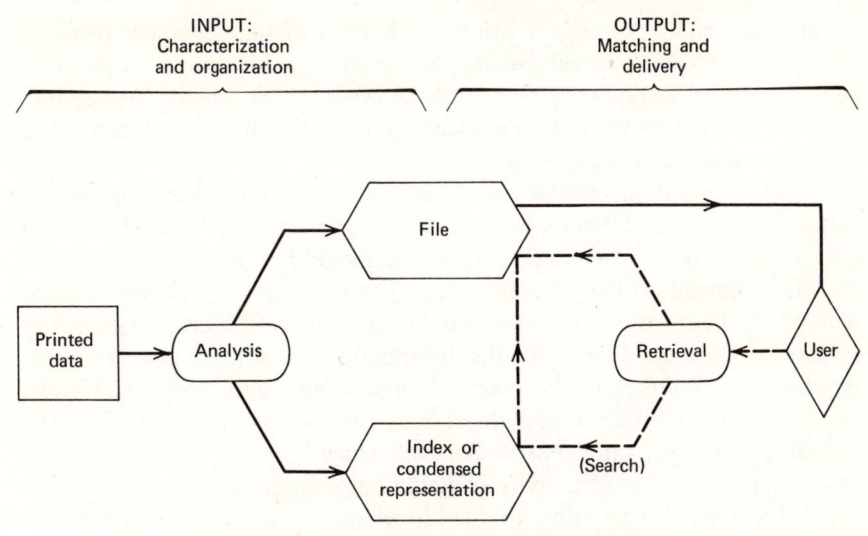

OUTPUT: Matching and delivery

Figure 7.1. The information framework.

It is at the *analysis* phase (oval box at left) that the characterization and organization of all information items is decided upon. At this phase, *index* terms are typically assigned, and one or more entries is added to some organized arrangement to be used subsequently in lookup; this can be anything from a printed index to a card catalog. Documents themselves are placed in a *file*, which is ordered usually according to one parameter (last name, for example) which is also yielded by the index as a pathway of entry to the file. These two elements, file and index, are present in almost every information system, and the routing of verbal data into them is shown via the bifurcation of the solid arrow path.

What happens in the output half of the system is determined by the actions of the *user* (right-hand box). The user's actions are shown in terms of two dotted arrow paths, indicating that he has a choice of consulting the index as a route of reference to the file or of approaching the file directly and looking up items according to the parameter(s) of organization. These actions are referred to as *matching*, because the user must match (in terms of mental recognition) the words that describe his information needs to words he encounters in the index or file. Many information systems have been built so that the machine (computer or special purpose device) does the matching, using words initially specified by the user. Where a system has feedback capabilities, the process of document search is more complicated than indicated by the dashed lines. At any rate, the final step is *delivery*, the solid path extending from the file to the user. All the user-governed processes on the right half are spoken of collectively as *retrieval* (oval box at right), though whether the delivery of the document is necessarily a part of the retrieval process can be an arguable point. People have been known to build working "retrieval systems" in which "successful" retrieval operations were accompanied by the news that the document is not, unfortunately, present in the file.

The information framework can serve as a simple, useful outline for bringing into focus the main parts of any information storage and retrieval system. Also, it will be used to help categorize new equipment research and development and their application. The examples of information systems given below should be viewed in terms of this block diagram. By essentially "walking through" the information framework in each case, these examples illustrate the essential processing similarities which exist in creating both library-type subject files, with their characteristic intellectual complexity, and commercial-type named object files, with their characteristic volume of activity. Thus, a basic frame of reference is provided for later interpreting the applications of machine research and development activities in the entire information system field.

The first example is that of a *local public library*. Here the printed data are the information recorded in books, periodicals, and other publications acquired or produced by the library. The analysis required to make this material usable involves the intellectual processes of examining each new piece of printed material, assigning classification numbers, and preparing title, author, and subject cards for inclusion in a card catalog. The index is then the accumulation of cards in the card catalog. This is usually the first place a user of a public library goes ot find a book and determine its shelf location. The document file is then the collection of publications themselves, filed on the shelves according to a prescribed order as indicated on each card in the catalog. The users are the library patrons, and their retrieval options are either to go directly to the stacks (direct request), or to consult the card catalog (search) or some other index (the reference librarian might qualify as an "index").

Another example is that of the *scientific research library*. Here the printed data may appear to be quite similar to that in the public library—books, periodicals, and similar publications. However, they will generally be more detailed, with much greater depth of coverage in the particular technical field. Data may include confidential reports, working papers, foreign literature, etc. The process of analysis again involves the intellectual effort of reading the document, assigning classification numbers or subject headings for each important fact, and preparing cards to be used in the index. The library operation may well require abstracts of the more significant articles, and these would be prepared and processed at this stage. The index then contains the data which result from the process of analysis. This index may be on manual cards, punched cards, magnetic tapes, depending on the complexity of operation and the volume of activity. The information in the index can include merely a reference to the location of the information in the document file or an entire abstract of the document. The document file itself contains the basic source material, perhaps in hard-copy form, perhaps on microfilm or even on magnetic tape. It is arranged in an order most convenient for access, usually by pre-assigned number. The document file will most often contain the full length document to which the index refers, but it may contain individual pieces of information grouped together in convenient form. The users of such a library are the researchers, workers, and employees of the organization which it serves.

A third example is a *personnel record file* such as would be maintained by commercial, governmental, or military organizations. The printed data consist of all recorded information or paperwork associated with the chronology of service for each man. This may include forms, correspondence, orders, efficiency reports, etc. The process of analysis involves the extraction from the source material of pertinent facts about each man, such as name, birth date, employee number, grade, and address. The accuracy of this process is crucial because spelling errors and numerical coding errors made at this time are almost certain to result in failures at the time of retrieval. The index is then a personnel record on each man which includes, in fixed subfields, key characteristics about the man. These may be either information vital for searching purposes or data subject to change through personnel activity. The manual cards, punched cards, or magnetic tape which may be used to store these data will be organized in a manner that will satisfy most retrieval demands. For such a situation, the document file will consist of the collection of source dossiers kept on each man. This will contain all the original documents affecting his service. The file is usually organized by an address system tied into the index record. The user activity results in additions, corrections, deletions to the file, and searches for information concerning the man and his past or present activities.

The fourth example is represented by the *title insurance* business. Here the printed data consist of recorded transactions and other legal actions affecting the rights of individuals to convey real property. They may include transfers of property or property rights, financial transactions and liens, court cases of several kinds, etc. [In one particular example (Title Insurance and Trust Co. of Los Angeles), these transactions amount to over 50 million covering a period of 100 years.] The process of analysis involves the identification of the property and the individuals affected. The relevant facts are then extracted from the source material in the form of an abstract. (In the case cited there are over 5000 such transactions each day.) The index is a record maintained for each parcel of land (over 2 million in the case cited), with a posting for each transaction affecting its status. The document file is then the set of abstracts of each transaction arranged in strict chronological order and grouped by daily activity. The index record defines the exact chronological position of the abstract. The users of this file include the title officers of the company, other company officials concerned with property data, and municipal employees. Requests are normally processed by reference to the index, producing a list of references to abstracts which are then collected for documentation as necessary to handle the request.

A fifth example is represented by the *cataloging* operation in the Department of Defense. The term cataloging is used by supply people in the military to describe the method by which material, such as equipment parts, is described and referenced in published indexes. Here the printed data consist of the description, both in words and pictures, of inventory items, including major assemblies, subassemblies, component parts. Each of these approximately two and a half million individual items is assigned a unique identification number. The purpose of the cataloging operation is to assign these numbers and provide them in response to requests. The process of analysis covers the description of items in standardized form for processing against the stored descriptions to determine whether the item has previously been assigned an identification number. These standardized item descriptions are based on a set of patterns, each suitable for a particular class of items. There are more than 12,000 such descriptive patterns. Each item description involves the specification of parameter values within the pattern appropriate to the item. This sequence of assigned parameter values is called the *signal* for the item and can be anywhere from 50 to 250 characters long, with the average of about 100 characters. A number of indexes are provided. One is in sequence by the assigned identification number so that the description can be quickly located if the identification number is known. A second is arranged in sequence by the part numbers of the various manufacturers so that the identification number for a specific part can be quickly located if the manufacturer's part number is known. The document file consists of a set of item descriptions arranged in sequence by their signals. This rather odd arrangement in effect treats the entire signal as though it were a number and arranges these numbers in increasing order. The users of this file are governmental groups and individuals concerned with the standardized identification of inventory items. To utilize the file they must process the item description and check its validity by comparison with standard permissible ranges of parameter values and their interrelationships. Each potentially new signal must then be compared with the signals stored in the document file to determine if it matches any one of them. If it does, the presently assigned identification number is used; if it does not, the new description is added to the file, a new number is assigned to it, and appropriate references are inserted in the index. The logical problem in determining whether a given signal matches any of the stored signals in an extremely complex one.

Chapter Eight

Information Retrieval Systems–Data

The bulk of the world's recorded information is stored and handled in two modes, either as formatted records or as documents.* Formatted information was not common in the world until after the period 1400–1450 A.D., wherein movable type and double-entry bookkeeping were developed. Before this, all information was stored in the free style of the document. With printing and with ease of replication, it became feasible to generate *forms*. It eventually became commonplace to use forms in business so that transactions could be recorded and stored in a methodical way. Business information—that pertaining to transactions, customers, or items of merchandize—has a character especially suitable for formatted storage: it tends to be limited in amount (per unit of storage) and it is usually quite repetitious in nature.

Formatting serves a purpose in information handling very similar to the purpose of military formations in handling large numbers of men; the typical geometry of a formatted file is suggestive of military rank and file. It is simple to request information (e.g., the eighth item of record 1017), and to make changes, additions, deletions, and other such operations, because the regularized structure of the information store is so easily

---

*Such items as paintings, maps, musical scores, movies, etc., are "information," but they are excluded from the discussion here because they are not commonly the focus of retrieval systems; where they are, retrieval is generally accomplished through indexing methods quite similar to those used for documents or data. This situation may change with the development of computerized pattern recognition.

comprehended by the user of the file. As with neatly arranged material possessions, it is easy to find items when "everything is in its place."

Formatting is among the oldest of retrieval tools. Its advantages are seen in the ordinary file cabinet, which is probably the most widespread and practical information storage and retrieval device. Formatted files have worked so well that one might wonder, "Why not format *all* information?" Unfortunately, the capabilities of formatting can accommodate only a part of the information our civilization needs and produces. Information must be limited in kind and amount for formatting to be efficient; however, one can merely look around him to observe that most recorded information is in the form of long and diversified units: books and documents. The flexible and narrative documentary structure is indispensible for written communication, and has its own peculiar kind of efficiency, antithetical though that can be to orderly processing of information.

The trend to mechanization of information processing naturally touched the most well-organized stores of information first. Thus, punched card machines were first used in connection with the tabular data of the U.S. Census (Chapters Three and Four). The rank-and-file structure of formatted files was readily mappable into the rows and columns of the Hollerith card; when computers came on the scene, the same regularities could be made compatible with the array structure of magnetic core memories. The regularity and the terseness of formatted information (relative to documented information) made it a "natural" for computerized treatment, and thus began *data processing*.

This chapter discusses aspects of the storage and retrieval of formatted data. Chapter Nine deals with the storage and retrieval of the more unmanageable variety of information, i.e., the document. These topics are dealt with separately because the dichotomy is a real-world one. Not only are there differences between the retrieval (and other techniques) in the two realms, but the professional populations dedicated to each subdiscipline are almost nonoverlapping.

We do, however, begin with a discussion of some factors that the two areas have in common.

INFORMATION STRUCTURE— UTILIZATION AND CONSEQUENCES

Recorded information exists in great quantity and diversity, and if it is to be utilized, it must be given structure. This fact affects both formatted data and documented information, in ways that are sometimes similar and sometimes different. For the present we center attention on the similarities, then we look more closely at the special nature of data structure.

Information—formatted or unformatted—comes in quantity, and therefore must be partitioned into manageable units of information. Because information is variegated in content and highly specific in its usefulness, these units of information must be labeled and organized. Only in terms of such labeling and organization can an information request be matched with that information unit having a high probability of fulfilling the need. This is the essence of information retrieval.

Information structures tend to be hierarchized. A store of formatted data (which is called a *data base* if it is used as computer input) is typically a collection of files. Files consist of records, which in turn are subdivided into items. Documented information has a similar hierarchized structure, with the individual document at the center of a scale running from small to large. At the small end of the scale, the structure (sections, paragraphs, etc.) is controlled by the writer or publisher. At the large end, the structure is controlled by the manager of the document collection.

Such structuring of information is effected for well-known utilitarian purposes, encompassing many aspects of information handling, e.g., inventory, addition or deletion, indexing, browsing, retrieval, and so on. The fact that the structure exists is so familiar to us that it can easily be taken granted or even escape notice in our thinking. As an important case in point, one might fail to realize that before a user of information can "consume" the information, he must first address some *unit* of information. This makes information retrieval at least a two-step process, but more typically it is a three-step process.

1. The user, having an expressible information need, queries the information system (by consulting an index or card catalog, by asking a question, etc.), and is provided with one or more *references*.
2. The reference is to some information *unit* that physically exists. The user is directed by the information system (or by the reference itself) as to what steps to take, as a result of which the user obtains the unit. (Note: The transition from 1 to 2 can be automatic.)
3. The user, having obtained the unit, proceeds to digest the information. (This may involve further iteration of steps 1 and 2, as in the familiar back-of-the-book index.)

Early builders of computerized document retrieval systems, preoccupied with the computer's ability to carry out step 1 with great speed, often neglected to consider that step 2 was needed for the ultimate satisfaction of the information need. The result, all too often, was the retrieval of a reference for which a document could not be obtained.

These early builders of computerized retrieval systems were in the presence of an important truth about information without realizing its (just cited) chief drawback. The truth is: the information structure can exist independently of the information store itself. Document retrieval using computers would be economically unfeasible if this were not the case. Expensive storage of entire text is not really necessary if only step 1 computerized. The "information structure," consisting of index-tagged references, is small enough to be dealt with in computer memory. As was discussed in Chapter Seven and will be again in Chapter Ten, it is also feasible to store enough information about the contents of the documents corresponding to the reference, so that a user may more carefully zero in on the documents of his choice before going on to the (as yet) noncomputerized steps 2 and 3.

The independence of the information structure from the information store has ramifications for data retrieval also. Formatted data bases are typically smaller, in terms of number of bits (Chapter Four), than collections of documents, yet they are commonly too large to be held in core memory all at one time. A representation of data-base structure, however, can be made small enough for core storage; the corresponding units of the data base, even though massive, may be kept available in auxiliary memory (tape, disk, etc.) and brought into core unit by unit as they are needed.

Such a mode of using auxiliary memory has been characteristic of data processing since its beginning. The first AN/FSQ-7 computers that were installed in 1956 as part of the U.S. Air Force's SAGE Air Defense System had core memories of only 4096 32-bit words, into which had to fit operating programs, control programs, and data being processed. The amount of information it was feasible to hold in core storage at any one time was equivalent to that on merely a single page of a telephone directory. Nevertheless it was possible to deal with thousands of radar blips, hundreds of aircraft coordinates, input/output to and from interceptors, etc., each minute, as a result of the fact that several dozen magnetic drums stood ready, each holding enough data to fill that part of core memory reserved for data, and each accessible in milliseconds. The total amount of information that could be processed in a few seconds was from 50 to 100 times as great as the capacity of core memory. The information structure, called the "sequence parameter table," was always present in core memory. It contained the names of all the units of the data base and all of the programs, and also indicated the sequence in which each program and data-base unit was to be called into core for use.

When it is economically feasible to have a large quantity of information in auxiliary digital storage, proceeding from step 1 to step 2 in the above sequence can be made automatic, and the request for data can be followed immediately by the delivery thereof. There are situations, however, where a user may not want delivery of data, but only references thereto. For example, in interrogating census data a user may have a query such as: What are the ten U.S. cities of population 50,000 and above having the largest percentages in the population of children aged five or less? An appropriate answer would be simply a printout of the names of the ten cities—information that can be derived from the information structure. The computer itself, of course, would have to inspect the numerical values in the data base, but need not print any of them out.

Bar-Hillel (1960) has made a distinction between "data-providing systems" and "reference-providing systems"; a system such as implied in the previous paragraph can.do both. Bar-Hillel was making the point, and it is still almost as true now as in 1960, that document retrieval systems were usually reference-providing systems. This state of affairs, as we have said, is mainly because of the economical unfeasibility of carrying full document text in digital storage, but also (not unimportantly) because the subunits of documents, especially paragraphs and sentences, were not meant to be retrieved in isolation from the whole document. Nevertheless, data-providing document retrieval systems are feasible in principle; experimental systems have been built, and some are even used (Chapters Nine, Ten). Thus, both data-providing and reference-providing capabilities are feasible and useful both in data retrieval and document retrieval systems. Because information structure is so often hierarchized, we can visualize data and reference providing at all levels of the structure. One can print out data from individual items that come from individual records, or one can retrieve references thereto; one can print out entire data bases, or references thereto. The desirability of being able to provide references is particularly evident in the latter case.

Complexity and Data Structure. Earlier in the chapter it was stated that the efficiencies of formatting depended on information being limited in kind and amount. Anyone who maintains and processes a data base over a period of time is fortunate if his store of data stays small and simple. But it is a more typical experience* to have one's data base grow—in size and in complexity. Such growth often whittles away at the advantages of formatting, and this tends to be so whether there is a computer in the picture or not.

Let us imagine a data base that starts out small and simple, and look

---

* It is also a typical experience to have massive data bases spring up full-grown, as from the head of Zeus.

at some of the ways in which it might diverge from this initial state—and note how the changes might affect processing efficiency. A data base at its smallest and simplest can be visualized as a large rectangle, having rows and columns of characters.

The data base might be a membership list of a professional organization.* Each member is given a row of 80 character spaces, including 20 for his name, 35 for his business or home address, 20 for his city and state, and 5 for zip code. These allotments for name, address, etc., are commonly termed *items*, or, when the data is on punched cards, *fields*. *A "key item" is one to which the record pertains (in this case "name") or one under which the record is cross-indexed.* If each row has the data for one member, then each column would correspond to a character position in some item or field, and this column would run through the entire membership list. The twenty-third column, for example, would be the third character position in the *address* item.

We note here that there are two *simple* ways for the data base to grow, either in number of rows or in number of columns. Number-of-rows growth would ordinarily not impair the efficiency of processing formatted files; it may even improve efficiency because of *economies of scale*. An example of an economy of scale is that fixed costs (such as the cost of writing and checking out the data-processing programs) and, in general, any task that has to be done only once are distributed over a larger and larger number of units of data as the data base grows, thus lowering per unit costs.

The second simple way of growth is in number of columns, and in the case we are considering, this amounts to an increase in the size of the record. One penalty is immediately apparent; growth above 80 characters means we can no longer store the membership list on IBM cards, at least not in a straight one-card-per-member fashion. There are a lot of reasons why a record will grow. The usual one is the desire to store more information about each key item (i.e., member). In addition to name and address, one might want member's telephone numbers, special interests, and other professional affiliations. This means more items per record which, in turn, usually means more character spaces per record.

Another reason for growth in record size is the expansion of the items themselves. Here, a distinction is made between *item* and *item*

---

* Ordinarily what we describe here would be spoken of in the data-processing profession as a *file,* and data bases typically consist of numerous files having different key items (e.g., names, cities, organizations). However, there is nothing incorrect about speaking of a data base having only one file; a part of the point of our discussion is that what begins as a one-file situation often develops into many files.

value; the zip code *item* is 5 character spaces corresponding to 5 columns in our format; the actual number that fills the spaces is the *item value*. Items can expand in size when a decision is made to increase the number of item values that may be entered; for example, the address space could be enlarged to permit two addresses per member. An item can also expand when item values come to exceed the amount of space allotted.

When the average length of an item value is greatly shorter than the maximum (allowed) length, many character spaces are unused, which can be a significant waste. Attempts to accommodate variable-length item values, however, constitute an example of the tendency of data bases to become more complex as well as merely growing in size. What we have been discussing is a *fixed format, fixed field* arrangement, where each record has the same layout of fixed-length items. (Note: the terms *item* and *field* are approximately synonymous in data processing.) It is the only feasible arrangement for the handling of large amounts of data on punched cards using electronic accounting machinery. Digital computers are more flexible, and at some cost in processing time can handle less regular formats. In particular, "fixed format, variable field," and "variable format, variable field" (and/or fixed field) configurations can be made use of. The former is a common way to deal with the problem of variable-length item values.

Figure 8.1 illustrates the mechanism by which items of variable length can be created. At the top, fixed length items of 20 characters (name), 35 characters (address), and 25 characters (city, state, and zip code) are shown. At the bottom are the same item values stored in variable-length items. Immediately preceding each item value are 2 digits that show the number of character spaces for that item (including those for the 2 digits themselves); the first 2 digits of the record show the total number of character spaces for that record (including those for all the digits). Using the digits of "length information," a program can compute where items begin and end, and can, for example, retrieve any of the item values in any record, by using the digits at the beginning of each *record* to calculate the location of the next record's digits, thus proceeding record by record until the requested record is found (either because of its known ordinal position or because of identification of a key item), then using the item digits to find the position and length of whichever item value is wanted from the record.

It is interesting to consider how much extra computation time is needed to retrieve a known item of a known record when comparing lookup in a "fixed format, fixed field" situation to lookup when a variable field is used. For a fixed field lookup, the address* of the item, in terms of

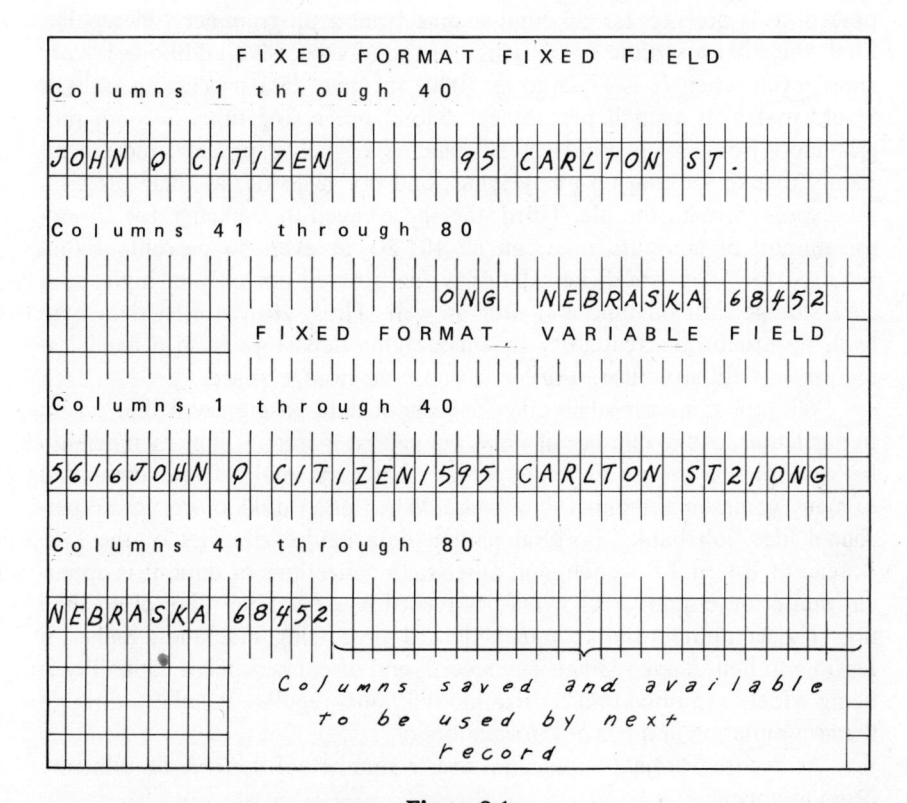

Figure 8.1.

```
FIXED FORMAT  FIXED  FIELD
Columns 1 through 40
JOHN Q CITIZEN        95 CARLTON ST.
Columns 41 through 80
                    ONG  NEBRASKA 68452
         FIXED FORMAT  VARIABLE  FIELD
Columns 1 through 40
56/6JOHN Q CITIZEN/595 CARLTON ST2/ONG
Columns 41 through 80
NEBRASKA 68452
              Columns saved and available
              to be used by next
              record
```

number of character spaces (bytes) from the beginning of the file, can be obtained in a single computation, $A_i = A_o + R(N-1) + C$. A_i is the address of the item, which equals A_o, the address of the beginning of the file, plus $R(N-1)$, the product of record length R and $N-1$ records which precede the Nth record in the file, plus C a column number that gives the position of the item in the record. In this case none of the preceding $N-1$ records have to be looked at. In the case of the variable field (item), all N records must be inspected, and the item's address must be computed by at least N successive additions. This is a fairly typical illustration of a tradeoff of computation time for storage space saved.

Contemplating the cumbersome procedure for looking up variable items, one may doubt that the space saved is worth the trouble. But the

---
* Addressing in computer memory is discussed in Chapter Four.

procedure is not necessarily cumbersome from a programmer's viewpoint. First, the total add time in carrying out the N successive additions is very short, even when N is as large as 1000. In most data processing tasks it would make up a small percentage of total processing time. Second, programmers bring many kinds of efficiencies to such a process, most commonly that of looking up many items, and not just one, as their program progresses through the file. Third, the space saved in exchange for a modest amount of compute time can be 10, 20, or even 50 percent of that required for fixed length items; this is space saved not only in high-speed core storage, but on tape and disk as well. Thus, growth of a data base leads to structural irregularity by encouraging departure from a fixed format, fixed field structure in order to conserve storage space.

We now consider some other aspects of data base growth that set in, in particular, as the number of items per record increases. The membership list example we have been using actually has very small records compared to many common personnel data bases. When one thinks of corporate personnel files, job banks, hospital patient data banks, the files of the U.S. Bureau of Internal Revenue, and other such collections of data, it is apparent that a large number of items per record is expectable more often than not. The computer, unlike punched card processing machines, makes it feasible to handle many items per record, and of course such a capability is being widely exploited in a civilization that must regulate its affairs through the accumulation and use of information.

As record formats expand in size, a number of sources of difficulty begin to appear.

1. The amount of computer time required to skip from item to item (via the procedure previously given) becomes commensurate with —and can exceed—time taken to move from record to record. This situation may be made less tolerable by the presence of *zero* values in many of the item spaces, either because information could not be obtained or because the item is of a type that often "does not apply" (e.g., spouse's residence, if different from 2b).*

---

* An interesting exception to the tendency to store zero items in large records is the U.S. Census data base, which, incidentally, grew from 70,000 pages in 1950 to 141,000 pages in 1960 (Wattenberg, 1965). The long questionnaire, which in 1960 was presented to 25 percent of the population, contained 79 questions. The answers to these questions were solicited by 160,000 census enumerators, all charged to obtain complete information; their battling average in 1960 was about 98 percent. Since the data available to the public is stored in *statisical* form pertaining to groups of blocks rather than individuals (for privacy reasons), there are very few *does not apply* cases.

2. Expanding the number of items per record focusses attention on differences rather than similarities. When records are small, information entries tend to be standard and unvarying in kind from record to record (e.g., name, rank, and serial number). As the number of items increases, so does the pressure to keep different kinds of information in records and to subcategorize the collection to make this convenient. In this way numerous subfiles can be created from one file each dealt with slightly differently from the others. Good examples of a data base in which this happens are criminal records. A crime file with small records might contain the bare essential data required for all crimes, e.g., time and place, name of reporting officer, name of victim(s), name or description of suspect(s), etc. As more information is stored in a crime report, however, its nature will tend to be influenced by type of crime; burglaries will require stolen property information but assault and battery cases will not; robberies or murders will require weapon information but grand theft auto will not; such variations of information required are endless. The end result will probably be a separate file on each major type of crime.

3. Collections of large records contain numerous instances of easily avoidable redundancy. As Figure 8.2 illustrates, one does not repeat a phrase such as "head of family" every time it applies, but uses a short numerical code (subscript)—reducing storage of such data by factors of 10, 20, or greater. But the number of item-value codes can be very large, so that those who have to use them to request data cannot possibly remember all the codes. Indeed, the Censac Users Guide (1972), from which the data in Figure 8.2 were taken, has in excess of 20 pages of item codes. One of the advantages of formatted data is that the user's access to the data base is streamlined by his ability to visualize its structure; when codes, subfiles, and other complexities obtrude, this advantage is seriously compromised.

There are ways to avert some of the difficulties of the increase in number of items per record. One way, for example, is to separate that part of a record that is consulted routinely from information that is stored merely because it might, under certain circumstances, be needed. "Routine use" records, made up of carefully chosen essential items, can be designed with speed of processing in mind; it can even be of "fixed format, fixed field" structure. Other information pertaining to these records can be encoded, compressed, referenced, and stashed in the cheapest available digital storage. It will be there when, or if, needed.

NAME	SUB-SCRIPT	DETAILED DESCRIPTION OF DATA ITEMS	NUMBER OF ITEMS
T23		POPULATION UNDER 18 YEARS OLD BY RELATIONSHIP AND FAMILY TYPE	10
	1	HEAD OR WIFE OF HEAD OF HOUSEHOLD	
		OWN (NEVER MARRIED) CHILD OF HEAD:	
	2	IN HUSBAND-WIFE FAMILY	
	3	IN OTHER FAMILY WITH MALE HEAD	
	4	IN FAMILY WITH FEMALE HEAD	
		OTHER RELATIVE OF HEAD:	
	5	IN HUSBAND-WIFE FAMILY	
	6	IN OTHER FAMILY WITH MALE HEAD	
	7	IN FAMILY WITH FEMALE HEAD	
	8	NONRELATIVE OF HEAD OF HOUSEHOLD	
	9	INMATE OF INSTITUTION	
	10	OTHER IN GROUP QUARTERS	
T24		POPULATION 65 YEARS AND OVER BY RELATIONSHIP	8
	1	HEAD OF FAMILY	
	2	WIFE OF HEAD	
	3	OTHER FAMILY MEMBER	
	4	MALE PRIMARY INDIVIDUAL	
	5	FEMALE PRIMARY INDIVIDUAL	
	6	NONRELATIVE OF HEAD OF HOUSEHOLD	
	7	INMATE OF INSTITUTION	
	8	OTHER IN GROUP QUARTERS	

Figure 8.2. Item-value codes from Censac Users Guide (1972).

There are cases in which it is obvious that some information, being too diverse and/or too unpredictable, cannot by any reasonable means be stored in a formatted way. This is an attribute of a kind of report used above as an example, i.e., a crime report. A report of a robbery will generally have two parts, a formatted part for information that is predictably required and a portion for narrative information which gives, for instance, the victim's description of the robbery. The information in the formatted portion would be used in processing the reports (e.g., in making statistical summaries or in retrieving individual reports) while that in the narrative portion would be simply kept in storage for retrieval as an integral part of the record. But we note, anticipating Chapter Ten, that the narrative material can be retrieved in terms of its own word content; experimental systems have been built for that purpose (Isaacs, 1965).

STORAGE PROGRAMMING

Data processing is a term that has been frequently used in this and other chapters. Chapter Four described its essentials, presenting examples of data and of some processing operations. Chapter Four, however, gave only a small-scale view of data processing, and did not speak of the necessities of dealing with hundreds or thousands of data items in core memory. It did not explain how all this data is to be arranged, and in what order it is to be processed, other than that of the straightforward programmer's tool, the index register. These topics were deferred until the present chapter because the theme herein—data retrieval—is thoroughly entwined with data storage and processing in a way that makes it awkward to explain them separately. Indeed, when a programmer designs a data-processing program, even he cannot deal with these functions separately, because how he retrieves will depend (to an extent greater than in document retrieval) on how he stores, and how he stores will in turn depend on what his major processing tasks are. Such interrelationships are inescapable, and take in auxiliary storage operations as well as those in core memory.

In the previous section we discussed arrangement of items within records, but not the arrangement of records within files. There is a reason for this divorcement of such closely related topics. In computer-stored files, as in the case of manual filing systems, records are ordinarily independent of each other. They may be arranged and rearranged, almost without restriction, to suit the needs of managing the file. This is much less true of items within records, the layout of which is governed by the need to have standardized forms, the need to have keying items more accessible than others, the desirability of grouping related items, and needs for minimization of storage space. As is the case in manual systems, the requirement for the maintenance of a record's integrity makes it a more convenient unit to manipulate than any of its components. One might say that if the item is the "atom" of data processing, then the record is the molecule.

Before we elucidate the various methods of organizing and accessing records, a distinction must be drawn between *logical* records and *physical* records. A logical record can be thought of independently of the physical form (holes in punched cards, cores in opposed states of magnetization, etc.) it may take; but physical records are not so thought of. Moreover, physical records need not necessarily correspond to logical records on a one-to-one basis, though it is convenient if they do. Physical records are created for efficiency in transferring data to and from auxiliary storage; such records are often *groups* of logical records, and they could just as well be *parts* of logical records (with the proviso that the reassembly of the parts is straightforward).

208   Information Retrieval Systems—Data

The concept of a physical record originated in relation to magnetic tape, for which it was necessary to group data into records separated by inter-record gaps to give the tape drive intermittent spaces in which to start and stop. Thus, physical records are said to be hardware-determined elements, and logical records to be software entities (CODASYL Systems Committee, 1971). In other words, the logical records are determined by what we (the users) want as units of our file; physical records are determined by hardware handling realities.

Sequential Organization. The primitive mode of organization of records in computer storage is quite similar to the physical ordering of records in a file. In fact, unless special reasons exist for changing the order, most computer-stored records are in the same order as they were when stored on punched cards prior to read-in. Usually (on punched cards or in computer storage) sequentially organized files are ordered according to some key item. In the case of personnel files this would probably be by last name or employee number.

Though storage organization methods have evolved to a complex state, sequential organization is still the most common way of storing data; one reason for this is that in many data-processing operations something must be done to every record. (This would be true, for example, in a company's payroll computations.) Data is simply read through storage processed, and written out (into some auxiliary storage unit) in whatever order it happens to be in.

Retrieval from a sequentially organized file is not difficult provided it is done in terms of the key item, and provided the data base is in core memory or at least on disk. One of the basic retrieval tools is called a *binary search*. Suppose, for example, one wants to determine the possessor of a given auto license number, which is the key item of a given file, the records of which are in order of the numerical portion of the license number. First the license number of the middle record of the whole file is examined and compared to the given number. If the given number is less, the numerically *greater* half of the file is eliminated from further search, and then the middle record of the *lesser* half is examined, with similar results. Each examination and comparison results in the elimination of half of the remaining possible records, and thus n comparisons will locate one item out of 2^n items. In more familiar terms, a file of 1000 records may require a maximum of 10 comparisons to find a record having a given value of the key item. This maximum applies only when the examined portions of the item values in the file are all different. When identical values of the examined digits occur, we must add to the maximum some number of extra searches that are needed to find the given value among the identical values. If, for example, we are looking for the license number 456 YCE, and if there are also records in the file for 456 SXG and 456 TWR, then (at most) two extra comparisons are needed.* The intrinsic speed of this mode of search is a strong factor in the success of highway patrol automated vehicle identification systems.

The binary search is by no means the most efficient way of searching sequentially ordered records. One can often compute the approximate location of a record within a given file by interpolation. This method is quite analogous to what people do in looking up a name in a telephone directory. When one looks up a name like "Carmichael," he opens the directory a tenth of the way through, rather than halfway as in a binary search, because he knows that the letter C is approximately a tenth of the way through the alphabet. Based on the results of the first cut, one can continue the interpolation method until the right page is found; a person of ordinary wit may require no more than four or five tries to find a name in 1000-page directory.

Indexed Sequential. Sequential organization sometimes entails sequential searching, a wasteful process in which each record must be looked at until the one sought is found. If a file contains m records, then on the average $(m+1)/2$ records must be examined in a sequential search, i.e., one must inspect half the file to find a particular record. One must examine the *entire* file to find all records having a given attribute. For example (and this applies to a manual file as well), where records are organized according to name, one must look through the entire file to find out how many other people represented therein have the same birthday as one's own.

Of course a sequential search is not needed for the key item, in terms of which the file is organized, and for which one can use binary or interpolative search techniques; it is needed only for nonkey items. Fortunately, there is a simple way to promote nonkey items to secondary keys, and this is to make an index based on that item's whole range of values. Here again, the principle applies both to manual files and computer-stored files. If it is found, in the practice of using a file, that many people must be looked up according to birthday, then one can construct an index ordered by date, with people's names or other record identification adjacent to the date that happens to be their birthday. Because birthdays tend to distribute themselves randomly throughout the year, interpolative searching of this index should be unusually efficient.

It is possible to construct such indexes for every *item* of every *record*

---

* To eliminate the need for such extra searches, one may simply order the records by alphabet within any block of identical numbers.

in a file. Thus, any record could be looked up in terms of *any* of its contents. One does not want to use this indexing power indiscriminately, for one pays a substantial price for the indexes: storage space. The aggregate indexes to a file could easily be larger than the file itself. Some indexes are so large that they have to be brought into core memory in segments (Lowe and Roberts, 1972). A collection of such indexes would constitute a burden of another sort whenever the file has to be updated: all of the indexes must be changed as well.

Direct Access. The indexes just discussed can be used in accessing unsequenced material as readily as sequenced. Indexing is one of a number of methods of *direct access*, also spoken of as *random access*, because successive recourses to storage need bear no positional relationship to one another. The first disk storage device, introduced in 1958, was called the RAMAC (RAndoMACcess). Though disks are not quite as intrinsically random in access as core memory itself, because economies result from doing as many read and write operations as possible without having to move the access arm, disks are so superior to magnetic tape (which can be accessed only serially) that their characterization as direct access devices is justified.

Dodd (1969) speaks of three common varieties of direct access: dictionary lookup (equivalent to indexing unsequenced records), direct addressing, and calculation. Direct addressing is commonly used by programmers, who, as a result of knowing what their programs do, also know in what core memory locations various kinds of data are stored. This location information is simply plugged in at appropriate points in the program. As Chapter Four explains, programmers do not have to work with the actual physical core memory addresses, but can place symbolic addresses in their programs, such as T001, T002, T003, etc., meaning "tables #1, #2, #3, etc.," and these symbols are converted into physical memory addresses when the programs are compiled. In other words, the computer itself performs the labor of counting memory registers so as to fit the tables properly in core storage.

The third method, calculation, uses the key item *values* to compute the addresses of each record. There are many methods of doing this, and most involve some kind of arithmetic. For example, consider the item "full name," and the item value "Fred L. Kane." Each of its letters can be converted into the number of its position in the alphabet, and then summed for the letters in "Fred L. Kane." Thus,

$$F\ R\ E\ D \qquad L \qquad K\ A\ N\ E$$
$$6+18+5+4 \qquad +12 \qquad +11+1+14+5=76.$$

The record pertaining to Fred L. Kane can then be assigned to address 76 (or, what is more usual, $T+76R$, where T is the address of the beginning of the file and R is the number of machine words occupied by a record). The computation of an address is performed at the time the record is initially stored, and on all later occasions where access to Fred L. Kane's record is desired.

The calculation method is obviously very efficient in terms of computer time, and even for space, because no dictionary has to be constructed for the key item. It is also a good example of the close relationship between storage and retrieval in data processing. The method, however, has two inherent difficulties, the overcoming of which is an integral part of the programmer's art. The first inherent difficulty is that some storage space goes unused. As a result of the computation method used for the storage of Fred L. Kane's record, hardly any records will be stored in the first 40 or so record spaces; now and then one will encounter an isolated record belonging to someone named "Abe C. Abba." This difficulty can be alleviated by appropriately altering the computation (e.g., subtract 40 from all computed address numbers greater than 40).

Another difficulty, almost unavoidable, is that some records will have the same addresses. The record for "Frank D. Lee" has to have the same address as that for Fred L. Kane because the names contain the same letters; but also, even the name "Abraham C. Black," though containing different letters, nonetheless has a computed address of 76. A programmer who knows his data base has many possible ways to encourage records to distribute themselves evenly in an allotted storage space; but regardless of the programmer's cleverness, some space will be unfilled and some records will be assigned to the same addresses.

When storage space is left unused, it can be accepted as the "cost" of using an efficient method, but when records are consigned to the same address, a remedy must be found, otherwise the latest record at such an address will be stored there and will erase the record previously stored, which cannot be tolerated. Here again, many remedies are available, usually involving the creation of storage space for overflow. The location of the overflow table is stored in the program, and it has, let's say, an absolute core memory address of 1501, and that each record fills 2 machine words of memory. Thereupon the procedure would be something like the following:

1. As each record's address is computed from its key item value, the storage space area at the computed address is tested. If it is empty the record is stored there.
2. If the space is not empty, the second record to be assigned to it is

placed at 1501, the beginning record of the overflow table. The address 1501 is now stored in an item of the original record assigned to the computed address. The number 1501 in this case is a *pointer*, because it will direct a subsequently operating retrieval program to the location of the second record. (We have more to say about pointers in the discussion to follow on list structure.)

3. The next time the overflow table is used, the program should not store the record at 1501, which is occupied. Since a record is 2 machine words in length, the available address in the table can be computed by adding 2 to the last occupied address. Thus, the number 1503 is stored in a special location to serve as a pointer the next time there is an address coincidence, and each time another overflow space is occupied the pointer value will be incremented by 2.

The use of overflow storage in this manner detracts somewhat from the efficiency of this method organizing data; however, if one is astute enough to invent a computation algorithm that will give every storage space a nearly equal probability of being occupied, the detraction from efficiency should be small.

List Structure. One of the curiosities of the history of programming is that stored-program computers were on the scene for more than 5 years before list processing was developed as a means of handling stored data. The *list*, as we are about to see, is a device elegantly suited to the handling of data in core memory. Evidently, many of the storage and processing techniques in computing's early days were anthropomorphic, i.e., analogues of a physical storage set-up that a programmer could visualize in terms of his own pencil-and-paper operations. And when there finally came a processing method uniquely suited to computers, it was heralded as a major discovery. To quote Sammet (1969):

> One of the most significant events that has ever occurred in programming was the development of the concept of list processing by . . . (Shaw) . . . Newell and Simon (1956) . . . [Its] first major use . . . was for proving theorems in the propositional calculus and . . . for playing chess. . . .

Clerical workers are familiar with the ease of manually adding and deleting records from an alphabetically organized file. Yet, oddly, until the advent of list processing there was not an easy way to perform this task with a computer. When adding a record manually to a file, one simply shoves the alphabetically greater records to the back of the file and inserts the new record. In core memory there did not exist a convenient electronic means of "shoving to the back of the file." Usually the process of adding new records was accomplished by reading the records into core from one tape, adding each new record in its place, and copying the entire file on a second tape. It is probable that *some* programmers, at some time before Simon, Newell, and Shaw, thought of the idea of using "pointers" for record insertion, a technique that can be carried out as follows:

1. Determine where, in an alphabetical file, a given new record should be inserted.

2. Store the new record in an arbitrary location (perhaps at the end of the file). Transfer the address of that location to a *pointer item* in the record alphabetically prior to where the new record would have been, had it been inserted.

3. When searching the file, later on, check the pointer item of each record to determine whether or not it is followed by an item added via steps (1) and (2). (Note: *Pointer* is the standard term for an item value that is the address of any subsequent record not immediately following a given record.)

This way of inserting records would be hopelessly cumbersome in a manual file. It is not, however, in core memory—whose random access construction makes a distant part of memory as quickly accessible as an immediately adjacent part.

The essence of list structure is that records do not have to be physically in sequence in order to be logically in sequence. This idea is illustrated in Figure 8.3, where the storage of records for fictitious racehorses is schematically depicted. The file has the appearance of being completely unstructured. But this is only an appearance, for each record has a pointer to the address of the next record in the file; if these pointers are traced from record to record, it will be found that the records are in alphabetical order. At the beginning of the file, at address 4000, two addresses are stored. The one on the left is the address of the first record, alphabetically, in the file. At the right is the address of the *space list*, for all the empty record slots are kept linked by pointers; we shall see why in a moment.

When a new record (that of a horse named "Salmonella") is added to the file, the procedure is as follows:

1. Starting with address 4031, procured from the left half of 4000, the program works its way through the file by following the pointers; the name "Salmonella" is compared with each name in turn until the proper alphabetical location is found. (Note: in a really large file a table of starting addresses for various portions of the alphabet can be maintained, so that it would be unnecessary to

214   **Information Retrieval Systems—Data**

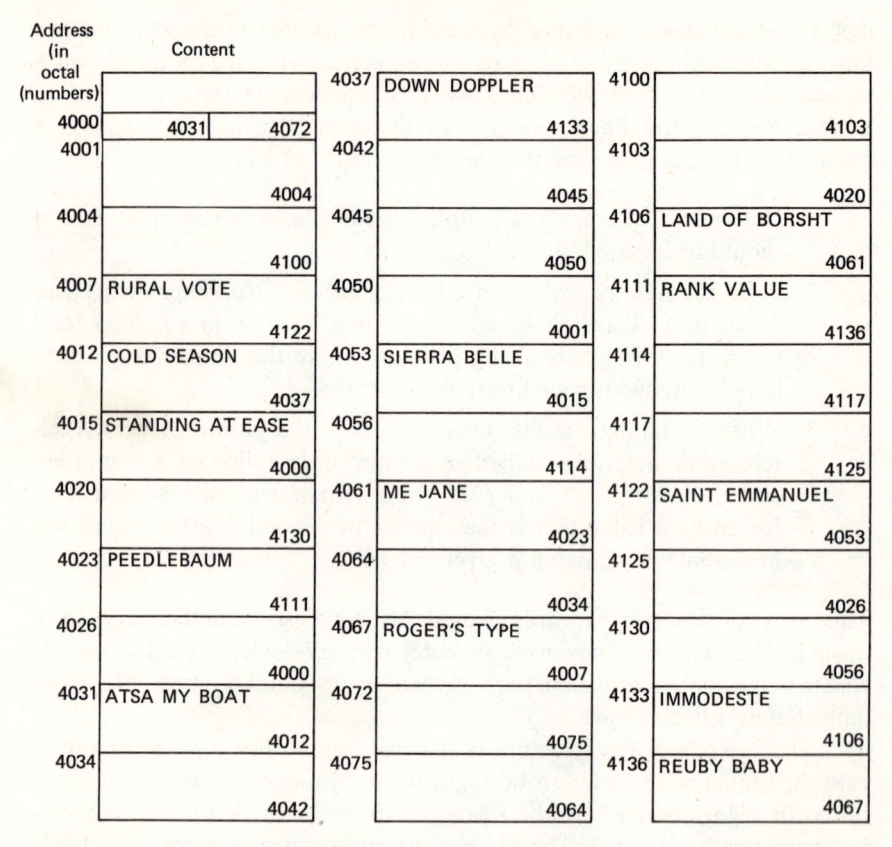

Address (in octal numbers)	Content					
4000	4031	4072	4037	DOWN DOPPLER	4100	
4001					4133	
			4042		4103	
						4103
		4004			4020	
4004			4045		4106	LAND OF BORSHT
		4100		4050		4061
4007	RURAL VOTE		4050		4111	RANK VALUE
		4122		4001		4136
4012	COLD SEASON		4053	SIERRA BELLE	4114	
		4037		4015		4117
4015	STANDING AT EASE		4056		4117	
		4000		4114		4125
4020			4061	ME JANE	4122	SAINT EMMANUEL
		4130		4023		4053
4023	PEEDLEBAUM		4064		4125	
		4111		4034		4026
4026			4067	ROGER'S TYPE	4130	
		4000		4007		4056
4031	ATSA MY BOAT		4072		4133	IMMODESTE
		4012		4075		4106
4034			4075		4136	REUBY BABY
		4042		4064		4067

Figure 8.3. List storage of Records for Racehorses.

compare a new record's key item with those of most of the records in the file.)

2. Once the alphabetical location of the "Salmonella" record is established, an empty space in which to store it is obtained by reference to the right half of address 4000, which contains the beginning of the space list. The record is stored at address 4072. The old pointer (4075) at that address is placed in the right half of 4000 to indicate where the next record is to be stored.

3. It has already been established that the "Salmonella" record is alphabetically between that for Saint Emmanuel and that for Sierra Belle. The pointers must be changed accordingly. The pointer belonging to Saint Emmanuel is changed from 4053 to 4072, and the value 4053 (which points to Sierra Belle) is stored in the "Salmonella" record.

For each record added to the list-structured file, 3 pointer values must be changed, that of the newly stored record, that of the record that alphabetically precedes it, and that stored in 4000 to indicate the beginning of the space list. The process of deletion can be seen to involve exactly the reverse steps. In the example given above, deletion of the "Salmonella" record would involve setting the pointer at 4072 back to whatever value is stored at 4000, changing the value at 4000 back to 4072, and re-establishing the link from Saint Emmanuel to Sierra Belle. Notice that, from a programming viewpoint, the "Salmonella" record need not actually be erased when it is deleted; once its address is put on the space list, the record is, by definition, not in the file. Actual erasing, of course, will take place the next time a new record is stored at that core memory location.*

One advantage of maintaining a space list can now be seen: it removes the need for erasing or otherwise flagging an available storage slot. If such flagging or erasing were used, the program would have to hunt for unoccupied space each time a new record is stored, and the hunt could prove lengthy in a nearly full file. With a space list, access to an unoccupied address is immediate every time. The program is able to sense when storage is completely filled because the pointer in the last remaining unoccupied space is set at 4000 (note address 4026 in Figure 8.3), which the program "knows" is a forbidden location for record storage. A consequence of always working with the *beginning* of the space list is that, as Flores (1970) points out, the very end of the space list rarely gets called into use—only when storage is almost full. Unaesthetic as that may be, one cannot really call it a problem.

The disordered appearance of the records in Figure 8.3 is what we might expect after many (several dozen or more) records have been added and deleted, more or less randomly. In this kind of storage situation, with many individual additions and deletions, it is hard to think of a more efficient system of managing the file and the space in it than the one just described. Even so, depending on the specific application, it is possible to improve list processing beyond the elemental method described. There are branching lists, lists of lists, and many other variations. In none of these variations does one need to be concerned with the layout or storage geometry, because all organization among records in a file is fixed by pointers, and the physical location of any given record in storage is of no consequence.

---

* One would want to erase in cases for which a non-list (e.g., serial) search capability is desired, for such a search could not distinguish a deleted item from a stored item.

Organization of Data by Linkages. Contrary to the remarks at the beginning of this section on storage programming, that files are relatively unstructured collections of records arranged primarily to suit the needs of processing efficiency, there is a growing trend toward structuring records as related entities. This kind of structuring is usually based on the list and pointer techniques we have just discussed, and these make possible complex interrelations of records that would be unthinkable in a manual system. (Notwithstanding, it is still true that simple file structure is the most common in data processing. The sweeping growth of business data processing has been possible because manual file concepts could be transformed straightforwardly into computerized processes, and this influence is continuing to be strong.)

How pointers can be used to interrelate records in a complex way is perhaps most easily visualized in terms of converting *indexed sequential* organization into an equivalent list structure. As indicated earlier, one of the drawbacks of indexed sequential organization is the bulkiness of the index; when all the items of each record are indexed, the aggregation of indexes can become larger than the file itself (especially where item values differ consistently from record to record).

Suppose, however, that an order (alphabetical or numerical) is created among the records for each item, through the use of pointers. Then each item would be required to contain both an item value and an address pointing to the record whose corresponding item value is the next alphabetically (or numerically) greater one in the sequence. Addresses are stored in binary, therefore not more than 2 bytes (16 bits) would ordinarily be required for each item's pointer. The space required to store item values is usually several times larger than 2 bytes, and thus the list index cannot take up more space than the file and is likely to be much more economical of storage space than a conventionally assembled index.

Such a list index is less efficient to use *by the computer* than an ordinary indexed sequential scheme, because direct access has been taken away; access to a requested item value can come only by traversing most of a list, or at least most of a segment of a list where interpolative entry points are provided. The list index, however, is highly effective as a means of generating printout indexes for manual use. This particular application is important in library data processing, allowing catalog data to be printed out by author, by subject, by title, by date of publication, by publisher, and by whatever data one wishes to provide for in a catalog record.

An increasingly common kind of record linkage is into families or *sets*, as described by Schubert (1972). A set, as he defines it, is a group of records one of which is designated an *owner* record, and the others of which are *member* records. Military personnel records would be an example of data for which one might use such record linkages. Owner records in such a case would probably be service records, which contain basic biographical and identity information (date of birth, names of parents, serial number, etc.). Member records would include those for payroll, medical history, promotional history, and so on.

In Schubert's scheme, member and owner records are linked by forward and backward pointers, so that one is always able to proceed from owner to member, and vice versa. Data processing programs can make direct use of the links in updating records. A large number of men in a given military unit, for example, are given raises, the data for which is used to update their service records. Forward pointers direct the program to update payroll records and possibly promotional history. Servicemen sometimes have their pay docked for this or that reason. A man's supply record may be updated to indicate that he damaged some equipment in a negligent way and duly signed a statement of charges. A backward pointer leads to the service record which in turn, via forward pointer, leads to the payroll record. (It is not implied here that any military service actually uses data processing in this way.)

Backward and forward pointers are only the beginning of the road to more complex linkage patterns. Members of sets are commonly linked laterally. Sets are linked together, sometimes directly (by linking owner records) or by having overlapping membership. An important type of inter-set link occurs when an owner in one set happens to be a member of another. This link can be the basis of hierarchies of sets, where there are superowners and subowners.

Figure 8.4 is a diagram of a complex structure of record sets, in which the boxes are records and the arrows are forward pointers from owners to members. The meaning of the inset *subschema*, according to Schubert, is a portion of the data base that cannot be accessed by programs that process the records outside of the subschema. He relates the subschema concept to *data privacy*, a facet of data processing which has been of growing concern in the past several years. Such subschemata may also be required simply as means of apportioning among several programmers the work of building the data processing programs. The asterisks represent entry points; as we saw earlier, the use of list structures can be made more efficient by providing these entry points, so that processing programs do not always have to traverse a chain of records from the beginning.

In a complex structure such as that in Figure 8.4, entry points are likely to represent various processing options, each involving only a portion of the data base. It is also to be pointed out that such list structures can constitute a part of the programming, fully as much as the paths and

218   **Information Retrieval Systems—Data**

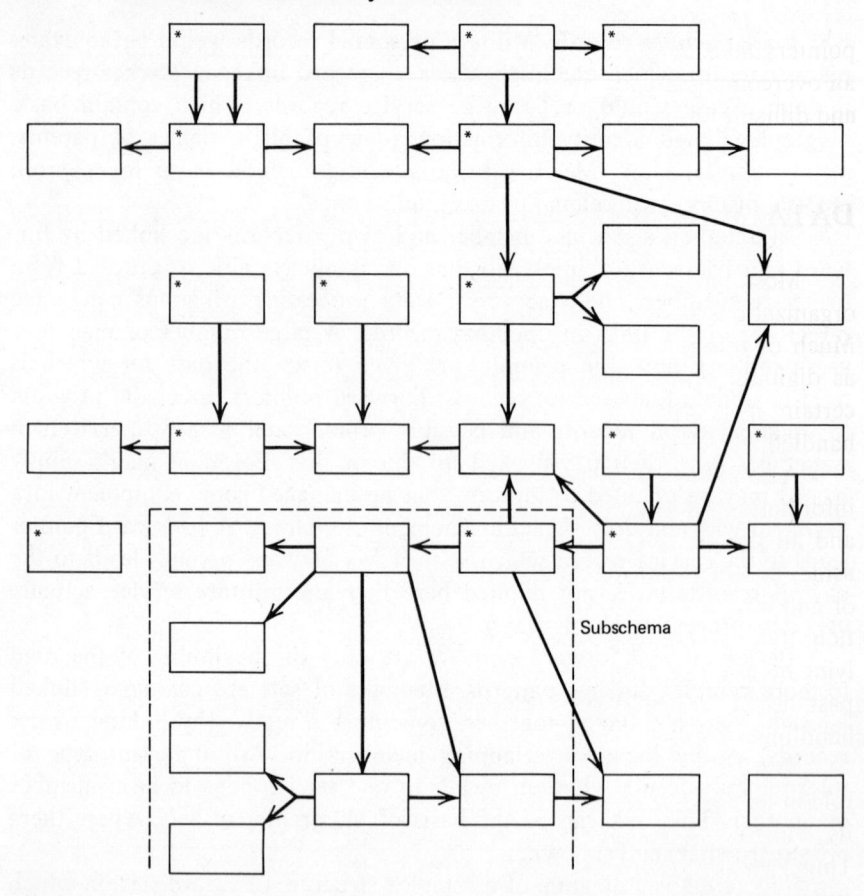

Figure 8.4. B.F. Goodrich Chemical Co. on-line order processing system network data structure. (Courtesy *Datamation*.)

branches in the processing programs themselves. It is thereby possible to separate nuts-and-bolts details of processing from the meaningful macro-decisions, including all the kinds of contingencies that nonprogrammers, who, however, are familiar with processing, can grasp. A representation of a list-structured data base can thus serve as a flow chart to be consulted by all concerned with the processing.

Complex linked data structures offer several different approaches to retrieval of individual records and items: direct access, ordinary sequential searches for specific item values, access by following pointers, and combinations of these. The fact that structure exists does not, after all, preclude the use of retrieval methods used for nonstructured data. Of course, one must use discretion in the provision of retrieval tools. Indexes and pointers take up storage space, and also—as programmers will advise—an overcomplicated data retrieval system is messy to design and check out, and difficult to comprehend and use.

DATA MANAGEMENT SYSTEMS AND LANGUAGES

Most businesses, governmental institutions, and other large, active organizations need to maintain and utilize accumulations of information. Much of this information is formatted and can be handled by computers as digitally stored files. The larger the organization is, the more nearly certain it is that the bulk of its formattable information will be so handled.

A company or other organization can be viewed as the sum total of its information processes. Concrete, glass, furniture, equipment, personnel, and all the nonsymbolic entities that make up a company can be placed aside, and attention focused entirely on the information—what it consists of and how it flows. If the leaders of a company can manage this information, they can manage the company. This, in brief, is the philosophy underlying *management information systems*, and has led many companies in the past decade to build their operations around computerized information-handling systems.

The philosophy is sound in principle, for information has a crucial role in business or in any other continuing, organized form of human activity, but the implementation of it has been a story of trial and much error. Thus, even after a decade of experience with management information systems, a *Business Week* (1971) article observes that the

> . . . day when a company president can tap a few keys on the computer console in his office and instantly monitor any tiny aspect of his far-flung business seems increasingly remote. The road to total, integrated management information systems [MIS] . . . has been hard-hit by washouts and abrupt detours.

A central problem in attaining success with MIS is that of developing an adequate balance between man and machine. The image of the company president pressing buttons at his console may prove to be the ultimate endpoint of MIS development, but it could not have been a proper starting point—as so many now know in retrospect. Some managers, like so many others who have hastily applied computers, succumbed to a "let the computer do everything" state of mind, and did not understand that computers are at their best at the mundane, nuts-and-bolts level of business—the part management is least concerned with (Eliason, 1974). In developing more consummate stages of MIS, one must work upward from the detailed level, until at the end of the development process it becomes clear what computerized aids the managers themselves need.

Oddly enough, the need for a progressive upward shift of the man–machine interface was understood by some at the outset, Bittel (1964), in his well-known book *Management by Exception* asserts:

> Viewed from a "system" approach, computers and (operations research) vary only in degree and intensity from the techniques and tools management has used and taken for granted for over fifty years. The basic process is one of collecting, analyzing and utilizing information. Older and smaller businesses do it with telephone and typewriter. The difference is in the relative employment of men and machines. In the simpler business operation, people accumulate data, do simple arithmetic, file, and remember; the manager accomplishes the necessary analysis in his head or with pencil and paper. As mechanical devices are incorporated into the process, people operate the machines and perform progressively higher-level analytical and managerial functions. In every case, the most effective system and best employment of men and machines represents a balance. . . .

The progressive evolution from a state of having to instruct computers in meticulous detail up to a state of being able to give computers sweeping commands has been traced out in Chapter Four, under the subsection on higher-level languages. We must briefly return to this subject, for the difficulty of developing languages which can be used by *nonprogrammers* to instruct computers has been a large part of the frustration in MIS. Management people, generally, would not be expected to have the computer knowledge of a programmer. If by chance a manager did have such knowledge, he would not have the time to put it to use. Writing programs is an inefficient way to communicate with computers—even for programmers, who, after all, originally developed higher-level languages to make their own work easier. But using higher-level languages (commonly called *procedural languages* because they are used to outline a sequence of processing steps that the computer will carry out) is still program writing, and is at the very least not the sort of activity in which a busy executive would want to get bogged down.

Developing a language that is both simple and understandable to any intelligent person, regardless of his specialty, and yet a language that enables one to tap nearly as much of the power and versatility of the computer as a programmer can tap has been a core problem in MIS—as, indeed, it has been a core problem in many other large-scale computer applications. Such a language must free one from having to think in terms of detailed procedures. A programmer using a precedural language will find himself thinking along lines such as: "Let's see, I will store this many bytes from disk track 22 at location 3000, changing the format from this to that, after which I will access it in such-and-such fashion to retrieve items satisfying this list of criteria." The question now is: Is there a way by which a nonprogrammer can make use of what the programmer has produced in this instance by typing via on-line keyboard something like: RETRIEVE (RECORDS): WITH (ITEM 4 less than 5.0) AND (ITEM 6 equal to 100) AND (ITEM 11 equal to SG-14).? Can a computer be instructed to do things in this manner, so that one need not worry about bytes, formats, storage locations, modes of access, and the exact sequence in which various things are done? The answer is a qualified "yes," qualified because, as we shall see, it gives the power of computer usage not so much to managerial people as to auditors and clerks. Still, this represents progress which may eventually lead to MIS in the sense visualized in the foregoing quotation from *Business Week*.

Making such a capability possible has been the purpose of numerous software packages called *data management systems*. The generic names for these packages are about as diverse as the individual packages themselves. The CODASYL (1971) Systems Committee uses the term "generalized data base management systems." Other generic terms are *file management systems, generalized information retrieval systems, information management systems*, and so on. Herein we use *data management systems*, because it is sufficiently specific, as to type of system, while also brief.* A term such as *information management systems* could be construed to pertain to systems that include nonformatted or narrative information, which is hardly ever true of this family of systems.

The CODASYL** Systems Committee's 1971 report, *Feature Analysis of Generalized Data Base Management Systems*, points out two major classes, host language systems and self-contained systems, the latter class being the more oriented towards use by nonprogrammers. Host language systems are usually built upon the facilities of an already existing procedural language, such as COBOL (Common Business-Oriented Language), and represent another milestone on the road to making data processing easier for programmers themselves to carry out. Contrasting the capabilities of self-contained systems with those of host language systems, the CODASYL report explains:

> The self-contained capabilities . . . are aimed at handling a certain *set* of data base functions in such a way that conventional procedural program-

---
* It is interesting and refreshing to find one recent book on computers in management whose index contains none of these terms (Lucas, 1973). The book is cited here for its different and seemingly valid point of view (see references at end of chapter).
** Conference on Data Systems Languages

ming is not required. A function in this set is always a high level one which might be programmed many times and which experience over the years has shown can be generalized—namely, programmed once with a high level language provided to express the various parameters of the function. The capability to mix conditions and actions as the programmer wishes is replaced by a preprogrammed or built-in processing algorithm so that the amount of writing required by the user is minimized. For this reason a system with such capabilities is sometimes called nonprocedural, to indicate that the user does not exercise control over the sequence of detailed steps the system uses to process his requirements. Most significantly, he has no control over the sequence in which data are examined and moved from one level of memory to another or even from one area to another within high speed memory.

. . . The most commonly provided self-contained capabilities identified by the Systems Committee are the functions of interrogation and update. Interrogation is here defined to subsume the processes of data selection, sorting, and report formatting. The interrogation function is one which has been very frequently generalized. . . . The language of the interrogation function is sometimes called a generalized query language. Systems providing this kind of function are also referred to as generalized information retrieval systems. . . .

In addition to interrogation and update, file creation and file restructuring are given as common data management functions.

The CODASYL report frequently uses the adjective "generalized" in reference to a data base function, and also speaks of the "various parameters" thereof. What they are alluding to here is an important factor that justifies the building of a data management system, i.e., generalizing its various processing capabilities so that they can be useful to many users with different kinds of processing to be done. We can illustrate what it means to generalize a function in terms of what the CODASYL report states is one of the most commonly provided capabilities, interrogation ". . . defined to subsume . . . data selection, sorting, and report formatting. . . ."

What, for this function, is the bare minimum that has to be done that will bring satisfaction to some user? First, some auxiliary storage area has to be specified (the data are unlikely to be already present in core memory), and an address therein provided. Then, an indication of the quantity (number of bytes, or words) to be selected is required, plus an indication of which item is to be the basis of a sort, plus a specification of what items are to be included in the output, plus, finally, a request for type of output (printer, CRT, etc.).

Most users will want more than this, but note that even in this simplest possible fulfillment of the function, certain choices have to be made by the user and a means must be provided to route these choices to the computer. Auxiliary storage addresses will often be indicated simply by giving the name of the file (the computer system will have a dictionary somewhere by which the actual address may be looked up). The sort item may be specified by giving its name, and so on. The user inputs names, numbers, or relational statements (such as "item value greater than or equal to 15") at a keyboard or other input device, and these specifications are what the CODASYL report refers to as "parameters." The program is written so that it can vary its action appropriately according to what the parameters are; for example, when a given body of data is stored in several widely spaced tracks (again, information likely to be found in a dictionary), the program is written to automatically perform several read operations instead of one. The user in such a case will not only *not* have to specify a change away from a single read operation, but is likely to be completely unaware of the fact that the computer is doing extra things for him. (Such things do, however, eventually show up in the user's bill for computer time.)

Many users will want more than a simple "get, sort, and list" service. For example, some users will not want *all* of a specified body of data, but some undetermined fraction of it—those that the program finds meet certain criteria given by the user, as parameters. Some users will have sorting requirements that are not straightforward; there must be a mechanism by which the user can express what sorting order he prefers, again through parameters. Some users might want output consisting of conditionally selected parts of the information on each record, and might want some of it on the first line of print, and the rest on a second line. The writers of such parameter-controlled programs try to anticipate as many *reasonable* user requirements as they can, and will include the corresponding routines. This, then, is the essence of a generalized, parameter-controlled program.

There is a price to be paid, however, if such programs become *too* generalized. As the number of user options grows, so does the complexity of the parameter system, and so does the thickness of the user's manual. Learning to use the available parameters can become such a chore that most users may restrict their scope to just a few of them—thus, losing the full generality of the system. This provides us with a glimpse, from another angle, of the great difficulty of giving a busy executive a convenient personal avenue to the computer. It is true that typing out a list of parameters may be far easier than specifying in detail each action of the computer. But there is still enough involved that a manager is likely to seek the usual solution: hire someone to learn the parameters and use the data management system.

What makes the foregoing even more likely is that managers, as Olle

(1970) reports, tend to have "unpredefinable" information needs. He states:

> ... The predefinable information needs tend to be those of the lower levels in the management hierarchy, and are therefore those most frequently handled with conventional programming techniques. However, several organizations are handling their predefinable needs to their satisfaction and are anxious to give a more timely response to their unpredefinable information needs, which usually originate from higher management echelons. In this case a timely response would often mean a matter or hours, rather than the several days or weeks which are usually required to write and check out a procedural program. ...

Unhappily, a "matter of hours" is still an appreciable amount of time, still distant from the instant MIS that people visualized in the beginning.

In the same article, Olle portrays a spectrum of data management system users, dependent to varying degrees on their knowledge of programming and of the detailed nature of the data base and the system that handles it. Olle's list,* in brief, proceeding from most knowledgeable to least, is:

1. *Data Base Administrator.* A data base that is shared by a number of users requires some one person who knows the data and the system well enough to have prime responsibility for it. This person has a background in conventional programming, and is able to create and change the data structure.
2. *Applications Programmer.* He is the typical user of host language systems and would be responsible for writing procedural programs which operate on the data base.
3. *Specifier User.* The user at whom self-contained systems are aimed need not be a programmer, but is required to make use of the data management system in a highly flexible or nonroutine way. This person, who probably would have some knowledge of programming, would be able to cope with most of the unpredefinable information needs mentioned above.
4. *Parametric User.* Many users now exist who have no knowledge of programming or the nature of the system, but whose jobs call for the more routine usages of data management systems. Very often they are on-line users at remote points. Examples of parametric

---

* Some people on the list are more in the role of serving users than of being users; it was evidently thought convenient to define anyone who accesses the data base, for whatever reason, as a user.

users today are airline clerks, stockroom clerks, bank tellers, and so on.

Data Management Packages—Some Examples. To round out the discussion of data management systems, we describe four software packages—one for a host language system and three for self-contained systems. *Package*, a term widely used in computer field, refers to those elements of a system or subsystem (program coding, terminology, manuals, format and other specifications) that can be abstracted from hardware; only in this way can software be marketed without also having to sell equipment. When a package becomes implemented on appropriate hardware, it then becomes a system. The specific packages to be described are (*a*) Integrated Data Store (IDS) of Honeywell Information Systems, (*b*) Time-Shared Data Management System (TDMS) of System Development Corporation, (*c*) User Language/1 (UL/1) of the Radio Corporation of America, and (*d*) System for Processing and Analysis (SPAN) of Becker and Hayes, Inc.* The data for the first three of these were excerpted (with deletions and slight changes) from the CODASYL (1971) report.

IDS, in its simplest sense, is a technique of data record organization which allows the application of specialized storage, retrieval, and update methods. The user defines the hierarchical relationships among the data elements (i.e., records, items) with which the application he is programming is concerned and specifies the methods of access to be applied. Thus, IDS is a data storage and retrieval system by which data structure is tailored by the user to particular application needs.

Typically, IDS implementations are designed to operate together with COBOL as a host language. Within this symbiotic relationship, language elements relating to IDS functions describe the storage, retrieval, and update functions relating to data stored on direct access devices. The host language facilities are used to define all other data manipulation, validation, and reporting functions.

Generation of the object code for the application can be looked on as requiring two phases. In the first, the IDS language elements are processed to produce host language coding reflecting the requirements of those elements. The second phase is a standard host language compilation. (See discussion of program compilation and/or high-level languages in Chapter Four.)

---

* Some of these packages are no longer in use. But the examples given are not intended to be a source of information for potential package users, but to illustrate what ingredients go into a data management system. These ingredients are bound to be present in contemporary systems. Potential package users should consult up-to-date books on business data processing or management information systems.

The options available to an IDS programmer are to a great extent defined by the host language and the operating system under which the generated code must operate.

The basic structural element of an IDS file is a *chain*. A chain contains one *master* group and any number of *detail* groups. The master groups contains a pointer which identifies the reference code of the first detail group. The first detail group contains a pointer which identifies the next detail group and so on until the last detail group, which points to the master group. (Note: Master and detail groups, in IDS terminology, are equivalent to owner and member records, discussed above under storage programming.)

Data contained in a master group applies to all details chained to that master. Detail groups contain variable information pertaining to the master. If specified by the user, each detail in a chain contains additional reference pointers to identify the prior details as well as the next detail and also the master of the chain.

IDS recognizes three group classes for storage and retrieval: calculated groups, primary groups, and secondary groups.

Storage/retrieval of a calculated group is based on the value of a data item stored within the group. Primary groups are retrieved based on a pointer furnished by the user. Secondary groups are retrieved based on their relationship to a specified master group. Secondary groups are accessed by first retrieving the master and then stepping through the detail chain to locate the desired group.

TDMS allows users to rapidly retrieve and manipulate data from large data bases to solve pressing everyday problems. It provides this capability in a direct and uncomplicated way that does not require the user to have a sophisticated knowledge of computer technology. With this system, the user can accomplish the folowing:

1. Describe large collections of data and enter them into the computer using only the real characteristics of the data—that is, name, type, and relationship to other items—without being concerned with computer functions.
2. Modify data items on-line through a terminal device or off-line if the volume of his transactions warrants this kind of operation.
3. Retrieve information by simply presenting queries to the computer or by requesting reports of various kinds to be generated—again either on-line or off-line (any data item or items can be used for selective retrieval, thus freeing the user from the necessity of specifying at data definition time which items are to be indexed).

4. Manage large data files—that is, subset, merge, sort and perform other data handling functions, using a convenient language.

With this data management system, the user constructs a file by defining the data he wants to store and then presenting the actual data values to the system in the accepted format. Errors in input data are auotmatically presented to the user for correction so that only correct data enter the file. If the user has a previously existing file in another format, the system provides special translation programs to achieve the necessary conversion. He is now ready to use the system to solve problems.

First, he gains direct access to the computer, typically from a remote console. He can call upon a file he has previously constructed, the names and contents of which he has determined himself or any other file in the system that he is authorized to use.

The user can then request that selected portions of his file be presented for his analysis. He can ask questions about the characteristics of his data (e.g., limits, number of items or certain types, average values, and so on); he can change values, perform arithmetic operations on the data and combine or rearrange groups of data.

UL/1 comprises a nonprocedural user-oriented language which may be used in communicating with files in a data base. The language may be used for interrogation, which involves retrieving information reports from a file, and also for updating the file. This version has facilities for converting into UL/1 format from fixed field, fixed record length files. When such files are established as UL/1 files, they may then be interrogated and updated. New files, namely files which are designed specifically for use with UL/1 may be defined having a structure with up to 15 levels of repeating groups and complete variability in item and record length. Two levels of user are supported. The first is the data base administrator who is responsible for establishing a file in the data base. The second is a specifier user who is able to specify interrogations and updates, and is closest to the current concept of an application programmer. A specifier user may query or update a single file in the data base. He will be able to extract information from the file in several forms. Printed reports may contain values from the file and the format of the report may be either standard or user specified. Other printed reports may be tables of the frequency of occurrence and co-occurrence of different values of specified data items. In addition to printed reports, subfiles may be extracted with either a standard record layout or with a user specified layout. In extracted files and in printed reports, sorting may be specified using any data items as sortkeys.

Interrogation may also be performed on sequential COBOL files without conversion. Interrogation in the initial release will cause sequential searching of the file stored on either tape or disk and updating will require copying the whole file. Updating may be specified on the record level, the data item level or on lower levels down to charatcers within an alphanumeric value.

Files which have been established into the UL/1 format may be revised. This means that new items may be introduced into the schema for each entry and numerous other modifications may be made to the file definition data.

Finally it is possible in interrogation and update to name and to define frequently used interrogations or updates in such a way that they may be invoked several times in the same run with only the name and parameter values specified.

SPAN provides a range of capabilities in file creation, file maintenance, report generation, computation, and documentation. File processing operations may be specified through a nonprocedural English-like control language.

SPAN data definition procedures enable a user to describe a wide variety of formats; files can be composed of uniform records or mixed record types; records can be fixed, variable, structured (i.e., having hierarchically grouped items), or dimensional (e.g., population breakdown by multiple criteria).

Data selection is of two types: (*a*) implicit data selection, in which an entire data base must be scanned for records or items which meet certain criteria, but whose identity is not generally known, and (*b*) explicit data selection, where record identity is named or where type of record is named; in explicit selection, therefore, one need not scan the entire data base. Report generation can be via standard format or according to a format specified by a user.

File processing capabilities include file writing, merging, matching, sorting, and reduction. A variety of computational facilities are available, including arithmetic, logical, and other mathematical functions, along with array operations (e.g., matrix multiplication). A computational language procedure is free-form with left-to-right interpretation; expressions may be nested up to 16 levels.

Building up a data definition can be a time-consuming procedure, therefore SPAN is provided with documentation routines by which all such definitions may be preserved so that future users do not have to repeat a given data definition effort; the routines can produce file layouts, cross-reference directories, and other forms of user-oriented data documentation.

Evolution of Languages. We have been speaking of procedural and nonprocedural languages, which are actually well along on the evolutionary chain of languages for data processing. It is interesting to take a look at the whole chain, past, present, and possible future, for nothing has quite so much of a bearing on the ability of man to utilize computers as the language of his instructions.

The earliest digital computers, in the late 1940s, were controlled by programs that were impressed on some medium that a computer could read: plugboards, punched cards, or punched tape. In retrospect, such methods seem like an appalling way to program. In a card-programmed calculator, for example, program execution could be no faster than the cards could be read; worse yet, iterative runs of the same sequence of instructions required someone to manually rerun the corresponding deck of instruction cards. Each instruction had to pertain directly to a part of the physical machine, i.e., to an absolute location in storage, to a specific machine register, or to a selected peripheral (input/output) unit.

In 1949 came the operation of the first stored program computer, EDSAC, by which programs could be operated directly from high-speed memory (Rosen, 1969). A stored program can modify itself or can be modified by another program; thus, stored program computers opened the way to the development of compilers, which could translate programs from a code convenient for the programmer to a code that could operate within the machine. Programmers could now write instructions having a rudimentary semantic quality. Suppose, for example, one writes a program to adjust bank accounts. Without the aid of a compiler he would have to write something like:

411	CLA*	1001
412	SUB	1301
413	TRM	424
414	STO	1141

An experienced programmer, not knowing the identity of the program containing such a sequence, would know only that something is being subtracted from something else and that the result, if positive, is stored somewhere. All the numbers in this sequence are absolute addresses in memory, those on the left the addresses of the instructions themselves and those on the right the addresses to which the instructions refer. Contrast this to:

CLA	ACCT
SUB	CHEK
TRM	34E
STO	NBAL

---

* Instruction codes given here in letters, would have to be written in strict machine-interpretable code—octal (Figure 8.5)

The original purpose of compilers, of course, was to save the programmer from the bookkeeping drudgery of having to keep track of absolute addresses; this was especially important in cooperative programming ventures where a central person determined the addresses of data to which other programmers had to refer. An important by-product was that it became possible for programmers to read each other's code without having to depend on exhaustive explanatory comments (which many programmers neglected to jot down). Such quasi-semantic designators as "ACCT" and "CHEK" could even help a programmer interpret his own programs—which is espeically important if he wrote the program, say, 6 months ago.

Those in the programming field soon realized the importance of having an instruction language with dual characteristics: (*a*) It can be translated effectively into reasonably efficient machine code, and (*b*) it can be written with economy of mental effort and partakes sufficiently of human language to allow the written program to serve as its own documentation. The first higher level procedural languages that were developed in the late 1950s, most notably FORTRAN and COBOL, were developed with these principles in mind.

These trends toward more language-like ways of writing instructions were not always regarded by those concerned as advances, and there was often a degree of backlash among programmers who were long accustomed to machine language. Sammet (1969) relates:

> ... The readability of COBOL programs would provide documentation to all who might wish to examine the programs, including supervisory or management personnel. Little attempt was made to cater to the professional programmer; in fact, people whose main interest is programming tend to be very unhappy with COBOL because so much writing is required. An attempt to achieve the somewhat contradictory objectives of minimizing writing and obtaining good documentation is the Rapidwrite system developed in England . . ., whereby people were able to write a very shorthand and formalistic version of COBOL and have the compiler turn out the actual . . . official COBOL program. . . .

Figure 8.5 shows what a profound change data-processing languages underwent in just the first two evolutionary jumps, first from absolute machine language to typical stored program machine language, and then to the first high-level procedure-oriented languages. The computation given is that of the length of the hypotenuse of a right triangle, the well-known $C = (A^2 + B^2)^{1/2}$; proceeding from left to right, one sees the program in primitive octal code, then in the much terser 709 program listing format, and finally in the much abbreviated JOVIAL code. JOVIAL is a procedural language originated at System Development Corporation in 1959, and the examples in Figure 8.5 were taken from the JOVIAL manual

OCTAL 709 PROGRAM			709 MACHINE-ORIENTED PROGRAM		PROCEDURE-ORIENTED PROGRAM
step	instruction	cell			
01	0560	100	1. LDQ	A	C = (A**2 + B**2)**0.5
02	0260	100	2. FMP	A	(**means that the num-
03	0601	77	3. STO	TEMP	ber to follow is an ex-
04	0560	101	4. LDQ	B	ponent)
05	0260	101	5. FMP	B	
06	0300	77	6. FAD	TEMP	
07	0601	77	7. SQRT		
10	0601	76	8. STO	C	
11	0500	77			
12	0241	76	LDQ	= Load MQ Register	
13	0131	0	FMP	= Floating Multiply	
14	0300	76	STO	= Store	
15	0241	75	FAD	= Floating Add	
16	0131	0	SQRT	= Square Root	
17	0402	76			
20	0765	3			
21	0100	26			
22	0763	3			
23	0400	76			
24	0601	76	Note on octal program: cell 75 contains the number		
25	0020	11	2; cells 76 and 77 are temporary storage locations;		
26	0500	76	cells 100, 101, and 102 contain A, B, and C, re-		
27	0601	102	spectively.		

Figure 8.5. Data processing languages. (Reprinted with the permission of System Development Corp.)

(1960). Note that instruction number 7, SQRT, in what is called the 709 machine-oriented program, corresponds to instructions 7 through 26 in the octal code. SQRT (i.e., square root) is a *macro* instruction, which can correspond to any number of machine-language instructions; thus, features of high-level languages were creeping into machine languages prior to the time when the first full-fledged high-level languages became available.

All three languages, the octal code, the machine language, and the procedural language, direct the actions of the computer in step-by-step fashion—but what a difference in the size of the steps! The two languages on the left give directions such as "transfer the number in storage location A to the MQ register, multiply by the same number, and store the product in location TEMP"; in the procedural language, however, there is no concern at all with what is stored in which location. A simple line of code says "take the square root of the sum of the squares of A and B." It also refers to this root as *C*, so that a later step might use the quantity *C* for some further purpose. The programmer has no interest in where the quantity *C* is stored in the meantime; the procedural language's compiler* takes care of that little chore. The procedural language depicted in Figure 8.5, JOVIAL (Jules' Own Version** of the International Algebraic Language), is much briefer in notation than COBOL, and more satisfying to programmers.

The reader might be prepared at this point to find that the next big jump in languages is from procedural to nonprocedural languages. The picture, however, is not that simple. Sammet (1969) observes:

> The term "nonprocedural language" has been bandied about for years without any attempt to define it. It is my firm contention that definition is not really possible because "nonprocedural" is actually a relative term meaning that decreasing numbers of specific sequential steps need be provided by the user as the state of the art improves. The closer the user can come to stating his problem without specifying the steps for solving it, the more nonprocedural is the language. . . .

The word *nonprocedural* thus is not a sharp boundary line that is crossed in going, say, from the first generation of high-level languages to the more powerful second generation. It is merely a trend that sets in as one goes to higher and higher levels of language, and has more to do with the "logic of doing things" than with the designed-in features of a programming language. After all, in no kind of a complex task is one totally free from procedure, that is, in doing a sequence of steps in an order that makes sense. The point is, in going to higher levels a user is increasingly freed from the detailed procedure of storing, adding, testing, branching—the kind of "leading the computer by the hand" so familiar to programmers—and instead can concentrate on a sequence of tasks familiar to a nonprogramming professional, dictated in a language that more and more resembles the terminology of such a nonprogramming professional.

Figure 8.5 illustrates what might be called the first three stages in the evolution of data-processing languages. The transition from the third to the fourth stage has some resemblance to the transition in Figure 8.5 between the second and third stage (machine language to procedural language). This similarity can be expected to apply to the fifth and subsequent stages, for each jump in language power brings with it greater condensation of whatever instructional notation has gone before, and therefore, of

---

* No high-level language can operate in its high level form, and therefore a compiler must exist which translates high-level expressions into machine code.
**"Jules' Own Version" pertains to Jules Schwartz, who—while an employee of System Development Corporation—led the JOVIAL development effort.

Data Management Systems and Languages

course, each jump implies that some compiler of the language will produce more octal computer instructions for each symbol written by the programmer or nonprogramming user. This progressive condensation of notation is the principal characteristic of the evolution of languages.

There is also a second characteristic of evolution, one, however, that is not consistently evident—that languages become more and more like the spoken or written language of the user. This observation must be qualified in two ways:

1. The user is often a professional man. His written language as a professional man may be as remote from the English language as programming code is. An obvious example of such a man is a mathematician. The right-hand expression of Figure 8.5 is a good example a programming language coming to resemble mathematical notation.
2. Many thoughtful computer people do not believe it is a good idea to have any computer language approach written English, or any other natural language, because language usage among humans is an informal and somewhat careless process. A human listener can sort out all the irregularities of the language; at present a computer cannot—or, to be more accurate, a compiler cannot. Though an English-like language can be made exact and unambiguous, the close resemblance to the spoken language, with all its informalities, might lead a user unwittingly to make use of some ungrammatical constructions. The use of a language appreciably different from English, according to this viewpoint, will encourage the user to exercise intellectual discipline in communicating with computers.

In spite of these considerations, communication with computers in conversational English is a popular idea, and one which poses an irresistible challenge to researchers. It is an area that should, in all seriousness, be thoroughly investigated, because if the outcome is to make it vastly easier for nonprogrammers to use computers, it will broaden the base of computer usage and thus better equip our civilization to solve some of its biggest problems, so many of which seem to involve the manipulation of huge amounts of information.

Chapter Ten will discuss question-answering programs and other ways to use computers in handling natural language situations. One such realm is inserted in the present chapter because it is an obvious extension of data management, namely the use of natural language in data retrieval. Many of the same principles of syntactic analysis to be discussed under machine translation of languages in Chapter Ten can be applied to the analysis of simple sentences used to make requests in a data management situation. Indeed, the employment of those principles can be made a far simpler matter than it has to be in machine translation, by the expedient of using a subset of English constructions, parts of speech, etc., that is free of ambiguities.

A problem to be solved in developing such a language—and it may not prove to be such a profound problem—is designing the language and picking the vocabulary carefully enough that a user is not led astray, e.g., led to use words in inappropriate senses. Many mistakes that a user might make can be anticipated as a result of experience with the system, and a repertoire of error messages corresponding to the most common kinds of mistakes can be included in the system. (This practice is followed, incidentally, in many on-line computer systems that are addressed in high-level programming-type languages.)

In general, the more rudimentary the subset of English is, the less chance there is for error. A number of data management systems do have a very elementary subset, as for example, the following from the CODASYL (1971) report:

```
SCHEMA NAME IS EMPFILE
RECORD NAME IS EMPREC
LOCATION MODE IS CALC USING EMPNO
SET NAME IS SKILLS
PRIVACY LOCK FOR REMOVE IS AUTHENTICATE
```

This is not very satisfying, yet it is closer to English-like addressing of computers than anything we have discussed so far in this chapter.

Experimental systems exist that employ considerably more advanced use of English-like address than this. Kellogg (1968) uses English to query files of U.S. Census data; his system, called "CONVERSE," can analyze and answer queries such as:

"What cities in California except Los Angeles and San Francisco have populations over 100,000?"

"Is El Cajon located in the state in which Fresno is located?"

Each word in these sentences plays its role in generating the process of lookup that will result in the delivery of whatever data will constitute an answer to the query. Words like "California" and "Fresno" are in a dictionary; the dictionary relates them to the data base—thus, opposite "Fresno" in the dictionary would be the cue that its data are a subset of "California," which is a state. This cue can be used directly in the process of answering the second question. Figure 8.6 schematically depicts the manner in which the query is broken into parts, and the way in which the parts are reorganized to form a data-lookup directive to the computer.

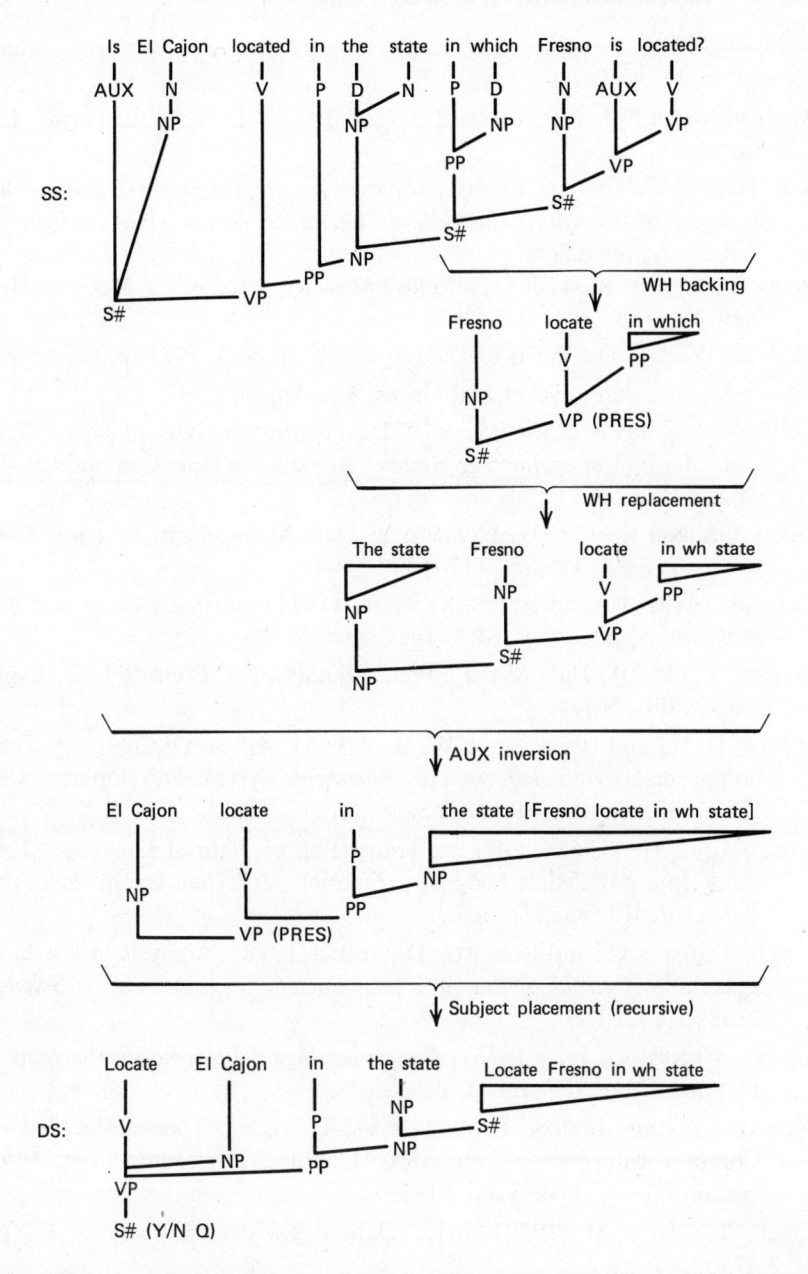

Figure 8.6. A Sample Surface Structure (SS) and Deep Structure (DP) Syntactic Analysis. (Note: NP=noun phrase; VP=verb phrase; and PP=prepositional phrase. WH backing is a structure-changing rule that moves a relative or interrogative pronoun into its underlying relation to a following verb.)

235

REFERENCES

ALMENDINGER, VLADIMIR (1972), *Span Digest*, Becker and Hayes, Los Angeles.

BAR-HILLEL, YEHOSHUA (1960), *Some Theoretical Aspects of the Mechanization of Literature Searching*, Technical Report No. 3, Hebrew University, Jerusalem.

BITTEL, LESTER R. (1964), *Management by Exception*, McGraw-Hill, New York.

Business Week, "The Perils of Data Systems," June 5, 1971, p. 62.

Censac Users Guide, Becker and Hayes, Los Angeles, 1971.

CODASYL Systems Committee (1971), *Feature Analysis of Generalized Data Base Management Systems*, Association for Computing Machinery, New York.

DODD, GEORGE G. (1969), Elements of Data Management Systems, *Computing Surveys*, 1:2, pp. 117–133.

ELIASON, ALAN L., and KITTS, KENT D. (1974), *Business Computer Systems and Applications*, SRA, Inc., Chicago.

FLORES, I. (1970), *Data Structure and Management*, Prentice-Hall, Englewood Cliffs, N.J.

ISAACS, H. H., and HERRMANN, W. W. (1965), *Advanced Computer Technology and Crime Information Retrieval*, System Development Corporation document SP-1927, Santa Monica, Calif.

KELLOGG, C. H. (1968), On-Line Translation of Natural Language Questions into Artificial Language Queries, *Information Storage and Retrieval*, 4:3, pp. 287–307.

LOWE, THOMAS C., and ROBERTS, DAVID C. (1972), Analysis of Directory Searching, *Journal of the American Society for Information Science*, 2:3, pp. 143–149.

LUCAS, HENRY C., Jr., (1973), *Computer Based Information Systems in Organizations*, SRA Inc., Chicago,

NEWELL, A., and SIMON, H. A. (1965), The Logic Theory Machine—A Complex Information Processing Machine, *IRE Transactions. Information Theory*, IT-2:3, pp. 61–79.

OLLE, T. WILLIAM (1970), MIS: Data Bases, *Datamation*, 16:15, pp. 47–50.

ROSEN, SAUL (1969), Electronic Computers: A Historical Survey, *Computing Surveys*, 1:1, pp. 7–36.

SAMMET, JEAN E. (1969), *Programming Languages: History and Fundamentals*, Prentice-Hall, Englewood Cliffs, N.J.

SCHUBERT, RICHARD F. (1972), Basic Concepts in Data Base Management, *Datamation*, 18:7, pp. 42–47.

SHAW, C. J. (1960), *The JOVIAL Manual: Part I. Computers, Programming Languages & JOVIAL*, System Development Corporation document TM-555, Part 1, Santa Monica, Calif.

WATTENBERG, BEN J. (1965), *This U. S. A.*, Doubleday, Garden City, New York.

Chapter Nine

Information Retrieval Systems–Documents

The previous chapter emphasized the clean distinction between information systems that handle data and those that deal with documents. This is a distinction that may fade in the distant future, as a result of the possible development of information methodologies that are far more comprehensive than anything now feasible (or perhaps even thinkable). In the immediate future, however, the distinction may actually sharpen, for computers have made faster, more complete inroads into data-handling systems than they have in the document area.

For various reasons computers may be kept at the periphery of document retrieval for some time to come. First, it appears prohibitively hard to separate documented information from *paper*, which is a natural medium for document dissemination. Paper is also a desirable storage medium. It is cheap,* convenient, and customary. Each of these attributes exercises its own peculiar veto power over transfer to another medium. As we saw in Chapter Two, even though microfilm is nominally superior in many ways to paper as a storage medium, the transition toward film has been slow largely because of the homely advantages of paper.

Second, documented information is perforce handled in large units—documents. The advantages of computer storage and manipulation are at a

---

* It would be more correct to say "ostensibly cheap," for many of the consequences of the use of paper in document processing systems make it more expensive than other media. Compare, for example, the cost of reproduction of a book in paper and in microfiche (Chapter Two).

maximum when units of information are at their smallest: numbers, names, easily formattable items, etc. Of course, many items of information *about* documents are small (titles, authors, publication dates) and even formattable to some degree, as one finds on a Library of Congress card. It is on such items that computer operations now focus, and, except for the typesetting of current publications, computer storage of entire documents will not be common until, perhaps, the era of networks fully arrives.

SYSTEMS FOR PROCESSING DOCUMENTED INFORMATION—GENERAL CHARACTERISTICS

The information diagram in Chapter Seven attempted to represent characteristics of all retrieval systems, whether for documents or data. But when data retrieval systems are left out of the picture, the list of common attributes among systems expands. Broadly, all document retrieval systems have the following attributes in common: (*a*) Natural language text is the predominant form of information; (*b*) The medium of the data base is primarily paper, even in systems where the commitment to microfilm is heavy (a factor which could change radically some years from now); and (*c*) Information is very loosely organized, and exists in more or less independent units called "documents."

The following outline illustrates the functions that are normally found in document processing systems:

A. Acquisition
   1. Locating/generating
   2. Selection
   3. Ordering/publishing
   4. Receiving
   5. Announcement
B. Initial processing
   1. Standardization
   2. Hardening/change of medium
C. Cataloging/analysis
   1. Derivative analysis (descriptive cataloging, abstracting, word indexing)
   2. Assignment analysis (classification, controlled subject indexing)
D. Immediate distribution
   1. Routing/dissemination
   2. Order filling

E. Storage/preservation

F. Retrospective search

Retrospective search,* commonly spoken of as *retrieval*, can be a major or a minor step in a document processing system. Generally, it is the definitive step that justifies the maintenance of an accumulation of documents over a period of time, and is the central problem in using such an accumulation. Steps preceding retrospective search can be regarded as subordinate thereto, because if the utility of retrospective search were to become zero, then there would be no need to maintain the file as an information resource. When the utility of an accumulation becomes very small, it is common to use the simplest of filing systems (by single subject, by date, or even by arbitrarily assigned numbers).

One of the aims of this chapter is to look at the retrieval step in the context of all the other functions in a document processing system. Some of these functions, for example cataloging/analysis, directly affect the retrieval process. In general, a total view of what happens in a document processing system is necessary in any systems approach to document retrieval.

When a document processing system is simple enough or small enough, most of the functions outlined above are not manifest; they are either unneeded or are unrecognizably informal or rudimentary. A small file of business correspondence would not be subject-indexed or abstracted, though it may be arranged in an ad hoc classification based on the concepts of the file keeper or user. But let the correspondence file become large enough and active enough, and the need becomes obvious for systematizing and formalizing the operations of the file-keeping process. Work has to be delegated, and hence arises the need for formalizing the procedures. The functions evolve in a familiar pattern. At the input end, someone has to take charge of screening, duplicating, and routing the incoming items, essentially performing steps A, B, and D in the foregoing outline. Step C requirements may call for more detailed breakdown of the files; if the correspondence is of enduring value, even subject-indexing may be necessary.

As a document file grows larger and procedures become more formal and complex, rigidities can creep into it that may hamper adaptation of the system to new uses or demands. Operators of document processing systems often face the painful prospect of changing a system while continuing to operate it; such changes are often hastily made, with very little considera-

---

* The term *retrospective search* came into existence to distinguish that kind of retrieval from selective dissemination and other current awareness mechanisms that can also be thought of as varieties of retrieval.

tion for the future, and soon, through unplanned growth, the system becomes encrusted and inefficient. Changing such systems in a thoughtful and orderly way is part of the responsibility of the systems analyst. The first task of systems analysis, characteristically, is to draw a detailed flowchart of the system-in-being, including a plot of document traffic and rate of use. Many of the answers to system change are indeed suggested by this initial study.

Systems analysis often reveals possibilities of change not realized by the operators or users of the system. For example, two document systems within a single organization might be advantageously merged, if their functional similarities are observed to be great enough. As another example, large subpopulations of documents may be found to need only low-grade processing, so that expensive clerical and other operations can be focused on those few documents that require such treatment. A real-life example of the latter cropped up in a hospital x-ray* system study, where an analyst planning microfilming of the x-rays (to save storage space) discovered that only a small fraction of the normal-sized x-rays are ever looked up after their first week of existence, and that it could generally be predicted which x-rays these would be. The overwhelming bulk of a hospital's x-rays, therefore, did not merit expensive processing involving careful photography, clean room conditions, sophisticated microfiche filing, and so on. The amount of money that can be saved by such findings is often impressive in cases where institutions are obliged to store millions of items.

For a detailed discussion of the functions and subfunctions of a document processing system, it is helpful to appreciate both the commonality and the range of diversity that we find in the realm of document processing. Think of the following systems: (*a*) a public library, (*b*) an encyclopedia publisher, (*c*) a large repository such as the Defense Documentation Center (DDC), (*d*) a metropolitan daily newspaper, and (*e*) a scientific and technical information center, such as one of those associated with the National Aeronautics and Space Administration (NASA). As we discuss the various aspects of document systems, we shall draw on these exemplars to illustrate both the diverse tendencies and the elements in common.

Acquisition. The acquisition function determines the volume and character of new information entering the document processing system. It has five subfunctions, which we discuss in the order of their sequence of occurrence in a typical system.

Information is acquired in two ways, by tapping outside sources or

---

* An x-ray is an unusual kind of "document," but this only emphasizes how some system principles apply in a very broad way.

by generating it internally. Some systems, such as libraries and document repositories, acquire information from outside sources only. Information centers and newspapers acquire most of their information from outside sources, but they also generate much of it from within. Such generation usually involves a synthesis of bits and pieces of information on hand, all of which may have originally come from outside sources. A newspaper morgue, for instance, can be used in the generation of information by weaving together current news with morgue-stored background information (most of which consists of clippings from old issues of the parent newspaper). At the opposite end of the spectrum from libraries are the encyclopedias, which tailormake all their information, usually by enlisting experts in specific fields to synthesize items conforming to the encyclopedia's style and format. This intensive processing of information at the input end distinguishes most publishing organizations from mere acquirers of information, such as libraries and repositories.

Where acquisition involves collecting documents and processing them minimally, the force of the activity can grade from passive to acquisitive. Some organizations, in other words, devote considerable effort to acquisition whereas others may accumulate documents unavoidably. DDC is a good example of the latter, because of the fact that the government requires all defense contractors to provide DDC with copies of documentation associated with their defense contracts. On the other hand, many libraries must search aggressively for new acquisitions. They must find out where outside sources are and must monitor them regularly. They strive to be on the mailing lists of publishers and document generators. They scan bibliographies and abstract journals. Newspapers are an evenly blended mixture of the tendencies: they usually get national and world news spoon fed via the wire services; adequate local news coverage, on the other hand, requires energetic seeking.

Most institutions that acquire documented information do so selectively. Libraries and information centers generally spell out an *acquisitions policy*, so that the breadth and depth of their coverage of different subjects can be kept in line with budgetary limitations. Such an acquisitions policy bears the closest possible relationship to the library's purpose, for through acquisitions the library becomes what it is: a public library, a research library, a law library, or whatever. Some groups, such as research libraries and information centers, tailor their acquisitions to the expressed demands or known requirements of their users; though this may seem to give the library a less firm hold on acquisitions policy, it may lead to a more valuable service for that library's clientele. In a few cases, acquisitions policy is determined neither by the librarian nor by the patron, but by some third group; the most common example of this is the school library, the acqui-

Systems for Processing Documented Information 243

sitions of which must support the curriculum, as determined by teachers and school administrators.

Once it is decided that a particular item is to become a part of the document collection, the next step is ordering. In the outline, this step is referred to as ordering/publishing, because in the event that a document is internally generated rather than located, "ordering" shrinks to the rudimentary formality of making the document a part of the system, which may mean little more than assigning it a number and a date. In branches of government and in many corporations, this formality can be thought of as the "publication" step, because it constitutes the first acknowledgement by the sponsoring institution that the document "exists."

Figure 9.1 is a flow diagram of the ordering subfunction. First comes the receipt of the request by an ordering department. Then a bibliographic search is made to ascertain what information is needed to order the document, and also, not unimportantly, to make sure that the document is not already in the collection. Third comes the filling out of whatever forms are

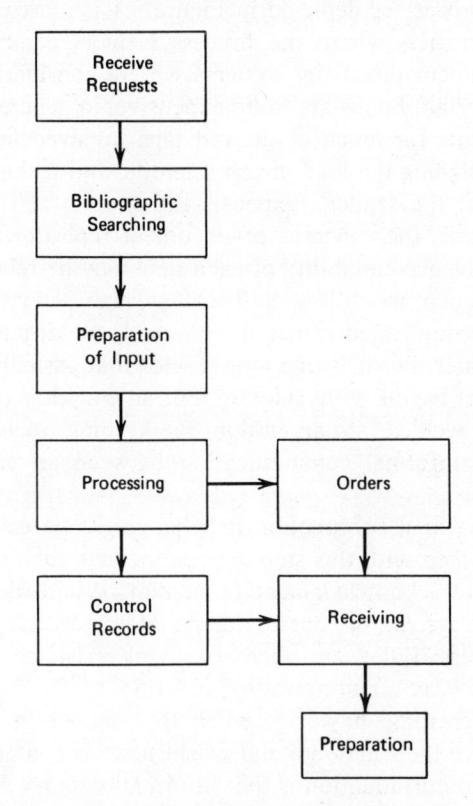

Figure. 9.1. The ordering subsystem.

required by the system; in addition to the order itself, there may be requests for funds to pay for the item, notifications to whomever placed the request for ordering, and so on. The next step, processing, is given in the diagram because this would be the logical point (if a flow diagram were given of the entire document processing system, rather than just the ordering subfunction) for the introduction of computer operations. The processes of shuffling information about a book order from one in-out basket to another are the ones most amenable to automation. Though the ordering flow chart may end with the receipt and inspection of an item, the need to keep current information about a book and its status, throughout its tenure in a collection, guarantees that much of the information connected with an order will become the nucleus of that book's representation in the computer file. This is not a trivial thought, for it seems characteristic of computer systems, especially in their infancy, that errors made at such beginning points in the computerized record have a way of being propagated, uncorrected, to other parts of the system.

The ordering process as depicted in Figure 9.1 is most representative of that used by libraries, where the process is most cumbersome. The other kinds of document processing systems we are considering have less of a problem in ordering. Books are more expensive, in general, than documents, which accounts for much of the red tape involved in library processing. Further lightening the load, much scientific and technical information is transferred at the sender's expense, rather than at the receiver's; under these conditions, the concerns of document repositories and information centers for the accountability of each item may be relaxed, and the paperwork per document much less. Still further, many scientific and technical documents are duplicated rather than loaned; we discuss this at the appropriate point, later, but it is one more factor that casualizes the keeping track process that begins with ordering. For an encyclopedia, where all items are eventually welded into an edition, the keeping track process may be little more than informal communication between an editor and an expert/author.

Receiving is the final subfunction in what might be called "acquisition proper." Associated with this step are routine acts such as inspection, logging, and possibly acknowledgment of receipt. Where documents are generated within the system, of course, the dichotomy ordering-receiving is somewhat meaningless. But even where receiving exists separately from ordering, it is by and large an uninteresting function.

It becomes interesting, however, when the manner in which newspapers usually receive their national and world news is contemplated. The first thing that strikes our attention is that information is received before it is selected; newspapers employ the wire services in such a way that they wind up with more information (much of it redundant) than they can possibly print in a day's run. The most profound aspect, however, of the way newspapers acquire their news by wire is that it may be looked upon as a prototype of how most document processing systems may some day (in the next century, perhaps) get their input. Up to now the economic constraints on the sending of large volumes of text via telecommunications have been severe; metropolitan dailies can afford such input only because the daily costs of using Teletype terminals can be passed on to several hundred thousand subscribers and advertisers. Declining costs of electronic and communications capabilities are changing the picture to the point that the use of telecommunications by libraries and information centers is just beginning to happen. Developments, however, will parallel the use of computers in document processing: first bibliographic-type information, and then, many years later, entire documents.

Announcing, which is listed as the last element of the acquisition process, is the process of alerting appropriate parties that a given item of documented information has been received. The importance of the announcement function is highly variable from system to system, and is dependent principally on two factors, (*a*) the degree to which the system deals in current information, and (*b*) the amount and kind of further processing that takes place after acquisition.

Announcements usually take the form of bibliography, consisting of readily available information about newly acquired items. The emphasis is on speed of spreading the word about the new acquisitions, so that, for example, branch libraries or satellite information centers can, in their turn, acquire the item. The document processing system doing the announcing was usually able to order the announced item in the first place by reading an announcement of some publisher or other document distributor. If the demand for a new book or document is widespread, a process almost resembling a chain reaction of announcement, subsequent acquisition, subsequent announcement, and so on, may ripple through an entire complex of document processing centers and branches.

Sometimes a library, for example, may wish to know what new books another library has just acquired so that it may be free *not* to order a book, relying on the interlibrary loan process in case a patron requests the book. Such is the principle of resource sharing, which is destined to increase in importance as the number of new books to buy keeps on increasing, as it tends to do, and as library budgets for new acquisitions fail to keep pace.

Announcement is thus the major process by which document processing agencies relate to each other. Sometimes it is also an avenue to users. Many public libraries announce new books to patrons by placing them on the new book shelf; where this is not done, perhaps because heavy borrowing of new books would render the process ineffective, a posted bibliography can serve the purpose.

Announcement to patrons is certainly a minor function in a library. In an information center, however, announcement can become a major fuction, overshadowing many others in the amount of effort involved. This is so because of the strong accent on current awareness existing there. Some extra pains, partaking of step C of our outline (analysis/cataloging), often go into the announcement process: NASA, for example, publishes STAR (Scientific and Technical Aerospace Reports) with each document indexed under an average of five terms. In 1965, the circulation of STAR was 9000 (Carter, 1967). DDC's TAB (Technical Abstract Bulletin) employs abstracts as well as index terms in the announcement of newly acquired documents (Hammond, 1965).

At the other end of the spectrum, document processing systems such as newspapers and encyclopedias have only the barest need for an announcement function. This is so in large part because all incoming information is directly routed to whatever editor is responsible for a given field, and each editor in turn has his own routing procedures within his department.

Initial processing. Each document processing system has a number of operations to perform for information items entering the system. There is less commonality at this point in the outline than at other points, so the vague term *initial processing* is used. Most operations under initial processing exist to make documents compatible with the system. They tend to divide into operations on the text of the document and operations relating to the medium.

Standardization refers to operations on the text; these can range from minor, such as library stamping its label on certain pages, to major, involving the most intensive kind of editing. In the most extreme cases, standardization can be a fertile field for application of computers. An encyclopedia has a horrendous standardization problem, in that new information about the world must reflect itself throughout a new edition; for example, when a statesman dies, the date of his death might not only have to be placed in the main article, but in all other references to him, throughout the edition, of a type: John Doe (1874–   ). Most standardization in newspapers concerns not the accuracy of the information, which is normally left up to the reporter or wire service, but homogeneity of style and in some cases editorial policy (the name Orson Welles was for years deleted from Hearst papers).

In the world of scientific and technical documentation, most editing is done at the source. Standardization here usually amounts to the addition of cover pages containing abstracts, routing slips, and other kinds of meta-information. Labels of security classification, though they may be applied at the source, are sometimes reapplied by the recipient to fit the local security system; sometimes this means overdue downgrading of a document's classification.

Hardening and change of medium depend both on the system and the form in which the document is received. Hardening comes into play primarily where documents are generated, and subsumes such obviously essential operations as typing up handwritten or telephoned information. When acquired documents are in nonpaper medium, such as microfilm, it may be necessary to produce hard copy for apt handling by the system. Many document processing systems go to the reverse road, changing from paper to some other medium; DDC, for example, microfiches each document announced in TAB, to provide for reproduction of copies on later request.

It is to be noted that once a document is changed to a digitized form, it is readily transformable to a wide variety of media situations. It can be directly printed out; it can be sent to a distant location via cable or microwave; or it can be displayed on a cathode-ray tube and microphotographed.

Cataloging/Analysis. Documents that are stored must be characterized and organized to permit retrieval according to subject. One might think that here, surely, is a realm in which the computer might come into play. There has, indeed, been numerous research on computerized analysis of documents, in cases where text has been digitized; we look at some of this research in Chapter Ten. But today such activities as subject analysis, indexing, abstracting, and classification—all of which have been researched as candidates for automation—remain primarily rote activities of the human intellect, as they have been right along. The computer's greatest inroads in these areas has been displacing manual indexing for certain kinds of documented material.

In the present discussion we are emphasizing that which is done in the document processing systems of today, primarily, with only passing references to the possibilities of the computer. (These will be taken up in the latter half of this chapter and in Chapter Ten.) However, for cataloging/analysis, it is useful to make a distinction that in fact originated with computer people, and that is between *derivative analysis* and *assignment analysis*. This distinction, first articulated by H. P. Luhn (1962) and later used by Mary Stevens (1965) to categorize automatic methods, happens also to be a meaningful distinction for manual/intellectual methods of analysis.

Derivative analysis pertains to any process in which information is characterized, e.g., indexed, outlined, summarized, etc., solely in terms of the information itself. A conventional abstract, for example, is normally derived only from the document it represents, and says nothing that the document does *not* say. It does not, for example, relate the information to knowledge in general, as conventional library classification does. On the other hand a review, in contrast to an abstract, may easily speak of information outside the document, and hence is not derivative.

The above outline of functions gives three examples of derivative analysis, descriptive cataloging, word indexing, and abstracting. Descriptive cataloging subsumes all those data about a document (author, title, publisher, etc.) that can be obtained directly from the document; sometimes this information includes the subject, but more often not—and at any rate it is more appropriate to discuss subject cataloging under assignment analysis, as we do in the pages to follow. (As concerns libraries, the distinction between descriptive and subject cataloging is treated in Chapter Five.)

Computers, lazy indexers, and/or indexers unaided by a thesaurus or other form of indexing language control tend to index documents according to words occurring therein. This kind of indexing is derivative. Any form of index language *control* brings information to bear from outside the document and therefore we discuss it under assignment analysis.

Hayes and Becker (1974) point out that there is a great deal of overlap between the concept of a *catalog* and that of an *index*. Clearly both are used for purposes of looking up information items. Hayes and Becker state:

> ... despite ... historical differences, there are good reasons for considering all forms of catalogs and indexes together. First from the standpoint of production of them by data processing equipment, the similarities are far more significant than the differences. Second, the semantic distinction is not really clear. There are, in fact, all kinds of catalogs and indexes—vendor catalogs as well as library catalogs, indexes to single books as well as to subject fields covered by many books. Finally, the apparent need to distinguish between catalogs and indexes merely emphasizes that each can be at any point in a broad spectrum of bibliographic description. By considering the entire spectrum, without regard to semantic distinctions, emphasis can be placed where it belongs: on real functional differences. . . . .

The present chapter, in discussing the various functions of such diverse systems as newspapers and libraries, is, of course, attempting to point out the existence in document processing systems of a large number of such "spectra" as quoted above. As a static entity, a catalog may appear superficially different from an index, primarily because each entry contains more or less complete bibliographic information, whereas an index entry may often contain only the bare minimum of information to permit one to locate or request the document. In the dynamics of use and maintenance, and in other important respects, it is the similarities rather than the differences that often emerge as having the greatest system implications.

As an example of a system implication, similarities often permit combination. One can have the best of both worlds, the complete information of the catalog together with the stripped-down, highly browsable format of the index. Many keyword-in-context (KWIC) indexes (Chapter Ten) achieve this objective by having an indexing section and a bibliographic section, the former to allow topical search and the latter to yield enough information about a document to permit a user to decide whether he wants it.

Such an index could go still further along the road to providing more complete information by including an abstract for each document, and this brings us to the third of the elements listed under derivative analysis. All the elements in this category, index entries, bibliographic entities, and abstracts, can be lumped together and termed "condensed representations" of documents, the automatic generation of which is to be discussed in Chapter Ten. The principle of condensed representation can extend even further—all the way, in fact, from the large (say, a *Reader's-Digest*-style précis) to the small (one characterizing word, such as the author's last name or the most frequent content word).

Various degrees of condensation can serve various purposes. Jonker (1958), talking about the small end of this continuum, pointed out that one-word items (e.g., uniterms) are most economical for indexing whereas somewhat longer items (consisting of several words) are more effective for searching. Jonker's paper was written before KWIC indexing was introduced to the world, but KWIC might have served as a good example to illustrate one of Jonker's points. KWIC's use of keywords in titles is an ultimate in indexing cheapness, whereas the presence of title-length entities to represent documents makes searching very efficient in two ways: (*a*) by providing enough information per entry to allow a user to judge relevance fairly reliably, depending on how good the titles are, and (*b*) by providing a degree of organization within blocks indexed by the same word.

Generally, the more topically remote an information searcher is from the subject matter he is seeking, the more value the small end of the continuum is to him. As of today, *only* the small end is useful in machine searching (e.g., coordination of uniterms or polyterms; discussed in Chapter Six) and, in prevailing practice, indexing terms seldom contain more than four or five words. Even in a KWIC index, whose entries contain titles, only one word determines each entry's location (remembering that there are as many entries per title as there are acceptable content words in the title).

250   Information Retrieval Systems—Documents

As a searcher narrows his search down to a few potentially relevant items, he begins to be interested in the intermediate part of the continuum, consisting usually of bibliography or abstracts. A title may tell a searcher that a document is potentially relevant; but an abstract may tell him enough that he can determine whether or not the relevance is actual. (This situation is discussed in Chapter Eleven on evaluation of retrieval systems.)

Even after a searcher is quite sure which documents are relevant and which are not, there are still important uses for condensed representations, because after all a searcher may not wish to read *all* of the relevant documents. It appears to be one of the facts of professional life today that people cannot afford the time to read everything that should be of interest to them. Figure 9.2, drawn up by Kent (1965), nicely points up the

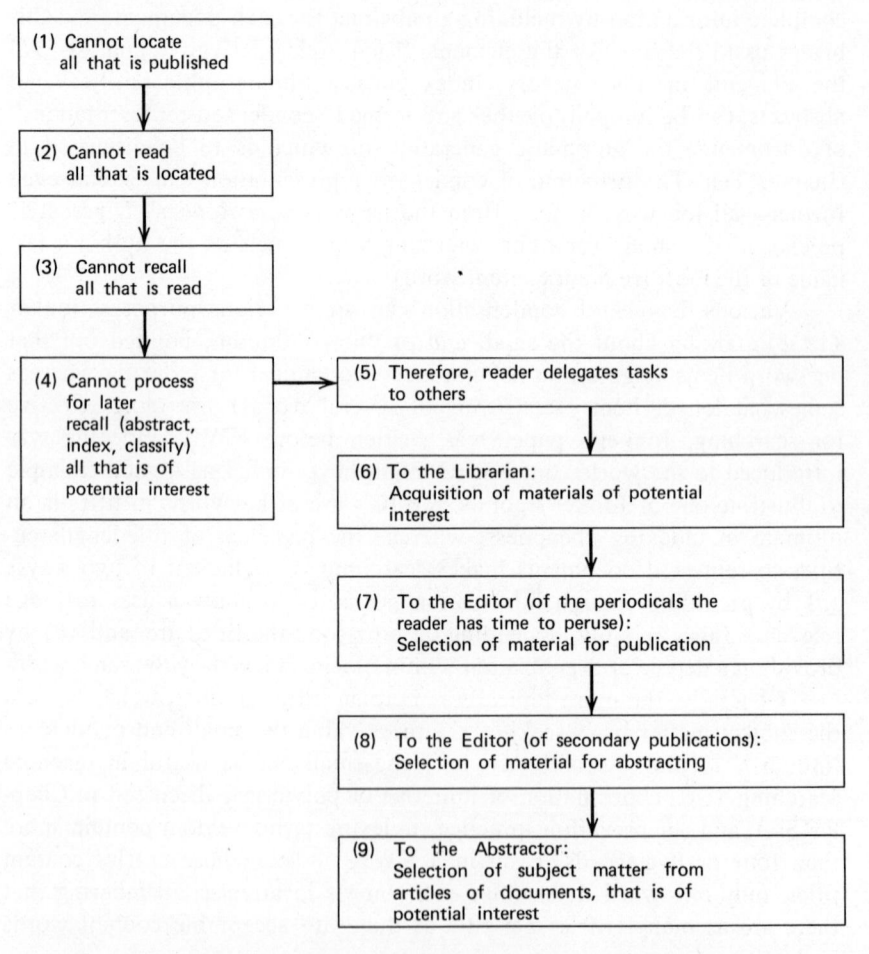

```
(1) Cannot locate
    all that is published
         │
         ▼
(2) Cannot read
    all that is located
         │
         ▼
(3) Cannot recall
    all that is read
         │
         ▼
(4) Cannot process          ──►   (5) Therefore, reader delegates tasks
    for later                          to others
    recall (abstract,                      │
    index, classify)                       ▼
    all that is of              (6) To the Librarian:
    potential interest              Acquisition of materials of potential
                                    interest
                                       │
                                       ▼
                                (7) To the Editor (of the periodicals the
                                    reader has time to peruse):
                                    Selection of material for publication
                                       │
                                       ▼
                                (8) To the Editor (of secondary publications):
                                    Selection of material for abstracting
                                       │
                                       ▼
                                (9) To the Abstractor:
                                    Selection of subject matter from
                                    articles of documents, that is of
                                    potential interest
```

Figure 9.2.   The reader's dilemma. (Courtesy United Publishing Corp.)

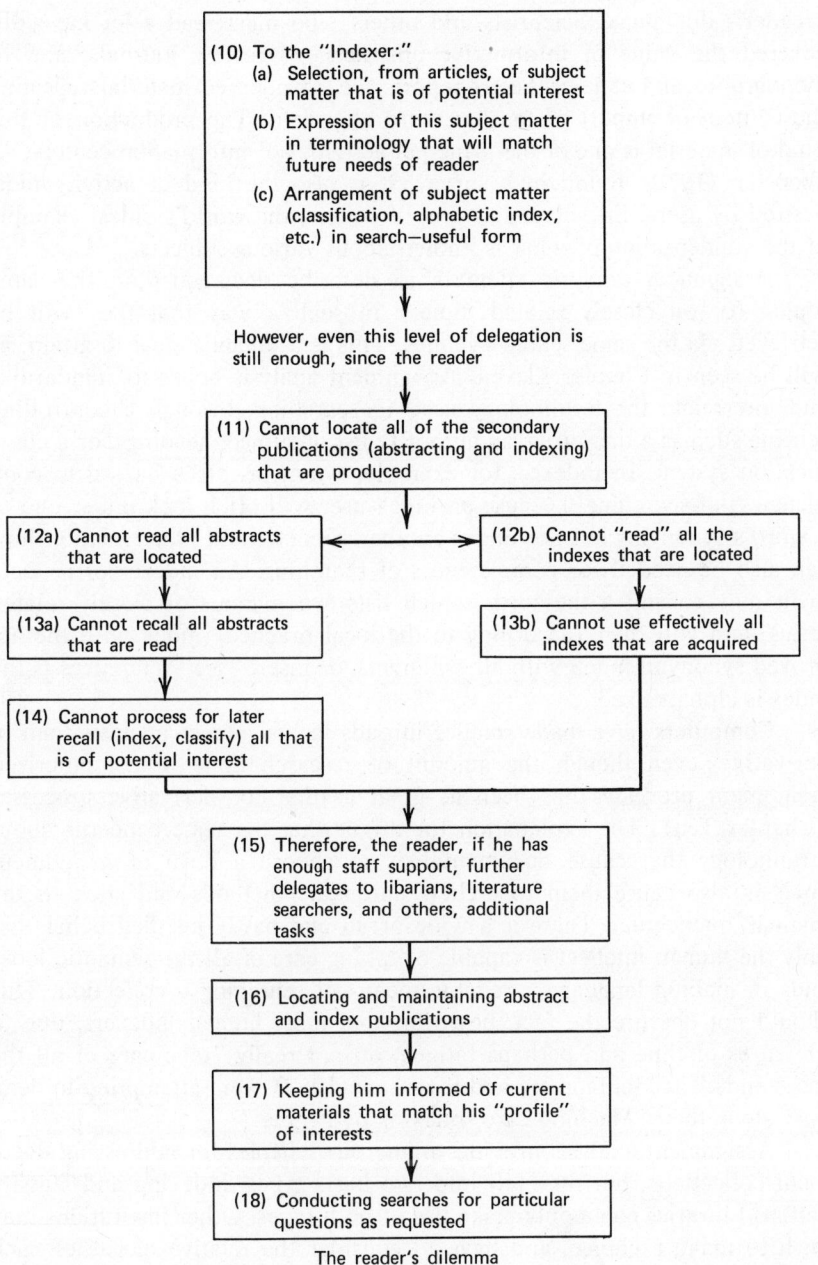

(10) To the "Indexer:"
  (a) Selection, from articles, of subject matter that is of potential interest
  (b) Expression of this subject matter in terminology that will match future needs of reader
  (c) Arrangement of subject matter (classification, alphabetic index, etc.) in search—useful form

However, even this level of delegation is still enough, since the reader

(11) Cannot locate all of the secondary publications (abstracting and indexing) that are produced

(12a) Cannot read all abstracts that are located

(12b) Cannot "read" all the indexes that are located

(13a) Cannot recall all abstracts that are read

(13b) Cannot use effectively all indexes that are acquired

(14) Cannot process for later recall (index, classify) all that is of potential interest

(15) Therefore, the reader, if he has enough staff support, further delegates to librarians, literature searchers, and others, additional tasks

(16) Locating and maintaining abstract and index publications

(17) Keeping him informed of current materials that match his "profile" of interests

(18) Conducting searches for particular questions as requested

The reader's dilemma

"reader's dilemma." Scientists and others who must read a lot have discovered the value of informative abstracts, of review journals, and of monographs and state-of-the-art reports, i.e., condensed material reflecting the content or import of the literature of a field. The production of this kind of material is one of the principal activities of information centers. As Wooster (1970) found in a survey, it is also the kind of activity most desired by users. Encyclopedias are, of course, the world's oldest example of the condensation of what is known about various subjects.

Assignment analysis attempts to describe documents on the same topics (or on closely related topics) in such a way that they will be retrieved via the same search avenues. This is a difficult ideal to attain, as will be seen in Chapter Eleven. Assignment analysis hopes to standardize and interrelate the terminology used in searching, through a controlling scheme such as a thesaurus, an authority list of subject headings, or a classification system. In indexes, for example, synonyms are a hazard to completeness of searching, because an index user will often look under one of a word's synonyms but not under another. Generic and other relationships can also be needed for completeness of searching. An indexer of a document may consult a thesaurus which lists synonymous or closely related terms, and will then (according to the local practice) index with the approved synonym, index with all synonyms, or insert "see" references if the index is alphabetized.

Computers have made smaller inroads in assignment analysis than in derivative, even though the amount of research done in computerized assignment processes has been as great as that for derivative processes (Chapter Ten). The explanation for this is that the same concerns about terminology that cause documentalists to choose a form of assignment analysis also cause them to eschew automatic methods and stick to the manual/intellectual. There is a widespread and partly justified belief that only the human intellect is capable of taking care of all the semantic loose ends in making language a reliable means of searching a collection. This should not obscure the fact, however, that most human indexers, due to pressures of time and perhaps fatigue, do not really "take care of all the loose ends," as Montgomery and Swanson (1962) were attempting to demonstrate in their "Machine-Like Indexing by People."

Assignment analysis provides numerous schemes for addressing document collections, but they fall into two basic types, indexing and classification. Libraries commonly make use of both types. Other institutions may wish to make a choice, and have to consider the relative merits of each way of doing things. For the smallest document processing systems, especially in business, indexing would ordinarily be chosen, for several reasons. One is that people who are likely to be hired as clerks are familiar with alphabetical order, whereas a classified arrangement of material would have to be learned. Another is that most business documents are looked up through cues whose classification would not have a great deal of meaning —last names, for example.

Classification is preferable to indexing when, on a large scale, it helps one make sense out of a large body of accumulated documented information and when, on a small scale, it aids file users in topical browsing. For these reasons, many sciences and other professional disciplines develop an early interest in classification, the number one historical example being biology. Chemists and nuclear physicists can classify much of their data by element or by isotope; the latter even have a two-dimensional classification of more than a thousand stable and radioactive isotopes. The "making sense out of accumulated information" aspect that scientists value is nicely depicted in an instance cited by Weinberg (1963):

> The best of the specialized information centers have contributed centrally and directly to the advancement of the science they serve. Mayer and Jensen's formulation of the shell model of the nucleus is an example. Probably the most important post-war discovery about nuclei was that neutrons and protons are arranged in shells, much like electrons in atoms. To deduce such a generalization required the most intimate familiarity with an enormous amount of nuclear data. This data had been accumulating, in isolated places, since the beginning of nuclear science. The systematic collection of data, under the direction of K. Way at the Nuclear Data Center, helped very substantially in establishing the regularities in nuclear structure that we now recognize as manifestations of the shell model. The handling of data in a meaningful manner in itself made possible a new science.

There are additional reasons, aside from those that affect scientific disciplines, why classification is so prevalent in libraries of all types, but especially in public and college libraries. One is the probable familiarity of the user with the system, which applies more to public than to college libraries. Some classification systems, such as the Dewey system, have practically become social institutions, and it is at this point of widespread familiarity with the system that classification attains its maximum value. Another reason, which may increase in its importance with the rise of automation and networks, is that no library need necessarily set up its own classification system or even make its own catalog cards, a factor that leads to great economies.

As Markuson (1970) states:

> ... One of the most important achievements in U.S. library history was the early effort to standardize catalog card records so that, theoretically at least, each book could be cataloged only once for the entire country with distribution of the data from a central agency to all libraries. Although this goal has

still not been completely attained, the tremendous growth, uniformity, and general high quality of U.S. libraries stem largely from this concept. Beginning in 1901, the Library of Congress (LC) began to distribute its catalog cards to other libraries. The subsequent impact of this service is almost incalculable in terms of man-hours of labor saved. At the present time LC catalog data are transmitted in a variety of ways: through distribution of individually ordered cards (about 63 million in 1968), through the printed *National Union Catalog*, through subscriptions . . . , and through various bibliographic and book trade tools. Since April, 1969, catalog data for current books in the English language are also available on magnetic tapes (the MARC program) distribtued weekly by the Library of Congress to more than 90 subscribers.

In summing up classification's advantages to diverse document processing systems even in situations to which the aforementioned specific advantages do not greatly apply, we quote Whatmore (1965), whose remarks on dealing with collections of news information are of quite general validity:

> . . . Press cuttings are different in nature from books and their range is wider. In addition, they are generally much more specific and require narrower subdivision. It is true that one cutting may cover several subjects, like a book, but whereas a book can only be classified in one place (usually the general, or embracing, subject), for a press cutting this would be wrong. The problem can be solved by filing several copies. . . . Speed is necessary, too, and arrangement becomes primarily a finding device.
>
> The qualities required of the scheme of arrangement may be summed up as:
>
> Easy to understand and remember
> Simple to operate
> Speedy access to information
> Permitting entrance of new subjects . . .
> Allowing for change of heading or emphasis . . .

In the foregoing discussions, the merits of classification have been dwelt on without much comment about those of indexing. In truth, though, classification should be viewed as a special case of indexing (which is universal and unavoidable in document retrieval) in which index tags are related, usually in hierarchical fashion. There are some costs associated with this, one of which noted in the foregoing quotation of Whatmore: most documents are much larger than press cuttings, and it is not practical to file duplicate copies in different parts of the classification structure. Libraries get around this by having both a classification system *and* an index; so, even though a book may be stored only in one place, the index permits the book to be located through more than one search avenue—

through as many search avenues, in fact, as there are subject headings for that book in the card catalog.

Classification has trouble accommodating new knowledge, especially when there is a lot of it, and even more especially when new *areas* of knowledge cross disciplinary boundaries. A topic such as an endangered species, for example, may have major aspects partaking of zoology, of law, of biochemistry, of agriculture (under pesticides), and of course of ecology. Such topical scrambling is inevitable, for it results directly from our efforts to apply what has been learned from the older, classical sciences. The effects of the fanning out of knowledge has been most keenly felt in areas of science and technology since World War II. The confusion factor has shaken the integrity of classification, and has driven many information specialists to more tractable free-form indexing procedures. Commenting on this, Shera (1957) wrote:

> As library collections grew in magnitude and complexity, and unanticipated relationships emerged among disciplines, and as new disciplines evolved, the structure of traditional bibliothecal classification began to crumble until not only the structure itself but the very idea of structure was condemned. This disillusionment with so-called "standard" classification has led many to rejection of classification as a valid technique for information retrieval.

Chapter Six has already described the responses of the documentalists to the challenge of the larger and more diverse supply of information. It is relevant at this point, however, to remark that fleeing from classification did not necessarily mean fleeing from assignment analysis. Though it is true that many information specialists adopted derivative methods based on the keyword principle (uniterm, KWIC, etc.), they often felt obliged after a while to introduce controlled vocabularies, in order to meet such problems as synonyms, subject scatter, retrieval of irrelevant material, and so on. As has been pointed out repeatedly by the classification-prone, some of the thesauri and authority lists that were developed to bolster keyword methods have quite a resemblance to classification-like structures. The entries in Figure 9.3, described by Fischer (1966), are an example; they make up a thesaurus that can be positioned at the beginning of a KWIC format to serve as an "index to the index."

However, it is notable that though KWIC indexing and its variants are now in widespread use (for the reasons to be explained in Chapter Ten), the use of thesaurus-like or classification-like aids is not common. Any large amount of manual/intellectual tinkering with the indexing language defeats the major purpose of keyword-in-context (cleverly suggested by its acronym KWIC) of delivery of cheap and rapid document-finding information to a group of users. Storrer (1963) suggests, moreover, that:

ACARICIDES
  (PEST CONTROL AND INHIBITING
    AGENTS)
  INCL: MITICIDES
  ALSO SEE: ANTIPEST IMPREGNANTS
    PARATHION
    PEST CONTROL

ACCELERATION
  (MECHANICS)
  ALSO SEE: DECELERATION

ACCELERATION INTEGRATORS USE
  ACCELEROMETERS

ACCELERATION TOLERANCE
  (TOLERANCES)

ACCELERATORS
  (PARTICLE ACCELERATORS)
  ALSO SEE: BETATRONS
    CYCLORTRONS
    ELECTRON ACCELERATORS
    ELECTROSTATIC ACCELERATORS
    ION ACCELERATORS
    LINEAR ACCELERATORS
    PARTICLE ACCELERATORS
    PROTON ACCELERATORS
    SYNCHROTRONS

Figure 9.3. Thesaurus aid to index searching.

". . . The KWIC listing when used as an index minimizes the need of a thesaurus in seeking references on particular topics. . . ." Yes, indeed. Though KWIC has been spoken of herein as a derivative method of analysis, because it indexes a document only under its own content words (usually the title), it can easily escape one's notice that each title appears in the context of many other titles within the same or nearby subject areas. Therefore the KWIC format suggests to the searcher, either directly or by mental association, many other indexing words that he might look under.

Immediate Distribution. Document processing systems have a greater variety of modes of distribution than is suggested by the outline at the

Systems for Processing Documented Information   257

beginning of this chapter. Some of them even have the distribution step precede the analysis/cataloging step; this is possible where the analysis is for retrospective search only. Among the kinds of systems we've been continually using as examples, this is most true of newspapers, about which Whatmore (1965) indicates:

> Newspapers themselves . . . do not regard it as part of their responsibility to provide for the public a key to their own past contents. Most of them, however, maintain a comprehensive reference service for their own use—consisting in the main of classified collections of press cuttings.

The analysis needed for morgue items is thus a leisurely process that may take place long after the paper has been distributed to subscribers.

Neither newspapers nor encyclopedias distribute their final product according to topic, and public libraries—normally having only one copy of each item—don't distribute their wares at all; a new book is treated just like an old book in its transfer from the collection to a user, although the circulation restrictions may be tighter when a book is freshly new.

The greater the value of current awareness is in a document processing system the more attention is given to immediate distribution. In science and technology, and in other professions too, there is so much more material to be currently aware of that the shift in demand toward more efficient vehicles for information dissemination has been almost dramatic. Compton and Garvey (1967) remark:

> . . . in view of the pressure for proceedings volumes and immediate accessibility of papers to which many societies are responding, as evidenced by a 2500 percent increase in the number of papers published in proceedings in a 20-year period by eight engineering societies, the role of the scientific journal becomes increasingly unclear. Its hold upon the scientists and scientifically oriented technologists is still great for reasons . . . [of] professional advancement, prestige, and priority. As a vehicle for the dissemination of scientific information, it is becoming increasingly an extremely late . . . and redundant type of communication.

Because of the heightening emphasis on current materials, the reality of many users wanting to check out the same new book or document will put ever greater pressure on information centers, research libraries, and other organizations serving professional people to build reproductive capability into their document processing systems. Where resources are to be shared among numerous centers, dissemination by reproduction becomes both a major opportunity and a system requirement. Avedon (1970) forecasts:

> In future networks of cooperating information centers, the concept of the *lending* library becomes technologically unwieldy and operationally unde-

sirable. Instead of lending primary materials, the future network will transfer photographic and electronic images of primary collections.

As pointed out early in this chapter, books are comfortable and customary; it is now an economic fact, however, that books are one of the less efficient means of distributing documented information—in comparison, for example, to microfilm. This economic fact has already manifested itself in many information centers. It will soon begin to affect college and university libraries. College presidents know that billions of dollars will be required in the coming years for new library facilities—billions whose source simply cannot be seen at present. We can expect to see more and more emphasis on interlibrary networks and on nonpaper media, such as Encyclopaedia Britannica's Microbook Library series.

Order filling and distribution-list routing have been traditional means of immediate distribution of documents. Distribution lists are found in many large or medium-sized corporations, as well as in institutions outside of the private sector (such as Atomic Energy Commission laboratories) whose internal information needs are shaped by the fact that they conduct a large number of more or less independent projects. Information needs tend to be compartmentalized, and it is feasible to arrange for one list of people to receive all documents for Project A, another list for all documents for Project B, another list for Project C, and so on. In the aerospace industry, almost everyone has heard stories of how hard it is to get off of document distribution lists, once on, and there is no doubt that the distribution-list method sometimes results in the overproduction of documents.

A more complicated but probably more efficient procedure is to couple the announcement function with distribution, to allow each user to order the documents he thinks he requires. If an organization produces documents internally, it can—at the time of the publication step—print bibliographic data for notifying potential users. Such information can be circulated daily in the form of a daily order sheet, on which users can check the documents they want. In this way the organization need not print any more copies than there is an expressed demand for. In general this arrangement produces substantial savings in documentation costs; on the other hand, organizations now and then have certain authors who like to be read, and who give their documents provocative titles, thereby expanding the order beyond what would have been printed up in a distribution-list system.

The reading of accession lists and bibliographies, unfortunately, is not very mentally stimulating to most people, and in situations where the daily document traffic is quite high there has been much groping for better approaches to immediate distribution than the traditional ones. The most popular new approach is selective dissemination of information (SDI), a technique that was pioneered at International Business Machines in the early 1960s. SDI and KWIC indexing are two of the most successful uses of computers in making information more accessible. In SDI each user makes up a list of terms to describe topics in which he has an interest; this list is called a *user interest profile*, or simply *profile*. The list may be modified to match the system's indexing vocabulary. The index tags of each incoming document are computer-matched to each user profile; one can easily see why a computer is needed: if there are 500 users and 4000 current titles a week, two million profile-document comparisons a week are indicated. These figures, which apply to the Ames Laboratory of the U.S. Atomic Energy Commission (Jordan, 1970), are not untypical; they are illustrative of the magnitude of the problem of distributing current information today.

A user can change his profile if his information requirements change. In some systems it is possible to adapt the user's profile to his needs continuously through feedback. The user is given a list of titles or abstracts of those documents that match his profile and then orders potentially relevant documents, and then later indicates which documents he ordered were not relevant. Thereupon, two kinds of information are available to use in changing his profile, the identities of the unordered documents and the identities of the ordered documents judged irrelevant. This procedure can also be used to evaluate the SDI system (Resnick, 1963).

The cost of SDI is apportioned among users generally on a per-profile basis; therefore some users having similar information needs can submit a group profile and split the cost among themselves. Some SDI operators have recognized that the group-profile principle can yield substantial overall cost decreases. It would appear that the grouping of expressions of information need represents a major future route of evolution for SDI systems. Brown and Jones (1968) report:

> ... NASA's experience with user turnover, project versus discipline interests, and cost of service for a large user community has led them into experimentation with less personally tailored dissemination systems. They have replaced the previous SDI system with SCAN (Selected Current Aerospace Notices), which provides what amounts to an annotated bibliography of current materials on a particular topic.

Commenting on the same system, EDP Analyzer (1970) states:

> SCAN is a modified SDI service that goes to over 8000 individuals in the NASA programs. Instead of using interest profiles of individuals, as in SDI, SCAN uses over 180 "subject profiles." These profiles are organized within

the 34 subject categories used in STAR (Scientific and Technical Aerospace Reports) and IAA (International Aerospace Abstracts). For instance, one of the STAR subject categories is "Computers." Within this category, SCAN has set up four subject profiles: digital and analog computers; computer software; data processing; airborne and spaceborne computers. Individuals may thus select the profiles that come closest to meeting their specific interests. Under SCAN, the individuals receive the selected citations that fit their profiles. These are the same citations that are published in STAR and IAA —but obviously require less time to review by the individuals.

It is interesting to contemplate the way in which document repositories and information centers complement each other in servicing current awareness needs. *Science, Government, and Information* (1963) observes:

> The centralized document depository is primarily a clearinghouse for documents; in general, it does not try to glean information from the documents it handles, but merely provides appropriate documents to users. But retrieval of documents is not the same as retrieval of information; . . . To retrieve information, as contrasted to documents, the technical community has devised the specialized information center.
>
> A specialized information center makes it its business to know everything that is being published in a special field such as nuclear spectroscopy or the thermophysical properties of chemical compounds; it collates and reviews the data, and provides subscribers with regularly issued compilations, critical reviews, specialized bibliographies, and other such tools. Its input is the output of the central depository.

(As was brought out in Chapter One, the *information analysis center* carries this principle still further.)

Storage/Preservation. Document retrieval, as it is usually conceived, consists of two separate steps, (*a*) the identification of which documents have a high likelihood of being relevant to a given search request, and (*b*) the actual physical retrieval of the document. Most discussion among people in information science concerns the first part of the process; the second part is very often taken for granted. The physical procurement of documents has not been what we would think of as a major problem to be solved in the document retrieval field.

Of course, when it comes to system design, no step in the total process —however mundane—can be overlooked. One can design "the perfect document retrieval machine," a machine capable of unerring identification of those documents precisely relevant to a request, but if someone has misplaced the document on the shelf, retrieval will be thwarted. This is the reason libraries do not like patrons putting books back on the shelf: a badly misplaced book is almost equivalent to a lost book, from the standpoint of locating it for someone who wants it.

Thus, the function of storage is not as uninteresting as one might think in the dynamics of retrieval systems, because care in storing an information item may have a great deal to do with success in getting it out of storage. A principal system fact about storage is there is often a tradeoff between compactness of storage and organization for physical retrieval. An absurd but easy to understand instance of this would be an overemphasis on compactness in library stacks to the point that most of the books are out of sight.

But the world of documented information is loaded with more subtle instances of this tradeoff. Consider, for example, for example, the problem of packing books on microfiche. Total film usage would require one always to begin the next book where the previous one ends. If one were packing a 1000-frame fiche and the first book on it were 673 pages (frames) in length, the next book would start at frame 674. If this book were 400 pages in length, 73 pages of it would have to spill over onto another fiche. From the standpoint of convenience of fiche handling, this spillover would be a very bad practice; in fact, it is practically never done, except in cases where low reduction ratios (or large book size) compel more than one fiche per book.

Even the preservation aspect of storage, as passive as that may seem, has system consequences. One of the foremost disadvantages of paper is the fact that it deteriorates with age. Furthermore, books deteriorate with use, so that a contradiction prevails between their very reason for existence (use) and their continuation of existence. This contradiction gives rise to the "librarian's syndrome," in which more care sometimes seems to be felt for the books than for the people who read the books.

One of the not-unimportant virtues of reprography is that it can largely remove the conflict between preservation and use, because the functions can be neatly separated. One population of documents can be designed never to be read, but to be kept—under the best possible conditions for their preservation—and used only as masters for duplication or microphotography.

THE LAST TWENTY YEARS IN INFORMATION RETRIEVAL

Part F of the outline lists retrospective search as the sixth major function of document processing systems. Though some document retrieval is associated with Part D, immediate distribution, it is generally agreed that the heart of the overall document retrieval problem is with retrospective search (which is why the terms are often used interchangeably). Ordinarily far more documents are present in an accumulated store than in any batch of current accessions, and a retrieval method that works well in retrospective search will yield even better results when applied to accessions, except in cases where terminology has just suffered an unlikely degree of drastic change.

It is appropriate to frame our discussion of document retrieval as a historical cross-section of aspects of the subject not already dealt with in Chapter Six. In the present chapter we cover the use of computers, and similar machines, in the retrieval or searching process. In the chapter to follow, we cover the use of computers for allied tasks, such as the generation of indexes, which are involved with manipulating units of English language in support of retrieval systems.

In the early years after 1950, when Calvin Mooers coined the term "information retrieval" (Mooers, 1959), the use of computers for document retrieval was seldom thought of as anything but a *mechanized searching* process. Not until 1958, when permuted title indexing and automatic abstracting began to be widely discussed, were other ways of computer use seriously contemplated by substantial numbers of people. Before that, the major question dividing investigators was whether *general purpose* or *special purpose* machines were better.

Use of General Purpose Computers. When work began on the use of computers in document retrieval, there were still very few computers in operation in the world—they numbered in the hundreds rather than in the hundreds of thousands. Most of these computers were located in aerospace firms or defense installations in the United States. Such organizations typically had documentation sections, with growing stores of documents and inadequate staffs for indexing and abstracting. The idea of making use of computers for document processing, in some way, was inevitable, for although these instruments were very expensive (compared to today), there was often idle time during which needs of a marginal nature (and documentation was usually so regarded) could be serviced. Early experiments in computerized document retrieval often represented joint efforts by one or two programmers with the assistance (sometimes reluctant) of one or two documentation personnel. Most of these efforts came to naught, in a practical sense, but, on the other hand, the fact they were undertaken was of much significance, because the results were published (often through such professional groups as the Association for Computing Machinery) and had wide impact. It became generally known what *not* to do with computers, as well as what could be done.

Probably the earliest experiment in computerized document retrieval was Bagley, in 1951, at the Massachusetts Institute of Technology. Since he concluded that special purpose computers should be used for document retrieval, we discuss his work later under that category. It was not until the mid-fifties that computers became common enough that retrieval projects were numerous. The first of a chain of them was Bracken and Tillitt (1957), at the U.S. Naval Ordnance Test Station at China Lake, California, who adapted coordinate indexing (Chapter Six) to an IBM 701 computer.

Today's on-line retrieval systems can pick references off of high-speed magnetic disks literally in milliseconds. We must remember that no such disks existed in 1957 if we are to fully appreciate the position of such parties as Bracken and Tillitt. They had to search magnetic tapes in an operation which, at worst, could take several minutes. But this capability, modest as it sounds now, was rather exalting then. From their point of view, in their hands was the ability to search, and inspect individually, tens of thousands of items in less than a minute; such a feat was out of the question manually, mechanically, or even electronically prior to computers of the speed and capacity of the IBM 700-series variety. For them, and for other such pioneers, it was not easy to believe that off-line tape searching as a means of document retrieval would ultimately prove grossly uneconomical as well as unsatisfying to users.

The tape format used by Bracken and Tillitt had index-term records arranged in sequence by index term and, within each term's record, document numbers in ascending order. The system allowed for an average of 8 index terms per document. The 701 program accepted up to 75 questions as input to the machine at the beginning of each search run. Each question was punched into tabulating cards which contained all information necessary to conduct a given search, that is, the index terms defining the subject, document number limits, etc. On input the program first sorted all questions by index term, and then the master tape was scanned completely once. During the scanning, all records on the master tape which corresponded with the sorted index terms were written magnetically on a separate tape. Thus, a working tape, consisting of only those portions of the master tape pertinent to all searches, was produced. By this technique the effective average time for any one search was considerably reduced.

The process of comparison was designed to handle only the simplest of logical interrelationships among the terms in a request. It therefore was concerned only with the concurrence of the same document number in the index record for those terms described in the request. For example, if a request called for "term A and term C but not term D," then a document number appearing in index records A and C but not on index D would represent a match, etc.

Document numbers which were found to match over the index terms defining a given search were immediately written on a result tape. The result tape therefore contained document numbers presumed relevant. It is these numbers that were printed out and furnished to the user. While the original search experiments were conducted on an IBM 701, Bracken and Tillitt looked forward to faster tape drive speeds and denser packing available on more advanced machines. Since then the search process has been successively reprogrammed for the IBM 704 and 709.

It is instructive to note how much more efficient this search procedure would become by utilizing a disk (the first of which, IBM's Ramac, came along the year following Bracken and Tillitt), where one need not search the entire store of index-term/document-number records, but only those records corresponding to the index terms specified in a given batch of search requests. Indeed, experiments of this very kind were conducted with the Ramac by Nolan (1958) and Firth (1958).

Disks, however, were not widespread for several years after Ramac's introduction, and others continued to expand on the tape-searching method. S. R. Moyer and Gwendown M. Bedford (1957), University of Pennsylvania, designed a search system utilizing the IBM 705. The file structure to be searched differed from that of Bracken and Tillitt, the information being grouped by document rather than by index term, a change which in principle makes little difference in the amount of scanning that has to be done in a tape search. (Note, however, that this file-searching scheme would not be transferrable to a disk, to any advantage, since all document records would have to be looked at in a search, rather than only *some* index-term records.) Moyer and Bedford's system also included more information per document than the Bracken-Tillitt system: the document serial number, bibliographic data (author, publisher, date, etc.), and a descriptor section containing an average of 30 index terms per document. Though this larger store of information resulted in a longer search time for the Moyer and Bedford system, it was held that the greater amount of information (per document) yielded on printout led to greater user satisfaction. This, in fact, was a rather important notion, and has cropped up again and again in the findings of other people. It is not satisfying to a user merely to be presented with a list of document numbers as the output of a computer search.

Some system developers brought greater efficiencies to their overall computerized systems by doing file maintenance and searching in the same tape pass. Barton and Caplan (1959) of General Electric evolved a system using the IBM 704 in which a master tape could be updated with new information while it was being searched for comparison with up to 99 different request criteria simultaneously. Output consisted of bibliographies grouped and printed on separate sheets for transmittal to requesters.

As experience accumulated in using the searching capabilities made possible by computers, doubts formed in many minds about factors of relevance of retrieved documents to expressible search requests. The broadest doubts, perhaps, were concerned with whether a human search requester could really choose a set of search terms that would result in the computer's selection of the optimum set of documents to fit his information requirement. In truth, some people worried about this question even in relation to ordinary manual searches of information files. These questions are so important that we devote a whole chapter to them (Chapter Eleven on Evaluation), but we also note them here to indicate their historical relationship to the development of document retrieval.

A more specific question dealt with the manner in which index terms were used in searching. Maron and Kuhns (1960) of Thompson Ramo Wooldridge, Inc. (as the much renamed company was then called), were concerned with the fact that in conventional manual indexing, tags or descriptions are applied to documents on a *yes* or *no* basis; likewise, in the computerized searches of that period, the tags were specified as criteria for retrieval on a yes or no basis.* Maron and Kuhns recognized that a given document was likely to have many degrees of relevance to a specified index tag, from complete germaneness (*the* document on the specified subject) to the most glancing relationship. This reality about the nature of indexing was then acknowledged neither by people who indexed documents nor by those who programmed searching systems. Surely a computer, with its ability to perform complex tasks, should make it possible to allow for degrees of relevance to be taken into account in indexing and searching.

Accordingly, Maron and Kuhns formulated *probabilistic indexing*, in which a document analyst assigning terms to documents applies a quantitative *weight* of the probable relevancy which each term is judged to have for the document. Such a weight could take any value from 0 to 1, representing an estimate of the probability that if a user specifies a given term in his request, he will be interested in that document. In this framework, traditional subject indexing or coordinate indexing are special cases in which a probability of 1 or 0 is assigned (i.e., the yes–or–no basis of assignment). By opening up the whole range of values between 0 and 1, then, one would expect indexing to lead to much more precise characterization of documents in degrees of relevance to the terms of an indexing vocabulary.

Maron and Kuhns experimented with this technique on a small col-

---

* The fact that the tags were typically used in Boolean-algebraic (i.e., and/or/not-connected combinations) does not affect the sharp-cutoff characteristics of the yes–no basis.

lection of articles chosen from *Science News Letter*, using five possible weightings from "very relevant" to "irrelevant." They indicated that their results showed the technique of weighted indexing, with suitable automatic elaboration of the search strategy, retrieved relevant documents that would not otherwise have been obtained.

More extensive discussions on the retrieval effectiveness of various ways of dealing with index terms are found in Chapter Eleven. It should be remarked here, however, that the weighting of indexing terms was not a passing fancy of the Maron and Kuhns era. Experiments on weighting have continued right up to the present. A significant recent one (Sparck Jones, 1973) studies three kinds of weighting:

1. Increasing the importance of a content word (or term) as its frequency (number of occurrences) in a document increases.
2. Increasing the importance of a content word when it is used a given number of times in a short document (as compared to a similar number of times in a long document), i.e., when the word has greater density of occurrence.
3. Increasing the importance of a word when its presence *elsewhere in the document collection* is less.

The outcome of this experiment was that the first two kinds of weighting were of little or no value, whereas the latter kind was of considerable value, in other words, *rare* words *are* more useful in retrieval.* It is interesting to note that this result was intuitively anticipated many years previously (e.g., Edmundson & Wyllys, 1961).

Weighted indexing is only one example of departures from what might be called "the main-line approach" in document retrieval by machine—straightforward, batch-process searching for various combinations of index tags. In reality there have been hundreds of such departures, and their variegated paths of evolution have become the major story of computer usage in document retrieval since 1960. At least four broad pathways of divergency, setting in at different times, can be picked out:

1. The development of special purpose devices. This movement started in the mid-1950s, and we discuss it in the section to follow.
2. Generation of indexes by machine. This line of progress had numerous noncomputer beginnings, but did not really take off until the period 1957–1958. We shall describe it at length in Chapter Ten on language processing.

---

* A fortunate outcome, because type 3 weighting can be used with manual indexing, whereas types 1 and 2 require computer operations on stored text (Chapter Ten).

3. The use of association (statistical co-occurrence) of index tags as a means of enlarging and sharpening the search. Maron, already cited, was the first to describe this approach in the open literature. Others were also at work in the period 1959–1960, and several different variants of the co-occurrence method soon appeared, which we discuss shortly.
4. Much later, when it became feasible in the late 1960s, on-line iterative searching was explored. This very promising avenue of development is taken up later in this chapter.

Use of Special Purpose Devices. Many came to feel that the general purpose computer, despite its great power and flexibility, was unsuitable for information retrieval. It seemed too expensive a device, with too much of its capability devoted to the computational area. (This rationale, much later in history, led to the devices which are now called minicomputers.) Furthermore, even considering its great speed, it was too slow a device because of its serial processing in executing one command at a time.

The beginning of this line of thinking came very early—as early as 1951 when Bagley of MIT prepared a master's thesis entitled "Electronic Digital Machines for High Speed Information Searching." The object of Bagley's thesis was to examine methods and machines designed to make possible the high-speed location of related items in a large body of suitably indexed material. He considered the application of a general purpose computer for searching a large-scale index on magnetic tape. His objective was to determine what kind of computer would be necessary to search a total collection of index records derived from 50 million documents. He concluded, using Whirlwind I as the sample general purpose machine, that a search of 50 million records of 30 index terms each would take 41,700 hours. Based on this fact, Bagley disqualified the general purpose computer as an effective searching device, since considerable time was spent internally in the machine due to its sequential nature and the need to move and shift information around in memory during the compare part of the search.

To overcome this disadvantage, Bagley proposed that a special purpose "information searching machine" be built which would be engineered to compare large blocks of information simultaneously, thus reducing overall search time. His calculations for doing substantially the same job as that contemplated on Whirlwind I resulted in an overall estimate of search time of approximately 11 hours.

The immediate basis of Bagley's conclusion, which involved the characteristics of the Whirlwind I computer, is no longer valid. Computers now have internal operating speeds and magnetic tape data rates

268   **Information Retrieval Systems—Documents**

greater by several orders of magnitude. However, many other people came to similar conclusions, resulting in a broad front of designing and experimenting with special purpose retrieval machines.

Three of the most significant approaches to special purpose searching devices were:

1. The COMAC (Continuous Multiple Access Collator) proposed by Taube (1957), a concept around which IBM designed its 9900 Special Index Analyzer, to achieve machine performance of coordinate-index searching (Chapter Six).
2. The Searching Selector of Western Reserve University (Shera, 1957), which was designed to utilize the particular coding technique of Perry and Kent, then at Western Reserve (see under "Formalized Abstracts" in Chapter Six).
3. The developmental avenue extending from the Minicard concept (originated by General Electric Company and matured by Eastman Kodak) to Computer Controls Company's Index Searcher (Kessel, 1959). This approach was significant because it attempted to join special-purpose digital machines and microfilm/photoelectric technology. The Minicard selector, shown in Figure 9.4,

Figure 9.4.   Minicard selector. (Courtesy Eastman Kodak Co., Rochester, N.Y.)

performs photoelectric searches of photographed digital-code fields (the regions having rectangular patterns shown in Figure 9.5) present on each minicard in order to select those cards conforming to a given search request. The cards generally contain information fields (as microfilmed documents or as magnetically stored digital information), although (as the bottom image in Figure 9.5 shows) it is sometimes the practice to put *all* the information on a card in the photoelectric-searchable form.

We have seen in earlier discussions that questions were being raised increasingly about the straightforward use of search terms (or Boolean combinations thereof) on general purpose computers. The same doubts were also applicable to the very similar methods employed on special purpose machines, but, unfortunately, the very special purpose nature of these

Figure 9.5. Minicard card formats. (Courtesy Eastman Kodak Co., Rochester, N.Y.)

machines meant that the search methods were to a great extent part of the hardware, and developers had very little flexibility to modify them.

These facts, coupled with the growing power and cheapness of general purpose computers, caused special-purpose approaches to lose ground rapidly. By 1965 little was found in the literature. In the first volume of the *Annual Review of Information Science and Technology,* then under preparation, little was described in special purpose machines (Cuadra, 1966). In the chapter on "New Hardware Developments" most of the equipment discussed was auxiliary to general purpose machines, a singular exception being the "associative-memory" or "content-addressable memory," a hardware element conceived with information storage and retrieval in mind. However, the paragraph on this subject concludes with: "An associative store . . . requires an amount of computing power proportional to the number of words in the store. . . . It is extremely unlikely that large and fast associative stores will become practicable in the near future."

A major thrust of this chapter has been that document retrieval ought not to be viewed in isolation, but as part (actually or potentially) of an overall system for handling documents. This leads us to, perhaps, a third reason for the eclipse of special purpose machines, i.e., the manifold tasks to be found in systems for documented information are numerous, diverse, and variable from system to system, and the call for general-purpose capability will inevitably emerge as such a system develops.

The *Annual Review* volume quoted above also mentions Eastman Kodak's Miracode,* which is a descendant of Minicard and one of the few survivors of the special-purpose retrieval era. Indeed, the development of Miracode appears to have kept pace with that of computers in general, having attained solid state circuitry in recent years (Micrographics News and Views, 1971). The coded searchable elements are shown in Figure 9.6, functioning as a photographic representation of binary code. One notes that the survival of Miracode is probably related to its aptness as a component of an overall microfilm handling system.

Use of Word Co-occurrence in Searching. If special purpose computers were not the answer to the sensed inadequacies of machine methods of searching for documents, one wonders if perhaps a solution might be found by taking more advantage of the fact that general purpose computers are general purpose, and, in particular, that general purpose computers *compute.*

A number of people were independently thinking along such lines in

---

* *M*icrofilm *I*nformation *R*etrieval *A*ccess *C*ode.

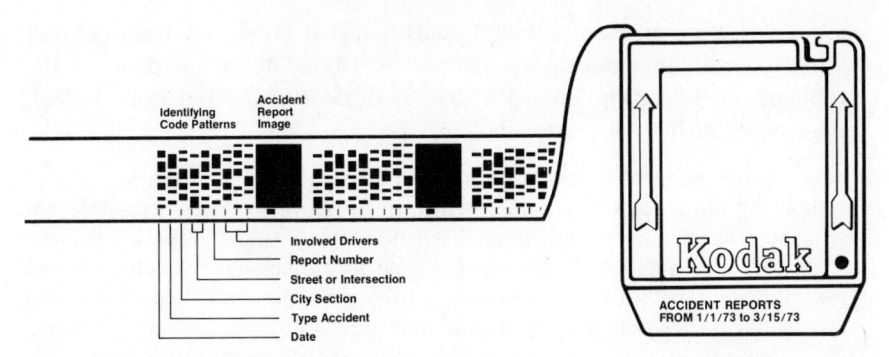

Figure 9.6. Miracode II coding scheme for retrieval of accident reports. Each microreduced accident report can be looked up according to any of its indicated identifying patterns. "Logical" searches are possible, such as "locate all reports with two *or* three involved drivers in the month of February." The electro-optical searching of the code elements is serial, but scanning rates range from 50 to 350 reports per second. Retrieved reports can be either displayed or printed out.

the late 1950s. They perceived that a manually prepared thesaurus (such as that shown in Figure 9.3) might be structured implicitly, through the co-occurrence of different index tags on the same documents, within any population of indexed documents, and might therefore be subject to automatic generation by computer. Of course, one has to assume that the most strongly co-occurring index tags are topically or semantically related, and that this relationship is useful in searching. If that be the case, one then has only to program a computer to determine or measure co-occurrence among many pairs of index tags (or other words describing a document) and print out or display the strongest aggregations of tags to have, in effect, an automatically generated thesaurus. Moreover, some realized, there might be ways to utilize these co-occurring index terms directly in a machine-searching procedure, so that the document requester need not be bothered with having to cope with the complexities of a machine-produced thesaurus.

Research in the use of index-term co-occurrence split into major paths, one of which became known as *associative retrieval* (because one might contend that strongly co-occurring terms are in fact associated), and the other of which became known as *automatic classification,* because it utilized the inter-document similarities that result from co-occurrence to produce meaningful groups of documents.

One of the best examples of how associative retrieval works in practice is the work of Stiles (1961, 1962), who used a fairly straightforward term co-occurrence approach. As raw material for his experiments, he used a collection of about 100,000 items that had previously been indexed with a coordinate indexing vocabulary of 15,000 terms. Explaining the problems of operating an IBM-705-based coordinate retrieval system, Stiles states in his 1961 article:

> ... by far the most serious difficulty in a large system ... is the problem of choosing terms for search which will turn up all of the documents relevant to the request. Our handicap has been that we ... must grope for just the right set of terms. Just as the indexer tried to use language which he hoped would be used by future requesters, so the requester must hope to use the same terms that were used by the indexer....

Stiles had read the work of Maron (1960), and hoped to apply statistical techniques to take some of the guessing aspects out of creating indexing and request terms. He investigated the co-occurrence behavior of some of the coordinate indexing terms, and found—after trying out different ideas—that a modified chi-square measure appeared to be the most appropriate measure of the co-occurrence of terms. Chi-square, a standard measure in applied statistics, determines the degree of unlikelihood that two terms can co-occur, to the extent that they do, by pure chance. Since document index tags are not randomly applied, Stiles was not surprised to find numerous large values of chi-square for every indexing term whose co-occurrence behavior he investigated.

For each indexing term, one can rank order the chi-square values, select the dozen or two most strongly correlated indexing terms and have them available for elaborating the search request. Stiles referred to such rank-ordered lists of strongly co-occurring terms as *term-profiles*. He evolved the following procedure for exploiting these term-profiles in a search:

1. For each term in the initial formation of a search request, the appropriate term-profile is obtained, which gives weighted values for those other terms that had significantly co-occurred with it.
2. The profiles of each term in a multiterm request are compared and those additional terms common to all or a specified number of the profiles are selected and added to the initial set.
3. The first generation terms resulting from step 2 are next treated as though they also were request terms, and steps 1 and 2 are repeated for them.
4. A selection is made from some reasonable proportion of the profiles associated with the first generation terms to produce the second generation terms.
5. The expanded list of search terms is then compared with the index

terms assigned to each document in the collection, and whenever a match is found, the weight of the request terms is assigned to the matching document term. These weights are then summed to provide a numeric measure of probable document relevance to the original request.

6. Documents responding to the expanded request are printed out in the order of document relevance scores.

Stiles sought independent estimates of relevance to test the effectiveness of the above procedure and reported:

... We asked a qualified engineer to examine these documents and specify which were related to "Thin Films" and which were not. ... This engineer was not familiar with our project ... yet ... found a remarkably high correlation between his evaluation and the document relevance numbers. ... We then check to see how the documents containing information on "Thin Film" had been indexed. We found that the first five documents on our list had been indexed by both "Thin" and "Film." Three more documents had been indexed by "Film" alone, and other related terms. Two documents had not been indexed by either 'Thin" or "Film," but only by a group of related terms, yet they contained information on "Thin Films" and had a high document relevance number. By using association factors and a series of statistical steps, easily programmed for a computer, we were thus able to locate documents relevant to a request *even though the documents had not been indexed by the terms used in the request.*

More recently Lesk (1969) evaluated the use of co-occurrence data in retrieval and concluded:

Experimental results with associative retrieval procedures indicate that ... [associative] retrieval is not an effective recall device but rather a precision device* in many cases, operating by increasing the weight of significant terms; and ... as a method of improving both precision and recall, a properly made thesaurus is generally preferable to associative procedures. ...

Lesk's data, however, show the thesaurus and associative methods to be fairly similar in effectiveness, even though the former may be slightly better. It is not to be forgotten that associative methods were conjured up in the first place in the hope of making unnecessary the large investment of human labor that the building and maintenance of a thesaurus requires.

Though we have spoken of special purpose devices for document retrieval and associative retrieval as representing almost diametrically divergent routes, it is interesting to note that some attempts have been made to design special purpose machines for associative retrieval. The foremost

---

* The concepts *recall* and *precision* are discussed at length in Chapter Eleven.

example of such a machine is ACORN (Associative Content Retrieval Network), developed by Giuliano (1963) and his associates at Arthur D. Little, Inc., and Harvard University. ACORN was essentially a network of resistors interconnected with various terminals in a manner that would reflect the pattern of word-document connectedness in a collection. A given word would be represented by a particular terminal, and a voltage applied to that terminal could be made to cause rises in voltages on other word terminals in proportion to the degree of co-occurrence. Special purpose document retrieval machines generally have not thrived, nor has associative retrieval in general gained much ground in the last 10 years. ACORN, thus doubly cursed, has been squirreled away, perhaps never to produce an oak.

At the bottom of term co-occurrence is the fact that document collections do not vary randomly in their pattern of index tagging, but divide into groups of various sizes wherein the similarities in tagging are high. This redundancy is reflected in the document-term matrix, and if one can derive associations between index terms by intercomparing the *rows* of the matrix, one can in like manner derive similarities between documents by intercomparing the *columns*. Early researchers were quick to see that both processes had significances for retrieval, term-term associations in expanding search requests, and document-document associations in splitting collections of documents into some number of groups such that within-group similarity is at a maximum—or in other words *automatic classification*.

Many people have equated the idea of classification with the manual/intellectual methods used in libraries, and therefore a somewhat outmoded idea. This is why, in the early years of document retrieval, computers were thought of primarily as searching instruments, and the idea that computers might also be used to advantage in doing classification was slow to take hold. But, as Borko (1964) pointed out:

> It is possible, especially with . . . high-speed computers, to eliminate classification entirely and to search the entire document file by using only the index terms or similar tags. However, we believe that this is an inefficient search strategy. The storage of a large collection of documents would require a number of reels of magnetic tape, and it would be time-consuming to search serially through all of these tapes. Certainly it would be more efficient if one could be reasonably certain that the desired documents are all located in one place. This is precisely what classification is supposed to accomplish. . . .

Actually, search operations can be made so rapid that subdividing the file is not so much important for the process of searching, as Borko implies, as it is for the process of *representing* the contents of a collection, or of any part of a collection, to a searcher, as we shall discuss in Chapter Ten on Language Data Processing. However, it appears that the majority of the workers in automatic classification have adopted the same assumption as Borko, which is why we are discussing their work here rather than in Chapter Ten.

Work in this area began in the period 1957–1959, principally by Parker-Rhodes and Needham at Cambridge University and by Tanimoto (1958) at International Business Machines in New York. Parker-Rhodes and Needham are noted for their "theory of clumps," regarding which Stevens, in a 1965 review of the automatic indexing field, explains:

> It is assumed, in the work on the theory of clumps, that we have a population of objects or items among which at least some classes or groupings do objectively exist, but that we do not have any bases for precisely determining class membership requirements. There may, therefore, be many possible ways of grouping and many possible definitions of clumps. On the other hand, such diverse definitions must conform to the extent of some similarities of membership in the clumps that they define if in fact that do define any of the existing classes. Assuming further that we are given information about properties ascribable to various members of the population, it is theorized that useful clumps can be discovered by investigating similarity connections between pairs of items, such as the number of co-occurrences of specific properties. Thereafter, only these similarity connections are considered, and the connection matrix is used as the basis for trial partitions of the population into various possible subsets.

Critics of efforts in automatic classification have often referred to the undeniable fact that computerized classifications of documents seldom turn out to be identical, or even similar to, the kind of groupings a human classifier might make. But Needham (1963) rightly points out that differences between human and computerized classifications may not matter in the practical functioning of retrieval systems:

> . . . It turned out that some groups were ones of which a human classifier would have thought (e.g., words concerning suffix removal for machine translation came together) while others were quite justified by the documents concerned, but would never have been thought of a priori. For example, the group: "phrase marker, phoneme, Markov process, terminal language" was entirely justified by the . . . contents of the library. It is groups of the latter kind that represent a success for clump theory, for they function usefully in retrieval but in no way form part of the structure of thought . . . which the human classifier's work is likely to reflect.

The foregoing point assumed a different kind of significance in 1964, when Borko, at System Development Corporation in Santa Monica, found that disagreement among human judges as to correct classification was of the same order of magnitude as the disagreement between any of the judges and the computer. Seemingly the only standard by which computerized classification could be appraised, i. e., decisions of the human intellect, was being undermined. It must be remarked, however, that some professional librarians have developed ways of achieving high degrees of consistency, which of course is not the same thing as accuracy.

This raises a question. There may be consistency of classification, but is there such a thing as classification accuracy, and if so, what is it? Suppose one formed a collection of items of time ordered material (such as progress reports), plus a collection of *segments* of documents on the same subject by the same author, plus a collection of documents by n different authors on the same subject—where each author has at least m documents present in the collection. Suppose all these items were then merged into one collection, and the key content words of each item listed and used as input to a classification program. Classification accuracy, in this case would appear to be:

1. Placing the time-ordered material in groups such that their time order is substantially restored.
2. Grouping the document segments so that the original documents are reassembled, possibly even in the right page order.
3. Forming n author groups each containing the appropriate m documents.
4. Neatly separating material in collections 1, 2, and 3, assuming the author in (2) is not one of the authors in (3).

An experiment like this was conducted by Doyle (1965) at System Development Corporation. Using the Ward and Hook (1963) hierarchical grouping procedure, he used lists of content words as input in a series of six runs, where the number of words per list was varied evenly from 12 to 36. This, in effect, determines classification accuracy as a function of number of words per list, i. e., amount of information per item. Later commenting on the results of the experiment, Doyle (1966) said:

> [The experiment] ... showed steady improvement in classification accuracy as the amount of information per document increased from 12 key words to 36 ... ; the data also implied that improvement should continue beyond 36 words. ... If classification does indeed improve with more information per document, it is implied that statistical programs can attain accuracy of topical assignment far beyond any need for it, much like some programs can compute the constant pi out to several hundred decimal places.

The Ward and Hook hierarchical grouping program that was used in the foregoing experiment was a typical matrix processing program, where every document must be compared to every other document to attain groupings of similar documents. Such programs characteristically use computer time in proportion to the square or cube of the number of items to be classified. Part of the reason for this becomes evident when one realizes that the number of document-document similarity matrix positions is $(n^2 - n)/2$ for n documents. To bring about a more reasonable, economical relationship between computer time and the number of documents, Doyle developed a program that would form a specified number of clusters of content word lists by using term-profiles (much like those of Stiles) as seeding points, each word list gravitating to that profile most similar to it in word content. A new generation of term-profiles can be formed simply by summing up the word content of all the lists in each cluster, and the process of seeding can then be repeated. After several iterations of this procedure, hopefully, equilibrium results such that there are no further changes in the cluster membership. Theoretically, such a procedure should use computer time in proportion to the number of documents times the logarithm of that number ($n \log n$).

Though this procedure usually converged to a set of stable clusters, it was not guaranteed to do so. Needham (1966) proved that convergence could be guaranteed for procedures of this type. Later Dattola (1969) explored improvements in the convergence characteristics of the procedure and concluded:

> Although the algorithm is not guaranteed to terminate, convergence has always been obtained in practice. In order to prevent the program from looping in cases of non-convergence, the algorithm can be modified to produce a maximum of n iterations, whether or not convergence is obtained. The results indicate that clusters change very little after about four or five iterations, so that this modification would not make much difference in the final clusters.

On-Line Retrieval Systems and Iterative Searching. Probably the greatest single impediment to the development of computerized retrieval of documents, aside from the expense of digital storage of document text, has been the long response time. This has been a great irony, because computers were contemplated as ultimate search and retrieval agencies—at the outset—because of their great speed. Nevertheless, until 1965 the necessities and the economics of the use of a large computer by many people required that jobs be batched. As often as not, before 1960 at least, computers were used primarily to solve problems in defense and space technology; document retrieval forays therefore had very low priority, and a requester usually waited 24 hours between his query and the receipt of a number of (possibly) relevant documents. For such mundane operational reasons,

278   Information Retrieval Systems—Documents

computerized document retrieval in the decade 1955–1965 had little popularity except among those who wrote papers on the subject for computer conferences.

The advent of time-shared computers has vastly changed the picture. As was explained in Chapter Four, a computer is time shared when it is able to shift its attention back and forth from one job to another on a millisecond-to-millisecond basis, so that dozens of users—each at his own input/output console—are being serviced apparently simultaneously by the same computer. Thus, if there are 100 users, each user has effectively 1 per cent of the available computer time. Though each user's program runs intermittently with all the others, the time slices follow each other so rapidly that the user ordinarily has the feeling that the computer is entirely at his disposal.

The idea of time-sharing was discussed among computer people for many years, but the first general-purpose time-shared system was not operational until 1963,* when Project MAC (Multiple Access Computer) was implemented at Massachusetts Institute of Technology. Shortly after that a time-shared system was installed at System Development Corporation in Santa Monica, California. The time-sharing field then expanded rapidly, so that as soon as 1965 as many as 30 systems were operating. It was a natural, of course, for university computing centers.

When a time-shared system is not overloaded or malfunctioning, responses to simple queries can be practically instantaneous, as long as the reservoir of information being queried is small enough to be contained in a disk file. A pool of index tags for a document collection is usually sufficiently small; the tags from 170,000-document MEDLARS collection, for example, fills only half a disk pack (about 14 million bytes).‡ The shortness of response time makes it possible for an on-line searcher to tune up his information request in two or three trials, based on information the query-processing program will give him. For example, the number of documents the searcher's query will retrieve might be too large; this information can easily be gleaned from the tag pool. As another example, the system can provide him with highly co-occurring terms by which to fill out his request. Where it is feasible to store bibliographic data along with index tags, titles and other data about each document can be displayed on a CRT to enable a searcher to assess the probable relevance of those documents whose tags

---

* Some time-shared systems, not usually thought of as such, existed before 1963. The 1956 SAGE (Semi-Automatic Ground Environment) Air Defense System allowed many simultaneous users (Air Force personnel) to keep track of aircraft on display consoles. SAGE could be regarded as a special-purpose time-shared system.
‡ While this book was being written, disk size for the SDC system was increased to 100 million bytes and later to 200 million.

match his request. When such information is fed back to the searcher after each successive refinement of his request, the man–machine interaction is called *iterative searching,* or—when no specific topic is being addressed—*iterative browsing.*

Those who are first exposed to on-line searching are at first perplexed, for it is an entirely new kind of information-foraging experience. As the flexibilities of on-line retrieval become more evident to them, they become impressed. As Cuadra (1971) comments: ". . . It's pretty hard to keep an information user down on the farm after he's gotten this kind of service. . . ." Arguing that the elimination of the middleman by on-line systems is a good thing, Cuadra continues:

> There is a limit to the extent to which one person—even a trained librarian or information specialist—can judge what a given user will regard as relevant to his information needs. There is nothing particularly magical about this; . . . there is something very personal about information needs, and every translation of those needs from one head into another, or from one language format into another, runs the risk of reducing the fidelity of the transmission.

Cuadra's referent system was the AIM-TWX (Abridged Index Medicus plus TWX communications network) service, based on an on-line system sponsored by the National Library of Medicine and set up System Development Corporation. More than 50 stations are connected to a central computer in Santa Monica, and each station has potential access to several hundred thousand medical documents. The system has a fast mode, in which brief information items can be obtained on-line, and a slow mode, in which long printouts, etc., are mailed. At present a dozen or so other subjects, aside from medicine, are accessible via the SDC system.

Lancaster and Fayen (1973) list about 30 such on-line systems that are being used for bibliographic searching in various fields of science, technology, and business. No doubt the figure 30 is already considerably out of date, for the doubling time in the proliferation of such systems is very short, in the neighborhood of 2 or 3 years. Most of the systems listed by Lancaster are in the United States, plus two in the United Kingdom and two in Western Europe, but this apportionment may change radically, for other advanced countries are now very quick to pick up on computer-system developments in the U.S.

How do users actually interact with such systems? Cuadra (1971) notes that persons doing iterative searching typically invoke a "3 x 4" transaction, which means 4 iterative formulations of 3 terms each. In this kind of searching foray, the time spent waiting for computer response totals about 30 seconds, but the total time spent at the console (due to the slowness of humans in reformulating requests) may be as much as 20 minutes. In a batch mode of computerized retrieval, however, the iterative searching process would have taken 4 days.

Salton (1968, 1971) found that the greatest improvement, from the standpoint of retrieval of most relevant documents, takes place between the first and second cycle of the iterative process. Improvement is much less for the third cycle, and by the fourth cycle there is little or no improvement. Thus, the meaning of the 3 x 4 pattern seems to be that 4 cycles are required to satisfy the user that he is not able to further improve his search statement. The 4-cycle limit would apply, however, only to searchers with preconceived objectives, and not to browsing searches, which could in principle be endless.

On-line retrieval still faces economic barriers. One of them is the raw cost of transferring bits of information from one place to another. As we saw in the previous discussion, bulky printouts are still sent by mail, rather than by electronic means. Locke (1970) reports:

> As with storage, a large cost differential divides conventional transportation from electronic transmission. John Simonds of Eastman Kodak has compared the cost of chartering a Boeing 707 and loading it with microfilm with that of using Telpak D to transmit the same number of bits from New York to Los Angeles. This works out to $10,000 for Boeing (.63 × 10^{-7} per megabit mile) versus $2,700,000 for Telpak D (.177 × 10^{-4} per megabit mile). Book rate parcel post at 24¢ per volume would be .53 × 10^{-5} per megabit mile. . . .

Historically, costs associated with electronic capabilities have decreased rapidly, and this is continuing. But for the time being the situation will be chaotic for anyone planning to design and implement a document retrieval system. As late as 1970 NASA, one of the most advanced experimenters with methods of dealing with documented information, was still performing 1000 searches a month in an off-line mode with a turnaround time of one week. Like other pioneers of on-line systems, NASA has undergone many growing pains for the past 8 years, and only recently has on-line retrieval begun to look like an institutional fixture. Mirrored in the following example is the growth of on-line retrieval itself. To quote *EDP Analyzer* (1970):

> Since 1965, NASA has been working on the design of an on-line system for improving the response time of demand searches. . . . NASA's first efforts in this direction were through a contract awarded to Bunker-Ramo Corporation in 1965. By November 1966, the system was using 23 consoles located at six points on the east coast. Benefits and difficulties of an on-line system were pointed up by this study. . . . Based on this experience, specifications

for an on-line system were revised and a contract was awarded to Lockheed Aircraft Corporation. This second pilot system was tested at Lockheed in mid-1967 and was then operated at NASA from late 1967 to the end of 1968; . . . The results of this study were incorporated in specifications for NASA's RECON (Remote Console) system. . . . Installation of RECON began in 1969. By the fall of 1969, 21 terminals had been installed at key NASA research centers. By next year (1971), NASA expects to have between 50 to 70 terminals in operation at NASA sites. . . .

As the reader may be aware, we regard the advent of on-line retrieval as the foremost development so far in the era of information storage and retrieval, and we do not confine our discussion of it to Chapter Nine. Chapter Eight has discussed on-line data management and man–machine dialogue. Chapter Ten will describe the potential of on-line display in document representation. Then, in Chapters Eleven and Twelve, we develop further aspects of on-line retrieval.

REFERENCES

AVEDON, DON M. (1970), Transmission of Information—New Networks, *Special Libraries*, 61:3, pp. 115–118.

BAGLEY, P. R. (1951), *Electronic Digital Machines for High Speed Information Searching*, Report R-200, Digital Computer Laboratory, MIT, Cambridge, Mass.

BARTON, A., SCHATZ, V. L., and CAPLAN L. N. (1959), Information Retrieval on a High Speed Computer, *Proceedings of the 1959 Western Joint Computer Conference*, IRE, New York.

BORKO, H., and BERNICK, M. D. (1964), Automatic Document Classification; Part II Additional Experiments, *Journal of the Association for Computing Machinery*, 11:2, pp. 138–151.

BRACKEN, R. H., and TILLITT, H. E. (1957), Information Searching with the 701 Calculator, *Journal of the Association for Computing Machinery*, 4:2, pp. 131–136.

BROWN, PATRICIA L., and JONES, SHIRLI O. (1968), Document Retrieval and Dissemination in Libraries and Information Centers, in Cuadra, C. A., ed., *Annual Review of Information Science and Technology*, Vol. 3, Encyclopaedia Britannica, Chicago.

CARTER, L. F., et al. (1967), *National Document-Handling Systems for Science and Technology*, John Wiley & Sons, New York.

COMPTON, B. E., and GARVEY, W. D. (1967), Dissemination Practices of Scientists and Engineers and Their Implications for Documentalists, in: *33rd Conference of FID and International Congress on Documentation,* Tokyo, September, 1967.

CUADRA, C. A. (1966), *Annual Review of Information Science and Technology,* Vol. 1, John Wiley & Sons, New York.

CUADRA, C. A. (1971), On-Line Systems: Promise and Pitfalls, *Journal of the American Society for Information Science,* 22:2, pp. 107–114.

DATTOLA, R. T. (1969), A Fast Algorithm for Automatic Classification, *Journal of Library Automation,* 2:1, pp. 31–48.

DOYLE, L. B. (1965), Is Automatic Classification a Reasonable Application of Statistical Analysis of Text, *Journal of the Association for Computing Machinery,* 12:4, pp. 473–489.

DOYLE, L. B., and BLANKENSHIP, D. A. (1966), Technical Advances in Automatic Classification, *Progress in Information Science and Technology: Proceedings of the American Documentation Institute,* Vol. 3 (Annual Meeting, Santa Monica, October 3–3), Adrienne Press, pp. 63–72.

EDMUNDSON, H. P., and WYLLYS, R. E. (1961), Automatic Abstracting & Indexing—Survey and Recommendations, *Communications of the Association for Computing Machinery,* 4:5, pp. 226–234.

EDP Analyzer (1970), Progress in Information Retrieval, 8:1 (January).

FIRTH, F. E. (1958), *An Experiment in Literature Searching with IBM 305 RAMAC,* IBM, San Jose, Calif., November 17.

FISCHER, MARGUERITE (1966), The KWIC Index Concept: A Retrospective View, *American Documentation,* 17:3, pp. 57–70.

GIULIANO, V. E., and JONES, P. E. (1963), Linear Associative Retrieval, in Howerton, P. W., ed., *Vistas in Information Handling,* Vol. 1, Spartan Books, Washington, D.C., pp. 30–46.

HAMMOND, WILLIAM (1965), Progress in Automation Among the Large Federal Information Centers, in Spiegel, J., and Walker D., eds., *Information System Sciences (2nd Congress),* Spartan Books, Washington, D.C.

HAYES, R. M., and BECKER, J. (1970), *Handbook of Data Processing for Libraries,* Becker & Hayes, Bethesda, Md.

JONKER, FREDERICK (1958), The Descriptive Continuum: A Generalized Theory of Indexing, *Preprints of Papers for the International Conference on Scientific Information,* National Academy of Sciences—National Research Council, Washington, D.C.

JORDAN, JOHN R. (1970), Let the Computer Select Your Reading List, *Datamation,* 16:2, pp. 91–94.

KENT, ALLEN (1965), *Specialized Information Centers*, Spartan Books, Washington, D.C.

KESSEL, B., and DE LUCIA, A. (1959), A Specialized Library Index Search Computer, *Proceedings of the 1959 Western Joint Computer Conference*, IRE, New York.

LANCASTER, F. W., and FAYEN, E. G. (1973), *Information Retrieval On-Line*, Melville, Los Angeles.

LESK, M. E., (1969), Word-Word Associations in Document Retrieval Systems, *American Documentation*, 20:1, pp. 27–38.

LOCKE, W. N. (1970), Computer Costs for Large Libraries, *Datamation*, 16:2, pp. 69–74.

LUHN, H. P. (1962), Automated Intelligence Systems, in Hattery, L. H., and McCormick, E. M., eds., *Information Retrieval Management*, pp. 92–100.

MARKUSON, BARBARA (1970), An Overview of Library Systems and Automation, *Datamation*, 16:2, pp. 60–68.

MARON, M. E., and KUHNS, J. L. (1960), On Relevance, Probabilistic Indexing, and Information Retrieval, *Journal of the Association for Computing Machinery*, 7:3, pp. 216–244.

MONTGOMERY, C., and SWANSON, D. R. (1962), Machine-Like Indexing by People, *American Documentation*, 13:4, pp. 359–366.

MOOERS, CALVIN N. (1959), The Next Twenty Years in Information Retrieval: Some Goals and Predictions, *Proceedings of the 1959 Western Joint Computer Conference*, IRE, New York.

MOYER, S. R. (1957), Automatic Search for Library Documents, *Computers and Automation*, 6:5, pp. 24–29.

NEEDHAM, R. M. (1963), A Method for Using Computers in Information Classification, in Popplewell, C. M., ed., *Information Processing 1962*, pp. 284–287.

NEEDHAM, R. M. (1966), *The Termination of Certain Iterative Processes*, RAND Corporation Memorandum RM-5188-PR.

NOLAN, J. J. (1958), *Principles of Information Storage and Retrieval Using a Large Scale Random Assess Memory*, IBM, San Jose, Calif., November 17.

RESNICK, A., and HENSLEY, C. B. (1963), The Use of a Diary and Interview Techniques in Evaluating a System for Disseminating Technical Information, *American Documentation*, 14:2, pp. 109–116.

SALTON, GERARD (1968), *Automatic Information Organization and Retrieval*, McGraw-Hill, New York.

SALTON, GERARD (1971), *The SMART Retrieval System,* Prentice-Hall, Englewood Cliffs, N.J.

Science, Government, and Information (1963), A Report of the President's Science Advisory Committee, The White House, Washington, D.C.

SHERA, J. H., KENT, A., and PERRY, J. W. (1957), The WRU Searching Selector, *Information Systems in Documentation, Advances in Documentation and Library Science II,* Interscience, New York.

SPARCK JONES, KAREN (1973), Index Term Weighting, *Information Storage and Retrieval,* 9:11, pp. 619–633.

STEVENS, MARY (1965), *Automatic Indexing: State of the Art Report,* National Bureau of Standards Monograph 91, U.S. Government Printing Office, Washington, D.C.

STILES, H. E. (1961), The Association Factor in Information Retrieval, *Journal of the Association for Computing Machinery,* 8:2, pp. 271–279.

STILES, H. E. (1962), Machine Retrieval Using the Association Factor, in *Machine Indexing,* American University, pp. 192–206.

STORRER, R. L. (1963), *KWIC and Dirty Information Retrieval,* paper read at the 1620 Users Group, Pittsburgh, Pa.

TANIMOTO, T. T. (1958), *An Elementary Mathematical Theory of Classification and Prediction,* IBM internal report, New York.

TAUBE, M. (1957), *The COMAC: An Efficient Punched Card Collating System for the Storage and Retrieval of Information,* AF OSR TN 58-365, AD 154 271.

WARD, J. H., Jr., and HOOK, M. E. (1963), Application of a Hierarchical Grouping Procedure to a Problem of Grouping Profiles, *Educational Psychological Measurement,* 23, pp. 69–92.

WEINBERG, A. M. (1963), Scientific Communication, *International Science and Technology,* pp. 65–74.

WHATMORE, GEOFFREY (1965), *News Information,* Archon Books, Hamden, Conn.

WOOSTER, HAROLD (1970), An Information Analysis Center Effectiveness Chrestomathy, *Journal of the American Society for Information Science,* 21:2, pp. 149–159.

Chapter Ten

The Processing of Language Data

In all of the methods of information organization and retrieval discussed herein, from the long-standing methods of library cataloging up to the most recent on-line techniques, we note that language and its units (words, terms, sentences) have major roles to play. Nonverbal guides to information, such as the Dewey and LC classification codes, have not fared well as a part of more recent inventions, a prime example being the Western Reserve *semantic factors,* discussed in Chapter Six. The trend, if anything, is toward more and more reliance on human language as a vehicle for access to stores of information, even in cases where the information is primarily numerical (Chapter Eight).

This is appropriate; ease and convenience of the information user are key factors in the overall efficiency of any system of making information available. One element of ease and convenience, of course, is to enable the user of information to make requests in his own language. Additionally, computers provide—potentially—ways to extract index-tag-length language units from a large reservoir of text, by which retrievable units (books, documents, etc.) might be characterized for future retrieval. The reverse side of this coin is that natural-language text might be searched directly by computer at the user's command (Barker, 1972).

Early in the history of computer applications two groups of people became interested in the computer as a language-processing machine. One group saw the computer as a means of access to information, and were also interested in the computer's potential for language processing. Much of the work we describe has come by way of this group's motivation. A second group that arose somewhat independently of the information retrieval movement consisted of those responding to the challenge of machine translation. To understand the peculiar development of the language-processing field, it is necessary to realize that though these two groups did interact and communicate to a degree, they never did blend into a single discipline (Montgomery, 1972).

Thus, today we have a bipolar situation. On the one side there is an information science pole that is primarily concerned with language as a "handle" on information, and on the other side is a computational linguistics pole whose interest is mainly in the structural-communicative nature of language (Sparck Jones, 1973). The work of the first group has been diffuse and pragmatic, and, of course, directly relevant to this chapter. The work of the computational linguists, semanticists, and others in the second group has not yet strongly affected that state of the art of computerized retrieval. The potential for doing so in the future, however, is very large, and we discuss this aspect in the latter part of the chapter.

Language and Computers. We learned in Chapter Three that typical alphabetical data from printed text can be represented in computer storage as numerical binary codes, and that, as far as bulk processing is concerned, there is almost no difference in effectiveness between the handling of virgin numerical data and of numerically coded text data. In the kind of detailed and selective processing we must do in connection with retrieval operations, however, there is a very substantial difference between the processibility of numerical data and of text data. This is so for reasons familiar to school children; numbers carry exact and reproducible information, whereas words and sentences ordinarily do not.

Whenever two identical sets of numbers are dealt with in the same way by the same sequence of operations, two identical outcomes will be achieved. This is the principle behind exact computation, and it holds true no matter how many numbers or operations are involved. A time came in the development of science and industry when needed computations that were therefore feasible in principle could not be done in practice because they were extremely long and repetitive, so that no person or group of persons could possibly carry them out in a reasonable length of time. As we know, these computational needs supplied the initial strong impetus for the invention and development of computers.

When an instrument that has been designed to function optimally in one problem area is adapted, as an afterthought, to a problem area entirely different in character, the prospects for success are likely to be much less than in the original problem area. Yet despite this, the digital computer has proved to be amazingly adaptable, and many of its present application areas are far removed from the highly iterative scientific and engineering calculations for which the computer was chiefly used in the beginning. But there are limits to the adaptability even of computers; and the problem of language processing is at the very outer edge of those limits. An understanding of the tenuous relationship between computers and human language will help one to appreciate both the great difficulty and the great fascination the workers in language processing have repeatedly experienced.

Of all the computers now in operation, which is is the most effective in processing human language? This is an important question to ask, and an easy one to answer: The most effective language-processing computer is the human brain. Digital computers, today, can do only a few things excellently with language, such as the alphabetization of index entries, or such as matching, counting, and looking up words on a list; it can do these things with great precision and speed. But the *raison d'être* of language is communication, and where satisfactory interpretation of a sentence is concerned, the performance of a six-year old child has yet to be matched by a machine.

The failure of computers, as yet, to handle language in a genuinely communicative way is not traceable to any deficiency in their design or circuitry. The failure is directly due to the fact that computer programmers do not yet know how to instruct a computer to deal with language, except in the most rudimentray or superficial ways. To understand this, let's consider a sentence a child might utter:

"Now I know why that door was locked that time Jim was here."

It would take about 3 seconds to say such a sentence, and perhaps less time than that for a human listener to understand it. But a computational linguist, for all his great knowledge about language, might take a full minute to draw a structural diagram of a child's sentence (even if he is permitted to draw the diagram without the words). The gulf apparent here, between *using* language and *analyzing* it, is certainly something to ponder, and is a commentary on the unique language handling capabilities that even a six-year-old human can exhibit.*

But a computational linguist can fudge in his analysis, for he is also a human language user. His fudging becomes painfully evident when he tries to write computer programs to duplicate his own ability to analyze sentences structurally. The sentence "They are flying planes" has often been used in linguistic circles as an example of a sentence having, from a

---

* Also something to ponder is the recent language performance of a 3-year-old chimpanzee named Lana (*Time* Magazine, 1974). It is conceivable that today's computers are not merely second-rate language processors, but actually third-rate.

computer's primitive point of view, more than one possible structure. Is "flying" an active verb, or is it an adjective modifying planes? A human listener, familiar with both usage and context, would know instantly which is the case. In the above sentence about the locked door, a computer program would have trouble with the missing word "that" (or "when") which should precede the word "Jim." Our language is full of such "incorrect" shortcuts or variations, which, however, cause human listeners almost no difficulty. (We consider the problem of determining sentence structure by computer in more detail later in the chapter.)

Processing language in terms of its meaning is far more difficult than processing it to determine sentence structure. The human brain, unlike the computer, can bring a terribly large amount of information to bear in interpreting a question like "Why was that door locked that time Jim was here?" The listener to such a question will undoubtedly know "which door," who "Jim" is, what occasion "that time Jim was here" refers to, and enough other factors about Jim and about whatever is behind the locked door to be able to give an intelligent answer to the question.

In fact, there is a vast and complexly interrelated storehouse of information in the mind of the listener pertaining to the tiny segment of reality designated by such a question. This storehouse includes the keys to recognition of many variant manners of speech (baby talk, dialects, affectations) and of vocal idiosyncrasies of one's individual friends and acquaintances. As Jakobson (1972) says, in something of an understatement, ". . . People usually display a narrower competence as senders of verbal messages and a wider competence as receivers. . . ." A human being can also contemplate endlessly, say, the ramifications of a fly crawling up a wall and not run out of fresh thoughts on the subject—or be unable to generate fresh sentences about the subject. It is this seemingly unlimited pool of knowledge, standing ready to embrace every word, phrase, and sentence heard by the human ear, that computer programmers do not yet know how to duplicate.

No one who has a modest understanding about how computers work and who, as well, has the barest insight into the complexity of his own thoughts should be surprised that success in using computers for language processing has been sparse. Yet, within certain limits, some quite useful computerized language processing methods have been devised, and there is a great deal of unmined gold slightly beneath the surface. But whether difficult or easy, problems in processing language pose an unavoidable challenge to be met if the fullest use of computers in information retrieval is to be attained.

At the present time much of the development in language processing is on a plateau (there are some who would call it an impasse). Apparently most of the easy ways of processing language have been worked and reworked. The more difficult formulations of the computational linguists appear to be losing their developmental momentum. Kay and Sparck Jones (1971), reviewing the field, state: ". . . Far less work has been done in computational linguistics during the past year than in any comparable period in the previous ten years. . . ." They also comment, meaningfully, ". . . The affluent 60s are gone, possibly never to return. . . ." Despite the impression given here, it seems unlikely that an area as important as language processing will remain static for long.

What is more likely is that the progress of language processing is at present poised between the first two levels of difficulty, out of three (at least) levels of difficulty:

1. Methods based on simple word matching, such as word alphabetization, counting, and finding.
2. Methods requiring the use of a dictionary, such as syntactic analysis and crude machine translation of languages.
3. Methods involving correlation of conceptual entities with units of language, such as question answering, computer-human discourse, etc.

Most of the pragmatically motivated work in the 1960s fell in category one, an important exception being machine translation, where dictionaries are essential. The methods of category one are discussed in detail in the section immediately to follow.

The construction of a dictionary is, of course, a laborious process. Up to the 1970s, therefore, only small experimental dictionaries were common (in machine translation, such a dictionary is termed a *microglossary*, and usually pertains to just one field of knowledge, most often technical). When truly large dictionaries become both common and interchangeable among language-processing workers, it can be predicted that a fresh burst of progress will take place. Indeed, this threshold is apparently just now being crossed. Olney (1972) reports the availability of machine-readable versions of *Webster's Seventh New Collegiate Dictionary*. Thirty users have been supplied with sets of this dictionary data, ranging in size from less than a million bytes to more than 100 million (remembering from Chapter Three that a byte is equivalent to one alphanumeric character). We are to discuss language processes that use dictionaries in the second section of this chapter.

Finally, there are methods of language processing in which some kinds of word-concept correlation must be employed. As might be guessed, the surface has hardly been scratched at this level of language-processing difficulty, although it is fair to say that it *has* been scratched. The applicability of any real progress at this level to information retrieval is obvious, though there is little at present that can be used. In the later sections in this chapter we briefly consider question-answering, coherent discourse, and the general problem of computerized "concepts."

PROCESSING BY SIMPLE MATCHING

It might surprise some to know how many useful computer operations involve nothing more than simple copying, comparison, and matching of words. In business data processing, for example, a vast amount of data is handled that consists wholly or partly of words. The numerical portion of such data is commonly the subject of a variety of arithmetic operations, but the alphabetic portion is most often simply copied from one medium or storage device to another (Chapter Three). Occasionally some of the alphabetic data (names, for example) will be involved in comparison and matching, for the purpose of lookup or other selective handling of records. This kind of language processing, together with the kind of bulk processing of text that is done in computerized photocomposition (Chapter Two) probably constitutes more than 99 percent of all the processing of words and sentences that is now being carried out.

This way of using the computer for processing language makes it just another dumb machine for handling information in bulk, not much more sophisticated in application than printing presses or card sorters. This of course explains the rapid spread of this methodology; the efficiencies of ever-faster and ever-cheaper computers can be quickly brought to bear with a minimum of research and development, and without the growing pains that accompany the initiation of entirely new ways of using computers.

There are some rather intriguing exceptions to this generalization. One is the use of the computer for hyphenation in photocomposition (Chapter Two), where some of the true difficulties of processing language are encountered, and where some form of dictionary lookup is required. Another is the detection of spelling errors, which is applicable both in business data processing and in publication.

The nature of the latter problem may be phrased: *if* a word is not in our dictionary, what is the likelihood that it is a spelling error, and not merely a potential new addition to the vocabulary? Spelling errors can always be dealt with in the time-honored way, by proofreading the input. This procedure requires that every line of material be scanned, a fatiguing eye exercise in which errors are often missed. But if computers can pick out instances that might be errors, then the attention of a human proofreader can be focused only where it is needed. And so, a fairly elaborate methodology has grown up for the detection of possible spelling or typographical errors in text data (Algebra, 1967). In some cases computers can make corrections without human help, although there are presently severe limitations to such a process. How would a computer be able to tell, for example, whether "Eire" is a mutation of the word "Erie" or whether it really means "Eire"? In cases like this we are face to face again with the difficulties noted at the beginning of the chapter. Damereau (1964) lists four of the most common kinds of typographical error: substitution of one letter for another, deletion of a single letter, insertion of a single letter, and transposition of adjacent letters.

The correction of spelling errors is, of course, only a small facet of the general problem of editing, and its performance via computer is likely to be affected by the way editing as a whole is done. At present the idea of a man–machine partnership is predominant in the editing of newspapers and other publications dealing with ordinary text. A typical such partnership is now achieved in many newspaper rooms by editors seated at display console, using blip and cursor methods (Chapter Three) to add, delete, or otherwise change text (*Time* Magazine, 1973). The computer's portion of the work is generally little more than shifting masses of text about from one location to another. Indeed, newspaper makeup itself is changing from a scissors-and-paste methodology to a kind of electronic text-shuffling in which editorial "gatekeepers" are able (with the help of a display scope) to select, from hundreds of available articles, the ones that are judged of most interest or value to the newspaper reader (Bagdikian, 1971).

Automatic Indexing. The use of computers for producing alphabetized indexes can be looked upon as the first form of language processing to experience widespread practical application. As Chapter Nine relates, thinking about computers in information retrieval at first concentrated on their use as *searching* instruments; this way of thinking *was* predominant until 1957–1958, when other viewpoints began to proliferate. In part the new thinking was a reaction to the delays of batch processing in giving service to information seekers (waits of 24 hours were common); there were then no general-purpose time-sharing systems, nor could any be seen on the horizon. Therefore, a method of using a computer to generate indexes that could be distributed so that people could consult them in their offices, the instant information needs arose, was an idea that made a great deal of sense (and, in fact, still does).

The first machine-produced indexes came to public attention in connection with the International Conference on Scientific Information (ICSI) at Washington, D.C., in late 1958. Independently, two developers, H. P. Luhn of International Business Machines and Herbert Ohlman of System Development Corporation, both planned to generate and distribute indexes

AUTOMATIC LEXICAL CODING OF MESSAGES—	6232	1603
RITER, A SYSTEM FOR THE LEXICAL PROCESSING OF STENOTYPE (ART	6343	4073
) THE JOVIAL GRAMMAR, A LEXICON (PROGLANG)=THE JOVIAL MANUA	6232	1664
PROGRAMMING FOR THE LGP-30 (DSGNGENL, FOREIGN-GERMAN)=	6012	0031
ACHINE, PROGRAMMING THE LGP-30 TO SOLVE PROBLEMS IN SYMBOLIC	6234	2103
REMARK ON A THEOREM OF LIAPUNOV (NUMRANAL)=A	6233	1996
T METHOD FOR GENERATING LIAPUNOV FUNCTIONS (NUMERAL)=THE V	6342	4030
REALTIME)=STABILITY BY LIAPUNOV'S DIRECT METHOD WITH APPLIC	6341	3455
RY (REALTIME)= (PART 2) LIAPUNCV'S METHODS IN AUTOMATIC CONT	6344	4310
Y (PROGLANG)=THE COBOL LIBRARIAN, A KEY TO OBJECT PROGRAM E	6236	3146
VAL AND THE PROBLEMS OF LIBRARIES (INFRETR)=INFORMATION STO	6232	1717
OKS IN THE YALE MEDICAL LIBRARY (INFRETR)=RECORDER USE OF B	6232	1719
ON AND USE OF A PROGRAM LIBRARY (PRCESSRS, FOREIGN-RUSSIAN)=	6235	2601
A LIBRARY FOR 2000 A.D. =	6236	3393
AND OF UTILIZATION OF A LIBRARY OF PROGRAMS (PROGGENL, FOREI	6341	3561
DUCE COSTS OF TECHNICAL LIBRARY OPERATIONS IN THE DEPARTMENT	6345	4568
ICATIONS OF MACHINES TO LIBRARY TECHNIQUES, PERIODICALS (INF	6235	2468
THE COMPUTER IN THE LIBRARY=	6342	3816
ABLE IN THE STATISTICAL LIBRARY=INDEX OF STATISTICAL PROGRA	6013	0122
ETRIEVAL (INFRETR)=THE LIBRARY-OF-CONGRESS LOOKS AT MECHANI	6236	3239
ES (SCIENTIF)=PERIODIC LIBRATIONS ABOUT THE TRIANGULAR SOLU	6345	4497
R THE UNITED-KINGDOM OF LIBYA BY ELECTRONIC COMPUTERS (SOCLS	6345	4519
ORIGIN AND SCOPE OF THE LIBYAN PILOT PROJECT (STATIST)=	6234	2278
ARY BUSINESS AND SOCIAL LIFE (STATIST, FOREIGN-GERMAN)=STAT	6343	4285
NAL)=THE LIFE AND WORKS OF A.K. ERLANG (NLMRA	6345	4621
AIRCRAFT ENGINE LIFE CYCLE SIMULATION (MATHPROG)=	6345	4600
BILITY PREDICTIONS FROM LIFE DISTRIBUTION DATA=SEMICCNDLCTO	6233	1913
N (COMPSYS)=TRANSISTOR LIFE IN THE TX-0 COMPUTER AFTER 10,	6235	2650
		LEA

at the conference. As it happened, both indexes were based on the *permuted title* principle (Figure 10.1) in which a large number of keypunched titles are individually rotated so that each major word in the title has a chance to appear in the alphabetized column. Consider, for example, the title "Automatic Lexical Coding of Messages," which appears in Figure 10.1. The title permuting process would permit 5 entries to be generated for this title:

```
PSYS, FOREIGN-RUSSIAN)=LINEAR DISTORTIONS IN DISCRETIZATION                            6232 1693
ING A CERTAIN PIECEWISE LINEAR DYNAMIC SYSTEM WITH THREE PAR                           6342 4025
    SYSTEM OF INCONSISTENT LINEAR EQUATIONS (MATHPROG, FOREIGN-                        6011 0007
  SYSTEMS OF SIMULTANEOUS LINEAR EQUATIONS (NUMRANAL)=AN ITER                          6123 0861
   ST SQUARES SOLUTIONS OF LINEAR EQUATIONS (NUMRANAL)=ON LEA                          6232 1791
      SOLUTIONS OF SYSTEMS OF LINEAR EQUATIONS (NUMRANAL, FOREIGN-                     6121 0552
= A PROGRAM FOR SOLVING LINEAR EQUATIONS AFTER THE METHOD OF                           6332 1786
                          LINEAR EQUATIONS AND MATRICES =                              6121 0546
     RANAL)=THE SOLUTION OF LINEAR EQUATIONS BY THE GAUSS-SEIDEL                       6121 0547
       SOLUTION OF SYSTEMS OF LINEAR EQUATIONS BY THE METHOD OF EX                     6236 3342
                      THE LINEAR EQUATIONS PROBLEM (NUMRANAL) =                        6014 0179
   OLUTION OF SIMULTANEOUS LINEAR EQUATIONS USING A MAGNETIC TA                        6015 0278
      SOLUTION OF SYSTEMS FOR LINEAR EQUATIONS WITH DEFINITE MATRI                     6346 4890
   D NUMERICAL METHODS FOR LINEAR EQUATIONS, POLYNOMIAL EQUATIO                        6346 4863
                         = LINEAR ESTIMATION AND RELATED TOPICS                        6236 3368
   IONS USING THE RATIO OF LINEAR FORMS=ALGORITHMS FOR CHEBYSH                         6234 2221
   AL NOMENCLATURE, INTO A LINEAR FORMULA (ENGRING)=AN ALGORIT                         6235 2431
     O COMPUTER SOLUTIONS OF LINEAR FUNCTIONS RELATED TO AUTOMATI                      6123 0739
              S (NUMRANAL) = LINEAR GRAPHS AND ELECTRICAL NETWORK                      6341 3707
     NUMRANAL)= THE USE OF LINEAR GRAPHS IN GAUSS ELIMINATION (                        6232 1792
    TCTIC POWER OF TESTS OF LINEAR HYPOTHESES USING THE PROBIT A                       6345 4663
     LES OF MATRICES AND THE LINEAR INDEPENDENCE OF THEIR MINORS                       6235 2812
                  INCIPLE = LINEAR INEQUALITIES AND THE PAULI PR                       6125 1096
    ATIONS OF THE THEORY OF LINEAR INEQUALITIES TO EXTERNAL COMB                       6125 1096
                            LINEAR INPUT LOGIC (LOGLDSGN) =                            6232 1740
A NEW METHOD OF SOLVING LINEAR INTEGRAL EQUATIONS OF THE FIR                           6125 1098
  IME) = ON THE ERROR OF A LINEAR INTERPOLATOR FOR A PROGRAM CO                        6121 0432
   ONCERNING ERRORS OF THE LINEAR INTERPOLATOR FOR THE DIGITAL                         6231 1335
                                                                                       LIN
```

Figure 10.1. KWIC index.

Messages. Automatic Lexical Coding of
tomaitc Lexical Coding of Messages. Au
 Automatic Lexical Coding of Messages.
xical Coding of Messages. Automatic Le
Lexical Coding of Messages. Automatic

(alphabetized column)

Not all entries are acceptable as part of the index. The title whose permutations are shown here would be indexed under its content words, "automatic," "lexical," etc., but not under function words such as "of," "the," or "which." The Luhn index, called Keyword-in-Context (KWIC), was generated on an IBM computer, wherein it was a simple matter to store a list (called a *stop list*) of the most common function words in memory and inhibit the generation of any entries alphabetized on those words (Luhn, 1960). Ohlman's index was not generated on a computer, but on ordinary punched card machines, with the aid of some tricky plugboard wiring by his colleague Lew Hart. Each permutation was a duplicate of the original title, punched on an 80-column card so that the indexing word was positioned at column 41 for alphabetization. Entries alphabetized on function words were deleted on inspection of the printout. As an interesting indication of how many minds were working along the same track, Ohlman (1959) pointed out that the permutation method (or methods similar thereto) was being worked on by at least six other people (including Luhn) scattered across the United States. He also acknowledged that a manual method of permuting titles was suggested as long ago as 1856 by Crestadoro, a British librarian (Stevens, 1965, p. 4).

Permuted title indexing, today most commonly referred to as KWIC indexing, was widely adopted by various information services in the years following 1958. Professional societies were especially attracted to it as a current-information guide for use by their membership, the Association for Computing Machinery and the American Bar Foundation being two examples. As early as 1962, 30 applications of the KWIC concept were in existence, including such examples as the *KWIC Index to Neurochemistry* and the *KWIC Index to the Science Abstracts of China* (Fischer, 1971). Herner (1962) comments:

> As a matter of fact, I am told that the American Chemical Society has never had a more successful basic science publication. The key to the whole thing is, I believe, the extreme currency of *Chemical Titles*. This in turn derives from the speed and simplicity of the KWIC process.

KWIC indexing is a good example of a language processing method at the easiest of three levels of difficulty, given above. KWIC also throws into bold relief three of the basic problems of language processing, one of which KWIC inherently solves, but two others of which require some form of human intervention either before or after the automatic process:

1. A given word *form* can have any number of meanings. This feature of language, known as *homography*, bedevils modern languages —English especially. Though homography makes a language elastic and highly expressive, it makes it also quite unfit for many

computer applications. The most well-known victim of homography is machine translation of languages. Such accidents as translation of the English phrase "hydraulic ram" into a Russian phrase "water goat" are very hard to avoid, even when a very large stored dictionary is available (Borko, 1968). An even more insidious kind of homography was pointed out by Bar-Hillel (1964), namely the difference in meaning in usages of the word "pen" in the phrases "the box is in the pen" and "the pen is in the box." In many cases there is simply no way for a machine to pick out the right meaning, however good the dictionary. The KWIC indexing method, however, has little trouble with multiple meanings because a word always appears in a contextual setting that makes its true meaning clear; this, of course, was the idea behind keyword-in-context.

2. A given word *meaning* can exist in a variety of forms, a condition familiar to us as *synonymy*. It is a more serious ailment for permutation indexing than homography, because it causes a group of entries which ought to be under the same heading to be scattered among several widely separated locations in the index. Material that one might look up under the word "law" might also be found under the words "legal," "jurisprudence," or perhaps "statute" or "statutory." Human intervention, in the form of post-editing the computer output or insertion of cross-references, is required to overcome this deficiency. It is interesting to note, however, that KWIC indexes partially offset the flaw of synonymy by providing leads to topically related words (which are often as valuable as synonyms as potentially relevant pathways). Note, in Figure 10.1, that in the block of entries under "linear," the index user's eye lights on the words "equation," "numerical," "solution," and "simultaneous," any of which might remind him of another place to look in the index. This strength of KWIC indexing could even outweigh its synonymy weakness, because any index user searching for something on a definite topic is highly likely to have need for closely related material. Put another way, every searcher is to some degree a browser.

3. A *title* is not an ideal index entry. This objection to the KWIC indexing principle has been advanced from the very start. Though the author of a document gives it a title to let possible readers know what it is about, he may not have planned on its being used for indexing purposes. Thus, some titles may not contain enough words; others may not contain any rich, specific terms; still other titles may be intentionally whimsical or enigmatic. The following

examples were found in the bibliography section of the chapter "Automated Language Processing" in Volume 4 of the *Annual Review of Information Science and Technology* (Montgomery, 1969):

(a) Is Linguistics Empirical? (Bever, Fodor, & Weksel)
(b) The Case for Case. (Fillmore, Charles J.)
(c) Referentials. (Hiz, Henry)
(d) Unpalatable Recipes for Buttering Parsnips. (Katz, Jerrold J.)
(e) Principia Mathematica. (Whitehead, Alfred N., & Russell, Bertrand)

Fortunately, many technical fields appear to have uniformly high quality titles containing numerous highly specific terms, for example, nuclear physics, biology, and metallurgy. In fields where such is not the case, it is often possible to solicit author cooperation in the production of better titling; Fischer (1971) reports on several such efforts and cites subtitles and augmentation of titles with indexing terms as remedies.

Much experimentation has been done with the KWIC index format to improve readability and information content. It may have already occurred to the reader that only a part of many of the titles can be represented in the format shown in Figure 10.1. Fischer (1971) presents a number of the variations that ensued to meet this and other problems of the permuted title format. Bell Telephone met the problem by simply extending the width of a line from 80 columns to 120 columns. Some titles are longer than 120 character spaces, of course, but the improvement in readability is much greater than the 50 percent implied by the change in length, and enables the index user to make decisions about a document's probable relevance much more freely than before.

Some information specialists were dismayed with KWIC's fragmenting most titles, and, of course, reversing the fragments. So to preserve the integrity of titles, the KWOC (Keyword-out-of-Context) index was developed. Very simply, the word on which the title would be alphabetized, in KWIC, is taken out of the title and placed at the left-hand margin. Then the title—in its natural order and including the alphabetizing word—is placed 20 or so character spaces to the right of the left-hand margin. A typical KWOC format appears in the lower half of Figure 10.2. Note that the meaning-conferring property of context is still present with the KWOC method. One drawback of KWOC, however, is that it hinders scanning for phrases or small groups of words (such as "Liapunov's Methods" and "Solution of Linear Equations" in Figure 10.1) that tend to group together in blocks under the regular KWIC method (Youden, 1963).

Sometimes a degree of control over the generation of KWIC entries is desirable that is much tighter than would be needed for word-rich technical titles. A newspaper headline is an example of a title that this characteristically somewhat lean in informative content words (Example: STATE SOLON GROUP HITS DRUG PROBE). Yet newspapers editors, whose pithy style of headline-writing is a necessary component of the newspaper art, also value whatever indexing cues are present as a means of access to morgue information. Figure 10.2 illustrates a method of man–machine action in which indexers mark useful words with asterisks, so that a computer can generate permutations only on those words (Davis, 1971).

Though title-indexing has held the spotlight in the 15-year history of automatic indexing, a rather large amount of work has been done on automatic processes of indexing document text in depth. Most people are familiar with the idea of a *concordance,* an index to practically every content-word occurrence in an entire text. Biblical concordances have been prepared since the twelfth century. Manually, the concordance-building process is most time-consuming, and could be justified only for a book of extraordinary and guaranteed usage. Strong's Concordance of the Bible took 30 years to compile (Carlson, 1963).

The process becomes quite easy and cheap when data processing is used, especially when the text is already in digital form for some other purpose, such as photocomposition. Unfortunately, concordances have the major drawback of being quite large. Indeed, if one combines the concordance and the KWIC technique, permuting sentences rather than titles, it can easily be seen that the index will be larger than the book. Therefore, for most *publishing* purposes, an automatic indexing technique would have to be much more selective than a concordance is.

Still there are some areas of endeavor where book and document texts are so information-packed that the concordance technique, for all its potential bulk, is economically justifiable. The concordance/KWIC combination is finding increasing use in the legal field. The problem of generating bulky publications is sidestepped by printing out only parts of the total possible KWIC format in response to individual requests. According to Beard (1971):

> . . . The user indicates the keywords that should be used in a search and can request a printout of the full text (of a statute), citations only, or a Keyword-in-Context . . . printout, which prints the keyword imbedded in approximately 70 characters of surrounding text, accompanied by the citation to the document in which the word appears. The system began with about half the statutes in Pennsylvania; by 1961, the complete Pennsylvania statutes were successfully stored and made available for search.
>
> The success of the Pittsburgh system led to its adoption by 23 states including New Jersey, New York, Ohio, Kansas, and Hawaii. It was also

1700916-03	CONTRACT TALKS RESUMED AS *SCHOOLS/OPEN'
1700916-05	CONTRACT LET IN *MINE FIRE/'
1700916-11	70,985 REGISTER IN PHILA. COUNTY (*VOTERS/)'
1700916-16	WHAT EXPO ''76 MIGHT DO TO TRANSFORM OUR CITY (*BICENTENNIAL/)'
1700916-18	*BLACK STUDENT/AID TO BE EXPANDED (*STUDENT AID/)'
1700916-19	PHILADELPHIA LAWYER TAKES REINS OF FTC; LONG CRITIC OF AGENCY (*KIRKPATRICK/)'
1700916-19	CLOSE *PRISON/OR IMPROVE IT, SUIT DEMANDS'
1700916-24	CUTTING THE *PRIME RATE/(*INTEREST/)'
1700916-28	MUSEUM HERE GIVEN *DORY/BY BRITISH ROWER (*MARITIME MUSEUM/)'
1700916-30	COLLEGE FEARS A ''TAKEOVER'' (*COMMUNITY COLLEGE/)'
1700916-41	*NEWARK/BUSINESSMEN CAUTIONED ON ''*BRIBES/'''
1700916-43	INDUSTRIES RAP *PGW/''S IN SEASONAL RATE (*GAS/)'
1700916-43	*BLATSTEIN/FACES NEW CHARGE (*STADIUM/)'
1700916-43	*ORCHESTRA/REUNITES FOR 71ST SEASON ON INTERRACIAL NOTE (*BLACK MUSICIAN/)'
1700916-43	TATE MAKES PLEA FOR 15 PCT. RISE IN *REAL ESTATE/*TAX/'
1700916-43	*POCRMAN/DENIES TESTIFYING THAT HE LIVES OUTSIDE PHILA.'
1700916-43	VOLPE WOULD PROHIBIT *ROADS/THAT ''DESTROY'''
INNER CITIES	1700920B26	STATE URGED TO ALTER SCHOOL SUBSIDY PLAN TO AID INNER CITIES
INSURANCE	1700916-44	PROBE URGED ON INSURANCE
INTEGRATION	1700925-03	COLOR UPHELD AS CRITERIA FOR NAMING SCHOOL CHIEFS (INTEGRATION)
INTEREST	1700916-24	CUTTING THE PRIME RATE (INTEREST)
INTEREST RATE	1700915-01	1ST PENNA. BANK CUTS INTEREST RATE TO 7 12%; MAY ESTABLISH TREND

JAIL	1700926-23	JUDGE URGES COURT USE IN CELL CROWDING (JAIL)
JAILS	1700925-03	CITY HALL JAIL CELLS FOUND CROWDED, UNSANITARY, HOT (JAILS)
JETS	1700924-33	JUMBO JETS WAVED OFF HERE; RUNAWAY COULD CRACK (AIRLINES)
JUDGE'S RECALL	1700915-17	POLICE WIVES WANT ISSUE OF JUDGE'S RECALL ON NOVEMBER BALLOT (LEVIN)
KIRKPATRICK	1700916-19	PHILADELPHIA LAWYER TAKES REINS OF FTC; LONG CRITIC OF AGENCY (KIRKPATRICK)
LAW	1700918-09	SHAPP DEFINES HIS STAND ON LAW, ORDER
LAWYERS	1700918-05	BAR EXAMINERS BIASED, PROBE IS TOLD (DISCRIMINATION, LAWYERS)
	1700920B01	CITY'S BLACK LAWYERS' CORPS CHARGES RACISM IN PROFESSION (LAWYERS)
LEVIN	1700915-17	POLICE WIVES WANT ISSUE OF JUDGE'S RECALL ON NOVEMBER BALLOT (LEVIN)
MAFIA	1700916-05	JERSEY PROBERS TO QUIZ BRUNO (MAFIA)
	1700925-01	MAFIA CHIEF GUILTY IN EXTORTION PLOT
	1700925-19	N.J. PROBERS DEFEND RIGHT TO CALL BRUNO (MAFIA)
MARITIME MUSEUM	1700916-28	MUSEUM HERE GIVEN DORY BY BRITISH ROWER (MARITIME MUSEUM)
MC INTIRE	1700917-39	TEMPLE PRESIDENT REJECTS MC INTIRE REQUEST FOR MALL
METROLINER	1700919-19	U. S. AGREES TO GIVE $4.6 MILLION FOR METROLINER PROJECT
MINE FIRE	1700916-05	CONTRACT LET IN MINE FIRE
MOLOTOV COCKTAILS	1700916-01	MOLOTOV COCKTAILS HIT ACLU OFFICES
MUSEUM	1700918-13	MUSEUM HONORS JAPANESE PRINTMAKER (EXHIBITS)
	1700920G07	RARE DISPLAY AT MUSEUM OFFERS PRINTS BY JAPANESE MASTER (EXHIBITS)
NARCOTICS	1700915-08	SHAPP SUPPORTS UNIT TO FIGHT NARCOTICS
NAVY	1700914-31	FOUNDER OF NAVY HONORED BY PARADE (BARRY DAY)
NEW HAVEN	1700924-17	PENNSY ASKS OK TO SELL NEW HAVEN
NEWARK	1700916-41	NEWARK BUSINESSMEN CAUTIONED ON 'BRIBES'
NUCLEAR PLANTS	1700927AO	11 NUCLEAR PLANTS ARE SPROUTING UP AROUND US (POWER)
OPEN HOUSING	1700921-29	15 AREA LEADERS SUPPORT PROGRAM OF RACIAL MIXTURE (OPEN HOUSING)

Figure 10.2. Output format.

adopted, ... by the Air Force. The ... Aspen Systems Corporation ... has available for computer searching the full texts of the statutes of all 50 states, the U.S. Code, as well as the text of all Pennsylvania Supreme and Superior Court Cases since 1960 and all third-Circuit and Supreme Court Cases since 1950. (John F.) Horty, who is president of Aspen, has commented that the primary users of the Aspen System ... are legislative bodies and government agencies. ...

The membership of a word in a title or sentence is not the only kind of context that is available to confer meaning on an otherwise ambiguous index term. In the familiar back-of-the-book index, ambiguity is seldom a problem, mainly because of the presence of many other index terms close by that are in the same topical area. The word "force," for example, would have companions like "field," "Faraday," and "free energy" on the same page in a physics text index, whereas similarly the presence of nearby terms in the index of a book on sociology, economics, or international relations would suggest that "force" is other than physical.

As already implied, a practical back-of-the-book index would have to be far more selective than a concordance technique, and would aim for index terms of unquestionable value, excluding those of marginal interest. And here, once again, we are up against the problem of the inadequacy of computers in dealing with language: How can a computer distinguish between an index term of unquestionable value and one that is marginal? In fact, this is a hard decision to make even by a human indexer; but nevertheless most human indexers feel they are competent to do it! As a result when people who do indexing professionally are led to use computers, the tendency has been to use them to take some of the drudgery out of the indexing process while leaving the ultimate decision-making power in human hands.

One way of doing this is to make use of a *go list*. We have already discussed the *stop list*, invented by Luhn (1960), as a means of eliminating useless function words as indexing words. The go list reverses the process: all words are eliminated which are *not* on the list. An adequate stop list need not have more than a hundred words in order to eliminate 99 percent of entries indexed under useless function words, as a mathematical consequence of Zipf's rank-frequency relation (Brookes, 1968)—provided, of course, that the hundred words are the most frequent function words. A go list, however, in order to be comprehensive in a given subject area must contain thousands of words and terms; furthermore, stop lists can be readily borrowed from others, whereas go lists must vary from field to field.

Because of the amount of human effort needed to construct machine-readable lists of many words and terms, the go list method might be thought of as semiautomatic indexing. Even so, in a setting where a large amount of text is stored digitally, a lot of labor is saved, because an indexer has to deal only with word *types* (i.e., word forms that may or may not be on the list) and not with each word *token* (i.e., each instance of a word form encountered in text). Unfortunately, again as a consequence of Zipf's rank-frequency law of distribution of words in text, most word types useful as indexing terms may not occur very many times as tokens, so efficiencies of computer use are not great. Armitage (1970), et al., report that their computer method will index in merely half the time required by the manual method.

It must be recognized, however, that the go list method, despite its inefficiency with respect to computer use, is a practical approach to defeating the synonym problem, one of the three language-processing problems mentioned above in relation to KWIC indexing. When a given variant of an approved term is encountered, the go list can contain the approved term itself which may be either assigned directly as an index or implanted next to the variant entry as a cross-reference (Artandi, 1969).

The cheapness and speed of purely automatic methods have served as a continuing motivation in quest of techniques of extraction of indexing words and terms from text by the unaided computer. A sample effort of recent times is told of in an article entitled "Experiments in Book Indexing by Computer" (Borko, 1970). Realizing automatically selected adjacent word pairs would probably make better indexing terms than single words, Borko explored the use of a program that would extract word pairs. He suggested that a given pair, such as "bulbar paralysis" could be used both as such and as "paralysis, bulbar," thus giving two access points. However, in sentences such as "After 1900 research on pyrochemistry gave way to attempts to achieve chemical transformations with the aid of catalysts," he saw no way to prevent the selection of inappropriate terms such as "1900 research" or "achieve chemical," aside from returning to the cumbersome go list method.

However, another worker (Brooks, 1965) alludes to the tendency of such useless terms as "achieve chemical" not to repeat in a text. The fact that words and terms *do* repeat in text is, indeed, the basis of a broad approach to automatic indexing that is just as long-standing (though not as successful) as the permuted title approach, and we now take up this topic.

Word Frequency Methods in Automatic Indexing and Abstracting. The same H. P. Luhn who was one of the originators of the KWIC technique also was involved in the initiation of another methodology of language processing (also at level one of the three levels of difficulty), based on the fact that if an author of a text uses a word often, it has something to do with his topic. Luhn, whose ideas have been so influential in information science that a book has been written about his life (Schultz, 1968), had an inventor's mind (and, indeed, held a large and variegated collection of patents). Like many inventors, Luhn was quick to see obvious principles that somehow escape the observation of most other people, and, as a longtime employee of International Business Machines, was in a position to try out what he saw. Thus, came a veritable explosion from his direction of operationally demonstrated and well-publicized new ideas during the years 1957 through 1963. In this chapter we are most interested in KWIC, already discussed, the word-frequency approach (Luhn, 1957), and automatic abstracting (Luhn, 1958).

It is convenient to talk about automatic abstracting first, because its development matured relatively quickly and has not evolved significantly since the early 1960s. The generalized word-frequency approach to language processing, however, was the start of a more diversified path, a part of which has to do with sentence structure and other level two processes we discuss later on.

The basic idea of automatic abstracting is that some sentences in an article are sufficiently rich, in words that are repeated throughout the article, that these sentences are capable of informing a reader what an article is about—as an abstract does. As can be easily imagined, the counting of the occurrences of various words in a text is about the easiest thing that can be done by means of a computer with language. Selecting the sentences having the highest concentration of the most frequent words is also a simple process. (An early Luhn abstract is shown in Exhibit 10.1. The abstract was the output of an IBM 704 program.) Unfortunately, the sentences do not fit together in a coherent way (it would be coincidental if they did!), and because of this some people have insisted that *automatic abstract* was not the proper term to describe the output of Luhn's process. Therefore the term *automatic extract* has come into currency. Since, however, no true automatic abstract, by this definition, has come into existence, no one will be confused if the term automatic abstract continues to be used.

Generally speaking, the steps followed in producing an auto-abstract under Luhn's program are:

1. The machine program separates the text in a way which insures that words and sentences are identifiable and available for subsequent processing on call.
2. A table lookup compares each word with those common words which rarely characterize meaning in English sentences, such as the conjunctives, articles, and prepositions, and causes them to be deleted.
3. The remaining notion words (i.e., verbs, nouns, adjectives, etc.)

are then sorted alphabetically so that the total occurrences of each can be tabulated.
4. A number of statistical calculations follow:
    a. Grouping of words having the same stem—to insure that variations of the word will still be treated as one occurrence.
    b. Tabulating the number of words at each frequency.
    c. Determining the number of words in a sentence and the average word frequency.
5. High frequency words are then traced back to their original sentences and their position noted.
6. Proximity rules determine which high-frequency words are close enough within a given sentence to be assigned to bracketed sections wherein the words are probably syntactically related.
7. Finally, the sentence is assigned a value corresponding to the square of the number of high-frequency noncommon words within

Exhibit 10.1
Source: Scientific American, Vol. 196, No. 2, 86–94, February, 1957
Title: Messengers of the Nervous System
Author: Amodeo S. Marrazzi
Editor's Subheading: The internal communication of the body is mediated by chemicals as well as by nerve impulses. Study of their interaction has developed important leads to the understanding and therapy of mental illness.

Auto-Abstract*
It seems reasonable to credit the single-celled organisms also with a system of chemical communication by diffusion of stimulating substances through the cell, and these correspond to the chemical messengers (e.g., hormones) that carry stimuli from cell to cell in the more complex organisms. (7.0)†
Finally in the vertebrate animals there are special glands (e.g., the adrenals) for producing chemical messengers, and the nervous and chemical communication systems are intertwined: for instance, release of adrenalin by the adrenal gland is subject to control both by nerve impulses and by chemicals brought to the gland by the blood. (6.4)
The experiments clearly demonstrated that acetylcholine (and related substances) and adrenalin (and its relatives) exert opposing actions which maintain a balanced regulation of the transmission of nerve impulses. (6.3)
It is reasonable to suppose that the tranquilizing drugs counteract the inhibitory effect of excessive adrenalin or serotonin or some related inhibitor in the human nervous system. (7.3)

---
* Sentences selected by means of statistical analysis as having a degree of significance of 6 and over.
† Significance factor is given at the end of each sentence.

SIGNIFICANT WORDS IN DESCENDING ORDER OF FREQUENCY (COMMON WORDS OMITTED).

46 NERVE	12 BODY	6 DISTURBANCE	4 ACCUMULATE
40 CHEMICAL	12 EFFECTS	6 RELATED	4 BALANCE
28 SYSTEM	12 ELECTRICAL	5 CONTROL	4 BLOCK
22 COMMUNICATION	12 MENTAL	5 DIAGRAM	4 DISORDERS
19 ADRENALIN	12 MESSENGERS	5 FIBERS	4 END
18 CELL	10 SIGNALS	5 GLAND	4 EXCITATION
18 SYNAPSE	10 STIMULATION	5 MECHANISMS	4 HEALTH
16 IMPULSES	8 ACTION	5 MEDIATORS	4 HUMAN
16 INHIBITION	8 GANGLION	5 ORGANISM	4 OUTGOING
15 BRAIN	7 ANIMAL	5 PRODUCE	4 REACHING
15 TRANSMISSION	7 BLOOD	5 REGULATE	4 RECORDING
13 ACETYLCHOLINE	7 DRUGS	5 SEROTONIN	4 RELEASE
13 EXPERIMENT	7 NORMAL		4 SUPPLY
13 SUBSTANCES			4 TRANQUILIZING

bracketed sections. After all sentences are assigned a value, they are ranked and the highest ones selected for the auto-abstract.

The experiments on automatic abstracting in other places are too numerous to mention here; it may suffice to give one example, the work of V. A. Oswald and his colleagues at Planning Research Corporation, reported in 1959. The objectives of Oswald's research were much the same as Luhn's—to isolate the sentences in an article which, in the language of the author, most completely expressed the subject content. Whereas Luhn stressed the word frequency count, and word correlation—the co-occurrence within a sentence of single noncommon high-frequency words—Oswald expanded this to include "all juxtapositions of meaning bearing forms of highest frequency" which he called *multiterms*. His hypothesis was that the most significant sentences in a document would be those in which the maximal co-occurrence of high-frequency multiterms would be found.

The research procedure was performed manually but was obviously suitable for computer programs. It operated as follows:

1. The text of the document was examined and all articles, prepositions, conjunctions, were culled. In addition, high-frequency qualifiers of minimal semantic importance like "good," "very," etc., were also discarded.
2. Occurrences of high-frequency words were posted and ranked, and multiterms were noted whenever two or more high-frequency words were in juxtaposition.
3. Significant sentences for display were selected each time a given sentence contained at least three multiterms.

Much of the research in subsequent years was evaluative in nature, aimed at demonstrating by some criterion (usually by comparison of machine output to the choices of human judges) which procedures produced the best automatic abstracts. We discuss one such effort, that of H. P. Edmundson (1969), in Chapter Eleven on Evaluation.

At this point, one aspect of the use of word frequencies has to be clarified. People in the field have occasionally expressed concern about the effect of suffixes on word counts. Note that the word-frequency list at the bottom of Exhibit 10.1 reveals plurals as well as singular forms, and also words ending in -ing, -ed, and other common suffixes. One would correctly suspect that some of the words on that list (for example, "cell," "synapse," and "impulses") exist both as singular and plural forms in the actual text. Also, one encounters such variants as "cellular" or "synaptic." Luhn's word-counting procedure took such variants as occurrences of the same word, and ordinarily (within the confines of a single article or singly authored document) this would be a safe assumption.

However, exceptions to this rule happen often enough that the outcome of a frequency count can in those cases be adversely affected. Words like "community" and "communication," which are not suffixed variants but (as far as common usage is concerned) are different words with different meanings. Yet Luhn's procedure would count them as instances of the same word.

When one takes a close look at how such incorrect counts affect output, however, it becomes apparent that one is mistaken to think that incorrect counts really constitute a flaw in the word-frequency approach. This also applies to other sources of counting error, for example, to failure to count synonyms as instances of occurrence of the same word. An example of this latter kind of error can be seen in Exhibit 10.2, which presents counts of frequent words and multiterms attained in the procedure of V. A. Oswald. Note that the word "orbit" and the word "path" mean essentially the same thing. (Good writers commonly make use of synonyms in reference to meanings that they have to use often. Too many occurrences of "orbit ... orbit ... orbit" in the same stretch of text makes for monotonous reading, so now and then the word "path" is used. In physics the word "path" is a somewhat more general term than "orbit," but a glance at the accompanying multiterms indicates that the author indeed used it as a synonym for "orbit.")

Suppose it were possible to count "path" and "orbit" as occurrences of the same "word." The count for that word would be 49+18, or 67, making it the most frequent word on Oswald's list. Also, the multiterms "elliptic orbit" and "elliptic path" would be combined to give a count that would cause that multiterm to rank higher than the term "equatorial orbit." Other synonyms can be found that will affect the counts (note "vehicle," a synonym both for "rocket" and, probably, "satellite"). What really happens if, for example, the words and multiterms are used to score word-rich sentences for selection in an automatic abstracting process? When synonyms are counted *separately*, "satellite" is the most frequent word, and sentences containing it are scored higher than sentences containing "orbit." When synonyms are counted together as the same word, "orbit" and "path" now constitute the most frequent word, and sentences containing them are scored higher. Clearly, no argument can be made as to which of these two variations of the process will produce a better result. If some inferior sentence lurking within the article has a high probability of being selected, one variation of the process is as likely to select it as the other.

Generally, the exact count of the occurrences of a word in an article is by itself insignificant. What matters in the word-frequency approach is the *identity* of the words that are frequently used. What matters even more

58	SATELLITE	13	ANGLE
6	EARTH SATELLITE	5	ELEVATION ANGLE
5	LOW-ALTITUDE SATELLITE	2	AZIMUTH ANGLE
49	ORBIT	2	COMPASS ANGLE
8	CIRCULAR ORBIT	12	CIRCULAR
5	EQUATORIAL ORBIT	12	MISSILE
4	ELLIPTIC ORBIT	3	BALLISTIC MISSILE
2	CIRCULAR SATELLITE ORBIT	3	ROCKET MISSILE
47	VELOCITY	12	SURFACE
16	EFFECTIVE LAUNCHING VELOCITY	11	EARTH'S SURFACE
5	BURNOUT VELOCITY	11	RANGE
4	INJECTION VELOCITY	3	FIRING RANGE
4	LAUNCHING VELOCITY	10	DIRECTION
3	ORBITAL VELOCITY	2	LAUNCHING DIRECTION
2	EXHAUST VELOCITY	10	ERROR
2	SATELLITE VELOCITY	10	VEHICLE
44	LAUNCHING	3	ROCKET VEHICLE
3	SATELLITE LAUNCHING	2	EARTH-ESCAPE VEHICLE
41	EARTH	2	RESEARCH VEHICLE
33	ALTITUDE	2	SATELLITE VEHICLE
6	ORBIT ALTITUDE		
2	INJECTION ALTITUDE		*ADDITIONAL MULTITERMS*
26	ROCKET		
2	LAUNCHING ROCKET	6	INJECTION POINT
21	INJECTION	4	ENERGY REQUIRED
18	PATH	4	LAUNCHING SITE
2	ELLIPTIC PATH	3	SATELLITE PROJECT
2	ORBITAL PATH	3	EARTH'S ROTATION
14	ENERGY	2	ROCKET ENGINE
4	LAUNCHING ENERGY		
3	POTENTIAL ENERGY		
2	KINETIC ENERGY		

Exhibit 10.2 Frequencies of Key Words and Multiterms—Oswald Study

than this is that the entire assemblage of frequent words gives an unmistakable indication of what the topic is, as is evident in Exhibit 10.2.

There does exist some experimental evidence on the question of whether one policy of regarding words equivalent is better than another. Specifically, Salton (1968) studied the effect of retaining or dropping suffixes on precision-recall measures of retrieval effectiveness. Salton concludes:

The results obtained ... are contradictory, in the sense that for two of the collections used (IRE-3 and ADI) the more thorough normalization inherent in the word stem process, compared with suffix s recognition alone, improves the search effectiveness; for the third collection (Cranfield), the reverse result appears to hold. For none of the collections is the improvement of one method over the other really dramatic, so that in practice either procedure might reasonably be used.

(Salton's work with the SMART evaluation system is discussed in Chapter Eleven.)

The waves of interest caused by Luhn's publicized ideas on the use of word frequency in automatic indexing and abstracting resulted in a number of people, all within the span of a few months it would seem, espousing approaches to word-frequency analysis somewhat more consummate than merely counting words.

Many of these, unlike V. A. Oswald, were not necessarily interested in automatic abstracting per se, but in achieving a generalized technology of automatic indexing, i.e., the selection of representative words and terms from text. An early example, the work of Phyllis Baxendale (1958) of the San Jose branch of International Business Machines, compared (*a*) straight frequency counting to (*b*) an inventory of words in topic sentences (usually the first sentence of each paragraph), and (*c*) a count of words in phrases following certain prepositions.

Like Luhn, Baxendale used a stop list, but also, interestingly, used a part of the stop list in the reverse way, allowing the presence of prepositions to govern the selection of words or groups of words. Wyllys (1968), reviewing work in the area comments:

> A rather surprising result (at least to the present writer) ... was the close similarity of the sets of representative words obtained by the three different selection processes. The same words, with very nearly the same relative* frequencies, tended to be chosen by all the methods. ... The similarity of these sets of representative words suggests that for uniformity of result there is no special reason for choosing one selection method over the others. ...

This observation accords well with the result of Salton and with the previous discussion about the effects of suffixes. Wyllys adds, however, that there would be practical reasons for preferring the topic sentence and prepositional phrase methods: less keypunching of text would have to be done. Sad to say, the possibility of a man–machine approach to automatic indexing suggested by the results of the Baxendale experiment was not intensively investigated during the 1960s when it could have had the

---

* Wyllys uses "relative frequency" to mean percent of all words tallied.

greatest value in overcoming the impediment posed by the need to keypunch.

Another significant mutation of the word-frequency approach was outlined by Edmundson and Wyllys (1961):

> Very general considerations from information theory suggest that a word's *information* should vary inversely with its frequency rather than directly, its lower probability evidencing greater selectivity or deliberation in its use. It is the rare, special, or technical word that will indicate most strongly the subject of an author's discussion. Here, however, it is clear that by "rare" we must mean *rare in general usage,* not rare within the document itself. In fact it would seem natural to regard the contrast between the word's relative frequency f within the document and its relative frequency r in general use ... as a more revealing indication of the world's value in indicating the subject matter of a document.

Edmundson and Wyllys therefore proposed the frequency ratio, f/r, as a criterion for a word's representativeness of the document containing it. An advantage of this criterion that can be most easily seen is that it does away with the need for a stop list in memory. Words like "of," "it," and "which" would have low values of f/r (in the neighborhood of unity) because the tendency of people to use them frequently would not change radically from one topic to another. However, such words as those in Exhibit 10.2 ("rocket," "satellite," etc.) can be expected to vary strongly with topic. The tendency of such words to concentrate in a few documents, incidentally, has been studied by quite a number of workers, a relatively recent one being Stone (1968). On the whole, there seems no doubt that f/r should measure what it is supposed to.

Unfortunately, the frequency ratio is an example of an idea which, though beautiful in concept, is not easy to carry out in practice. In making this observation one cannot help but be aware of an even broader one, i.e., that frequency methods in general have not been as successful in application as the automatic indexing ideas (especially KWIC) we discussed earlier. A central reason is one of economics. Up until recently most language data had to be keypunched, an expensive way to place words and sentences in computer storage. The fact that titles are *short* removed keypunching as an economic barrier to their processing. The keypunching of entire documents was prohibitively costly, and up until about 1965 only people engaging in research on language processing would do it.

Now, with the rise of photocomposition, much digitized text can be obtained cheaply as a by-product. As the economic barrier to whole-document storage becomes ever smaller, we can expect to see much greater interest in the practical application of frequency methods. Such conditions, auspicious to language data processing, have been a long time coming. (If the people who were thinking about relative frequency in the 1959–1961 period had known just *how* long, they would have been dismayed indeed.)

Whatever factors have stifled the word-frequency approach up to the present have had a vastly greater effect on relative frequency because of the problem of determining r in the frequency ratio f/r. Determining general usage for every word and term—even for those of one field—is an enormous undertaking technically, as well as a difficult one methodologically. The background sample would have to be at least as carefully and widely selected as that for the as yet unmatched 18-million word manual count performed in the 1930s (Thorndike & Lorge, 1944). No one to date, it appears, has had an occasion to assemble a stratified sample of text of such a large magnitude. Even if such a sample were to be assembled, there would remain several difficult problems regarding the method of totaling. The most severe of these is how to deal with homography. A number of technical fields have numerous quite common words in their jargon. Mathematics has words like "set," "square," "curve," and "integration," that are used frequently in other realms of discourse. Chemistry has "weight," "bond," and "heat," each in its own right a well-defined technical term. Physics has "mass," "motion," "wave," and of course "light"—the visible kind. Any such words would tend to be downgraded by use of the frequency ratio and be relatively unavailable for indexing. It is not unvaryingly the case that esoteric terms are best for indexing. The only kinds of general usage counts that could cause the relative frequency approach to work as intended would be one which permitted a computer to decide: Is this usage of the word "bond" as a chemical bond or some other kind of bond? (Of course, if the problem of homography could be conquered, we could also do high-quality machine translation and a lot of other things now unfeasible in language processing.)

The true importance of relative frequency was not what was accomplished with it per se, but the fact that people working with language processing at level one (of the aforementioned three levels of difficulty) shifted their attention away from merely analyzing individual documents in isolation to the idea of analyzing documents against a background of other documents—in other words, analyzing document *collections*.

Chapter Nine presented part of the story of document collection analysis as one of the branches of evolution taken by computerized information retrieval systems. Much of that portion of document collection analysis— that concerning associative indexing and automatic classification—operated through processing *index tags*, or facsimiles thereof, and did not operate directly on document text. Thus, it is somewhat at the fringes of language processing. The part of the story that has more to do with direct analysis of text we have saved over for this chapter.

In the years previous to 1958, numerous document collections had been amassed for experimental and even operational activities in computerized retrieval. But these were usually manually indexed collections, and only the index tags (most often uniterms) became involved in computer storage and retrieval. Then, partly because of Luhn's and Ohlman's dramatic introduction of permuted indexing at a major conference, and also partly because of a number of active research projects in machine translation were attracting attention, people began thinking of document collections as aggregates of text which could be computer stored, analyzed, and retrieved.

For some reason, much of the initial activity in analyzing the text of collections concentrated in the Los Angeles area, possibly because at that time more large computers were in use there than elsewhere—a state of affairs that no longer holds. Maron, whose work we discussed in Chapter Nine, experimented with a collection of *Science News Letter* articles. Don R. Swanson, a colleague of Maron's at Thompson Ramo Wooldridge in Los Angeles, had assembled a number of keypunched articles in nuclear physics. His research, which compared manual, library-type retrieval to machine searching of text, was one of the first intensively evaluative efforts in the field of text analysis, and for this reason we discuss it in Chapter Eleven.

It must be made clear at this point that neither Maron nor Swanson viewed their accumulations of text as anything more than collections to be retrieved *from*. Maron, however, did utilize the collection as a source of information about the relatedness of indexing tags, and his thinking was one of the beginning points of the idea of rounding out inadequate search requests by mobilizing highly co-occurring terms. Another researcher who just happened to be thinking along the same lines was Doyle (1959) of System Development Corporation in Santa Monica. His view of the value of word or term co-occurrence was as a source for the generation of browsing aids or as a means of feedback from computer storage in a man–machine iterative-searching system. A computer, through analysis of the word content of the entire corpus of a document collection, could present to an information searcher—via cathode-ray display—an "association map" (Doyle, 1962) consisting of words or terms that co-occur strongly, and "drawn" on the scope face so that links are placed to show appropriate co-occurrences. Figure 10.3 shows a final stage of an iterative search in which words within individual documents are related to words (in bold type) that a group of closely related documents have in common. The "diagrammatic representations of individual documents" are intended to contain enough terminological information to permit some degree of relevance judgment by the searcher, thus functioning as abstracts. In one of

312   The Processing of Language Data

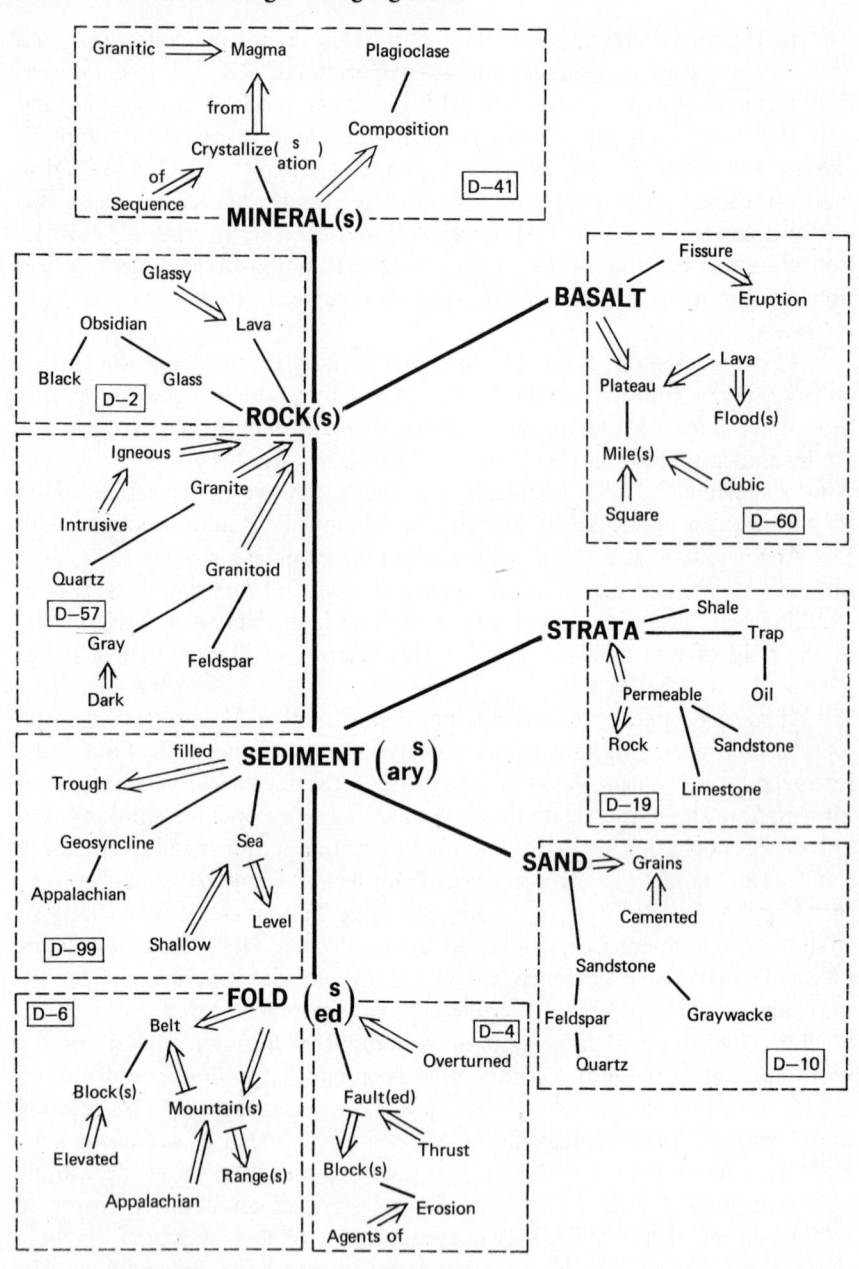

Figure 10.3.

those twists of fate that sometimes occur in the development of a new area, two workers also at System Development Corporation (see reference to Ford and Holmes at the end of Chapter Eleven), unknown to Doyle and for reasons entirely unconnected with his project, began a project to evaluate various kinds of intelligence summaries in which they compared the effectiveness as retrieval aids of conventional abstracts to hand-drawn "term diagrams" (looking much like those in Figure 10.3). The outcome of their work is described in Chapter Eleven. A program was actually written and run, in an effort sponsored by Rome Air Development Center (Doyle, 1965), to produce association maps on printout paper, generated from most-frequent-word input. But like other ideas involving the word-frequency approach, the association map was ahead of its time.

Recently, however, the idea has begun to revive in various forms, as display scopes are becoming increasingly available as peripheral equipment, particularly in on-line systems. One example is Treu (1968), who, in an article entitled "The Browser's Retrieval Game," advances the concept of remote file browsing, based on the ability of the searcher to explore and probe the index vocabulary of the system for highly associated terms. An experimental system was tried out, though not in an operational setting. A more recent example of a display-scope based retrieval system is described by Thompson (1971). In this system, as shown in Figure 10.4, an on-line searcher works his way down a hierarchy from a highly general level (categories such as biological, social, and behavioral sciences) through intermediate levels (circulatory, respiratory, digestive systems) to very detailed levels (arteries, veins, capillaries).

These arrays of categories were not derived from frequency counts, however, and thus not from the text of the documents to which the diagrams refer, and one would perhaps not be inclined to call the methodology *language processing*. But by this way of defining it, neither was KWIC indexing language processing, since titles, in a sense, are not necessarily any more derived from the document text than subject heading hierarchies would be. We can satisfy the issue by saying that the display diagram shown in Figure 10.4 is, like KWIC, a legitimate starting point on the road to language processing. It is interesting to note that a complete technology package existed at System Development Corporation in 1966 for deriving hierarchical displays directly from text. Unfortunately, it was in two separate pieces. One was the BOLD system (Bibliographic On-Line Display—Borko and Burnaugh, 1966), and the other was a hierarchical labeling system programmed by Blankenship (Borko, Blankenship, and Burket, 1968).

At the end of the 1960s at least two experimental systems were in being that offered the potential to display frequencies and co-occurrence data directly from text. One is Salton's SMART system at Cornell Univer-

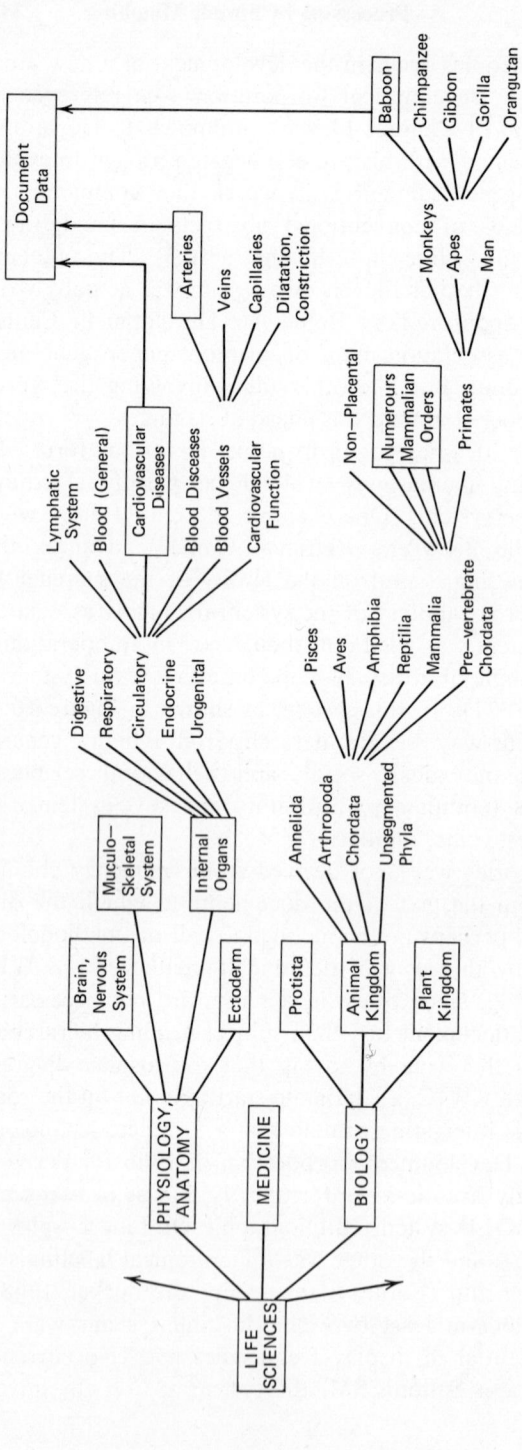

Figure 10.4. Illustration of a possible index tree display in which a searcher, using CRT, can selectively work his way from general to specific, with the option of making coordinations (such as "baboon," "arteries," and "cardiovascular disease") at any level of specificity. The hierarchies shown here are well-known but most would not be, and the display would convey information as well as guidance.

sity, which we discuss in Chapter Eleven. The other, called IRMA (Internal Report Management Aid), is at Arthur D. Little, Inc., in Boston. Curtice and Jones (1969), commenting on the history of automatic indexing, point out:

> Four major changes have taken place since the bulk of the early work was done, and these changes figured importantly in our determination that the use of the techniques in an operational system was becoming feasible and cost/effective:
> a. Disk storage units have become rather commonly available for use as storage media and as scratch space for sorting.
> b. The cost of computer operations has continued to fall, and many of the practical problems of time-sharing and multiprogramming have been solved.
> c. Display technology has matured to the point where using such terminals is convenient and the cost is moderate.
> d. The cost of people has continued to rise, and the investment in salaries has increasingly been recognized as a *major* system cost....

The ultimate promise of word-frequency techniques is that through them an information searcher can use a computer to browse at any level of detail in text, and over a much greater general-to-specific range than is shown in Figure 10.4. Realization of this potential is what caused so many to take, perhaps, a prematurely vigorous start. (In 1964 the National Bureau of Standards held a symposium on statistical methods of text analysis featuring 25 papers and attended by more than 100 registrants—Stevens, 1965.) Part of the languishing since then has been due to a downturn in research funding that has affected language processing as a whole as well as countless other comparable realms.

There are at present great differences of opinion as to what one might conclude about word-frequency methods, as evidenced by the contrasting viewpoints of Annual Review chapters covering the area:

1. ... The particular point we seem to have reached is the realization that statistical methods for textual analysis are inadequate. This is evidenced by the absence of reports of work along these lines.... It is disappointing that the early and ingenious ideas of H. P. Luhn for matching terms against text on a purely statistical basis have proved to be abortive, for here was promise of the possibility of eliminating the enormous problems of syntax and semantics.... (Sharp, 1967)
2. [In direct response to Sharp's appraisal] ... It is this writer's guess that the ideas of Luhn, far from being abortive, may really come into their own within the next few years. The simple language processing methods, including small stored dictionaries, appear to be far more

powerful than was originally thought possible; such methods will likely be used for most of the language processing tasks actually implemented on computers, including applications in library science and information retrieval. More refined methods, including semantic and syntactic analyses, are needed for some applications such as language translation. . . . (Salton, 1968b)

Salton's statement interrelates all of the three levels of language processing difficulty, that we have alluded to, and now we discuss the second level of difficulty, which includes among its elements dictionaries and syntactic analysis.

PROCESSING BY STRUCTURAL ANALYSIS OF SENTENCES

The history of computerized language processing may be looked upon as a monument to getting the cart before the horse. Normally, a new line of research and development will begin its attack on two levels; (*a*) the mobilization of what is already known for the sake of solving practical problems, and (*b*) the pursuit of basic lines of research, serving the longer-range objectives of enabling the profession to solve more difficult practical problems. In fact, language processing did not begin with either path, but, in dead earnest proceeded at once toward attaining practical solution of what has turned out to be one of the most difficult of language-processing tasks: machine translation of languages.

When the first work on machine translation began at Georgetown and Harvard Universities in the early 1950s essentially no knowledge existed on the use of computers for syntactic, semantic, or statistical analysis of text. Of course, the need for such knowledge soon became recognized by those conducting such projects (more than ten of which existed by 1960); but forays into syntactic and other forms of analysis, which otherwise might have been made for their own sakes, tended to be begrudged by-products of the main effort. What has been realized in nearly all quarters by now is that *fully automatic high-quality translation* (as it has been frequently termed) is at the third level of difficulty in language processing. In other words, to attain it a computer would have to be supplied with the labyrinthine background knowledge of a human translator (Bar-Hillel, 1964, p. 182).

The subject of machine translation of languages has only a glancing relationship to information storage and retrieval. We allude to it mainly to explain the developmental history of language processing. In particular, the spreading awareness of the difficulties and frustrations of machine translation gave a large thrust to the study of sentence structure, and to the field of computational linguistics, whose main concern has been sentence structure. At the end of Chapter Eight, in Kellogg's CONVERSE, we saw one example of the applicability of syntactic analysis of sentences to an information retrieval problem. We are now ready to discuss the subject per se.

Syntactic Analysis. Many people have had an experience or two in parsing a sentence in high school English. Those who remember the experience probably also remember their bewilderment of having to decide which words were nouns, and which were other parts of speech, (verbs, adjectives, prepositions, etc.). Then one would decide which is the subject, which is the predicate, and which are the dependent and independent clauses. The fun part (for some but not for others) would come in drawing a neat diagram consisting of the sentence's words and lines between them. The sentence's structure, or syntax, would then have been analyzed.

A student, no matter how difficult he finds it to analyze an English sentence, has an enormous head start over any computer program written to parse a sentence; he can generally determine his parts of speech *first*, before he does anything else. Consider the sentence:

"I am going to court if their rent checks bounce."

A parsing program will have a dictionary available, and it can therefore "know" immediately that "I" is a pronoun, "am" is a verb, and "if" is a conjunction, because this information has been implanted by the programmer in the dictionary entries for "I," "am," and "if." But the dictionary says that "court" can be either a noun or a verb, and there is not much in the sentence to help decide which. If "court" were preceded by an article, or followed by suffixes -ed or -ing, only a small amount of information would be needed in storage for deciding the issue. As the sentence stands, "court" could easily be a verb, giving a sentence of the form: "I am going to (flip) if their rent checks bounce." It could also give a more idiomatic parsing of the form: "I am going to (see if) their rent checks bounce."

The sentence-parsing student knows immediately, however, that "court" is a noun. Otherwise the sentence doesn't make sense. He also knows that "checks" is a noun and "bounce" is a verb. But the computer must reckon with the possibility that "checks" is a verb and "bounce" is a noun ("more bounce to the ounce"). A point to note here, as an assist to the computer program, is that if "bounce" is determinate, then "checks" also is, and vice versa. If the sentence had read: "I am going to court if their rent checks *the* bounce," then (if the reader will momentarily ignore the fact that the sentence now doesn't make sense) "bounce" would be decidable as a noun (being preceded by "the") and "check" would have to be designated a verb, otherwise it would not be possible to analyze the structure of the "if" clause, since evey clause must have a verb. We shall shortly appreciate the function of a verb in sentence structure. But before that, the point is rounded out that a computer program, not having the means of determining in one pass *all* of the parts of speech in a typical sentence, must operate differently from the student at the blackboard. Characteristically, a program will determine as many parts of speech as it can in one left-to-right pass through a sentence. Then, using information gleaned in this pass, it can often subsequently resolve the remaining ambiguities. In any given pass through a sentence, a program can only work on one word at a time. (Despite the fact that today's multiprocessing technologies permit computers to do a number of things simultaneously, programming's nature has not changed.) Therefore, in the last sample sentence, the first left-to-right scan encounters the word "checks" before it has the ambiguity-reducing information it will acquire from "the bounce," and a second scan will be needed to properly designate "checks."

A wide variety of different techniques for parsing sentences by computer are being practiced. Collectively, they are called *grammars*. One of the best existing grammars* to use in explaining how a computer can determine sentence structure is an *immediate constituent grammar*. In computational linguistics and allied branches of mathematics, any linear sequence of distinct words or symbols is known as a "string." A sentence, then, is a string. An immediate constituent grammar regards the string representing a sentence to be made up of a number of hierarchically related substrings. In a grammatical sentence, it is always possible to break the string, or any of its substrings, into two component parts, and these parts may be (*a*) two words, (*b*) a word and a substring, or (*c*) two substrings. Normally, for purposes of syntactic analysis, the word is the lowest level of breakdown. A computer program, however, synthesizes this structure from the word level up, so perhaps the word "breakdown" is slightly misleading. Consider the sentence:

"The man from the insurance company stands at the front door."

On the first pass, a parsing program looks for nouns and verbs, and tries to form substrings consisting of 2 words. "The man" is the first obvious candidate, and it is bracketed as a possible noun phrase. So is "insur-

---

* A good discussion of major types of grammar may be found in Bobrow's chapter of "Automated Language Processing" (Borko, 1968).

ance company." The word "stands" could be a noun, and this possibility must be taken into account, tentatively at least. "Company stands" is bracketed. Here, however, one of the basic rules of immediate constituent grammars is called into play: structure must be hierarchical,* which means that the substring categories cannot overlap. "Company stands" is still a legal possibility, but it must be considered as a *separate parsing* from the one having the constituent "insurance company," to avoid overlapping on the word "company." (Later on, however, the parsing built around "company stands" will be rejected because under that interpretation no verb can be found in the sentence.)

After the two-word constituents have been listed, the basis is at hand for generating 3-word constituents. At this point it is time to state that the program has a system of rules available for generating substrings. These rules specify what combinations of parts of speech and *substring types* (verb phrase, noun phrase, etc.) are permissible. The following rules apply to the sentence we are considering:

1. Sentence = $NP + VP$
2. $NP = NP + PP$
3. $NP = T + N$
4. $VP = V + PP$ ($VP = V + NP$, quite common, is not used in this example.)
5. $PP = P + NP$
6. $N = A + N$

(NP = noun phrase, VP = verb phrase, PP = prepositional phrase, T = article, N = noun or modified noun, A = adjective, V = verb, and, P = preposition.)

On the first bracketing pass, only rules 3 and 6 could be used, since no substrings (NP, VP, PP, or modified noun) had yet been formed. On the second pass, some modified nouns and one NP had been formed, and due to the latter, rule 5 becomes available for use. On the second pass, ignoring the substring "company stands," a parsing that will eventually be thrown out, rule 3 makes it possible to form "the insurance company," and "the front door," and on the third pass rule 5 permits the formation of "from the insurance company" and "at the front door." In such a manner are larger and larger substrings built up until, finally, rule 1 permits the joining of subject and predicate.

---

* In a hierarchical structure, a subcategory must be wholly contained within a category. Partial containment (overlap) is not allowed.

The gross bracketing pattern can be represented as:

$$\{(\text{THE MAN})\,\{\text{FROM}\,[\text{THE}\,(\text{INSURANCE COMPANY})]\}\}$$

$$\{\text{STANDS}\,\{\text{AT}\,[\text{THE}\,(\text{FRONT DOOR})]\}\}$$

The words, plus the bracket assignments, plus the code (*NP, VP,* etc.) associated with each pair of brackets, are all that is required to represent the complete sentence structure. For blackboard purposes, however, it is more common to represent the sentence as a labeled "tree structure," i.e.:

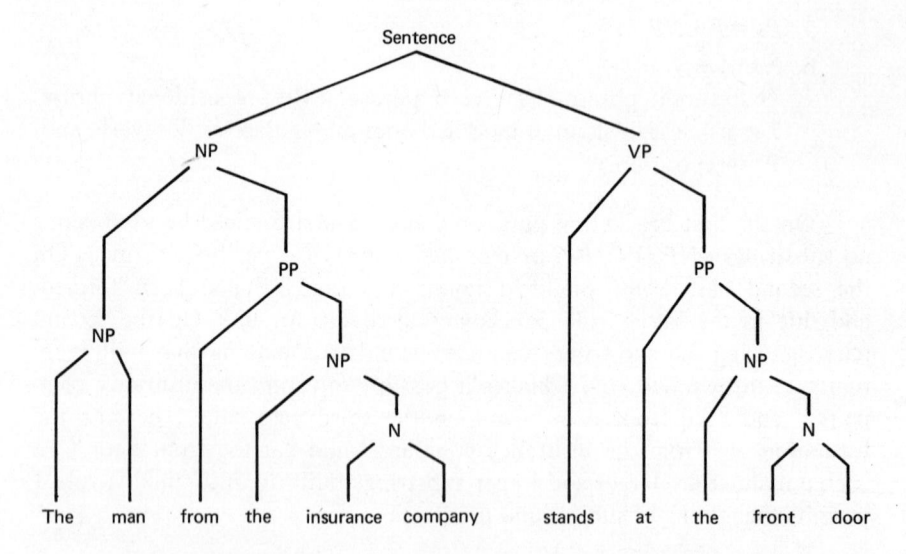

An immediate constituent grammar, in the terminology of computational linguistics, is a context-free phrase structure grammar. It is context-free because the rules for forming substrings use *only* part of speech and substring type (*NP, VP,* etc.) as a source of information to govern the process. A context-dependent grammar would allow the rules to be applied differently when certain types of context are sensed. An example of where a context-dependent grammar might come in handy can be found in the sentence: "He stands knocking at the front door." When this sentence is compared to another similar one: "He stands knocking very well," the possibility of two different interpretations can be seen. A context-sensitive grammar might resolve such an issue by permitting the word "knocking" to be a gerund-type noun in all simple situations, but allowing a compound verb interpretation (stands and knocks at the front door) whenever a prepositional phrase follows the would-be verb. The reader is invited to think of a case where a context-dependent grammar *always* resolves such ambiguities (it's difficult!).

A further kind of grammar is shown as *dependency analysis* (Hays, 1961). Taking the place of the substring-forming rules of an immediate constituent grammar is a system of dependency relationships, so constructed that the predicate verb is the only word in a sentence that is not dependent on another word. The subject noun is dependent on the verb, and this is represented graphically by slanting a line from the noun upward to the verb. Adjectives are dependent on nouns, articles on nouns, adverbs on verbs, adjectives, and adverbs, prepositions on whatever words the prepositional phrase modifies, and nouns in prepositional phrases on the preposition, and so on. Each dependency is shown as a line slanting down to the dependent word. One can thereby build a dependency tree with the verb at the top:

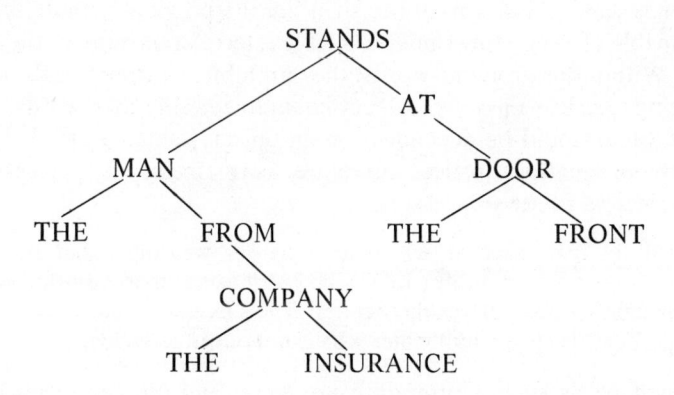

```
                    STANDS
                   /      \
                  /        AT
                 /           \
              MAN            DOOR
             /   \          /    \
          THE    FROM     THE    FRONT
                   \
                 COMPANY
                 /     \
               THE    INSURANCE
```

We have chosen to consider a dependency grammar because through it can be explained one interesting (and potentially relevant to information retrieval) facet of syntactic analysis, namely, the generation of original grammatical sentences by computer. Suppose one had a list of a large number of English words in computer storage, with indications of parts of speech by each word, along with a set of dependency rules and a set of random numbers. The selection of the next random number would determine how a given sentence might be added to. One would start with a verb, of course, and build the sentence on it. For a 2-word sentence like: "Birds are," one might have a number table from zero to nine, e.g.,

>   0 = Add period, sentence complete.
>   1 = Add an adjective.
>   2 = Add an article.
>   3 = Add a preposition . . . and so on

from which one picks the next step by chance, that is, by picking a digit from the random number table. Dependency rules would determine which word of the sentence should be modified by the added word. Selection of any given part of speech from the stored list would also be by chance.

Now as the reader can well imagine, such a "mindless" process of building sentences could not be expected to produce anything intelligent, nor even intelligible. Something should result like: "The terribly kind-hearted foresight is under asparagus which is ordinarily granulated in the strap shapes." However, the dependency rules will guarantee that a grammatical sentence will result.

Klein and Simmons (1963), however, managed to generate discourse randomly that was surprisingly intelligible—and even having a plot, so long as not too many sentences in a row are generated. First of all, they selected a sufficiently small number of words which (unlike the words "asparagus" and "kindhearted foresight" in the previous sample sentence) were capable of suggesting understandable interrelationships to the average person. Within this group of words, they prohibited certain kinds of words from being too close on a dependency chain to certain other words. A color (yellow, blue) could be dependent on an object (table, shirt), but not on a concept or quality (justice, curvature, correctness). The results were more or less as follows:

> A beautiful homewrecker who was a dancer wearing a hat is beautiful Helen. Successful unfaithful John who is a businessman who killed a bullfighter fighting bulls drives the Bentley. The successful husband of a beautiful dancer suspects the bullfighter who is unfaithful to Helen.

Unfortunately, as such a procedure grinds on and on, the result changes from interesting to confusing, redundant, and contradictory. What is significant here is that a technology is possible that can generate a series of highly readable sentences. The sort of *macro rules* that Klein used to control nonsense can be carried to almost any lengths. We have more to say about this at the third level of difficulty.

In considering the sentence generating process as explained in terms of random selection of words, a while back, one can see a possible advantage of the immediate constituent grammar over the dependency grammar, in that the latter is forced to add words to a sentence it is generating one word at a time, whereas the former can build prefabricated phrase structures (*NP, VP*), for which it then has combining rules.

Syntax as an Aid to Noncognitive Question-Answering Systems. In Kellogg's CONVERSE system (Chapter Eight), we saw one way in which syntactic analysis could be used in the retrieval of information. In that system, a question containing words from a selected vocabulary could be transformed into a data retrieval routine, partly by virtue of the correspondence between the major content words of the question and units of the data base. One can also design systems to perform somewhat parallel operations on text. This was done experimentally by Simmons (1967) in a system called *Protosynthex*, which could retrieve individual sentences and paragraphs from a children's encyclopedia.

The system was operated at one of the first time-sharing installations, that sponsored by the Advanced Research Projects Agency (ARPA) at System Development Corporation at Santa Monica. In this type of system, at the beginning of the questioning procedure a first try question is typed on a Teletype console, and this is responded to by a printout of related words, rather than by an answer. For example, the question, "What animals live longer than man?" elicits a display such as:

Word	Words of Related Meaning
animals	mammals, reptiles, fish
live	age, inhabit, exist
longer	greater, larger, older
man	men, person, people, human

The printout also contains information on which of the words coexist in sentences; this feature allows the question to be properly reworded to correspond to sentences actually in the stored text.

The next time a question is typed in, it and those sentences containing the words that might be an answer to it are analyzed syntactically—in this case by means of a dependency grammar. All sentences having inappropriate dependency relations are screened out. As an example, if the question had been, "What do worms eat?", only sentences in which "worm" occurs as a subject and is dependent on "eat" would be acceptable. A sentence such as, "Small birds eat insects, worms, and seeds" can be suppressed.

This approach to question-answering is not very effective, for a variety of reasons. The simplest and most practical reasons are:

1. No corpus of digitally stored text is likely to contain enough information to provide answers for more than a fraction of questions that might be asked (a limitation that should recede as time goes on).
2. There is much information in a given store of text that cannot be tapped by simple sentence-retrieval approaches. (Example: An encyclopedia might state, "Some tortoises are believed to attain an age of 300 years," which could constitute an answer to, "What animals live longer than man?" The required inference may be a simple one, but it cannot be made by the system described above.)
3. Much information in text is implied rather than stated. ("Boll weevils cost cotton farmers four million dollars annually" is capable of answering a question about what boll weevils eat. Indeed, so does the term "boll weevil"; they eat cotton bolls.)
4. Short of an as yet unrealized true cognitive language-processing system, a selective printout or display format based on the key words of a request (e.g., the sort of on-line KWIC generator discussed earlier in the chapter) is likely to represent a more effective man–machine balance than any of the more machine intensive processes achieved so far.

PROCESSING BY MEANS OF SEMANTIC OR CONCEPTUAL SCHEME

Text was designed for people to read, and not for indexing or for information retrieval. Anyone who has worked very long on either the first or second levels of difficulty of language processing knows what this means. The human mind contains an enormously complex and intricate model of the world, encompassing not only the aspects of a human being's own experience, but including all imaginable universes to which one individual might have given any attention over his lifespan from fleeing galaxies at the edge of the cosmos down to angels dancing on pinpoints. Any person who writes text, for other people to read, knows that he is addressing this huge model, and to be comprehensible he must write according to his own, hopefully accurate, notion of the state of his typical reader's knowledge.

Processing by Means of Semantic or Conceptual Scheme 325

A pertinent point about writing readable text is that a writer should contrive to use as few words as possible to achieve a given communicative effect. For example, he doesn't keep repeating key content words: he may at the outset say, "information retrieval system," equating it with "library" or "index" or some other concept he is sure will be a part of his reader's mental model of the world. Later in his text, he will shorten that to "retrieval system," and still later to "system." A point may occur at which the writer simply says "it" to avoid monotonous repetition of the word "system." (A legal document is an example of the text that results when an author does not follow such practices.)

Such use of pronouns and pronominal nouns like "system" is only one aspect of the writing art. The writer takes advantage of his reader's concepts by making use of images and analogies. He moves his level of discourse form generic to specific levels and back again. He gives examples of what he is discussing. All these ways of taking advantage of what he knows the reader knows contribute to the diversity of language units and structures, and make language—as discussed at the beginning of this chapter—unsuitable for processing by any mechanism other than the human brain. (However, the computer can be used to help humans process language in an analytical way. A field exists—stylistic analysis—in which features of written language can be inventoried by computer. But the brain of the human analyst is then needed to figure out what the computer results mean. (Sedelow, 1971)).

Computerized processing of language at what we have been calling "the third level of difficulty" involves attempts to design, store, and use cognitive structures or networks that can interrelate meanings of words in a way resembling the human brain's own ability to interrelate meanings and concepts. Though the human brain is able to store vast amounts of information relating to each word or concept, a computational linguist (or semanticist) is likely to try to see how far he can get in simulating cognitive processes by storing a modest amount (i.e., realistically, "now feasible" amount) of information per word or concept. Anaphoric analysis can sometimes get this information directly from text. For example, in the sentence: "Give the bananas to the monkeys although they are not ripe," the occurrence of the pair "ripe bananas" but not "ripe monkeys" elsewhere in the text would decide the ambiguity. A linguist is more apt to develop a scheme in which he himself can store information in a somewhat more generic way. Thus, Wilks (1973) builds networks of templates by which one can decide not only that "ripe" applies to vegetable entities and not animal, but also that "whisky" is a liquid and can be contained in "glasses" and "stomachs," thus removing the ambiguity in the sentence:

"John drank the whisky from the glass and it felt warm in his stomach."

Two general comments can be made about the plight of those who have attempted to work at the third level of difficulty:

1. They have not had to start from scratch. By the time people began to simulate cognitive processes on computers, psychologists and psycholinguists had already stored up a great deal of thought and research on how the brain deals with information and meaning. Two of the most well-known examples of work in the area are *A Study of Thinking* (Bruner, 1956) and *The Measurement of Meaning* (Osgood, 1957).
2. The chance of any now-living language-processing worker duplicating even a minor fraction of the brain's ability to handle concepts and meaning (and hence language) is almost nil. On the other hand, it is essential to pursue such work, not only because it is the kind of research that yields unanticipated by-products, but also because men must gain experience in *dealing with complexity* if they are to approach full utilization of computers—and obviously the complexity of human thinking is an important kind of complexity.

The processing of language in a cognitive or human-like way is subdiscipline of *artificial intelligence*, a field that subsumes the simulation of numerous intellectual activities in which humans engage, such as chess playing, theorem proving, puzzle solving, and so on. The prospects for equalling or surpassing human abilities in some realms of artificial intelligence are quite good, for the simple reason that the *amount of information* that has to be brought to bear in some of these realms is much less than the human brain characteristically must avail itself of. An extreme example of "much less" is the simulation of a student doing arithmetic (Bobrow, 1968).

Unfortunately for researchers in artificial intelligence, "amount of information" is not the only issue involved in the apparent superiority of the human brain over computers. Another issue is the human brain's uncanny ability to choose appropriate problem-solving strategies from among hundreds, thousands, or even millions of possible strategies.

This ability is brought out when researchers try to simulate human chess-playing on a computer. As is well-known to chess players, white has 20 possible opening moves, to which black has 20 possible replies, leading to a possible 400 different first move combinations. There are actually more than 100,000 possible two-move sequences (two each by white and by black), and this number expands quickly into the millions and billions in the third and fourth moves. A computer program, having no rules to guide it save those of chess itself (i.e., which moves are legal), would have to execute billions of operations to duplicate human ability to look several moves ahead (and, as we know, some humans can see five, six, or seven moves ahead). A large part of the problem of computerized chess is to find ways of cutting down the search space from billions to some manageable number. (A human being apparently does this by simply refusing to think about most of the *possible* moves—but how does one decide which moves not to think about? Therein lies the problem.)

Simulation of human language-using ability involves *simultaneously* coping with the "amount of information" issue and the "cutting down the search space" issue. The widely acknowledged first step is to simulate the human brain's capability to make inferences. As a simple minded example of both the thought-saving and knowledge-saving power of inference, consider the question: "How many Wednesdays have fallen on July 4 since the year 1836?" First, one does not have to store the entire calendar from 1836 to the present to answer this question; today's day and date plus the rules of calendar (occurrence of leap years, etc.) are the only information necessary. Second, one does not have to inspect every possible calendar date to see if it is both a Wednesday and a July 4; one can compute how many July 4th's are Wednesdays. (Some humans can do this quite easily.) Inference is important for fact retrieval systems because it can both cut down the amount of information that has to be stored as well as the number of operations required to obtain specified information (Travis, 1973).

A general question in artificial intelligence has been that of when a computer can be said to equal or surpass human ability. Need a computer actually defeat a human in some contest? A spokesman of the artificial intelligence field predicted in 1958 that in ten years the world's chess champion would be a computer. Fifteen years have now passed, but, as everyone knows, Bobby Fischer is not a computer. However, mastery may not be a fair test of duplication of human capability. The most widely accepted test is probably the "Turing test," as explained here by Weston (1970):

> ... Regarding the outward identifying characteristics of an artificial "intelligence," the public idea is essentially the same as that of the researchers, and in substance amounts to the requirement that such a thing must act human. This was once stated by A. M. Turing as the *Turing test*. This test postulates that a machine can converse with a human through any appropriate means, cathode-ray displays, Teletype, simulated voice, or whatever, and if the person, not knowing that a machine is at the other end of the channel, is still satisfied after however long he wishes to maintain the conversation that it could be a person at the other end, then the machine has passed the test and can be considered intelligent. ...

If, then, a computer today can yield a game of chess indistinguishably different from that of a mediocre human chess player, it may be considered "intelligent" at chess. It does not have to beat Bobby Fischer. The importance of meeting the Turing test in the processing of language is that man–machine interaction will be considerably enhanced once this is achieved. Moreover, passing the Turing test need not *necessarily* depend on solving all of the problems connected with the complexity of the brain and its processes of interrelating meanings and concepts. A routine that would generate a long string of sentences that pass the Turing test could be coupled with a nonhuman, relatively conventional information retrieval system (such as Kellogg's CONVERSE—Chapter Eight) to yield an information facility not too much different, in palatability of interaction at least, from a human expert.

Weizebaum (1967) refers to a "computer therapist" that produces responses eerily suggestive of what human therapists say in response to a patient (or, at least, of what the public has been led to believe they say). Example (S=statement by human, R=response by computer therapist):

S: I thought it would be a good thing to talk to you.
R: I see. But why do you really want to talk to me?
S: Well, my boyfriend made me come here.
R: Your boyfriend made you come here?
S: He says I'm depressed much of the time.
R: I'm sorry to hear that you're depressed.
S: It's true. I am unhappy.
R: Do you think coming here will help you not to be unhappy?
S: Perhaps I could learn to get along with my mother.
R: Tell me about your mother.

An important condition in the Turing test is that the person (S) must be still satisfied after "however long he wishes to maintain the conversation that it could be a person at the other end." It is doubtful that any existing language-simulating system could satisfy that aspect of the Turing test. Human therapists, who need not worry about their jobs, soon store up impressions and memories about a patient to the point that their responses become more and more tailored by what they know about a specific patient. The above computer therapist, however, after several hours of exchanges with a given patient, would probably still respond to a sentence of S such as, "Yesterday I had another quarrel with my mother," with an understanding electronic nod and, "Tell me about your mother."

Though cognitive language processing is a fascinating area, and full of much future potential, it would not be appropriate to continue discussing the various lines of development in detail, because none of them have yet impinged on operational retrieval systems. Aside from the possibility of lubricating the man-machine interface by the kinds of human-like sentence-generating capabilities we have discussed, there does not seem to be many other ultra-software packages evolving from this area of research. The major roadblock to the utility of language processing at the third level of difficulty is the enormity of the information structures that would have to be built, even to cover the requirements of a narrow realm of discourse. As Quillian (1968) points out:

> ... [The] problems of what is to be contained in an overall, humanlike permanent memory, what format this is to be in, and how this memory is to be organized have not been dealt with in great generality in prior simulation programs. ... In sum, relatively little work has been done toward simulating really general and large memory structures, especially structures in which newly input symbolic material would typically be put in relation to large quantities of previously stored information about the same kinds of things. ...

REFERENCES

ALGEBRA, CYRIL N. (1967), String Similarity and Misspellings, *Communications of the Association for Computing Machinery*, 10:5, pp. 302–313.

ARMITAGE, J. E., LYNCH, M. F., PETRIE, J. H., and BELTON, M. (1970), Experimental Use of a Program for Computer-Aided Subject-Index Production, *Information Storage and Retrieval*, 6:1, pp. 79–87.

ARTANDI, SUSAN (1969), Computer Indexing of Medical Articles: Project Medico, *Journal of Documentation*, 25:3, pp. 214–223.

BAGDIKIAN, BEN H. (1971), *The Information Machines*, Harper & Row, New York.

BAR-HILLEL, YEHOSHUA (1964), *Language and Information*, Addison-Wesley, Reading, Mass.

BARKER, FRANCES H., VEAL, DOUGLAS C., and WYATT, BARRY K. (1972), Comparative Efficiency of Searching Titles, Abstracts, and Index Terms in a Free-Text Data Base, *Journal of Documentation*, 28:1, pp. 22–36.

BAXENDALE, P. B. (1958), Machine-Made Index for Technical Literature— An Experiment, *IBM Journal of Research and Development*, 2:4, pp. 354–361.

BEARD, JOSEPH J. (1971), Information Systems Application in Law, in Cuadra, C. A., ed., *Annual Review of Information Science and Technology*, Vol. 6, Encyclopaedia Britannica, Chicago.

BOBROW, DANIEL G. (1968), Natural Language Input, in Minsky, Marvin, ed., *Semantic Information Processing*, the MIT Press, Cambridge, Mass., pp. 148–226.

BORKO, HAROLD, and BURNAUGH, H. P. (1966), Interactive Displays for Document Retrieval, *Information Display*, 3 (September/October), pp. 47–90.

BORKO, HAROLD, BLANKENSHIP, D. A., and BURKET, R. C. (1968), *On-Line Information Retrieval Using Associative Indexing*, System Development Corporation Document TM-(L)-3851 (RADC-TR-68-100).

BORKO, HAROLD (1968), *Automated Language Processing*, John Wiley & Sons, New York.

BORKO, HAROLD (1970), Experiments in Book Indexing by Computer, *Information Storage and Retrieval*, 6:1, pp. 5–16.

BROOKES, B. C. (1968), The Derivation and Application of the Bradford-Zipf Distribution, *Journal of Documentation*, 24:4, pp. 247–265.

BROOKS, F. P., JR. (1965), Review of "The Microstatistics of Text," *Computing Reviews*, 6:1, pp. 13–14.

BRUNER, J. S., GOODNOW, J. J., and AUSTIN, C. A. (1956), *A Study of Thinking*, John Wiley & Sons, New York.

CARLSON, W. H. (1963), The Holy Grail Evades the Search, *American Documentation*, 14:3, pp. 207–212.

CURTICE, R. M., and JONES, P. E. (1969), *An Operational Interactive Retrieval System*, Arthur D. Little, Boston.

DAMEREAU, F. (1964), A Technique for Computer Detection and Correction of Spelling Errors, *Communications of the Association for Computing Machinery*, 7:3, pp. 171–176.

DAVIS, C. H., KEARNEY, W. R., and DAVIS, B. M. (1971), A Computer-Based Procedure for Keyword Indexing of Newspapers, *Journal of the American Society for Information Science*, 22:5, pp. 348–351.

DOYLE, L. B. (1959), Programmed Interpretation of Text as a Basis for Information Retrieval Systems, in *Proceedings of the Western Joint Computer Conference*, San Francisco, pp. 60–63.

DOYLE, L. B. (1962), Indexing and Abstracting by Association, *American Documentation*, 13:4, pp. 378–390.

DOYLE, L. B. (1965), Is Automatic Classification a Reasonable Application of Statistical Analysis of Text?, *Journal of the Association for Computing Machinery*, 12:4, pp. 473–489.

EDMUNDSON, H. P. (1969), New Methods in Automatic Extracting, *Journal of the Association for Computing Machinery*, 16:2, pp. 265–285.

EDMUNDSON, H. P., and WYLLYS, R. E. (1961), Automatic Abstracting and Indexing—Survey and Recommendations, *Communications of the Association for Computing Machinery*, 4:5, pp. 226–234.

FISCHER, MARGUERITE (1971), The KWIC Index Concept: A Retrospective View, in Elias, Arthur W., ed., *Key Papers in Information Science*, American Society for Information Science, Washington, D.C., pp. 121–134.

HAYS, D. C. (1961), Grouping and Dependency Theories, *Proceedings of the National Symposium on Machine Translation*, Prentice-Hall, Englewood Cliffs, N.J.

HERNER, SAUL (1962), Methods of Organizing Information for Storing and Searching, *American Documentation*, 13:1, pp. 3–14.

JAKOBSON, ROMAN (1972), Verbal Communication, *Scientific American*, 227:3, pp. 72–80.

KAY, MARTIN, and SPARCK JONES, KAREN (1971), Automated Language Processing, in Cuadra, C. A., ed., *Annual Review of Information Science and Technology*, Vol. 6, Encyclopaedia Britannica, Chicago.

KLEIN, S., and SIMMONS, R. F. (1963), Syntactic Dependence and the Computer Generation of Coherent Discourse, *Mechanical Translation* (August).

LUHN, H. P. (1957), A Statistical Approach to Mechanized Encoding and Searching of Literary Information, *IBM Journal of Reseach and Development*, 1:4, pp. 309–317.

LUHN, H. P. (1958), The Automatic Creation of Literature Abstracts, *ibid.*, 2:2, pp. 159–165.

LUHN, H. P. (1960), Keyword-in-Context Index for Technical Literature (KWIC), *American Documentation*, 11:4, pp. 288–295.

MONTGOMERY, C. A. (1969), Automated Language Processing, in Cuadra, C. A., ed., *Annual Review of Information Science and Technology*, Vol. 4, Encyclopaedia Britannica, Chicago.

MONTGOMERY, C. A. (1972), Linguistics and Information Science, *Journal of the American Society for Information Science*, 23:3, pp. 195–219.

(OHLMAN, H.): CITRON, J., HART, L., and OHLMAN, H. (1959), *A Permutation Index to the "Preprints of the International Conference on*

Scientific Information," System Development Corporation Document SP-44, Santa Monica, Calif.

OLNEY, JOHN, and RAMSEY, DONALD (1972), From Machine-Readable Dictionaries to a Lexicon Tester: Progress, Plans, and an Offer, *Computer Studies in the Humanities and Verbal Behavior*, 3:4, pp. 213–220.

OSGOOD, C. E. (1957), *The Measurement of Meaning*, University of Illinois Press, Urbana, Ill.

(OSWALD, V. A.): *Interim Report, the Automatic Extraction and Display of the Content of Documents*, PRC-R-91, March 15, 1959.

QUILLIAN, M. ROSS (1968), Semantic Memory, in Minsky, Marvin, ed., *Semantic Information Processing*, The MIT Press, Cambridge, Mass., pp. 227–270.

SALTON, GERARD (1968a), *Automatic Information Organization and Retrieval*, McGraw-Hill, New York.

SALTON, GERARD (1968b), Automated Language Processing, in Cuadra, C. A., ed., *Annual Review of Information Science and Technology*, Vol. 3, Encyclopaedia Britannica, Chicago.

SCHULTZ, CLAIRE K., ed. (1968), *H. P. Luhn: Pioneer in Information Science; Selected Works*, Spartan Books, New York.

SEDELOW, SALLY Y. (1971), Computers and Language, *Iowa Alumni Review*, June–July, pp. 6–7, 18–19.

SHARP, JOHN R. (1967), Content Analysis, Specification, and Control, in Cuadra, C. A., ed., *Annual Review of Information Science and Technology*, Vol. 2, John Wiley & Sons, New York.

SPARCK JONES, KAREN, and KAY, MARTIN (1973), *Linguistics and Information Science*, Academic Press, New York.

SIMMONS, R. F. (1967), Answering English Questions by Computer: A Survey, in Kochen, M., ed., *The Growth of Knowledge*, John Wiley & Sons, New York.

STEVENS, MARY E. (1965), *Automatic Indexing: A State-of-the-Art Report*, National Bureau of Standards Monograph 91, Washington, D.C.

STONE, D. C., and RUBINOFF, M. (1968), Statistical Generation of a Technical Vocabulary, *American Documentation*, 19:4, pp. 411–412.

THOMPSON, DAVID A. (1971), Interface Designs for an Interactive Information Retrieval System: A Literature Survey and a Research System Description, *Journal of the American Society for Information Science*, 22:6, pp. 361–373.

THORNDIKE, E. L., and LORGE, IRVING (1944), *The Teacher's Word Book of 30,000 Words*, Bureau of Publications, Columbia University, New York.

Time (December 17, 1973), Press Section.

Time (March 4, 1974), Science Section.

TRAVIS, LARRY, KELLOGG, CHARLES, and KLAHR, PHILIP (1973), *Inferential Question Answering: Extending Converse*, System Development Corporation paper SP-3679, Santa Monica, Calif.

TREU, SIEGFRIED (1968), The Browser's Retrieval Game, *American Documentation*, 19:4, pp. 404–410.

WEIZBAUM, JOSEPH (1967), Contextual Understanding by Computers, *Communications of the Association for Computing Machinery*, 10:8, pp. 474–480.

WESTON, PAUL (1970), Man-like Machines: the Language Barrier, in Garvin, Paul L., ed., *Cognition: A Multiple View*, Spartan Books, New York.

WILKS, YORICK (1973), *Natural Language Inference*, Stanford Artificial Intelligence Laboratory Memo AIM-211, Stanford University, Palo Alto, Calif.

WYLLYS, RONALD E. (1968), Extracting and Abstracting by Computer, in Borko, H., ed., *Automated Language Processing*, John Wiley & Sons, New York.

YOUDEN, W. W. (1963), Characteristics of Programs for KWIC and Other Computer-Produced Indexes, *Automation and Scientific Communication*, American Documentation Institute, Washington, D.C., pp. 331–332.

Chapter Eleven

Evaluation of Information Retrieval Systems

As the concept of information retrieval grew up during the 1950–1960 decade, and as numerous new methods of access to information were developed, documentalists and others soon realized that it was not easy to appraise the workability of these new methods. The situation became more acute as computer people began taking an active interest in the information retrieval problem. Their swift, new systems gave rise to claims such as, "We can do 100 simultaneous searches of 10,000 documents in 20 seconds." Some of the more mathematically inclined among them spelled out ornate theoretical treatments, based on hastily adopted assumptions about how computers would be used in information retrieval.

In many instances it was felt that these newcomers were missing the point in regard to the information problem, and the corps or ardent advocates of the new systems became opposed by an equally ardent group of critics. The climax of the debate may have been reached in 1960 when Bar-Hillel's Technical Report Number 3 was issued. Bar-Hillel said:

> The prospects for efficient use of computers for information retrieval have so far been greatly hampered by inept theorizing, by pointless attempts to "apply" prestige-carrying scientific, and especially mathematical, disciplines . . . and by greatly underestimating the intellectual effort required to arrive at a good abstract, a good index set, and good judgment as to the closeness of topics. . . .

Soon the notion became widespread that the advocates of new ideas should prove their worth by evaluating them—by giving their systems a rigorous shakedown, making use of real document collections and impartial searchers and judges of document relevance. The system evaluation route appealed to government agencies that supported research in information areas, and as a result evaluation studies began to multiply. During the 1950s only three papers appeared in the journal *American Documentation* having to do with evaluation. Then the evaluation movement began in earnest, and by 1969 *American Documentation* was featuring evaluation-oriented papers at the rate of three *per issue*.

The onset of the evaluation era was not solely a reaction to the proliferation of new ideas inspired by the computer; it only appears so on the surface. To understand other equally significant factors, especially in view of the fact that information-finding systems existed long before the 1960s, we must ask: "Why haven't system evaluation approaches been extensively tried before?" A large part of the answer to this question is that until recently the world of information handling changed slowly enough that traditional methods of filing, indexing, etc., could nearly always be adapted to the solution of new problems. Slow change meant that people who needed to manage large record files or book collections had time to develop experience with relatively unchanging procedures; younger people could be taught such procedures in colleges or schools of business.

In business enterprises, the methods of dealing with information could be "evaluated" in the same way all other business operations were evaluated—in terms of cost. Information specialists outside the business world, such as librarians, though not quite so cost conscious, also used economic rules of thumb as criteria for their operations. Even today such criteria are feasible in public libraries, which tend to have numerous procedural carbon copies of themselves scattered around the country, and which therefore have a huge reservoir of shared experience to draw on, a situation that may even withstand the transition to library automation.

The new methods, subsumed under documentation and information retrieval, did not arise in those areas having a backlog of common experience or precedent. They arose mainly in connection with unprecedented expenditures by government and industry for research and development, which led to the production of enormous collections of scientific and technical documents. Thus, these methods, in addition to being themselves new, had to function in new information environments. Economic criteria have been largely nonexistent in these environments, and could not be easily developed. (As will be seen later in the chapter, it is not a straightforward matter to decide what the economic loss becomes when a scientist does not retrieve a needed item of information.)

In addition to the need to appraise new methods and the need to deal with the precipitously growing literature of science and technology, there is a third factor underlying the evaluation era—the inherent difficulty of adequately indexing documents. Most reported evaluation studies which deal with the retrieval of documented information have come up against the demon "indexing" in one way or another.

As was made clear in Chapter Eight, the only sure route to the easy indexing and retrieval of information items is through formatting. However, civilization has an insatiable need for information items that are too complex and/or too unique to format. For these items it is not feasible to provide a "type of information" tag for every single datum in storage, as is the case with formatted information.

In a flight of imagination, one might think: "Why not index a document under every one of its content words?" This solution, sometimes referred to as *maximum-depth indexing*, has often been discussed as a possible application of computers. For much-used works, the solution has been applied manually as in concordance of the Bible. But for whole-document retrieval, the most apparent difficulty of such a method is that it would lead to the generation of several hundred index tags for each typical technical document. Facing a collection of such multifariously tagged documents, a literature searcher cannot express his information request in any normal manner, i.e., in 3 or 4 logically joined words or terms. If he did so express himself, he would find that a large fraction of the documents in the collection contained the corresponding content words. Ways of using maximum-depth indexing in the retrieval of whole documents have been tried out, with interesting results (Swanson, 1960) to be discussed shortly, but require most judicious and imaginative selection of search words, and have not yet been shown to be economically feasible or workable in practice. Practitioners of indexing methods found workable in practice know that the use of even as few as 30 index tags per document leads to the retrieval of much material of marginal or low relevance (Herner, 1962).

Document indexing, as it has been conceived up to the present, requires one to represent an information item of 5 to 10 thousand words, or larger, by a relative handful of words or terms—seldom more than a dozen. Once these representative tags are decided on (whether by indexer or by computer), there exists no other avenue to the retrieval of the parent document by topic, except through these few tags. The intrinsic unsoundness of this situation is easily seen, once one starts considering all the words and terms in the document that were *not* chosen as index tags. The indexer, by not choosing those words and terms as tags, is actually decreeing those words and terms are not of potential use by someone in searching for this document. The indexer may really know better than to believe they are not of potential use; the point is, the indexing procedure, restricting him to only a few tags, compels him to behave as if he so believed.

The searcher, of course, does not know which words or terms an indexer chooses and which he condemns to oblivion for a given document. The probability is quite high that the searcher will use one or more of the rejected terms in specifying his information need; it is also quite high that he will fail to use some of the terms accepted by the indexer. The need to represent documents by a small group of index tags thus *invites mismatch* between the characterization of a document by the indexer and the request statement by the searcher. A large part of the developmental history of information retrieval is the groping for strategies to diminish this inherent tendency toward mismatch (Chapter Nine). Though the quest to minimize mismatch has not been without progress, it remains true—to date—that the retrieval of documented information has much in common with the operation of a penny arcade shovel.

EVALUATION PARAMETERS

In the mid 1950s it was Perry and Kent (1957) who first brought into the open a framework for evaluation of retrieval systems. They defined several measures of retrieval effectiveness which related the total number (N) of documents, the number (L) of retrieved documents, the number (C) of relevant documents, and the number (R) of documents that are both retrieved and relevant. The measures included:

L/N = the resolution factor* $(N-L)/N$ = the elimination factor
R/L = the pertinency factor $(L-R)/L$ = the noise factor
R/C = the recall factor $(C-R)/C$ = the omission factor

The great majority of retrieval system evaluators who later made use of the parameters N, L, C, and R discarded all of the above measures but two, R/C, which is now termed simply *recall*, and R/L, which has come to be known as *precision* rather than as *pertinency*. As we are to see in later discussions, a good number of evaluators have found fault with the idea of *precision* and use instead the measure $(L-R)/(N-C)$, appropriately called *fallout*.

Some of the first open discussions of the effectiveness of retrieval systems occurred in relation to coordinate indexing and the problem of "false drops," i.e., the retrieval of large numbers of irrelevant documents (Chapter Six). One of the curiosities of the history of information retrieval is that in the early years the problem of low precision (retrieval of irrelevant

---

* We have altered Perry & Kent's notation slightly for the sake of notational consistency within this chapter.

338   **Evaluation of Information Retrieval Systems**

documents) was a matter of more concern, seemingly, than low recall (failure to retrieve relevant documents). Today low recall is the more strongly emphasized. But in the beginning many of the modifications of coordinate indexing, such as polyterms, and many of the principal features of alternative methods of indexing, such as roles and links, were devised to improve precision.

It was shortly realized however, that efforts to improve precision, however well-conceived, had an unavoidable tendency to diminish recall. It was realized that the recall-precision tradeoff was a central matter for experimental investigation, and it was at this point that evaluators began to plot recall and precision as co-variables. Figure 11.1 is an example of a recall-precision plot and reflects the experience of Lancaster (1968) in regard to how recall and precision vary as a function of average number of index terms assigned per document.

Figure 11.1 expresses recall and precision as percentages; the more usual practice is to use the simple ratios R/C and R/L, each of which then has a maximum value of 1.0. In the recall-precision graph one can readily see the effect of increasing the number of index tags on both recall and precision. At 5 terms per document, roughly half the documents judged relevant in the collection are actually retrieved, assuming normal search requests containing combinations of 3 or 4 words/terms are used. Slightly less than half of the retrieved documents are relevant.

If one then increases the number of index tags to 10 per document, in the interest of improving recall, one thereby degrades precision, as the graph illustrates. About three-fourths of the relevant documents are now retrieved, but at the cost of lowering precision to 30 percent and, by defini-

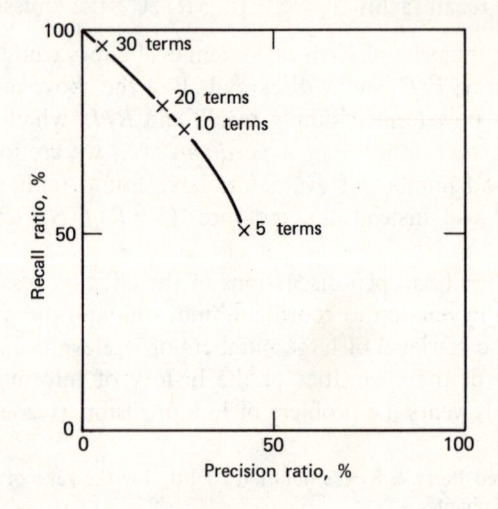

Figure 11.1.

tion, increasing the irrelevant retrievals to 70 percent. The graph shows that, as observed previously in this chapter, the placement of as many as 30 tags per document results in the retrieval of nearly all of the relevant documents, but these have to be winnowed out of a large pile of retrieved documents, 95 percent of which are irrelevant.

Cleverdon (1967) speaks of two kinds of devices to improve indexing, recall devices and precision devices. Examples of recall devices are:

1. Control of synonyms.
2. Alphabetical term indexes to bring root forms together (weld, welded, welding).
3. Generic relations.

Examples of precision devices are:

1. Use of additional coordinating terms.
2. Links (indicators of *which* of a document's index tags can be meaningfully coordinated).
3. Roles (CH_3OH: solvent; CH_3OH: product; CH_3OH: impurity).

However effective a recall device or a precision device might be, the precision-recall tradeoff seems inescapable. On the other hand, the possibility exists that if recall and precision devices can be blended in a suitable way, recall-precision curves such as that in Figure 11.1 might well be movable upward and/or to the right, so that less overall degradation of retrieval results. Some evaluators have succeeded in achieving this result, of which we have more to say later.

SOME LANDMARKS IN THE EVALUATION ERA

Evidently the earliest experimental testing of retrieval methods was done in 1953, when personnel of Documentation, Inc., compared the effectiveness of their uniterm method of coordinate indexing to that of a conventional catalog (Taube, 1953). This rather massive pioneering venture, involving 15,000 documents and 100 search requests, led to uncertain conclusions, largely due to the fact that "firsts" in a new area of investigation have to contend with underdeveloped methodology.

The era of evaluation truly started in 1957 with the ASLIB-Cranfield Research Project in England, supported by the National Science Foundation and under the direction of the Cranfield College Librarian, Cyril Cleverdon (Richmond, 1963). An 18,000 document collection was divided into quarters, each of which was indexed by one of four methods, (*a*) Universal Decimal Classification, (*b*) conventional alphabetic subject indexing, (*c*) faceted classification, and (*d*) the uniterm method of coordinate indexing. It is to be noted that (*c*) is the mod version of (*a*), and (*d*) relates similarly to (*b*).

The results featured notably high values of recall, ranging from 74 to 82 percent, and also appeared to show that the new, unconventional systems were not an improvement over the conventional. Critics pointed out, however, that Cleverdon derived his recall data from the retrieval of "source" documents, subsets of the document collection designated in advance as "relevant." The practical reason, at Cranfield, for working with source documents was that it provided a means to evaluate recall without going through the entire 18,000 document collection to see which ones should have been retrieved. Nevertheless, as the critics insisted, and as was soon borne out in a later experiment by Swanson (1960), source documents inspire the wording of the search questions intended to retrieve them, and the natural result is an increase in recall rates.

Unsurprisingly—in view of the massive effort required to index 18,000 documents—half of the search failures were traceable to inadequate indexing. Most of the remaining failures were due to errors at the searching end of the experiment. (Later workers, as we are to discuss shortly, made elaborate breakdowns of causes of failure.)

Swanson (1960) conducted a study at Thompson Ramo Wooldridge, sponsored by the Council on Library Resources, that is widely regarded as a classic in retrieval experimentation. The aim of the study was to explore the feasibility of storing the texts of entire documents in computer-searchable media for purposes of search and retrieval. One hundred articles on nuclear physics from *Physics Review* were keypunched in their entirety, and plans were made to compare computerized searching of the text with searching using conventional subject headings.

In order to make the comparison as objective as possible, two groups of knowledgeable people were formed, one to make judgments of relevance of each of the 100 articles in relation to each of 50 search questions, and the other to formulate and carry out the searches. The conventional subject headings were prepared by a librarian who also had been trained in physics. The text searches were accomplished in terms of statements logically relating words and phrases from physics (e.g., "All articles with the terms 'charge polarization' or 'charge distribution,' *and* the words 'scatter,' 'scattered,' or 'scattering' "). In order to bend over backwards to avoid fudging in favor of computerized text-searching, conventional subject headings were liberally supplied, with an average of about five headings per document.

Each of the 50 search questions was inspired by some particular article in the collection. These articles were designated source documents. The probability of retrieval of a source document via the question it inspired can be expected to be high; therefore Swanson tabulated the corresponding data separately from the rest, and did not include it in the graphical representation of his data.

Swanson's relevance judges worked in terms of *relevance weights* rather than rating the articles on a yes-no relevance basis.* His retrieval data, therefore, are not strictly transformable into a recall-precision framework. Recall, for example, is no longer a simple R/C, but the ratio of the sum of the relevance weights of retrieved documents to the sum of all relevance weights (for that question) in the collection. As in the Cranfield studies, Swanson achieved high recall figures—up to 86 percent—where source documents were being retrieved by the questions they inspired. On the other hand, the highest recall values for nonsource documents were not more than 30 percent. If, however, only nonsource documents with *high* relevance weights for a given question were considered, recall values were much higher. (The corresponding data were not openly published, but were given in the Thompson Ramo Wooldridge project documentation.)

From a strict high-recall standpoint, thesaurus-aided machine searching of text performed best (recall 30 percent), while searching via subject heading and unaided machine searching came off less well (recall less than 20 percent). When precision is considered, unaided machine searching triumphed over the other methods, having much less of a tendency to produce irrelevant retrievals. It is to be noted that Swanson's low recall rates may have been due to the exquisitely narrow topical spectrum worked with, a matter that those who work with multithousand document libraries of broad scope ought not to overlook. In such a narrow spectrum, relevance distinctions are particularly difficult.

In his concluding paragraph, Swanson states:

> In terms of these measures, the effectiveness of all information search techniques tested on the model was found to be rather low. Text search by computer was, however, significantly better than a conventional nonmechanized subject-index method. Thus, even though machines may never enjoy more than partial success in library indexing, a small suspicion might justifiably be entertained that people are even less promising.

After 1960, evaluation projects proliferated. Bourne (1966) tabulates 19 retrieval evaluation studies pursued during the years 1963–1965, lead-

---

* Relevance weights generally vary from a maximum of one to a minimum of zero.

ing to 37 papers and reports. Though not clearly discernible as a "landmark," the work of Montague (1964) stands out as a representative solid investigation of that period. The du Pont project evaluated retrieval from a collection of more than 5000 patents, divided into chemical and nonchemical patents so that their data could be tabulated separately. A notable feature of the corpus was the great depth of indexing, from 70 to 90 terms per document; apparently such an indexing practice is not unusual when dealing with patents.

As might be expected from such great depth of indexing, recall was quite high, often exceeding 90 percent. Good precision was obtained, however, only for chemical information (80 percent), and this was attributable to the rigor with which it could be described; the situation approaches the orderliness of formattable information. For nonchemical information precision ratios were in the neighborhood of 20 percent.

A great many effects were investigated in the study, and the conclusions are quoted here:

1. From comparison of two coordinate indexing systems:
   a. Recall is affected by depth of indexing, vocabulary control and generic searching.
   b. Relevance* is affected by links and roles.
2. From comparison of coordinate indexing with classification:
   a. Coordinate indexing is faster.
   b. Coordinate indexing provides higher recall.
   c. Coordinate indexing costs more for input, less for searching.
   d. Coordinate indexing missed half its references due to indexing errors and half due to search strategy.
3. Links:
   a. Represent 4 percent of total indexing cost.
   b. Do not affect recall nor appreciably improve relevance.
4. Roles:
   a. Represent 11 percent of total indexing cost.
   b. Appreciably increase relevance but reduce recall through errors in application.
   c. Accurate use of roles requires technical indexers.
   d. Increase relevance for chemical information more than for nonchemical information.

---

* Note: Montague used the word "relevance" to mean R/L in lieu of "precision," as numerous people did then; this caused confusion, since "relevance" is also "that which relevance judges judge," and therefore the term "precision" soon prevailed as meaning R/L.

5. Depth of indexing:
   a. Appreciably affects recall as well as cost.
6. Chemical information can be retrieved with higher recall and relevance than nonchemical information.

If the evaluation of retrieval systems is a science, and if the recall-precision graph is its paradigm, then the chief normal scientist is surely Gerard Salton (1971) of Cornell University. Using the SMART retrieval system, which operates on an IBM 360/65, the Cornell group has probably turned out more recall versus precision curves than any other single agency. SMART was implemented in 1964 (on an IBM 7094). The system stores document text and matches the words and phrases in search queries to words in the text, much as Swanson's program did. SMART is capable of performing a great variety of operations to enhance the matching process. Some examples:

1. It will look up synonyms and other thesaurus-related words to augment search requests and thereby increase recall.
2. It will display portions of the system's vocabulary to help the searcher formulate his request (or reformulate it if the original request seems insufficient).
3. It will inform the searcher how many times the words in his request occur in all the documents. (One can attain greater precision by using less frequent words.)
4. It will compute correlation coefficients or other statistical measures of word co-occurrence. (As described in Chapter Nine, strongly co-occurring words can be used to enhance search requests.)
5. It will split suffixes (record-s, record-ed, record-ing) and perform syntactical analyses.

None of these functions are unique to Cornell, but it is unusual to have such a large number of them available to one system.

SMART is not merely a retrieval system; it is a scientific instrument, which, among other things, is capable of comparing the effectiveness of any retrieval method against that of any other retrieval method. Moreover, the comparison need not be done entirely with the SMART system; Salton has borrowed corpora that have been used in retrieval experiments in other institutions, in order to test other people's methods against those of Cornell. One example is Salton's comparison of the manual indexing methods of MEDLARS to SMART automatic indexing processes (1969).

It is interesting to consider the exact manner in which SMART is used to generate a recall-precision curve. Typically, a group of documents whose members have already been judged as relevant or not relevant to some search request, Q_1, are placed in computer storage and *scored* according to how well the words in the text match the words in the search request, or match words *related* (by thesaurus, statistical co-occurrence, etc.) to those in the search request. The documents are then *ranked* according to this matching score.

This ranking is illustrated at the top in Figure 11.2. At the far left

RECALL-PRECISION AFTER RETRIEVAL
OF N DOCUMENTS

N	(X = RELEVANT)	RECALL	PRECISION
1	558 x	0.2	1.0
2	589 x	0.4	1.0
3	576	0.4	0.67
4	590 x	0.6	0.75
5	986	0.6	0.60
6	592 x	0.8	0.67
7	984	0.8	0.57
8	988	0.8	0.50
9	578	0.8	0.44
10	985	0.8	0.40
11	103	0.8	0.36
12	591	0.8	0.33
13	772 x	1.0	0.38
14	990	1.0	0.36

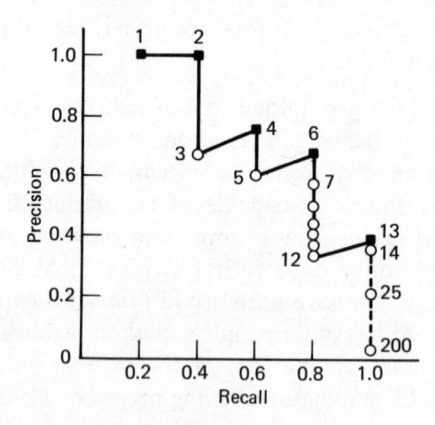

Figure 11.2. (E.M. Keen, 'Evaluation Parameters,' in George Salton, ed., *The Smart Retreival System: Experiments in Automatic Document Processing,* 1971. Reprinted by permission of Prentice-Hall, Inc., Englewood Cliffs, N.J.)

is the rank; proceeding towards the right, one sees a column of document numbers of the ranked documents plus an x indicating relevance. The next two columns, recall and precision, contain values that are computed progressively as one steps downward by rank. For example, at rank one recall is 0.2 because there are five relevant documents in the collection and one has been retrieved; precision is naturally 1.0, because there are yet no irrelevant documents. At rank two is another relevant document, bringing the recall to 0.4, and leaving precision unchanged. At rank three is an irrelevant document, leaving recall unchanged but reducing precision to 0.67. For each successive value of rank, recall and precision are recomputed.

At the bottom of the table in Figure 11.2 is the recall-precision curve that results when the tabulated data are plotted. Of course, one does not take seriously a recall-precision curve based on one search request Q_1. For any given method of searching the document collection, one averages the data *corresponding to each rank* for many different search requests, Q_1, Q_2, Q_3, ... Q_n, where from a dozen to 100 or more searches might be involved. To reduce unnecessary computation, points are plotted only for those ranks where the recall value changes, and thus the resulting recall-precision curve loses its sawtooth character and becomes smooth, such as the ones in Figure 11.3, each of which averaged over 17 search requests.

The averaged recall-precision curves can be printed out either as tables or as graphs. Computer time for 50,000 document-request matches (e.g., 50 search requests against 1000 documents) is of the order of 15 minutes.

Figure 11.3 illustrates the sort of comparison between retrieval methods of which the Cornell group has partaken (seemingly) countless times. The "word stem" method matches requests and documents straightforwardly on the basis of their suffix-normalized word content. The thesaurus, which lists synonyms and closely related concepts for each word of a search request, is invoked here in four different ways: (*a*) in scanning titles only (apparently the worst method—with apologies to KWIC-index fans), (*b*) in employing thesaurus terms on a yes-no basis (logical vectors), (*c*) in employing them on a numerically weighted basis (numeric vectors), and (*d*) in using the thesaurus method with the word method on an "equal contribution to rank" basis. Finally, the statistical phrase method accords higher weight to instances where words used in the request happen to co-occur within sentences or other subunits of a document (when this co-occurrence happens with great frequency, it is nearly always because the co-occurring words are part of a term or phrase). The success of the statistical phrase method at the high-recall end of the graph is apparently because of its tendency to exclude documents that do *not* have instances of co-occurrence, even though they may contain the words. (In a sense, statistical phrases have a precision-enhancing effect similar to links.)

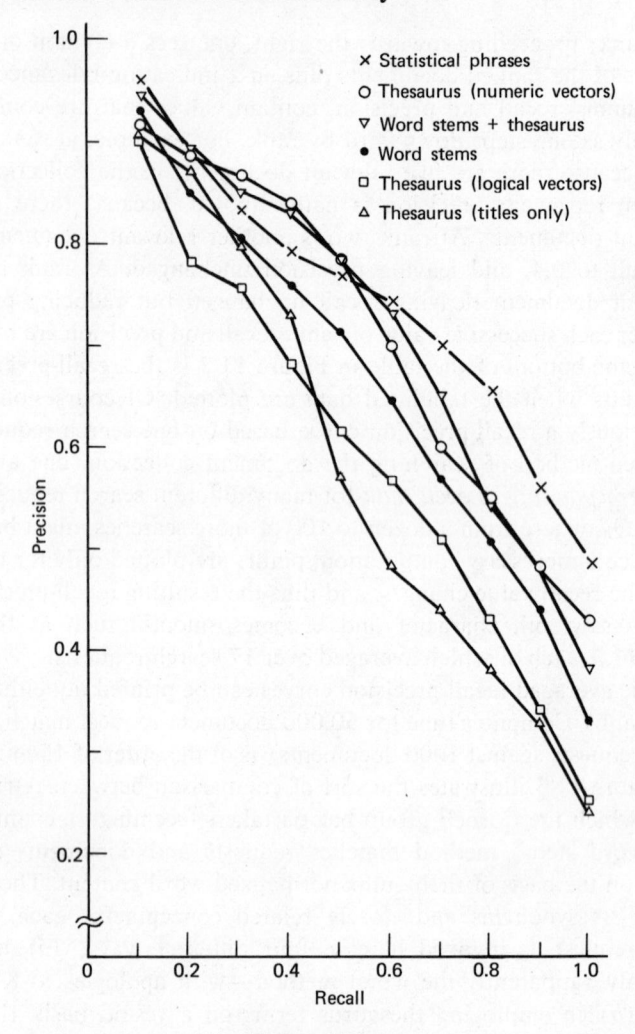

Figure 11.3.

The SMART work herein thought to have the greatest eventual significance for the use of computers in information retrieval is that dealing with interactive on-line retrieval systems. Figure 11.4 diagrams *relevance feedback*, a process for allowing a searcher at an on-line console to change his search request in ways to reflect his experience with the document collection and the system in meeting his particular information need. There are many ways a searcher might upgrade his request, e.g., by using more specific terms, by using words or terms he is reminded of by the relevant items he retrieves, or, as Figure 11.4 suggests, using negative information

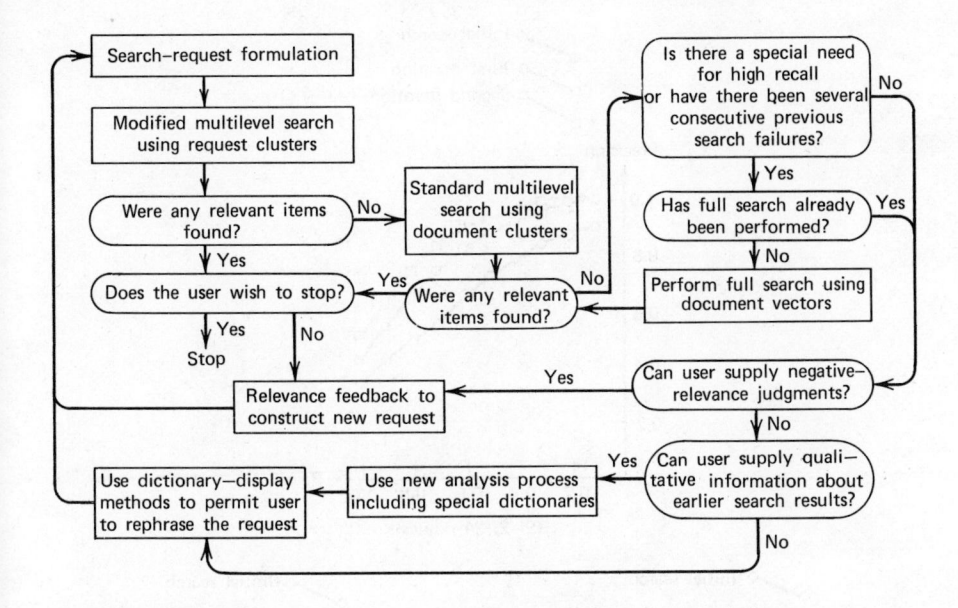

Figure 11.4. Sample search strategy using multilevel searches and relevance feedback. (E.M. Keen, 'Evaluation Parameters,' in George Salton, ed., *The Smart Retrieval System: Experiments in Automatic Document Processing,* 1971. Reprinted by permission of Prentice-Hall, Inc., Englewood Cliffs, N.J.)

to exclude possible documents that are clearly irrelevant (thus upgrading precision).

Figure 11.5 shows the results of some evaluative runs as a function of the iteration. The upward migration of the recall versus precision curve is what we might well expect of an interactive retrieval process; it would be surprising if it had proved otherwise. Also not unexpected is the law of diminishing returns that quickly sets in beyond the first iteration; the improvement between the second and third iteration appears so marginal that it is hard to imagine what might be gained from a fourth iteration.

SMART has thus revealed itself as an important facility for gaining better knowledge of what can happen at the man-machine interface. It is to be hoped, however, that possessing such observational tools does not render one too preoccupied with quantitative data—like the microscopist who refuses to note or understand anything that he cannot measure via the reticule in his lens. Fortunately, there appears little danger that—in the field of evaluation as a whole—the qualitative aspects of information searching will be overlooked.

A recent example of qualitative observation on a fairly large scale is

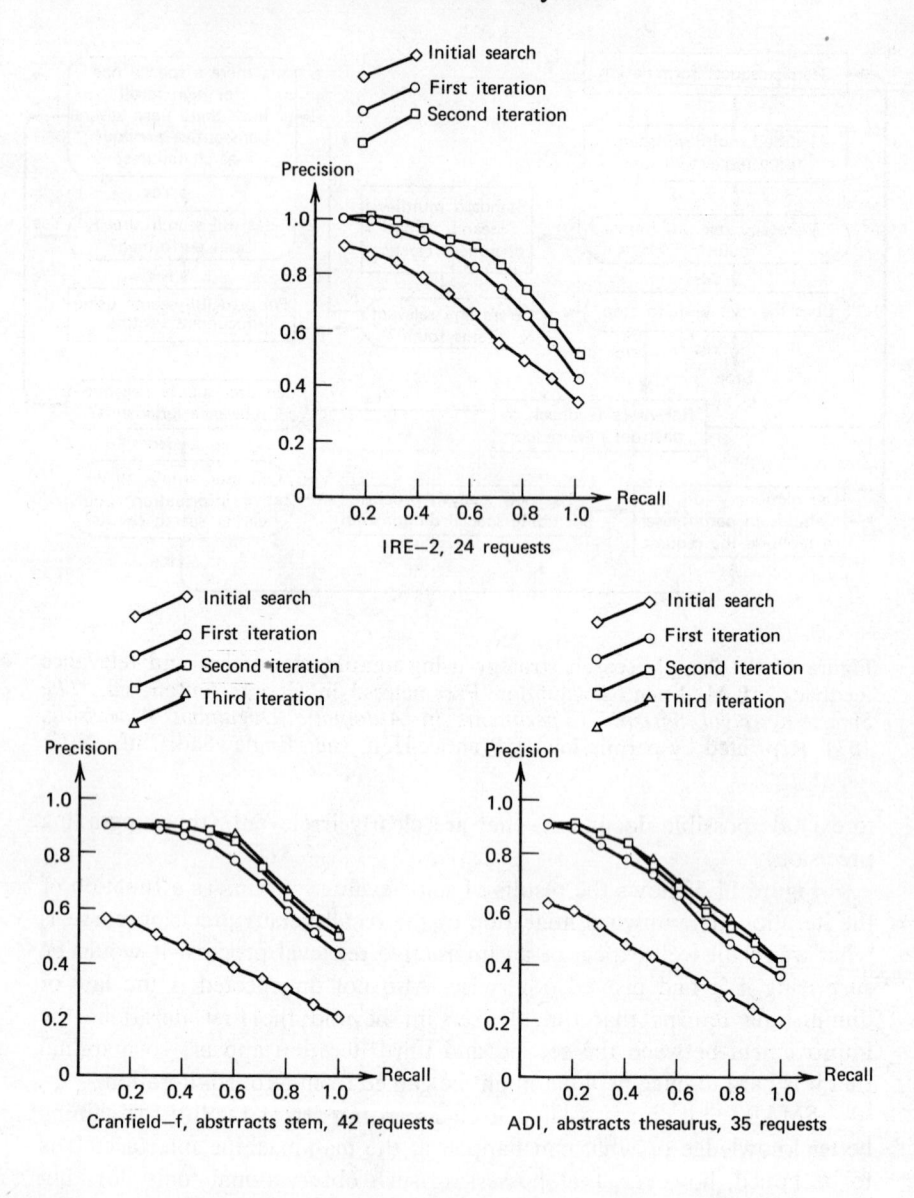

348 Evaluation of Information Retrieval Systems

Figure 11.5. Comparison of initial search with iterated search process using relevance/feedback. (E.M. Keen, 'Evaluation Parameters,' in George Salton, ed., *The Smart Retreival System: Experiments in Automatic Document Processing,* 1971. (Reprinted by permission of Prentice-Hall, Inc., Englewood Cliffs, N.J.)

Some Landmarks in the Evaluation Era

the work of Lancaster (1968), who analyzed and tabulated the nature of several thousand retrieval errors in the operation of MEDLARS (Medical Literature Analysis and Retrieval System) at the National Library of Medicine. He describes the major classes of error as follows:

	Recall Failures	Precision Failures
Index Language	Lack of specific terms (entry vocabulary) Inadequate hierarchical cross-reference structure Roles, or other relational indicators, causing over-preciseness	Lack of specific terms (index terms) Defects in hierarchy False coordinations Incorrect term relationships
Indexing	Lack of specificity Lack of exhaustivity Omission of important concepts Use of inappropriate terms	Exhaustive indexing Use of inappropriate terms
Searching	Failure to cover all reasonable approaches to retrieval Formulation too exhaustive Formulation too specific	Formulation not sufficiently exhaustive Formulation not sufficiently specific Use of inappropriate terms or term combinations
User/System Interaction	Requests more specific than actual information needs	Requests more general than actual information needs
Other	Computer processing Clerical	Computer processing Clerical Value judgment Inevitable retrievals

The error data are given here without percentage breakdown because, we stress, the percentages are bound to vary widely from one retrieval system to another, or from one document collection to another, depending on indexer skill, collection size and specificity, adequacy of search mechanisms, and uncountable other factors. It may be interesting, however, to report that for MEDLARS:

1. The most frequent cause of precision failures was the indexing language, with "lack of specific terms" and "false coordination"

leading the parade (historically, false coordination or "false drop" was one of the first symptoms of retrieval failure to be commonly discussed). The second greatest cause resided in the searching process, in particular that the search formulation was either not specific enough or not exhaustive enough. (Lancaster defines "exhaustivity" as the use of a sufficient number of coordinated terms; thus, he implies, the two major ways of improving precision in searching is in using highly specific terms or, if this is not feasible, coordinating—in the logical "and" sense—a sufficient number of more general terms.)

2. The most frequent causes of recall failures were in indexing and searching. A typical cause of failure at the indexing end was under-tagging, and of course indexing as a process is inherently vulnerable to this; on a practical level under-tagging is often simply a result of indexers not having enough time per document. At the searching end the most common recall error was "failure to cover all reasonable approaches to retrieval." This failure is usually attributable not necessarily to the laziness of the searcher, but to sheer inability to know all the possible search terms that can be effectively employed.

Some of the error data from the MEDLARS evaluation project have led to improvements in the system. Unfortunately, regardless of one's knowledge of what is behind the retrieval failures of a given system, it is still true that attempts to improve recall generally lower precision, and vice versa. Thus, though the recall-precision curve can often be displaced upward, as noted under the foregoing discussion of interactive systems, the need to make the recall-precision tradeoff is still with us, and under current conceptions one cannot at the moment predict that it will ever be otherwise in dealing with document collections.

RELEVANCE AND OTHER ISSUES

The establishment of methodology has been a necessary concomitant to the evaluation movement because no ready-made methodology for such a task existed in neighboring fields. In the beginning attempts were made to borrow statistical, engineering, and other concepts; for example, people educated in psychological statistics used to conceive of recall as related to Type I Error (rejecting a true statistical hypothesis) and precision as related to Type II Error (accepting a false hypothesis). Such superficial analogies were abandoned when it was realized that document retrieval was a problem area whose major puzzles were unique to itself. Though such measures as recall, precision, fallout, etc., are common-sense concepts of a type found in many other fields, the apparent similarity ends as soon as one begins to use these measures in studying the dynamics of indexing and document retrieval.

The reasons for this are not hard to see. For one, the currencies treated in other fields might be coin tosses, genetic traits, test scores, or radioactive particles, but in the evaluation of retrieval systems the currency is language—words, terms, and phrases occurring in text and/or used as index tags. Language is a system of signs and symbols with highly unique properties and interrelations among its component parts. Furthermore, in information retrieval situations, language is being dealt with in a peculiar way—not as a linguist would deal with it, not as a psychologist would, and certainly not as a poet would. In effect, language is being used to address and penetrate library-sized accumulations of itself, a most singular state of affairs.

On still further thought, one realizes that language is ill-designed for such purposes as addressing libraries. What we know about language suggests that it has evolved to suit the needs of humans communicating among themselves, and it is very efficient for that purpose. It is, as yet, not efficient for information retrieval. The latter statement can best be appreciated by comparing the process of retrieving information from a well-motivated human expert to that of retrieving from a document collection.

So, with regard to the brand new, unique problem of evaluating retrieval systems, new concepts, new measures, and new methodologies were needed to supplement whatever might be legitimately borrowed from other fields. With this newness came false starts, mistakes in application, confused and changing terminology, and above all arguments about which concepts or methods are correct or important. No field that we presently call an established science has become so without going through such birth pangs. A close look at the dynamics of conceptual development of retrieval evaluation is required if we are truly to understand the issues and the difficulties therein.

Relevance. Information retrieval has often been defined as "the provision of relevant responses to requests for information." Relevance in itself is not a new idea, but the emphasis which has been given to it by the evaluation movement is new; relevance is the standard in terms of which retrieval performance is appraised. Understandably, as the word "relevance" began to increase in the frequency of its usage among retrievalists and documentalists, soon people began to wonder, "What is relevance, really? Is it after all a suitable standard by which to assess retrieval?"

Evaluation of Information Retrieval Systems

Up to about 1960 the idea of relevance was taken for granted among librarians and documentalists, and even among the computer-oriented newcomers. Then Swanson's full-text retrieval experiment worked in terms of relevance weights, and Maron (1960) carried the concept of weighting further, maintaining that a yes-no, either-or approach to relevance no longer bound people in the computer age. There could be *degrees* of relevance, and perhaps relevance could even be measured. Maron also abandoned a yes-no basis of index-term assignment; a term could be assigned to a document on a weighted basis, the amount of the weight depending on the *probability* that a searcher using that term would find that document relevant. Maron appropriately called his new approach "probabilistic indexing."

With his elaboration of the search request, Maron was on the same track as Stiles (1961), a phase of retrieval development already gone into in Chapter Nine. The point being now developed is that relevance was becoming a quantity, perhaps even a measure, rather than merely the condition of being found relevant. The idea caught on rapidly among computer people, many of whom had already been primed for the idea by Osgood's *The Measurement of Meaning* (1957).

The idea of measuring relevance spread to the Cranfield project, thus becoming a part of the new-born evaluation movement, but did so in an unfortunate way—typifying the confusion that can result within a new methodological area. The "relevance" that Cranfield was actually measuring* was not the same "relevance" that Maron was talking about measuring.

The effect of the confusion is clearly evident in Taube's (1965) attack on the quantification of relevance, where he said:

> The Cranfield studies not only recognized the difficulty of measuring relevance, but also indicated that there was a very real question concerning the ability of a librarian or information office to "recognize a relevant document when he sees one." Having thus established the difficulty of measuring relevance, the Cranfield studies nevertheless have no hesitation in concluding, "With the aid of the set of documents and the set of questions, it will be possible to test each index language device in turn and so get *precise figures* for their effect on recall and relevance." Some way or another, a vague, hardly recognizable, and admittedly difficult notion has turned out to be precisely measurable.

Taube evidently did not realize, here, that the Cranfield writer was switching definitions of relevance in midstream. In the main Taube's argu-

---

* See footnote for Montague earlier in this chapter.

ment against the quantification of relevance struck at the conceptual core of what was then happening.

At the same time Taube was preparing his paper, Goffman (1964) was suggesting that relevance is intrinsically not a measure, because it is not additive. If Goffman's mathematical analysis is correct, then one cannot average a series of relevance estimates, due to lack of additivity. If we are dealing with a true measure, then the average of 0.2 and 0.9 should be exactly the same as the average of 0.5 and 0.6. The implication is that this is not so for relevance judgments—that a situation wherein one judge says a document is 0.2 in relevance weight and another judge says 0.9 is basically not equivalent to the situation wherein two judges almost agree (0.5 and 0.6).

The acquisition of methodology often leads its appliers to feel obliged to measure and weigh entities—even though it is possible to be methodical without always being quantitative. Perhaps the real question that should have been asked, in those times, was not, "How much relevance has a document to a search?" but, "In what sense is a document relevant to a search?"—in other words, not *how* relevant, but *why* relevant.

If relevance judgments are not additive, and hence relevance not truly a measure, methodologists need not make a wholesale retreat to an "either relevant or not relevant" appraisal. Perhaps one can rank relevance judgments, or place them on a nonquantitative scale, so that, at least, one can speak of equivalent degrees of relevance.

But soon even this stance toward relevance came under fire. Fairthorne (1969) summarizes the situation in the late 1960s:

> . . . we are faced with the difficult but attainable target of how to assess to what extent two documents are about the same things. . . . Many people, especially Cuadra, Katter, and Rees, have shown that the assessment of "sameness" depends upon many things other than those connected with the document and its retrieval environment. . . .

Katter (1968) probed the effect of the type of scale used on relevance judgments, and revealed differences based on whether the scale was (*a*) a rank-order scale, (*b*) a category scale (e.g., maximum relevance, near maximum, very strong, strong, etc.), or (*c*) a magnitude-ratio scale (e.g., twice as relevant, three times as relevant, etc.

In 1967 Cuadra and Katter published a paper appropriately titled "Opening the Black Box of Relevance," in which they reported the effects of varying the instructions given to relevance judges, by informing them what the retrieved documents are to be used for. Examples are: (*a*) Use in stimulating ideas, creative approaches, etc. (*b*) Use in relation to a specific task. (*c*) Use in preparing an exhaustive bibliography. The authors conclude: ". . . Thus it is possible to obtain higher or lower relevance scores simply by telling judges how documents are expected to be used. . . ." It is evident that *without* instructions on use expectations, relevance judges are free to make their own assumptions about use, thus leading to hidden variation within the "black box of relevance."

Some people have questioned the worth of the very idea of relevance. A part of the skepticism about "the relevance of relevance" sprung from the fact that, in most evaluation experiments, the relevance judges have not been actual information users with live needs. The artifice of using relevance judges is, of course, compelled by the necessities of rigorous experimentation, where copious data, consistently obtained, are required.

Even in situations where relevance judgments can be obtained from live users, as in selective dissemination (Resnick, 1961), there are reasons not to take the judgments at face value. Taylor (1962), taking a penetrating look at what the structure of a user's information need might be, points out four levels on which an information requirement might be formulated.

1. The visceral need: that part of the information need which *exists*, but is either unexpressable or very difficult to express; the visceral need definitely comes into play when a retrieved document is finally perused.
2. The conscious need: the conscious within-brain description of what is being sought.
3. The formalized need: the statement of the question for communicative purposes.
4. The compromised need: the question after having been translated into the language of the information system.

Taylor's analysis raises doubts about the utility of relevance, as currently conceived, and it hints at the true complexity of a user's need as he approaches an information system. It has often been said that "the perfect retrieval system is one that will retrieve *all* and *only* those documents a searcher himself would choose if he looked through the entire document collection." The naive concept of the searcher reflected here actually underlies all the work which has been done in retrieval system evaluation. This concept of the searcher is inadequate in at least two ways:

1. It assumes that the process of choosing "those documents that the searcher himself would choose" will have no effect on his search request. In other words, it assumes that awareness of what is in the document collection will do nothing to change the information requirement or the statement thereof. Taylor's portrayal of need

structure guarantees—if the four levels of structure really exist—that awareness of collection content is highly likely to change the search statement, as anyone who has watched himself in a difficult search knows.
2. It assumes that a searcher approaches the information system totally preoccupied with a single information need for which there exists single optimum search statement. In reality, a searcher is apt to approach the system with several search needs in his immediate awareness and dozens more in the back of his mind. Thus, evaluators, through their casually adopted model of the searcher, may actually be evaluating their way towards better retrieval systems for one-track minds, in consequence putting aside the possibility that retrieval systems to satisfy a multiplicity of needs (in one fell swoop) might be conceivable.

The nature of the information user is a new area of study which, like evaluation, has mushroomed in the past 10 or 15 years; this area of study will be discussed at length in Chapter Twelve. We talk about the complexities of user needs at this point, however, only to air the legitimate question of whether a simplistic view of users is capable of turning the evaluation movement on a route that does not adapt retrieval systems to real users.

Such questions were being raised by numerous parties in the early and middle 1960s. Rees (1965) discusses such questions, and gives a typical evaluator's response to them:

> Tests based upon the assessment of relevance of documents to questions do not provide a measure of the amount of satisfaction provided.... However, research to develop a methodology for assessing the impact of a retrieval system upon the cognitive processes of users has yet to be performed. No practical alternative to the use of relevance exists at the present time.

Many evaluators appear to say, "We do not believe one ought to be concerned about those information problems for which a methodology of solution is not at hand." Accordingly, many information-seeking situations of contemporary importance are thrust outside the circle of that which may be conscientiously investigated. By the same token, as we shall see in the upcoming discussion about consistency among indexers, situations where methodology is especially easy to apply are investigated long past the point of diminishing returns.

When the use of a tool such as the KWIC index is investigated by a typical evaluator, it is investigated in the customary way, by starting out with a set of cast-iron search-request statements, for which subsets of documents have been judged relevant. One may never evaluate processes by which most users actually use KWIC indexes. A user, for example, does not really have to formulate a search request, but only to know his information need. But one cannot get a methodological handle on this situation, and therefore it is ruled out as a respectable avenue of study, as is browsing and many other significant modes of information access. Fortunately, as we see in Chapter Twelve on user studies, there are some people who will conduct research in areas lacking firm methodology, and of course when methodology does come in their areas, it will be *they* who invent it.

One or two things more must be pointed out about the evaluator's side of the relevance issue. For one, many problems that have been worked on are probably invariant with respect to either the validity or the quality of relevance judgments; in other words, the value of such work may be unaffected by how the relevance debate turns out. Both Lesk (1968) and Troller (1969) have observed that the relative effectiveness of compared methods of retrieval does not change when sets of relevance judgments derived from different groups of people (e.g., experts, nonexpert judges, etc.) are used as criteria. If any halfway decent relevance judgment will do, generally, it's good news for the evaluators.

Additionally, the possibility that some of the user study people may join forces with some of the evaluators offers the potential for a right-angle turn for everybody, and the built-up methodological skill in the evaluation field can hopefully be brought to bear in a more powerful way than it has up to now. Both groups will have an interest in what happens in on-line systems, and in particular they will be interested in what goes on between that initial search and that first iteration. Whatever it is, anything that can make a recall-precision curve jump so far surely deserves study—whether subject to existing methodology or not.

Precision. *Precision* is the fraction of retrieved documents judged relevant. At face value, it is the measure of the work still to be done in screening out irrelevant material at the next level of search.

However, anyone who begins to wonder about why irrelevant documents are retrieved soon feels disturbed about precision as a measure. Irrelevant documents are retrieved, usually, because they contain combinations of words, terms, or phrases that matched those in the search request. The point of substance here is that there are countless reasons why a document should be aptly tagged yet fail to measure up—such is the diversity of information. Each retrieval of irrelevant document is, in a true sense, an accident: an unanticipated, undesirable event.

Looking at the issue this way, one can view each irrelevant document in a collection as a potential accident waiting to happen. If one retrieves from a 1000-document library, and there are in fact 10 relevant documents present, the remainder consists of 990 potential retrieval accidents—some of which happen when retrieval is performed. What about a 10,000-document library containing 10 relevant documents? Now, all other things being equal, we should expect ten times as many retrieval accidents as for a 1000-document library, just as one would expect ten times as many accidents among 10,000 motorists as among 1000 motorists.

What, then, will happen to precision when the library increases in size by a factor of ten? In the simple case in which the number of relevant documents remains the same, going from small to large, precision will decrease to 10 percent or less of its value in the smaller library.

However, if the library increases tenfold, should we not also expect the number of *relevant* documents to expand tenfold? Possibly. Unfortunately for this line of reasoning, libraries tend to become more general as they become larger. This is especially true in science and technology, for anyone who maintains a small or modest collection of documents usually does so in response to the specialized needs of some sponsoring institution.

Such realizations have brought many people to conclude that such parameters as library size and topical specificity influence the number of irrelevant retrievals more strongly than they influence the number of relevant retrievals; it follows that precision cannot be used in comparing the retrieval effectiveness in one library with that in another of substantially different size or specificity.

A number of people, such as Robertson (1969), consider the measure known as *fallout*, $(L-R)/(N-C)$, to be a more meaningful quantity than precision, and adherents of this view plot recall-fallout curves rather than recall-precision curves. Even fallout, however, is subject to doubts somewhat similar to those affecting precision. Fallout, clearly, is a reliable measure only if the probability, per document, of an accident (irrelevant retrieval) remains the same, as one moves from a small to a large library. There is considerable doubt that this is the case. Cleverdon (1971) makes the following pregnant observation:

> Where small sets of documents have been used in experimental tests, it has been a matter for argument whether the results would be applicable in large collections. It would be expected that generality would have an adverse effect on precision, so that it might well be intolerably low. There was a prediction made a few years ago that large document collections (100,000+) could not perform satisfactorily for this reason, yet in the evaluation test there were many cases in which the MEDLARS system could select just a few documents in a collection of 700,000 and was able to average 50 percent precision, as against the 5 percent precision considered possible. . . .

Thus the precision/fallout issue is one that appears far from resolved.

358   Evaluation of Information Retrieval Systems

Lancaster and Gillespie (1970) bring out a point that weighs against the importance of precision in an entirely different dimension:

> ... For example, in evaluating the results of a ranked output we may need to modify recall and precision and substitute other measures as Salton has done in some of his studies. In the evaluation of on-line systems, also, precision ... may be less useful as a performance paramenter. In testing on-line systems we will be more concerned with establishing the amount of effort expended in search time to obtain a particular recall ratio.

Indeed, on-line systems may diminish the concern about precision, and about irrelevant retrievals in general, not only with regard to use of on-line systems but in other retrieval systems too. Evaluation of on-line systems is likely to produce a shift in viewpoint that is transferable elsewhere. Those formerly despised irrelevant retrievals may well be discovered to be of more use to an information searcher than hitherto imagined. Here are some likely possibilities:

1. The use of negative relevance in supplying exclusion feedback to searching systems, as implied by the right-hand, next-to-bottom box in Figure 11.4.
2. The use of data from documents of marginal relevance to supply a backdrop against which possibly relevant documents can be viewed; note discussion of association maps in Chapter Ten.
3. Use for counting purposes: if output is ranked, one can use "number of consecutive documents deemed irrelevant" as a criterion for stopping the search—with practice, of course.
4. Last but not least, display of surrogates (abstracts, etc.) of the irrelevant documents might easily result in some of them being found relevant to an unexpressed information need of the searcher.

Recall. Though some people have taken specific aim at recall as a measure, far and away the major problem with recall is the problem of getting an accurate value of it, even by those who accept is as a measure. Attainment of a true value of recall seemingly entails a complete pass through all documents in a collection, to be sure of counting all unretrieved relevant documents. For large collections this is "exceedingly impractical," one might say.

Salton (1968) suggests a number of alternative methods of obtaining reasonable approximations of the number of unretrieved relevant documents:

1. Use of sampling techniques.
2. The designation of source documents (the disadvantage of which was earlier discussed).

3. The scanning of condensed formats indexed by one of the "anded" words in the search request (example of condensed format: a KWIC index) to discover which documents in the collection *might* be relevant; then, if worth the trouble, further investigation of just that subset of the collection.
4. Conducting a number of searches using the *same* search request but *different search methods* (word stem, thesaurus, statistical phrase, etc.), assuming that all of the methods, collectively will retrieve all the relevant documents; though this probably will not produce true or even approximate values of recall, it may suffice for certain types of experimentation.

EVALUATION OF COMPONENTS

Only about half of the evaluation-related projects reported in the open literature are concerned with the information retrieval process as a whole. The remaining half is a mixed bag, part dealing with relevance, recall, precision, and other such evaluation parameters, which we have already discussed, and part dealing with a variety of other matters, including consistency among indexers, evaluation of extracts, selective dissemination, and so on. Few of these areas have come to nearly as definite a focus, methodologically or in terms of results, as have the areas already discussed. But we take up the most prominent ones not only "because they are there," but because they represent attempts by various people to zero in on troublesome (or otherwise significant) aspects of the total retrieval problem.

Interindexer Consistency. The largest category of work on components of the information retrieval process is that of evaluating the consistency of manual indexing. There are a number of reasons why so much attention has been given to this category:

1. In almost every document retrieval system there is indexing, and, presently, most of it is manual indexing.
2. If poor work is done at the indexing stage it is very difficult to undo, and crops out later in the form of poor retrieval.
3. Consistency, as opposed to relevance, is easier to measure; experiments in interindexer consistency are relatively easy to set up and carry out.
4. A consistency experiment is a tempting way for people who are managing information services (which nearly always employ people in an indexing capacity) to get into the evaluation act.

Zunde and Dexter (1969) review 11 consistency studies and find wide variation (from as low as 10 to 80 percent) in the data reported. Generally, higher consistencies occurred where indexers were most constrained in vocabulary choice and other indexing practices. The lowest consistencies occurred in experiments involving mixes of experienced and inexperienced indexers, and also where no thesauri, schedules, or other indexing aids were available.

As in the case of retrieval evaluation, some people see little significance in the consistency numbers game, and indicate the need for qualitative breakdowns such as given above. Hurwitz (1969) observes:

> It does not seem possible for a system to retrieve documents effectively if they are not indexed consistently. Once this point is recognized, the problem becomes not to eliminate inconsistencies, for this is impossible, but to discover what types of inconsistencies occur and the best ways to minimize the effects of these on document retrieval.

It is possible to argue that indexing inconsistency need not *necessarily* produce bad retrieval. One usually thinks of inconsistency in terms of one individual choosing to use term A but not term B for a given document, whereas another individual uses term B but not term A for a document on the very same subject. If term A or term B are equally appropriate in describing the documents' subjects, it is impossible to tell from this example which choice will lead to better retrieval; this will depend on the accident of the searcher's choice of term. On the other hand, if the limitation of the number of index tags per document is loosened, both indexers are free to choose both term A and term B, and the whole consistency issue becomes displaced to the region of marginally applicable terms.

It is not surprising, then, that some people consider indexing consistency something of a phantom issue. In an appraisal titled "Is Interindexer Consistency a Hobgoblin?", Cooper (1969) states: "Now, the phenomenon of interindexer consistency is devoid of practical interest unless it can be shown that it has something to do with indexing quality and ultimately with retrieval effectiveness. If it does not, it is merely a hobgoblin which should not be permitted to haunt discussions about indexing any longer." Cooper then points out the importance of indexer-requester consistency, and suggests that many methods of increasing interindexer consistency do so at the cost of indexer-requester consistency.

Indeed, the concept of indexer-requester consistency is one that is not very often mentioned in the evaluation literature. This concept silhouettes a flaw underlying much of the component evaluation work (including that which we have yet to discuss), and that is the danger of suboptimizing: of trying to get a component to do its best in isolation rather than as part of a system. Indexer-requester consistency is a concept that reminds us that the indexer does his work in a system context, and that even the attainment of 100 percent consistency will be in vain if the requester's vocabulary is substantially different from the indexer's. Devices to enlighten requesters in regard to the indexer's vocabulary now become more significant than agreement among indexers.

Use of Surrogates in Determining Relevance. The possibility of using surrogates (titles, abstracts, etc.) to represent documents to permit a searcher to rapidly "eyeball" many potentially relevant items is one that surely has been with the information retrieval field from year one. The presentation of titles to a searcher, for example, is a possible solution to the problem of low precision in situations where high recall is desirable; it could also be an avenue to highly selective browsing by those with multiple information needs within a specialized area. Thus, there has been concern for whether titles, abstracts, or other condensed representations can safely serve as stand-ins for whole documents.

Though the evaluation of surrogates is an important area, less attention seems to have been given to it than to interindexer consistency, which is one of the numerous curiosities in the development of information retrieval. Some of the first observations about surrogates came with the rise of selective dissemination systems (Chapter Nine). A selective dissemination system is a convenient place to make observations about many aspects of information retrieval, because it possesses a number of passive clients who use the system in the most casual possible way, i.e., by removing items from their in-baskets and resubmitting or responding via outbasket. In contrast, retrospective search systems often have a small number of active clients who are impatient to get on with their searches. With selective dissemination (SDI) it is possible to collect much data unobtrusively from numerous people.

Resnick (1961) took advantage of this characteristic of IBM's SDI system to determine how satisfactorily titles and abstracts, singly or in combination, enabled system users to estimate relevance. The entire procedure, briefly, is:

1. The collection of index terms assigned to a new document is compared to each user's profile (i.e., fairly lengthy list of terms, sometimes weighted, delineating topics of regular interest to the user). To each user are routed titles and/or abstracts for documents having a certain number of terms in common with the user's profile. The routed information is designated *notification of acquisition*.
2. On receipt of a notification of acquisition, the user decides, based on the title/abstract information, whether or not he wants the document.

3. When the user receives a document, he appraises its relevance and returns his appraisal to the system.

The method presented here is unusual, as a method of evaluation, in that real users in live information-consuming situations were used, rather than relevance judges. Employing live users may seem a sounder way to conduct retrieval evaluation; but unfortunately, the grip on the relevance handle is no longer firm, because live users can, and do, decide a document relevant (in step 3, above) on some basis other than what they might have had in mind when making the decision of step 2. Circumstantially, this factor might well have affected Resnick's data in a decisive way: he found that titles were as satisfactory as abstracts in enabling users to judge relevance.

Making relevance judgments after a document has been retrieved is a *no-no* in current evaluation methodology, which, however, had not crystallized at the time of Resnick's work. Yet despite the later advent of relevance-determining methodology, Resnick's precedent is still followed for evaluating SDI-type systems in terms of the satisfaction of live users.

In a follow-on experiment to the above-mentioned machine-searching evaluation by Swanson (1960), Black (1965) found searches based on titles slightly superior, in terms of recall, to the other methods tested by Swanson, even though all methods were improved in the follow-on runs. Furthermore, Maizell (1960) found that titles contained 58 to 70 percent of the terms under which they were indexed. Later evaluators were not able to make titles look quite so good as they looked in the experiments just described. The result of Salton, shown in Figure 11.3, is somewhat typical of later work.

It must be pointed out that there are two variables that can make a whale of a difference in the adequacy of titles in representing the subject matter of documents. One is, of course, the title itself. Titles range all the way from the meticulously descriptive ("Diffusion of Fission-Product Elements from Uranium-Impregnated Graphite In Vacuo at Temperatures from 1500°C to 1900°C") to the cryptic and whimsical ("Of Monkeys and Typewriters"). It is noted that both Resnick and Black worked in areas of physics, where titles tend toward the meticulously descriptive. A title is *potentially* capable of representing a document well enough to provide topical discrimination from every other document in a large library, for even a six-content-word title contains trillions of bits, in the information theory sense.

The second variable affecting the adequacy of a title in representing a document is percentage information loss in transition from full document to condensed representation. Any degree of condensation of a document entails some information loss. However, as we shall see within a few paragraphs, it is possible to condense a document to 10 percent of its original length while sacrificing very little information pertaining to its "aboutness." A short abstract is capable of containing enough information for the satisfaction of most topical searches.

How about a title? Recent experiments seem to show that titles, such as they are, contain only enough information to faithfully represent a document's main aspect. Katter (1971), using a multidimensional scaling technique in establishing dimensions of judgment of content, on the part of 172 students of medical and physical sciences, confirmed other workers' results concerning the adequacy of titles to represent a document's major dimension. However, he says:

> ... the power of titles to represent the second and third (weaker) dimensions was much less than the power of other types of representations. Digests, on the other hand, showed considerable power to represent all three of the strongest dimensions ..., with the strongest dimension being represented with the most fidelity, the next strongest with the next most fidelity, and so on. ... Index term assignments showed approximately equal fidelity in representing the first, second and third dimensions, but their overall level of fidelity was low.'...

Katter's strongest dimension is clearly the one in terms of which most relevance judgments are cast. An abstract, which is long enough to include reference to second, third, and lesser dimensions may possibly detract from relevance judgments with respect to the strongest dimension. Most studies comparing titles and abstracts as document surrogates do not allude to this possibility.

A rather unique surrogate evaluation study is that of Ford and Holmes (1962), part of an intelligence-oriented project to investigate the adequacy of surrogates in helping intelligence system monitors keep track of a changing world situation. Newspaper articles about African nations were used as a data base, each containing from 500 to 1000 words. Two types of surrogates were prepared, NL-10 abstracts (where NL-10 means "10 percent of original length in natural language") and term diagrams (a rectangular diagram with content words on the right and left connected by arrows labeled with either function or content words).

The surrogates were rated according to three criteria, (a) ease of preparation, (b) usefulness in retrieving the original article, and (c) adequacy in making inferences in lieu of the original article. The NL-10 abstracts were easier to prepare, but otherwise term diagrams were rated more highly. It was also found that, using a term diagram, an operative was able to infer up to 80 percent of the content of the full-size article. It is notable that recent articles discuss methods of programmed generation of term-diagram-like structures (Strong, 1974).

Evaluation of Extracts. The field of automatic abstracting, or *extracting* as some prefer to call it, has been almost static since the flurry of interest in it in the period 1957–1963. Evaluation in the area is close to nil. One study, however, stands out not only as a singular investigation of extracting, but as a model of its kind in the evaluation of computerized natural language output, that of Edmundson (1969).

A comparison was made between two processes of generating abstracts:

1. Human subjects were given instructions for preparing *target extracts*, i.e., were told to select sentences from an article reflecting the concern of the article's author with the topic, author purpose or intent, conclusions, implications, etc.
2. A computer was programmed with various classes of rules for selecting sentences from an article.

The objective in this study was to use the human-prepared target extracts as a standard, and to evaluate various computer rules or combinations of rules in terms of *percentage coselection* of the sentences by the rule and by humans in forming the target extracts.

Types of rules by which the computer selected sentences were:

1. The keyword method: the original Luhn method (Chapter Ten) in which sentences were selected on the basis of the number of most frequent content words they contained.
2. The cue method: the selection of sentences containing words from a specially prepared cue-word dictionary, such words and phrases as "conclusion(s)," "is hypothesized," "future research," and so on.
3. The title method: selection of sentences containing keywords, where title words or words in major headings are given extra weight.
4. The location method: selection of sentences occurring under certain headings (like under "Results"), or selection of paragraph topic sentences.

When sentences were randomly selected from the articles, it was found that a 25 percent coselection (with the target extracts) resulted. The keyword method was not much better, leading to 37 percent coselection. The combined cue-title-location method proved to have the highest coselection, 55 percent. (Curiously, the addition of the keyword method to the combination actually diminished the coselection percentage.) Edmundson concluded that though the keyword method might be fine in automatic indexing, where words and terms are picked out of text, it "may not be as useful" for extracting.

Other Directions. It is beyond the scope of this chapter to be in any sense thorough about the evaluation of all the would-be bits and pieces of information retrieval systems. But certain directions need to be touched on, with perhaps a paragraph, because enough work is being done therein to give persistence, and, for all we know, ultimately to yield greater significance.

Aside from the indefatigable Cornell group under Salton, numerous people have been checking out the performance of statistical and co-occurrence methods, such as are discussed in Chapters Nine and Ten. One example is Jones and Needham (1968), who are noted for their decade of work with *clumps*, statistically derived clusters of indexing terms. In a retrieval evaluation in which the effectiveness was sought of terms alone, clumps alone, and clumps plus terms, it was found that the latter functioned most effectively. Clumps alone worked least well because "many terms didn't clump." Another Jones (Jones and Curtice, 1967) evaluated various measures of word co-occurrence in documents to ascertain, through a system of mathematical analysis, which measures were recall-oriented and which precision-oriented. The mathematics is not difficult to follow, and the paper is most intriguing, suggesting that choice of a co-occurrence measure should depend on whether one is at an early or late stage of a retrospective search.

Several people have evaluated the use of either KWIC (Keyword-in-Context) or KWOC (Keyword-out-of-Context) indexes. The typical practice appears to be to compare the keyword indexes with conventional approaches, often in the hope that if the keyword index compares favorably enough, the cheapness of the keyword indexes should decide the issue. Brodie (1970) studied the effectiveness of KWIC as a means of access to library literature; the results did not favor KWIC. On the other side of the coin, Jahoda and Stursa (1969) compared KWOC to alphabetical subject indexing and found remarkable equalities, both in recall and precision. The only sense in which KWOC lagged was that its use was sometimes slower than that of the subject index.

We now briefly note a number of peripheral roads of evaluation. Salton, it appears, has not only compared everything with everything else, but has also *combined* everything with everything else, a recent example being (1970) the finding that increased retrieval performance is attained by combining citation indexing with automatic keyword indexing. Wooster (1969) evaluates microfilm systems by excerpting from several hundred letters received from interested users. Borko (1968) describes a test of five variables, type and depth of indexing, classification algorithm, homogeneity of document collection, and order of data input on the stability of automatic classification; only the latter variable had a statistically significant effect. O'Hara (1970) considers the significance of the corners and edges of the recall-precision diagram, concluding that the 100 percent edges can be occupied by data points but the 0 percent edges cannot.* And so turns the crank in the era of evaluation.

THE VALUE OF INFORMATION

Anyone familiar with the daily life of a professional person knows that information has value. As will be discussed in Chapter Twelve on The User of Information, the word "scientist" in one of its senses comes close to being synonymous with "information processor." More broadly, information has been spoken of as a "national resource."

Large corporations hiring numerous scientists and engineers are particularly concerned to see that avenues to needed information are efficient; not many of them really believe the adage current in the last decade that "for any research project costing less than $100,000 it is cheaper to go ahead and do it than it is to search the literature to find out if someone else has done it."

On the contrary, most organizations worry about the hidden losses that could occur in research and development resulting from lack of information. Some of them sponsor studies to find out specifically what happens on a project when the information pipeline malfunctions. Lancaster (1968) cites an investigation conducted at Lockheed Aircraft Corporation, where it was found that:

> ... once the need for information arises an engineer's productivity drops rapidly until the information has been obtained. Some men, working on a single job, virtually stop altogether. The typical engineer slows down, tries to find alternative ways of solving his problem, or seeks alternative sources of information—usually by means of consultation. Efficiency was found to drop 25 percent in the typical waiting situation and to cost the company around $2.50 per hour. Obviously, under these conditions, a dollar value could be placed on a successful retrieval. ...

In another case, Jordan (1970) reports that after installing a selective

---

* Because if $R/L = 0$, then R/C must $= 0$, and vice versa, except for the special case where the library has no relevant documents, in which event R/C is meaningless (as well as indeterminate).

dissemination system, a large company found that each user was saving 3 hours a week in literature searching activity. Assuming an hourly rate of $7.00 per hour, the company estimated savings of $1000.00 per year per man, whereas the cost of the dissemination system was $250.00 per year per man.

However obvious it may be that information has value, it seems very difficult to package it as a commodity. This is especially the case in science and technology, partly for the reasons explained at the beginning of this chapter, namely that each science seems to have unique information needs and problems that do not allow it readily to profit by the information-cost experience of another science. Though the uniqueness argument is coming under some challenge (Landau, 1969), it has surely inhibited the exchange of cost data.

There may be a serious reason for actually avoiding putting a price tag on specific information transactions in science and technology, even if it could be done accurately. The reason is connected with the number of options available to the user, i.e., the information channels spoken of (Chapter Twelve) in models of the user as an information processor. Evidence indicates that whenever a user is inhibited, frustrated, or in some way dissatisfied with a given information channel, it is easy for him to switch to an alternative channel. Direct charge for an information channel can be, of course, an inhibition. It seems very likely that the means of financing information services, by government, by corporations, by coeducational and other institutions, has become as complex and as indirect as it is *because* it is in the interest of the sponsoring organizations to promote —rather than inhibit—the use of information. Looking from this angle, it is apparent that though information may have value, a large part of this value may consist of information's liquidity, as an asset. If a given channel seems sufficiently important to a user, he may pay for it (as many do in subscribing to journals), but perhaps it is a good thing that no user is entirely dependent on having to pay for information.

The institutions that foot the bill for information services are compelled to be interested—one would think—not only in the value of information, but in the cost of information and of the means of access to information. Yet in the two decades since scientific and technical information handling became a nine-figure item in the national budget, there has been, until quite recently, a surprising scarcity of material on costs in the literature of information science and allied fields.

Some sample observations:

1. "Despite the widespread interest in the economics of computer storage and retrieval of scientific information—specifically the cost

of performing searches and preparing reports—there is little definitive discussion of this subject in the open literature. . . ." (Marron and Snyderman, 1966).

2. ". . . A somewhat disturbing discovery was made when volumes 1 and 2 of the *Annual Review of Information Science and Technology* . . . were consulted for references. Neither of these two volumes had the term "cost" in their subject indexes. . . ." (Landau, 1969).

Commenting further, Landau observes:

It appears possible to this reviewer that cost figures are omitted from the literature for three basic reasons:

1. Writers do not consider them to be of value or interest to the reader.
2. Writers prefer not to divulge cost figures . . . for fear their costs are too high and . . . not justifiable.
3. Writers (i.e., managers) do not in most cases really know how to measure costs and therefore cannot accurately report on them.

. . . It is this reviewer's opinion that hypothesis 3 is probably closest to the truth for the majority of papers. . . .

The Resurgent Interest in Cost. The story told by Landau seems to be changing, at least as far as the field of information science is concerned. Though the field's *Annual Review* does, indeed, have no "cost" entries in its 1966 and 1967 volumes, successive year volumes have had, respectively, 1, 6, 55, and 25 page references in their subject indexes to either "cost" or "cost effectiveness." A parallel shift is found in the *Annual Review* chapters having to do with "design and evaluation of information systems," where the 1966–1968 editions had a total of 2 paragraphs on costing, and 1969–1971 had a total of 6 pages. The 1973 edition features an entire chapter on the subject.

The increase in the amount of material on cost and cost effectiveness within the literature of information service has such a finger-pulled-out-of-the-dike character, that one is inclined to wonder not only why the trend was so long in developing, but why it has been developing so rapidly. A part of the answer to the mystery may be that enough data are now in, in the era of evaluation, to permit a large number of people to "evaluate evaluation."

What we have seen, starting with the ASLIB-Cranfield experiments of Cleverdon, through the various debates on relevance, and through the works of Salton up to the present, adds up to an image—an image that one perceives again and again in Salton's 1971 book on the SMART retrieval system: a recall-precision diagram having two, sometimes three or four, recall-precision curves running quite close together. One sooner or later gets the impression that a great many methods of retrieval give more or less equal performance. There are important exceptions, to be sure. The gap between the recall-precision curves of an original search and its first iteration on an on-line system is really there, and is very significant. Also, some methods of retrieval are markedly poorer than others, but usually for easily identifiable reasons. However, if all the recall-precision graphs ever drawn were put together on one chart, each drawn with a very fine line, the overall appearance would very likely be suggestive of Huygens wave-front envelope (or, for those who have not had high school physics, a wind-tunnel photograph of a complex shock wave). The point of interest would be that the wave front would be on the upper side of the recall-precision diagram. Looking at this wave front, one would surely suspect that the recall-precision diagram has served its purpose in showing the way to better retrieval, and that the law of diminishing returns must already be eating away at this mode of retrieval system evaluation.

An Old/New Approach to Evaluation. Earlier in this discussion, we spoke of the risk of inhibiting retrieval system users by directly charging them for information transactions. But there is one kind of retrieval system for which the risk is minimal—the on-line computer system. Generally speaking, on-line systems are set up so that charges accruing to customers are recorded automatically, in a way very similar to the recording of one's expenses in using the telephone (and, as any telephone user is aware, the inhibition of having to pay is at a minimum, for some telephone users disastrously so). With on-line systems, evaluation can be global, for we have the opportunity to evaluate it not merely as a retrieval system, but as a general information-computational service. Every possible system response can be appraised relative to every other possible response. But what should be the method of evaluation?

A mechanism for relating the discrete responses to the service costs of providing them is desirable. In economics, the market is considered as the mechanism which adjusts the price of goods and services to reflect their relative value. The relation of these prices to the costs of production in turn determines the amount of productive capacity which will be allocated to the various commodities. Repetitive operations in the market adjust the supplies and prices until they are in line with the demands and costs. Essentially, by providing circumstances in which commodities are sold in competition with others, the market serves to accumulate the microdecisions concerning the value of a commodity to a buyer and its cost to a seller. Although there are both theoretical and practical limitations to the market mechanism, it remains one of the most satisfactory techniques available for determining prices.

If such methods of evaluation work for on-line systems, they may well be generalizable to other kinds of information systems. As we know, it is not now the practice to provide information services through a market, that is, those who consume the services on a daily basis do not pay for them. In general, information consumers are but remotely associated with the people who make support decisions, that is, those who decide how much information service will be available. There is lack of feedback between the consumers and the information suppliers, and also lack of communication between the consumers and those paying for the services. There is also no reason to believe that the suppliers and those paying them are any more closely coupled. The poor communication and long delay times render such a system useless as a market mechanism.

The tremendous operating success that market and cost accounting mechanisms have had throughout our economy makes it desirable that careful attention be given to the possibilities of developing and applying such a mechanism to the information services. The costs of information services would no longer be hidden in a gross overhead percentage and thus they would no longer be considered as free goods. In such a case the project manager would become concerned with the use of information services as a productive factor in his project performance. On the policy level, data would be provided on the total utilization of information services and the comparison used to adjust the criteria on service.

The costing data would also provide knowledge of differing approaches to information utilization. Over a period of time, guidelines may be established which would indicate when a proposed usage appeared radically out of line. Also, this knowledge could be made public and would promote quantitative knowledge and experience in the field. The increased stimulation could conceivably lead to improved information systems on a nation-wide basis.

REFERENCES

BAR-HILLEL, YEHOSHUA (1960), *Some Theoretical Aspects of the Mechanization of Literature Searching*, Technical Report No. 3, Hebrew University, Jerusalem. (Also in: Bar-Hillel, Yehoshua, "Language and Information," Addison-Wesley, 1964, Reading, Mass.)

BLACK, DONALD V. (1965), Automatic Classification and Indexing for Libraries?, *Library Resources and Technical Services*, 9:1, pp. 35–52.

BORKO, HAROLD, BLANKENSHIP, D. A., and BURKET, R. C. (1968) *On-*

Line Information Retrieval Using Associative Indexing, System Development Corp., Santa Monica, Calif. (RADC-TR-68-100) (TM(L)-3851).

BOURNE, CHARLES P. (1966), Evaluation of Indexing Systems, in Cuadra, C. A., ed., *Annual Review of Information Science and Technology*, Vol. 1, John Wiley & Sons, New York.

BRODIE, NANCY E. (1970), Evaluation of a KWIC Index for Library Literature, *Journal of the American Society for Information Science*, 21:1, pp. 22–28.

CLEVERDON, CYRIL (1967), The Cranfield Tests on Index Language Devices, *Aslib Proceedings*, 19:6, pp. 173–194.

CLEVERDON, CYRIL (1971), Design and Evaluation of Indexing Systems, in Cuadra, C. A., ed., *Annual Review of Information Science and Technology*, Vol. 6, Encyclopaedia Britannica, Chicago.

COOPER, WILLIAM S. (1969), Is Interindexer Consistency a Hobgoblin?, *American Documentation*, 20:3, pp. 268–278.

CUADRA, C. A., and KATTER, R. V. (1967), Opening the Black Box of "Relevance," *Journal of Documentation*, 23:4, pp. 291–303.

EDMUNDSON, H. P. (1969), New Methods in Automatic Extracting, *Journal of the Association for Computing Machinery*, 16:2, pp. 265–285.

FAIRTHORNE, ROBERT A. (1969), Content Analysis, Specification, and Control, in Cuadra, C. A., ed., *Annual Review of Information Science and Technology*, Vol. 4, Encyclopaedia Britannica, Chicago.

FORD, J. D., JR., and HOLMES, E. H. (1962), *A Comparison of Human Performance Under Natural Language and Term Diagram Procedures for the Production of Report Summaries*, TM-662, System Development Corporation, Santa Monica, Calif.

GOFFMAN, WILLIAM (1964), On Relevance as a Measure, *Information Storage and Retrieval*, 2 (December), pp. 201–203.

HERNER, SAUL (1962), Methods of Organizing Information for Storage and Searching, *American Documentation*, 13:1, pp. 3–14.

JAHODA, G., and STURSA, MARY LOU (1969), A Comparison of a Keyword from Title Index with a Single Access Point per Document Alphabetic Subject Index, *American Documentation*, 20:1, pp. 92–94.

JONES, PAUL E., and CURTICE, ROBERT M. (1967), A Framework for Comparing Term Association Measures, *American Documentation*, 18:3, pp. 153–161.

JONES, KAREN SPARCK, and NEEDHAM, R. M. (1968), Automatic Term Classifications and Retrieval, *Information Storage and Retrieval*, 4:2, pp. 91–100.

JORDAN, JOHN R. (1970), Let the Computer Select Your Reading List, *Datamation*, 16:2, pp. 91–94.

KATTER, R. V. (1968), The Influence of Scale Form on Relevance Judgments, *Information Storage and Retrieval*, 4:1, pp. 1–11.

KATTER, R. V., HOLMES, E. H., and WEIS, R. L. (1971), *Interpretive Overlap among Document Surrogates: Effect of Judgmental Point of View and Consensus Factors,* System Development Corporation, Santa Monica, Calif., SP-3573.

LANCASTER, F. W., and GILLESPIE, C. J. (1970), Design and Evaluation of Information Systems, in Cuadra, C. A., ed., *Annual Review of Information Science and Technology*, Vol. 5, Encyclopaedia Britannica, Chicago.

LANCASTER, F. W. (1968), *Information Retrieval Systems: Characteristics, Testing, and Evaluation*, John Wiley & Sons, New York.

LANDAU, HERBERT B. (1969), The Cost Analysis of Document Surrogation, *American Documentation*, 20:4, pp. 302–310.

LESK, M. E., and SALTON, G. (1968), Relevance Assessments and Retrieval System Evaluation, *Information Storage and Retrieval*, 4:3, pp. 343–359.

MAIZELL, R. E. (1960), Value of Titles for Indexing Purposes, *Revue de la Documentation*, 27, pp. 126–127.

MARON, M. E., and KUHNS, J. L. (1960), On Relevance, Probabilistic Indexing, and Information Retrieval, *Journal of the Association for Computing Machinery*, 7:3, pp. 216–244.

MARRON, HARVEY, and SNYDERMAN, MARTIN (1966), Cost Distribution and Analysis in Computer Storage and Retrieval, *American Documentation*, 17:2, pp. 89–95.

MONTAGUE, BARBARA A. (1964), Testing, Comparison, and Evaluation of Recall, Relevance, and Cost of Coordinate Indexing with Links and Roles, *Proceedings of the American Documentation Institute: Parameters of Information Science*, Vol. 1, (Annual Meeting, Philadelphia, October 5–8), pp. 357–367.

O'HARA, F. M., JR., (1970), The Corners and Edges of the Precision-Recall Square, *Journal of the American Society for Information Science*, 21:2, pp. 166 (brief communication).

OSGOOD, C. E. (1957), *The Measurement of Meaning*, University of Illinois Press, Urbana, Ill.

PERRY, J. W., and KENT, ALLEN (1957), *Documentation and Information Retrieval*, Interscience, New York.

REES, ALAN M. (1965), The Evaluation of Retrieval Systems, in Elias, A. W., ed., *Technical Information Center Administration*, Spartan Books/Macmillan, Washington, D.C.

RESNICK, A. (1961), Relative Effectiveness of Document Titles and Abstracts for Determining Relevance of Documents, *Science*, 134:3484, pp. 1004–1005.

RICHMOND, PHYLLIS A. (1963), Review of the Cranfield Project, *American Documentation*, 14:4, pp. 307–311.

ROBERTSON, E. E. (1969), The Parametric Description of Retrieval Tests, Part I: The Basic Parameters, *Journal of Documentation*, 25:1, pp. 1–27.

SALTON, GERARD (1968), *Automatic Information Organization and Retrieval*, McGraw-Hill, New York.

SALTON, GERARD (1969), A Comparison between Manual and Automatic Indexing Methods, *American Documentation*, 20:1, pp. 61–71.

SALTON, GERARD (1970), Automatic Text Analysis, *Science*, 168:3929, pp. 335–343.

SALTON, GERARD (1971), *The SMART Retrieval System*, Prentice-Hall, Englewood Cliffs, N.J.

SARACEVIC, TEFKO (1970), The Concept of "Relevance," in Saracevic, T., ed., *Introduction to Information Science*, R. R. Bowker, New York, pp. 111–151.

STILES, H. EDMUND (1961), The Association Factor in Information Retrieval, *Journal of the Association for Computing Machinery*, 8:2, pp. 271–279.

STRONG, SUZANNE M. (1974), An Algorithm for Generating Structural Surrogates of English Text, *Journal of the American Society for Information Science*, 25:1, pp. 10–24.

SWANSON, D. R. (1960), Searching Natural Language Text by Computer, *Science*, 132:3434, pp. 1099–1104.

TAUBE, MORTIMER (1953), Evaluation of Information Systems for Report Utilization, in *Studies in Coordinate Indexing*, Vol. 1, Documentation, Inc., Washington, D.C.

TAUBE, MORTIMER (1965), A Note on the Pseudo-Mathematics of Relevance, *American Documentation*, 16:2, pp. 69–72.

TAYLOR, ROBERT S. (1962), The Process of Asking Questions, *American Documentation*, 13.4, pp. 391–396.

TROLLER, CHRISTINA E. (1969), *Comparative Performance of Two Indexing Languages for an Operating Information System: Measurement of*

Differences in Content and Construction, General Electric Co., Knolls Atomic Power Laboratory, Schenectady, N.Y. (KAPL-M-7056).

WOOSTER, HAROLD (1969), *Microfiche 1969: a User Survey*, Air Force Office of Scientific Research, Washington, D.C. (AFOSR 69-1847 TR).

ZUNDE, PRANAS, and DEXTER, MARGARET E. (1969), Indexing Consistency and Quality, *American Documentation*, 20:3, pp. 259–267.

Chapter Twelve

The User of Information

Information science would be much simpler if authors, the generators of information, were solely in charge of determining who their readers should be. In an author-controlled information flow, perhaps nothing more complicated than the postal system would be required for adequate distribution of information. As we well know, no author can predict with assurance what set of individuals will find his work of value. Therefore, except for a few readers he knows will be interested, the author determines his readers by adding his document to the great mountain of other documents, hoping that appropriate readers will somehow retrieve it.

The whole function of retrieval is thus brought into existence because the information user, by and large, needs to make his own choices of the information he acquires. The user is rightly regarded as the key person in the information retrieval picture. All of the machines, materials, methods, and systems discussed in this book exist for the ultimate service of this key person. (Note that if authors could unerringly route their documents to the proper users, all of the boxes in the information flow diagram presented in Chapter Seven would vanish except those for the document and its user.)

Axiomatic in information science today is the realization that one courts error, in the design of an information system or facility, if he does not know what its user will be like. Knowing the user, however, is not an easy process. Users have complex and changing motivations. Users are diverse, both as human beings and in the professional roles they occupy. A user could be a doctor looking for a case history; a reactor engineer needing to know the cross-section of an isotope of strontium; or just an apartment seeker looking in the classified ads. Indeed, it often appears that the only common denominator among users is that very gross one: the need for information.

SCIENTIFIC AND TECHNICAL INFORMATION USE

Most of the methodical studies of user behavior in seeking information, over the past 20 years, have taken place in scientific and engineering fields. The primary reason for this is a consequence of the large research and development expenditures since World War II—the generation of enormous accumulations of scientific and technical documents. The change in the quantity and quality of scientific and technical information was so great in the 1940s and 1950s that existing institutions and methods were completely unsuited to deal with it. As we saw in Chapter Six, an entirely new profession came into prominence—the documentalist. Documentalists have characteristically dealt with scientific and technical information. The need for entirely new methods and new systems was seen, and it was also soon seen that these new ways were likely not to succeed without a solid concept of the user in scientific and technical fields.

The nature of science itself promotes interest in the scientist-user. Arnett (1970) observes:

> It may come as a shock to many research chemists to realize that, from one point of view, all of their activities are concerned with chemical information—its acquisition, evaluation, storage, retrieval, and transmission. Unlike the chemical engineer or the chemist concerned with applications, the research chemist produces no material product. The gathering and manipulation of information is his *raison d'être*.

When chemists (research or otherwise) keep track of how they spend their time, the importance of information transactions again looms large. Ackoff et al. (1958) presented the following typical chemist's time allocation:

Percent	Activity	Percent	Activity
33%	scientific communication (writing, reading, discussion)	6%	equipment setup
		23%	equipment use
		6%	data treatment
10%	business communication	16%	(other)
6%	thinking and planning alone		

If scientists and engineers are the most intensively studied groups of users, then who does the studying? In the beginning, most often, the people managing the information system or facility were those most concerned. Many librarians have long kept use statistics, for the relatively primitive motive of justifying the existence of this or that aspect of the library service. More serious and direct studies of the user arose during the 1950s among documentalists facing the novel problems caused by the mushrooming scientific and technical literature. In the 1960s, however, people outside the information service area, such as psychologists and operations researchers, have been conducting user studies in ever-increasing numbers, and as a result the entire area of study has taken on a much more sophisticated look than it had 10 years ago.

We pause to impress upon interested readers that user studies do not usually deal with actual use of information items, but, typically, with the acts of searching, retrieval, and acquisition (etc.) thereof. This apparent misfocus is the historical consequence of the concern with information retrieval per se on the part of those who have conducted user studies.

METHODS OF CONDUCTING USER STUDIES

When the hundreds of user studies and surveys whose results have been published are examined, five major ways of gathering data about the user are revealed: diaries, questionnaires, interviews, direct observation, and analysis of existing data.

Diaries. The diary method of gathering data about user access to information is among the oldest of methods, perhaps because it is so straightforward—you observe yourself seeking information. Systematic self-observation is capable of yielding fine results if conscientiously applied—and therein lies the rub. In practice the method is difficult to extend to a large number of users, none of whom is likely to be as deeply interested in observing and recording his own behavior as is the person conducting the study.

A more intrinsic objection to the diary method is that it is subject to the "Hawthorne effect," i.e., the effect whereby an *act of observation* may have an influence on the subsequent behavior to be observed.

Some students of the user have noted that the reverse effect also impinges: the absorption in the primary task of looking for information erodes the observation process after a short time, for most people. Where one becomes most engrossed in searching operations he is least likely to be observant. As Jahoda (1966) points out, there are many situations where one does not like to break a train of thought, such as in performing an index lookup while conversing with someone who happens to be in the office, or as in using an index just before going home, etc.

Still a further criticism of the diary method is the possibility of acquiring a biased user population. Working with a subset of users who volunteer to observe themselves (which tends to leave out, for example, busy people) is not equivalent to working with a randomly chosen sample.

Questionnaires. *Questionnaires, interviews,* and *observations* differ from the diary technique in that a second party is partially or wholly involved in the role of observer. These approaches are more palatable to the behavioral scientist, who, after all, has been trained to be a methodical observer of human behavior. As one might suspect, the questionnaire method is the least well-regarded of the three methods, because the role of observer is confined to choosing the questions and evaluating the answers.

Questionnaires, however, are often the only feasible way to gather user information, especially when users are geographically scattered. Generally, a properly designed questionnaire is capable of yielding valuable and highly revealing data; and, like the diary method it is capable of thrusting most of the work on the subject being investigated (especially when the questionnaire forms are designed so that the responses may be sensed and tabulated via computer).

But the basic imperfections and the practical difficulties of the questionnaire method are numerous. Like the diary method, it may report on a biased user population, i.e., those who are willing to return questionnaires, properly filled out. As Wood (1969) suggests, there is a lack of knowledge about the respondent's state of mind or his understanding of the questions. Questionnaires are too often amateurishly prepared, and as an example of what can easily happen, Wood (1969) cites the question: "About what percent of useful information on your subject do you get from abstracts, journals, books, etc.?" The concept of useful information is fuzzy; one wonders, "percent of what?" and thus one may never be sure exactly how the respondent interpreted the question.

Interviews. Face-to-face interviews are capable of easing some of the shortcomings of questionnaires. Immediate feedback inheres, so that doubts about the meanings of either questions or answers can be quickly cleared up. Though both the interview and questionnaire techniques (in contrast to the diary method), tend to depend on the user's long-term memory, interviews can probe memory and partially offset error from this factor. An interviewer can have more control over his population of respondents than can a questionnaire sender, because, by persistence, an interviewer can reduce the nonresponse rate to a low level.

The interview is most easily carried out with a tape recorder. There is the hazard that, unless frequent use of an on-off switch is made, much irrelevant data will be collected. In general, the need to transcribe and select may make interview data more difficult to compile than data from a questionnaire.

The combination of a broadly distributed questionnaire with a selective interview follow-up is most interesting to consider, in that it is capable of reducing much of the uncertainty associated with questionnaire responses.

Direct Observation. This method, much preferred by the behavioral scientist, neatly separates the functions of observing and being observed. It is a superb, here-and-now means of determining in detail what an observed user does; when one envisions instruments such as movie cameras, the power to collect sheer masses of data becomes impressive. A period of direct observation followed by an interview probably contains the greatest potential of any methodology to probe user behavior in great and significant detail.

The chief disadvantage of direct observation, which need not be a serious one, is that the user subject must be continually within range of observation. This difficulty is at a minimum when one user is being observed in one location. In user studies which are deliberately set up in such a way that not all data can possibly be collected, as when one observer monitors a number of people in a library, there is the danger that a biased set of observations might be made. This flaw can be eliminated if attention is paid to randomizing or at least regularizing the procedures of observation. Randomizing techniques were found quite useful by Martin and Ackoff (1963) in improving the *diary* method. In the *random alarm* method, scientist-users carried alarm clocks during their waking hours, and were instructed to describe what they were doing or experiencing at the moment the alarm sounded.

As behavioral scientists are aware, observation of the user need not be passive. Experiments can be set up to test facets of information gathering that are difficult to observe passively. One such facet is motivation, the *why* behind information-seeking acts, as described by Parker (1966).

Analysis of Existing Data. All of the user study methods described to this point are subject to a common criticism: the user is aware he is being observed. In none of the four methods can the Hawthorne effect be ruled out, except for acts of observation that are deliberately covert, such as a candid-camera approach.

Much data exists in our information environment by which one may build highly interesting pictures of user behavior without ever confronting the user himself. Such data are often in a state of high availability. For example, one might easily check the frequency with which various books are borrowed by browsing through the stacks in a public library. Librarians themselves are in a good position to gather use data, and many do so.

A form of data which has proved strongly interesting to students of the history of science are citations in books and periodicals. Citations are often clues in the search for key scientific contributions and in determining productivity patterns within a professional field (Westbrook, 1960). Another use of citations is in determining the obsolescence rate of the literature in various fields. Price (1965) found that in science as a whole, 75 percent of all references are to papers less than 10 years old. Use of citations is one of the few ways of comparing user behavior today with user behavior 50 or 100 years ago.

Without much thought it can be seen that analysis of existing data is not a particularly penetrating way to study the user. One may not be able to find out *why* a certain book was borrowed. A paper might well have been cited because it happened to be on the citer's desk rather than because it was the ideal paper to cite. The danger of arriving at unwarranted conclusions is at its highest in this method of user study.

The most noteworthy feature of existing data analysis as a method of user study is its future potential, especially in relation to the use of computer-centered information systems. In principle, almost every significant user action can be recorded in a time-shared computer system. The abundance and detail of the data can be so great that much correct meaning can be read into it; when supplemented by interview, such data collection can become a powerful method of acquiring a knowledge of users. Note that the sequence (*a*) extended data collection, (*b*) interview, (*c*) extended data collection is a promising means of assessing the magnitude of the Hawthorne effect.

Relating Typical Users to Ideal Information Systems. Though users are diverse, they also have enough in common to profitably influence system design. The information about what the typical user is like comes, of course, through user studies. Unhappily, user studies are so numerous, so varying in quality and focus, and so difficult to relate to each other, that one who hopes to gain a composite picture of a typical user, merely by amassing several dozen papers about user studies, is in for more hard work and hard thinking than he imagines. Because of the effort involved, studies of user studies are valued contributions to the literature, and are therefore increasingly frequent.

As an example of such a review of user studies we have chosen that by Carter et al. (1967) because it so nicely relates each user characteristic found among 58 selected user studies to a corresponding aspect of an "ideal national system" to serve the user:

    1. *Principle of Least Effort.** People in general expend as little energy as possible in pursuit of their particular goals. We would

---

* Reprinted with the permission of System Development Corp. © 1967 System Development Corp.

not expect people to depart significantly from this behavior pattern when seeking scientific and technical information.

System Implication. The system should be easy to use. It should optimize providing the right number of documents in the right form to the right person at the right time with the least effort on the part of the user.

2. *Resistance to Change.* Except in cases in which a man is highly motivated, changes in his behavior occur rather slowly.

System Implication. Changes in the system which directly affect the user should be evolutionary—not revolutionary, unless a critical need is perceived by the user or the system change is clearly easier to user.

3. *Quantity of Information Consumed.* There is a wide range among users in the quantity of information needed or consumed. This varies both between and within disciplines. This variability is related to such factors as individual motivation and capacity, nature of tasks, etc.

System Implication. The system should be designed so that the range of its services meets the needs of the most, as well as the least, motivated and productive members of the community.

4. *Research Scientists Prefer to Do Their Own Searches.* Most research scientists presently prefer to do at least part of their own searches and request or require hard copy. Since this appears to be related to their own need for assurance that an adequate search has been accomplished, they will most likely continue this practice in the future.

System Implication. The system should be designed to facilitate efficient searching by the scientist and to provide hard copy of all needed documents, both foreign and domestic, within any reasonable specified time.

5. *Professional and Trade Publications.* Most scientists, engineers, and technicians read professional and trade publications within both their own and related fields. Many of these are personal subscriptions particularly through membership in their professional societies, but more often the publications are furnished by the employing agency. These publications play an important part in keeping the professional worker abreast of current research and development and frequently stimulate him to new ideas and research. Most often journal articles are read only because they are immediately available in a field of interest. Research scientists consider this the most important single source of information, although oral communication is not significantly less important than journal articles as an information source.

System Implication. Provisions should be made for the scientist and practitioner to have easy access to current professional and trade publications in their own and related fields.

6. *Information Lag.* About 20 percent of scientists and practitioners admit to information gaps or duplication of work caused by the lack or inability to locate information in informal and formal publications.
System Implication. The system should make provisions for disseminating information about current research projects and unpublished reports, and reduce the time lag in formal publications.

7. *Users' Needs Vary.* Information requirements vary with the individual scientist, practitioner, and engineer as to his role, discipline, project, and environment.
System Implication. The system should be capable of supporting a variety of different user configurations.

8. *Quality of Information.* The quantity of information available in many fields is exceeding the capacity of the individual to consume it. There is an expressed need for better rather than more information.
System Implication. The system should provide for an improvement in the quality of documentation produced, the condensing of information, and the purging or retiring of files and document stores of unused materials.

9. *Age of Journal Articles.* The frequency with which an article from a serial publication is used is inversely related in a linear fashion to the age of the article. Approximately 95 percent of all journals consulted are less than twenty years old, and approximately 50 percent are less than five years old.
System Implication. The system should provide for storing documents infrequently used because of age to facilitate the distribution of more used documents and to better preserve the old.

10. *Awareness of Information Services.* Many users are unaware of information sources, how to utilize them, or what services are available to aid them with their problems.
System Implication. The system should be designed and operated so that its retail services and responsibilities can be clearly understood by the scientific and technical community. It should provide for the educating and training of users and prospective users (students) in its services.

11. *Quality of Services.* The user often is disappointed with the quality of service rendered by libraries, information agencies, and their associated personnel. Collections are sometimes inadequate.
System Implication. (*a*) The system should provide a mechanism for obtaining competent qualified personnel. This should include periodic review of position descriptions, specification of training

Methods of Conducting User Studies 383

requirements, review of manning levels, and sponsoring of training program development, both within the system and in the academic curriculum. (*b*) The system should provide for quality assurance programs designed to measure the efficiency of its services.

12. *User Studies.* Research programs to determine user needs have been hampered in the past by lack of funds, lack of coordinated planning, lack of quality, and lack of sufficient recognition of their value. Programs for the systematic study of user patterns in present information agencies are almost nonexistent.
System Implication. The system should provide for a broad program of research that includes particular attention to determining user needs and user satisfaction. Such a program should strive for improving techniques for measuring user behavior as well as the behavior itself.

13. *Foreign Publications.* Users frequently find difficulty in obtaining foreign documents and translations of these foreign publications.
System Implication. The system should provide for easy access to all important foreign publications, preferably with English translations.

14. *Oral Communication.* Oral communication plays an important role in the dissemination of scientific and technical information.
System Implication. The system should provide for facilitating the dissemination of scientific and technical information through oral communication media. . . .

How can one further boil down the foregoing statements about the user, and how can one proceed from there to be a little more specific about the system implications that ensue?

Suppose we try to sum up user characteristics in one paragraph, placing numbers in parentheses to indicate correspondence with 12 of the 14 foregoing statements:

Users are diverse (3, 7). Users have conflicting traits and attitudes in pursuit of information. On the one hand they are hungry enough for information to strive to do what they believe is necessary in satisfying their information need (4, 5, 14) and they express awareness of how much their environment falls short in supplying their information (6, 8, 11, 13). But on the other hand they display perhaps inherently human resistances in accommodating to information systems (1, 2, 10).

Broadly rephrasing, the user wants to be captain in managing the satisfaction of his information requirements. He wants to be himself, which leads to his diversity and reluctance to change or to adapt to the admonishments of information service personnel. He wants to be at the forefront of his own information search, and has a reluctance to delegate.

What does this picture of the user imply in system requirements? In answering this question, suppose we resolutely ignore cost factors and considerations of social or institutional inertia, in order to attain an ultimate view of the sort of information system that would best serve the user as we have pictured him. The following system properties are suggested.

Impediments of Time and Space Minimized. Typical users today must go places to get information and must often wait for it—two examples of time and distance barriers that inhibit the pursuit of information. The central aim of system design, ultimately, should be the reduction of such barriers to insignificant dimensions.

Miniaturization and communications are two avenues in the compression of time and space. In an ultimate information system, the user's office would be rich in information-finding capacity, implying remote computer terminals, telephone, and closed-circuit television. Microfilm is a means of both time and space compression. With a large library in one's own office—omitting time necessarily consumed in the retrieval step—delay time in acquiring information is almost nil. What would otherwise be walking through the stacks becomes reaching across a desk. Given a sufficiently good CRT image (or microfilm printer), backed up by an efficient interlibrary network, one might also abolish time and space barriers in the availability of a large fraction of the world's literature.

Finding and Summarizing Aids Provided. Putting a library in a user's office solves only part of his problem. In addition to compressing time and space, system design ought to effectively compress the amount of information. One ideal is a document surrogate that would satisfy both informing and finding functions. Neither a catalog card nor an abstract seems entirely adequate as such a surrogate. An entity longer than a title but substantially shorter than an abstract, so that its meaning can be taken in at a glance, could be the basis for rapid, low-fatigue browsing. The structure of it should reflect what has been learned about human cognition. Such entities would have maximum utility when easily rearrangeable, say, as in a CRT display in response to an on-line search request (Chapter Nine). We shall continue to discuss finding and summarizing aids under the next system property.

Responsiveness to Individual Preferences. If a system is built around a computer with remote terminals, one could include feedback mechanisms in the system that would provide a kind of market-like response to patterns of use. Information summaries of one kind or another will become more and more essential to users as the world supply of information (as well as the supply of information *available* to each user) continues to grow. There are many ways of summarizing the literature, of course; at the present time summarizations are produced more or less arbitrarily; when such items are furnished via computer systems, however, such parameters as depth and breadth of coverage, type of summary, and so on, could be made responsive to what users find most useful.

If large collections of microfilm are present in an office, standard indexing and retrieval tools (easy to learn and use) will be needed, such as those described for the Microbook Library (Chapter Two). Such standard tools need not preclude subcollections of microfilm organized according to the user's individual requirements; indeed, that would be contrary to the vision of Bush (1945), who strongly advocated capability for each user to easily organize his own material.

THE USER AND EXISTING NEW INFORMATION SYSTEMS

It has been 30 years since Bush (1945) conceived "memex," his idea of a desk-drawer library; it may well be another 30 years before users have anything like the concentrated access to information just pictured. Nevertheless, the trends are in that direction. Moreover, the applicable equipment is with us today, and it is not so costly that it cannot be used in certain environments.

Arnett (1970) speaks of computer-based current awareness services now operating from several chemical information centers in the United States and abroad. Selective computer printouts can be generated from header material in *Chemical Abstracts*, such as author, title, key words, author's location, etc. Chemists are said to be eagerly using this service to monitor areas peripheral to their major interests. Thus, the user's desire to browse and to conduct his own searching is revealing itself as a driving force which will sooner or later lead to the ultimate capability we have discussed.

Lancaster (1968) asserts: "Personal searches tend to be browsing searches . . ." and concludes: ". . . In the next few years we are likely to witness the demise of the 'one chance' delegated machine search and a return to the personal, nondelegated browsing search. In future systems, the researcher will be able to browse through extremely large data bases, at rapid speeds, using a multiplicity of possible networks of associations."

Lipetz (1970) cites a study of NASA users in which it was revealed that 334 university students were willing to pay for computer searches of a 360,000-document collection at the rate of $5 to $15 per search. The search questions were prepared jointly by the student and a NASA staff engineer. Evidently 70 percent of the students felt they had received their money's worth. (Interestingly, the 70 percent figure was obtained by means of a questionnaire which, after some prodding, achieved a 90 percent return.)

It is not the purpose of this chapter to cover the entire waterfront, neither of new system usage nor of user studies in general. The instances just cited merely illustrate a vital segment of reality that has only recently come into being. Ten years ago, people were thinking about computer-based document retrieval systems, and some were even building and operating them. Unfortunately, it has taken user enthusiasm for such systems a long time to build up, principally because in the early days systems were not built with the user sufficiently in mind. All that has changed now, and large numbers of people are using computer-based retrieval systems and even paying to use them.

We observe, in concluding this section of the chapter, that nowhere are user studies of more crucial value than they are in relation to use of the systems made possible by new technology (whether computer-based or otherwise), because such systems—still in relative infancy and therefore malleable—will evolve in sounder directions as a result of painstaking observations of the user's successes and frustrations in using the new systems.

THE SCIENTIST-USER AS AN INFORMATION PROCESSOR

As has already been brought out, user studies have tended to focus on scientists and engineers, especially the former. Scientists are the right arm of progress; because of the nature of science as an activity, how well the scientist copes with his problem of getting and using information has a high overlap with how well he does his job. Therefore, understandably, a great deal of effort has been spent by students of the user to build up a detailed image, if not a model, of the scientist-user.

The Invisible College. Price (1963) pointed to the fact that each science or subscience has cores of people who maintain contact among themselves, communicating frequently by mail, telephone, and attending meetings. The term *invisible college* has come into use to pertain to a core of people who, by continual professional intercommunication, exchanges of working papers, data, etc., constitute an information processing machine within a discipline.

Within a sufficiently small field of activity, such an invisible college can come close to satisfying the bulk of the current information requirements of the group. However, as such a group becomes larger in its membership, additional, quasi-institutional entities are needed to supplement the highly effective—but informal, and therefore a bit undependable—information processing of the invisible college. Sciences have published journals for more than two centuries, as one example. Another example from more recent times, is the information center (Chapter One). When a comparison is made between the information content of several years' accumulation of journals and the information content of a 700,000-document library as serviced by MEDLARS, it is a comment on the degree to which science as a whole has grown.

When a given science is looked at as an organization of people and activities, it can generally be seen that it has *structure*. Chemistry divides into organic, inorganic, and physical; further subdivisions occur, often down to very narrow levels of specialization, such as flame photometry. A great deal of interest has been shown in recent years in the possibility that the invisible college phenomenon may actually determine the structure of science.

Citation tracing, discussed earlier in this chapter under the heading "analysis of existing data," can be used as a means of charting the structure of science. People within an invisible college have a strong tendency to cite each other's papers. Each invisible college has its neighboring, closely related invisible colleges, and citation tracing can be used to show the pattern of such relationships.

Earle and Vickery (1969) studied 65,000 citations in the social and natural sciences, and in technology, in a 10 percent representative sample of material published in the United Kingdom during the year 1965. A notable finding was that citation patterns in the social sciences had greater scatter than in the other areas studied. Papers within social science as a whole cited *other* social science papers in only 58 percent of the citations; the corresponding figure for technology was 81 percent. The comparison held when subgroups of science and technology were looked at (only 36 percent of the citations in the field of education, for example, were of other papers in education).

The obvious implication of such data is that the invisible college structure is weaker in the social sciences than in other areas. Other studies have pinpointed the humanities as having weak structure. Crane (1971), referring to the humanities and the soft sciences, comments:

> ... Their citation patterns tend to resemble a kind of "random raiding of the entire archive of the literature." There is some indication that, when social organization emerges in these fields, it does so in an attenuated form. ... Information-seeking is probably more difficult in such a field than in the basic sciences but also perhaps less imperative.

Scientific progress, as well as science itself, tends to have a structure. Kuhn (1962), in his analytical book *The Structure of Scientific Revolutions*, presents the notion of a *paradigm*, an idea or thesis that underlies a branch of scientific activity. Explaining how a paradigm tends to structure scientific progress, Kuhn states:

> . . . Newton's *Principia*, Franklin's *Electricity*, Lavoisier's *Chemistry*, and Lyell's *Geology* . . . served for a time implicitly to define the legitimate problems and methods of a research field for succeeding generations of practitioners. They were able to do so because they shared two essential characteristics. Their achievement was sufficiently unprecedented to attract an enduring group of adherents away from competing modes of scientific activity. Simultaneously, it was sufficiently open-ended to leave all sorts of problems for the redefined group of practitioners to resolve. Achievements that share these two characteristics I shall henceworth refer to as "paradigms," . . .

The paradigm is thus veiwed as having a charter-like relationship to a corresponding science or subscience, because scores of others in the field take it as a mandate, or at least as a challenge for further research and experiment. Citation tracing can be used as a means revealing paradigmatic effects in science—or the lack of such effects. Strong intercommunication and the accompanying strong mutual citation patterns within a group of adherents to a paradigm are manifest in the literature, and generally point backward in time to some one paper, article or book that announces the paradigm.

In scientific areas where such tight citation patterns do not exist, one suspects a lack of paradigms acceptable to members of the science. Recalling once again the tendency for citations to scatter in the social sciences, we note the observations of Brittain (1970):

> When a paradigm exists, new knowledge can be evaluated. Material that is worthless or discrepant can be disregarded, and valuable material left to accumulate. In the absence of a paradigm, a discipline must proceed by trial and error, never knowing whether unusual or discrepant research findings are adding to knowledge or side-tracking major issues. In the social sciences there is no lack of important problems to study . . . , but it is doubtful, even when the problems can be clearly identified, whether much progress will be made until the social sciences have their own paradigm. . . ."

Then, in the very next sentence, Brittain states, and brings us full circle to the point being developed, ". . . In the pre-paradigmatic stage the information requirements are particularly difficult to assess, and to meet. . . ." We now see each science not only as an information processing organism, but as one whose information needs and processes are likely to be distinctly different from those of other sciences. Apparently Kuhn's paradigm is itself a likely candidate as a paradigm for the field of information science. The structure and state of development of a science has very much to do with its character as a generator and consumer of information.

Katter (1963) reviewed some user studies from various fields of science and found the following relative differences in information use characteristics between broad areas of science:

TABLE 12.1 Pattern of Information Use. (Reprinted with the permission of System Development Corp.)

	Wide Variety	Few Types	Longer Life[a]	Shorter Life	Specific Need	Non-Specific Browsing	More Processing[b]	Less Processing
Old		✓	✓		✓		✓	
New	✓			✓		✓		✓
Applied	✓			✓	✓			✓
Basic		✓	✓			✓	✓	
Soft	✓		✓			✓	✓	
Hard		✓		✓	✓			✓

Characteristic of Field

[a] "Longer life" referes to greater age of document before it is used or cited.
[b] "Processing" includes activities such as indexing, cataloging, and other kinds of ordering or characteristics.

The finding that hard sciences are characterized by "less processing" and soft sciences by "more processing" is in interesting contrast to the recent discovery of Earle and Vickery (1969) that, as measured by citations, the average use of an item of natural science literature is several times greater than the average use of an item of social science literature (note: it seems generally agreed that social sciences are within the "soft sciences," possibly excepting some branches of psychology).

Modeling the Scientist. So important is it regarded for people in the field of information science to have an accurate view of the scientist-user that painstaking attempts are being made to synthesize what is known about scientists and the process of "doing science" into a useful conceptual framework. The word *model* is often used in relation to such a framework. Although this is, perhaps stretching the meaning of "model" considerably, it underlines the seriousness of the aim involved. The hope is that the thought exercise involved in making the synthesis will offset the casual attitude toward the scientist-user that information systems designers have characteristically shown.

An entire review chapter (Paisley, 1968) has been outlined in a manner congruent with such a conceptual framework. It is worthy of describing at some length. In the chapter, the scientist is seen as a part of his information environment, which we might think of schematically as a dot within a family of concentric circles. As one proceeds outward from the dot successively to each larger circle, one goes to broader and broader sectors of the information environment. The dot is termed "the scientist within his own head"—since that's where his information processing takes place. The smallest circle is the work team of which the scientist is a member. Then, working outward, we encounter the scientist's formal organization, his invisible college, his nation (or other significant political unit), and his culture.

A: *The Scientist Within His Own Head.* The mental functioning of a scientist-user seeking and evaluating information is a matter of basic interest in every user study. But some user studies deal with mental processes per se, and Paisley lumped them together in this section of his review chapter. Most of such papers that year, 1967, dealt with the relevance and utility of information (which subjects are treated at length in Chapter Eleven). The papers of that year tended to show, more than before, just how difficult it is to decide how relevant a document is to an information need. Experimentation up until then blithely assumed that one could meaningfully use relevance judges as stand-ins for real users; now there is considerable healthy doubt. The uniqueness and complexity of the scientist-user's appraisal of the relevance and utility of a document, a highly individual mental process, is now better appreciated than it was 5 years ago.

B: *The Scientist Within His Work Team.* The cluster of people working on the same project or within the same laboratory appears to be more significant in technology than in science. Engineers appear to seek more information from people in their immediate environment than scientists, who tend to look outward. In some research groups, looking outward for information often evolves so as to concentrate in one or two individuals, who are termed *technological gatekeepers.*

Of course, no one restricts his information input to that from a single source or group of people. There are always numerous choices, the bookshelf in the next office, the telephone, the company library, a consultant, and information center, etc. Senior people, who know "who's who" in a field or organization, may prefer informal contacts—meetings, phone calls, visits; new people are more dependent on journals or on company documentation. It is becoming increasingly common, in the field of information science, to refer to these alternatives as *information channels,* and of course there are both output and input channels.

C: *The Scientist Within a Formal Organization.* As was the case with studies of work team behavior, those studies focusing on in-organization behavior are often interested in the user's tendency to look either in or out of his company, university, etc. Studies such as the relation between the use of outside consultants and the quality of proposals written are examples. The use of company libraries or technical information facilities is often looked into; such a service costs money, and many are therefore interested in such questions as why a user bypasses company facilities, preferring other information channels. Some studies focus on such matters as the effect of company policy toward long distance telephoning, travel, etc., on research output or on information adequacy.

D: *The Scentist Within an Invisible College.* So much attention is being paid to the invisible college concept that considerable data has collected—much of it conflicting and confusing. A lot of the confusion apparently springs from two factors: (*a*) It is possible for a given scientist to belong to more than one invisible college—in fact, to as many as he can manage; and (*b*) Invisible colleges are often not cleanly separated, and in some cases networks of communication seemingly go on and on. (At this point we are beginning to get a vague idea of how complicated our model of the scientist-user is going to have to be in order to provide a complete description of him as an information processor.)

E: *The Scientist Within His Science.* At this point Paisley's framework becomes more complicated than what is presented here which is simplified for brevity's sake. At this level, rather than one concentric circle, Paisley has two not-quite concentric circles, a reference group and a (somewhat larger) membership group. A reference group is generally one that is congruent with the area in which the scientist reads or keeps a file, and the membership group is likely to be an entire professional society. This part of the framework pushes close to the frontiers of the scientist's regular information channels. It focuses on such information processes as conventions, major journals, abstracting and indexing services, etc.

F: *The Scientist Within a Political Unit.* A barrier around a nation can be a formidable one in its effect on information transfer. An American scientist who may be quite satisfied that he is aware of what people in his field are doing in England is apt to feel uncomfortable about his corresponding awareness of activities in France or Germany, still more so about Japan. The overstimulation of science, the waste and duplication of effort, etc., produced by international tension, strongly affects processes of information flow. Despite the importance of this level, relatively few studies could be assigned to it in 1967, and it is not easy to see in them any central foci.

G: *The Scientist Within His Culture.* It is perhaps misleading to think of this level as a concentric circle slightly larger than that for political unit. It would probably be better to think of this realm as lying in a totally different dimension from the others. An example of works done at this level can be found in the question: What happens to several collaborating scientists after one of them wins the Nobel prize? (Answer: They bust up.) Studies in this realm tend to deal with scientists as cultural beings and the information implications thereof. Such matters as prestige, visibility, and effect of the number of publications on promotion and salary, etc., are hereunder dealt with.

OVERVIEW

If the reader has followed the discussion of the chapter this far, and feels in a state of confusion, this is appropriate. User studies up to this point have so thinly scratched the surface in fathoming the use of information that confusion is a healthy state of mind to be in when undertaking any project related to the user. As Chapter Nine points up, one should think of all the misdirected effort that has gone into the invention and design of retrieval systems, a large number of which failed at the point where real users entered the picture. (As we now appreciate, it is so easy for a user to select a different channel.) So, if the reader is confused, he is much better off than he was at the end of Chapter Seven, where the user was no more complicated than a single box in an information flow diagram.

REFERENCES

ACKOFF, R. L., and M. H. HALBERT (1958), *An Operations Research Study of the Scientific Activity of Chemists,* Case Institute of Technology, Cleveland.

ARNETT, EDWARD M. (1970), Computer-Based Chemical Information Services, *Science,* 170:3965, pp. 1370–1376.

BRITTAIN, J. M. (1970), *Information and Its Users,* John Wiley & Sons, New York.

BUSH, VANNEVAR (1945), As We May Think, *Atlantic Monthly,* 176, pp. 101–108.

CARTER, L. F., et al. (1967), *National Documentation-Handling Systems for Science and Technology,* John Wiley & Sons, New York.

CRANE, DIANA (1971), Information Needs and Uses, in Cuadra, C. A., ed., *Annual Review of Information Science and Technology,* Vol. 6, Encyclopaedia Britannica, Chicago.

EARLE, PENELOPE, and VICKERY, BRIAN (1969), Social Science Literature in the UK as Indicated by Citations, *Journal of Documentation*, 25:2, pp. 123–141.

JAHODA, G., HUTCHINS, RONALD D., and MILLER, D. M. (1966), Analysis of Case Histories of Personal Index Use, in Black, Donald V., ed., *Progress in Information Science and Technology, Proceedings of the American Documentation Institute; 1966 Annual Meeting, October 3–7, Santa Monica, California,* Adrianne Press, Woodland Hills, Calif., pp. 245–254.

KATTER, R. V. (1963), *Research Bases of Language Data Processing System Design*, System Development Corporation TM-1199, Santa Monica, Calif.

KUHN, T. S. (1962), *The Structure of Scientific Revolutions*, University of Chicago, Chicago.

LANCASTER, F. W. (1969), MEDLARS: Report on the Evaluation of its Operating Efficiency, *American Documentation*, 20:2, pp. 119–142.

LIPETZ, BEN-AMI (1970), Information Needs and Uses, in Cuadra, C. A., ed., *Annual Review of Information Science and Technology*, Vol. 5, Encyclopaedia Britannica, Chicago.

MARTIN, M. W., and ACKOFF, R. L. (1963), The Dissemination and Use of Recorded Scientific Information, *Management Science*, 9:2, pp. 322–336.

PAISLEY, W. J. (1968), Information Needs and Uses, in Cuadra, C. A., ed., *Annual Review of Information Science and Technology*, Vol. 3, Encyclopaedia Britannica, Chicago.

PARKER, E. B., and PAISLEY, W. J. (1966), Research for Psychologists at the Interface of the Scientist and his Information System, *American Psychologist*, 21:11, pp. 1061–1071.

PRICE, D. J. DE SOLLA (1963), *Little Science, Big Science*, Columbia Press, New York.

PRICE, D. J. DE SOLLA (1965), Networks of Scientific Papers, *Science*, 149:3683, pp. 510–515.

WESTBROOK, J. H. (1960), Identifying Significant Research, *Science*, 132:3435, pp. 1229–1234.

WOOD, D. N. (1969), Discovering the User and His Information Needs, *Aslib Proceedings*, 21:7, pp. 262–270.

Index

Abrams, Peter, 118
Abstracting, 8, 16
Abstracts, as document surrogates, 248, 311, 362, 363, 384
Abstracts, automatic, 61, 262, **302-308, 364-365**
Accumulator, 121, 133, 138
Accuracy (classification), 276
Ackoff, R. L., 376, 379
ACORN (**A**ssociative **C**ontent **R**etrieval **N**etwork), 274
Acquisition, 146, 167, **241-246**
Add instruction, 121
Add time, 204
Adding machine (**See** Calculator, desk)
Address calculation, 203, 210
Address tags, 123
Addressing,
  core memory, **120-126**, 135, 203, 212, 213, 229
  direct, 210
  disk, 96, 98
Adelson, Marvin, 11
Administrative data processing, 167
Advanced Technology/Libraries, 46, 108
African nations, 363
Aids for the blind, 69
AIM-TWX (Index Medicus), 279
Alexandrian Library, 5
Alfred, E. N., 396
Algebra, Boolean, 264
Algebra, Cyril, 291
Allen, Thomas J., 10
Alphabet, in digital form, 56, 290
Alphabetical sorting, 57
Alphanumeric characters, 80, 103
American Bar Foundation, 294
American Chemical Society, 294
American Documentation, 180-183, 335
American Documentation Institute, 145, 172

American Libraries, 28
American Library Association, 147
American Medical Association, 11
American Society for Information Science, 145, 172
American Society of Metals, 180
Ames Laboratory (AEC), 259
Ames Research Center (NASA), 101
Ammonia (in duplication), 34
Analytic infixes, 180
Anaphoric analysis, 325
Anderson, L. H., 86
Andersson, P. L., 26, 75
AN/FSQ-7 computer, 199
Announcing, 8, **245-246**, 258
Annual Review of Information Science and Technology, 270, 296, 315, 368
Aperture card, 37, 38, 43
Arcata Microfilm Corp., 50
Archival storage, digital, 102
Arithmetic and control unit, 132, 133, 138
Armitage, J. E., 301
Arnett, Edward M., 376, 385
ARPA (Advanced Research Projects Agency), 323
ARPANET, 101
Artandi, Susan, 301
Arthur D. Little, Inc., 274
Artificial intelligence, 326-327
ASLIB (Association of Special Libraries and Information Bureaus), 145
ASLIB-Cranfield project, 186, 339, 352, 368
Aspen Systems Corp., 300
Assembler (computer instructions), 131
Assembly language, 130-131
Assignment analysis, 247, **252-256**
Association for Computing Machinery, 262, 294
Association map, 312-313
Associative indexing, 310

395

396   Index

Associative memory, 270
Associative retrieval, 271, 273
Assyrian writing, 142
Atomic energy applications (data generation), 106
Atomic Energy Commission, 8, 43, 258, 259
Attaché case terminal, 86
Audio coupler, 86, 110
Audio recording, 67
Audio signals, 61, 79, 90
Auerbach Task Force, 88
Author alterations, cost, 23
Author compensation, 27, 29
Authority list, **152-155**, 252, 255
Automatic abstract, 61, 262, **302-308**, **364-365**
Automatic classification, 271, **274-277**, 310, 366
Automatic extracting, 302, 364
Automatic indexing, **291-301**, 365
Automobile license lookup, 209
Autopositive process, 33
Auxiliary memory, 62, 89, 98, 133, 199, 207, 222-223
Avedon, Don M., 107, 108, 257

Babylonian writing, 142
Back-of-the-book index, 300
Backspacing, 87
Bagdikian, Ben H., 4, 13, 291
Bagley, P. R., 262, 267
Bandwidth, 92, **110-111**
Bank of America, 72
Bar-Hillel, Yehoshua, 200, 295, 316, 334
Barker, Frances H., 285
Barton, A., 264
Batch processing, 78, 139, 277, 291
Battelle Memorial Institute, 8
Baxendale, Phyllis, 308
Beard, Joseph, 297
Becker, Joseph, 59, 100, 110, 167, 225, 248
Bedford, Gwendolyn M., 264
Behavioral scientists (**See** Psychologists)
Bell Telephone Laboratories, 296
Benjamin, Curtis G., 29
Benson-Lehner Corp., 39
Bernick, Myrna, 281
Bershadskii, R., 2
Best fit character recognition, 71

Biblical concordance, 297, 336
Bibliographic information, 243, 245, 248
Bibliographic searching, 279
Bibliographies, 26, 149, 242, 258
Bibliography, annotated, 259
Binary digits, 57
Binary numbers, **53-59,** 103, 270, 286
Binary search, 208
Bishop, W. W., 148
Bi-stable elements, 54, 69
Bittel, Lester R., 220
Black, Donald V., 362
Blankenship, D. A., 313
Blowback, 44
Bobrow, Daniel G., 318, 326
BOLD (**B**ibliographic **O**n-**L**ine **D**isplay), 313
Book, concept of, 143
Book catalog, 26, 49, 107, 150, 168
Book deterioration, 2, 48
Book duplication, 48
Book output, world, 3
Book production process, 23, 26
Book publishing, 29
Book titles, 5
Bookkeeping, double entry, 196
Boolean algebra, 265
Borko, Harold, 274, 275, 295, 301, 313, 318, 366
Bourne, Charles, 11, 341
Bowker Annual, The, 2, 4
Bracken, R. H., 263, 264
Braille, 69
Braille books, 2
Brain, human, 287-288, 325
Branching instructions, 122-125
British Museum, 16
British Standards Institute, 159
Brittain, J. M., 388
Broadcasting, 5
Brodie, Nancy, 365
Brookes, B. C., 300
Brooks, F. P., Jr, 113, 301
Brown, Harrison, 3
Brown, Patricia L., 259
Brown, Richard M., 101
Brown University, 88
Browsing, 315, 361, 384
  and classification, 253, 311
  iterative, 279, 313, 385

Bruner, J. S., 326
Budgetary function (library), 167
Buffer unit, 78, 80, 110, 133
Buffered entry, 63, 64
Buffers (disks, cassettes), 65
Bulk processing of information, **16**, 290
Bunker-Ramo Corp., (**See also** Thompson Ramo-Wooldridge), 280
Bureau of Internal Revenue, U.S., 204
Burnaugh, H. P., 313
Burroughs TD-700 display, 86
Bush, Vannevar, 6, 39, 164, 385
Business automation, 167
Business data processing, 216, 290
Business Week, 27, 219, 221
Bytes, 57, 103, 216

Cable, coaxial, 5, 13, 111, 247
Calculator,
 card programmed, 119
 desk, 71, 118-119
 pocket, 83
California Computer Products, 108
Call number, 148, 156
Cambridge University, 275
Cameras, 21
 microfiche, 107
 microfilm, 39, 45
 rotary, 37, 43
 step-and-repeat, 44, 46
Canning, Richard G., 105
Caplan, L. N., 264
Card (**See** Punched card)
Card catalog, 43, 144, 145, **150-153**, 192, 253, 255, 384
Card punch, 71
Card-to-tape converter, 64
Carey, Robert F., 64
Carlson, W. H., 297
Carter, Launor, F., 8, 246
Cartridge, tape, 67, 102
Casey, R. S., 178
Cassette, tape, 67
Catalog, dictionary, 147, 148, 150
Catalog, union, 144, 150, 254
Cataloging (**See also** Book catalog; Card catalog; Descriptive catalog; Subject cataloging), 2, 145, **147-148**, **150-153**, 167
Cataloging/analysis, 240, **247-257**

Catalogs,
 and organization, 5, 248
 merchandise, 108
 parts, 49, 194-195
Categories, 7
Cathode-ray tube (CRT), 12, 13, 21, 22, 23, **80-89**, 103, 104, **106-109**, 247, 278, 311, 314, 384
Censac Users Guide, 205-206
Census data,
 and punched cards, 60, 118, 197
 storage and retrieval of, 204, 234
Chain indexing, 185
Chain printer, 105
Channel,
 communication, **109-111**
 in magnetic storage, 93, 96
 information, 390-392
Channel capacity, limits of, 59
Character generators, 22, 82-83
Character print mechanisms, 79-80, 104-107
Character readers, photoelectric, 12
Character recognition,
 magentic, **72-73**
 optical, 44, 60, **74-77**
Characters per second, 64, 80, 89, 93, 99, 103, 105-107, 112
Charactron tube, 80, 107
Chemical Abstracts, 22, 385
Chemical information, 342-343
Chemical Titles, 294
Chemists, 253, 376
Chess and computers, 326-328
Chi square, 272
Chimpanzee, 287
China, ancient paper making, 143
China, science abstracts of, 294
CIM (**C**omputer-**I**nput **M**icrofilm), 44, 109
Circulating (C) library, 48
Circulation control, 69, **149**, 167
Citation indexing, 365
Citations, 379-380, 387-388
Class number, 148
Classification, 144, 145, 148, **153-161**, 162-163, 177, 184-187, 252, 253, 254, 255, 342
Classification, automatic, 271, **274-277**, 310, 366

Cleanroom conditions, 46
Clerical functions (library automation), 166
Cleverdon, Cyril, 339, 340, 357, 368
Clumps, 275, 365
Cluster, 277
COBOL (Common Business-Oriented Language), 221, 225, 227, 230
CODASYL (Conference on Data Systems Languages) Systems Committee, 208, 221-223, 225, 234
Codex, papyrus, 143
Collator, 60
College of Aeronautics, Cranfield, 186
Colon classification, 184
Color copying, 34, 35
COM (Computer-Output Microfilm), 44, 53, **106-109**
COMAC (Continuous Multiple Access Collator), 268
Communication,
  in digital form, 58, **109-113**
  measure of efficiency, 59
Communication systems, **110-111**, 190
Communications, declining cost, 13
Communications satellites, 5
Competence, 288
Compiler, 123, **130-132**, 229-233
Compiling, delay in batch processing, 78
Composition (**See also** Typesetting), 16, 17, **21-27**
Compton, B. E., 257
Computational linguistics, 286-289, 318, 325
Computer control, 132, 229
Computer Decisions, 68, 110
Computer-human discourse, 289, 328
Computer instructions, 121, 130, 138, 229-233
Computer time, 125, 140, 203-205, 211, 277, 278, 345
Computers,
  and bi-stable elements, 54
  and document retrieval (history), 262-265, 267, 270
  and human language, 286-287
  and optical input, 69
  in typesetting, 19, 21, 26
  memory storage in, 120
  need for auxiliary storage, 89

Computers (cont.)
  on-line inefficiencies, 88
  time shared, 78, 278
Computerworld, 26
Computing,
  declining cost of, 13, 315
  growth of, 5, 12
  remote location, 5
Computing power, distribution of, 89
Concept coordination, 173
Concordance, 297, 300, 336
Condensed representation, 249, 250
Congress, U. S., 12
Consistency, interindexer, 355, **359-361**
Constitution, U. S., 118
Contact copying, full-size, **30-31**, 34
Contact duplication, microfilm, 27, 44, 46
Content-addressable memory, 270
Context-dependent grammar, 321
Control Data Corporation,
  3300 computer, 76
  915 optical scanner, 74, 76
CONVERSE (data retrieval system), 234, 317, 323, 328
Cooccurrence, word, term, **270-277**, 311, 313, 343, 345, 365
Cooper, Wm. S., 360
Coordinate indexing, **173-177**, 265, 268, 272, 339, 340, 342
Copying,
  eye-legible, 30
  full-size, 12, 27, **30-36**
  office, 29, 35
Copying Methods Manual, 30
Copyright, 27, 49
Corbato, F. J., 140
Core memory, 103, **132-139**, 197, 199, 207, 213
Cores (**See** Magnetic cores)
Cornell University, 313, 343, 345, 365
Correlation, 343
Coselection, 364-365
Cost accounting, library, 167, 168
Cost of computing, 13, 315
Cost of indexing, 342
Cost of information service, 335, 366-370
Cost of telecommunications, 13
Council of Library Resources, 145, 340
Crane, Diana, 387
Cranfield College, 186, 339, 341, 352

Credit card processing, 71
Crestadoro, A., 294
Criminal records, 205-206
Cross-indexed storage, 96, 98, 201, 228
CRT (**See** Cathode-ray tube)
Cuadra, Carlos A., 270, 279, 353
Cue-word method, extracting, 364
Cuneiform writing, 142
Cursor (display keying indicator), 87, 291
Curtice, R. M., 315, 365
Cutter, C. A., 172
Cutter author marks, 161

Daily newspaper, as document system, 241, 242, 244
Daily newspaper, automation of, 27
Daily order sheet, 258
D'Albe, Fournier, 69
Damereau, F., 291
Dana, John Cotton, 145
Dancer, J. B., 36, 45
Data base, 198-206
Data base administrator, 224-227
Data cell (IBM 2321), **98-99**
Data communications, 5, 59, **109-113**
Data definition, 225-228
Data management packages, 225-228
Data management systems, **219-228**
Data processing, 61, 88, 118
  central mechanics of, 133, 207
  origins, 197
Data processing power, distribution of, 89
Data providing systems, 200
Data retrieval, 170, **196-237**, 239
Datamation, 77, 80
Dataproducts Corp., 106
Dattola, R. T., 277
Davis, C. H., 297
Davis, Sidney, 67
Debug, 126
Decentralized publication, 26
Decimal numbers, 55, 103, 120
Decision making, information in, 11
Defense Documentation Center (DDC), 44, 241, 242, 246, 247
Defense Metals and Ceramics Information Center, 8
Department of Defense, U. S., 194

Dependency analysis, 321
Depth of indexing, 336, 342, 343
Derivative analysis, **247-252**, 256
Descriptive cataloging, 147, 248
Destructive readout, 138
Deterioration of books, 2, 48
Developing solution, 33
Dewey, Melvil, 172
Dewey Decimal Classification, 7, 145, 148, **156-158**, 179, 253, 285
Dexter, Margaret E., 359
Diagonal striping, 45
Diary method, user studies, 377-379
Diazo method, copying, 31, 36, 44
Diazotypy, 32, **34**
Dictionaries, in language processing, 289, 290, 315, 316, 317, 364
Dictionary catalog, 147, 148, 150
Digit, display, cost of, 86
Digital representation, 53, 247
Digitizing from microfiche, 44
Digits, binary, **53-59**
Diode,
  light-emitting, 83, 107
  laser beam readout, 102
Diptych, 143
Direct access,
  in digital storage, **210-212**, 225
  in microfiche, 38, 40
Direct method, contact copying, 30
Direct observation, user studies, **379**
Disk (**See** Magnetic disk)
Disk pack, 66, 96, 278
Diskette (**See** Floppy disk)
Display, 21, 53, 68, **80-89**, 278, 314
  interactive, 83, 86-89, 291, 313, 315
Dissemination,
  by reproduction, 257
  microfiche, 43
  selective (SDI), 240, **259**, 361, 367
Distribution lists, 258
Dittberner, Donald L., 13, 110
Ditto process, 33
Document collection analysis, 310
Document-document similarity matrix, 277
Document processing systems, **239-261**
Document repository, 241, 242, 244
Document retrieval, 40, 170, 200, **262-281**, 285

Index

Document-term matrix, 274
Document transport, 70
Documentalists, 171, 189, 334, 352, 276, 277
Documentation, 171, 335
Documentation, Inc., 339
Documented information, 197
Dodd, George G., 210
Doebler, Paul D., 26
Domains, magnetic, 135
Dorn, Philip H., 64
Dot matrix characters, 82, 86, 113
Double-entry bookkeeping, 196
Doubling time, information parameters, 2-5
Doyle, Lauren B., 276, 277, 311-313
Drafting, electronic, 88
Drum printer, 105-106
Drums (**See** Magnetic drums)
Dry silver process, 33
Duodecimal numbers, 55
Duplicates, microfilm, 45, 108
Duplicating (D) library, 48
Duplication (**See** Copying, Reprography)
Duplication of effort, 7
DuPont Co., 342

EAM (Electronic Accounting Machinery), 37, 60, 71, 202
Earle, Penelope, 387, 389
Eastman Kodak Co., 37, 39, 40, 268-270, 280
EBCDIC (Extended **B**inary-**C**oded **D**ecimal **I**nterchange **C**ode), 57, 59
Ecology and information, 10
Economies of scale, 201
Edge-notched cards, 179
Editing, 291
Edmundson, H. P., 266, 305, 309, 364-365
EDP Analyzer, 76, 110, 259, 280
EDSAC computer, 229
Education and information growth, **10-11**
Egyptian papyrus, 142
Egyptian writing, 142
Eichner process, 34
Ektafax process, 34
Eldredge, K. R., 72
Electric pencil, 70
Electrical conductivity, in copying, 32
Electrofax process 31, 34

Electrolytic processes, **33-34**
Electronic draftsman, 88
Electronic microfilm searching, 39
Electronic watches, 83
Electrophotography, 32, **33**
Electrostatic duplication, 30, 32
Eliason, Alan L., 219
Elimination factor, 337
Encyclopaedia Britannica, Inc., 45, 49, 258
Encyclopedia, as a system, 241, 242, 244, 246, 252
Engineering drawings, 37
Engineering Research Associates, 40
Engineers,
  education, 10
  productivity, 366
  seeking information, 390
England (**See also** Great Britain, United Kingdom) 230, 339
English language, 294
  in programming, 233
Enlargement, photographic, 31
Erasing, 65, 83, 93
Error correction, 22, 64
Error detection (input), 60, 65, 290-291
Error messages, 234
Evaluation of retrieval systems, 273, **334-370**
Evaluators of retrieval systems, 337, 338, 339, 355, 356
Exact match character recognition, 71
Extracts, automatic, 302, 364-365
Eye-legible copying, 30
Eye-legible titles, 38, 43

Faceted classification, **184-187**, 340
Facsimile transmission, 28, **111-112**
Fair use doctrine, 29
Fairthorne, Robert A., 353
Fallout, 337, 351, **357**
False drops, 176-178, 350
Farmer, Vic, 133
Farrington 3030, 74
Farrington recognition code, 73
Farrington scanner, 70
Fayen, E. G., 279
Federal Communications Commission, 110
Federal Government, U. S., 11, 38

Index 401

Federation Internationale de Documentation (FID), 145, 161, 172
Ferromagnetic domains, 135
Field (Item), 202
File cabinet, 197
File integrity (microfiche), 45
File management, 222, 228
File organization, 96, 98
Files (as data base units), 198, 201, 205, 207-219
Financial data processing (libraries), 167
Firth, F. E., 264
Fischer, Bobby, 327-328
Fischer, Marguerite, 255, 294, 296
Fixed format, fixed field file arrangement, 202, 204, 205, 227
Fixed format, variable field file arrangement, 202
Flexowriter, 61
Flip (Benson-Lehner), 40
Floppy disks, 67
Flores, I. 215
Flow diagram, 126, 241
FMA, Inc., 40
Ford, John D., Jr, 313, 363
Ford Foundation, 145
Formatted information, 6, 87, 196-206, 222, 336, 342
Fortran, 132, 230
Franco-Prussian War, 37
Free, John, 35
Frequency of words, index terms, 266, **301-316**
Frequency ratio, 309, 310
Full-size copying, 12, 27, 29, **30-36**
Function words, 294, 300
Future Shock, 6

Gannett, Elwood K., 29
Garvey, W. D., 257
General Electric Co., 73, 140, 264, 268
General purpose computers and document retrieval, history, **262-265,** 267, 269, 270
Generalized capability (data management), 222-224
Generic relationships, 252, 339
Generic requests, 177
Generic searching, 342
Germany, 43

Georgetown University, 316
Giuliano, V. E., 274
Glasser, E. L., 140
Go list, 300, 301
Goffman, William, 353
Goodrich Chemical Co., 217
Gordon, Ronald F., 45
Grammar,
 context dependent, 321
 immediate constituent, 318
 phrase structure, context-free, 320
Graphic CRT displays, 80, 82
Great Britain (**See also** United Kingdom), 144, 145
Group profile, 259
Growth,
 computing, 5
 data base, 210-206
 information, **2-14,** 170
 population, 3, 4
Gruenberger, Fred, 5
Gutenberg, Johannes, 143

Haavind, Robert, 68
Hammond, William, 246
Hard copy, from microforms, 29, 31, 33, 37, 44, 45, 247
Hardening, 247
Hart, Lew, 294
Harvard University, 274, 316
Hawken, William R., 30, 32, 34
Hawthorne effect, 377, 379, 380
Hayes, Robert M., 110, 167, 225, 248
Hays, David, 321
Heilprin, L. B., 36, 48
Henry, Nicholas L., 29
Herner, Saul, 294, 336
Herschel, Sir John, 33
Hexadecimal numbers, 55, **103-104**
Hierarchical structure, 6, 200, 276, 319, 349
Hieroglyphics, 142
High-level languages, **130-132,** 220, **230-235**
Hillegass, John R., 79
Holland, 42, 43
Hollerith, Herman, 59, 119
Hollerith card, 197
Holmes, Emory, 313, 363
Holography, 100

402 Index

Homography, 294, 310
Honeywell Information Systems, 225
Horty, John F., 300
Hospital,
 medical records and OCR, 76
 x-ray system analysis, 241
Host language systems, 221, 224, 225
Hot metal composition, 22
Human brain, 287-288, 325
Hurwitz, Frances I., 360
Huskey, Harry D., 54
Hyphenation, 21, 290
Hysteresis loop, 135

IAA (International Aerospace Abstracts), 260
IBM (International Business Machines), 60, 119, 259, 275, 302, 308, 361
IBM 026 and 029 keypunch machines, 60
IBM 2280 character generator, 22
IBM 2321 data cell, 98-99
IBM 2740 and 2741 on-line terminals, 79-80
IBM 360-series computer, 56, 57, 73, 123-124, 343
IBM 3850 mass storage device, 102
IBM 602 calculator, 119
IBM 700-series computer, 230, 231, 264, 272, 343
IBM card (See also Punched card), **57-58**
IDS (Integrated Data Store), 225-226
ILLIAC IV computer, 101
Immediate constituent analysis, 318-320
Immediate distribution, **256-260**
Impact printer, **104-106**
Index,
 as indirect organization, 5, 254
 concept of, vis á vis catalog, 248
Index production vis computerized typesetting, 26
Index register, 122-125, 133, 207
Index terms, in tape seraching, 263-265
Indexed sequential organization, 96, 98, **209-210**, 216
Indexing,
 automatic, **291-301**, 343, 365
 depth of, 336, 342, 343, 350
 manual, 252, 266, 300, 336, 343, 359-361
Indirect method of optical copying, 32
Inference, 327

Information analysis center, **7-10,** 170
Information and language, 287-288
Information center, **7-10,** 44, 170, 241, 242, 244, 252, 253, 257, 260, 387, 390
Information channels, 390-392
Information growth, **2-14**
Information measure, 58
Information science, 172, 286, 363
Information structure, **197-206**
Information system, **189-195,** 238-239
Information theory, 59, 190, 309, 362
Information user needs, 354-355, **375-392**
Information value, **366-370**
Informative abstracts, 252
Infrared radiation, in copying, 31
Initial processing, **246-247**
Input, 23, **59-89**
Input/output equipment, 16, 133
Institute International de Bibliographie, 171
Instructions, computer, 121, 130, 138, 229-233
Intelligence summaries, 313, 363
Intelligent terminals, 68, **88-89**
Interactive displays, **87-88**
Interactive retrieval systems, 140, 346
 (see also On-line systems)
Interest profile (SDI), 259, 361
Interface, man-machine, 220, 348
Interindexer consistency, 355, **359-361**
Interlibrary communication, 167, 168, 384
Interlibrary loan, 149, 245
International Algebraic Language (IAL), 232
International Business Machines Corp. (See IBM)
International Conference on Scientific Information (ICSI), 291
Interpolation, 209, 216
Interrogation, 222, 227, 228
Intertype Co., 18, 19
Interviews, in user studies, **378-379,** 380
Inventory catalog, 153
Invisible college, 10, **386-389**
IRMA (Internal Report Management Aid), 315)
Irrelevant documents, 337, 339, 341, 345, 347, 357, 358

Isaacs, H. H. 206
Item, of data, 198, 201-205, 207
Item value, 202, 205, 208, 210-213
Iterative browsing, 279
Iterative searching, **277-281**, 311

Jacquard, J. M., 118
Jahoda, G., 365, 377
Jakobson, Roman, 288
Japan, 4
Johnson, Elmer D., 142
Jones, P. E., 315, 365
Jones, Shirli O., 259
Jonker, Frederick, 249
Jordain, Philip B., 140
Jordan, John R., 259, 366
Journals, 259, 367, 387, 390, 391
JOVIAL (**J**ules' **O**wn **V**ersion of **I**nternational **A**lgebraic **L**anguage), 230, 232
Judges, classification (**See also** Relevance judges), 275-276
Justification (in typesetting), 18, 21

Kalvar process (microfilm duplication), 31, 36, 44
Katter, Robert V., 353, 363, 389
Kay, Martin, 289
Kellogg, Charles, 234, 317, 323, 328
Kent, Allen, 179, 184, 250, 268, 337
Kertesz, Francois, 7
Kessel, B., 268
Key items, 201-202, 207, 209
Key-to-disk input, **65-66**, 89
Key-to-tape input, 13, **64-66**
Keyboard, linotype, 17
Keyboard input, **60-69**, **78-89**
Keyboard verification, 22, 23, **60**, 64, 78
Keypunch operator, 60, 77, 121
Keypunch replacement (by OCR), 77
Keypunching, **60-61**, 66, 76, 78, 119, 308-309, 340
 of aperture cards, 37
Keyword-in-context (KWIC) indexing, 259, **292-301**, 313, 324, 345, 355, 356, 365
 design concept, 249
 format, 255-256, 359
Keyword-out-of-context (KWOC), 296-299, 365

Klein, Sheldon, 322
Knuth, D. E., 55
Kolb, Edwin R., 21
Kuhn, T. S., 388-389
Kuhns, J. L., 265
Kuney, Joseph H. 22
KWIC, KWOC (**See under** Keyword)

Lancaster, F. W., 279, 338, 349-350, 358, 366, 385
Landau, Herbert B., 367, 368
Language, natural, 239
 processing, **285-329**
 translation by machine, 286, 216
Lap reader (microfilm), 49
Laser memories, **99-102**
Laser transmission, 100, 110
Legal search, 297
Legislative Reference Staff, 149
Legislators and information, 12
Lending library concept, 257
Lenin State Library, 2
Lesk, M. E., 273, 356
Letterpress printing, **17-19**, 21
Lettieri, Larry, 105
Librarians, 16, 39, 261, 276, 340, 352, 376, 379
Librarianship, **144-146**, 171
Libraries, duplicating vs. circulating, 48
Library automation, **166-168**
Library equipment, 33
Library functions, **146-149**
Library network, 168
Library of American Civilization, 49
Library of Congress,
 cataloging, 147, 151, 239
 classification, 145, 148, 153, 158, 285
 list of subject headings, 148, 152, 153
 service (MARC), 254
 size, 2, 48
 staff, 149
Library profession, **144-146**
Library shelf integrity, 260
Library tools, **149-161**
License search, 209
Light-emitting diode, 83, 107
Light pen, 87
Line printer, 21, 79, 103, **104-106**, 108
Linguistic competence, 288
Linguistic performance, 287

Index

Linguistics, computational, 286, 318, 325
Links (address), 98, 213, 216-219
Links (subject), 177, 338, 339, 342, 345
Lintotype, **17-19**, 23, 27, 61
Lipetz, Ben-Ami, 385
List processing, 212-215, 217
Locke, W. N., 280
Lockheed Aircraft Corp., 281, 366
Lodestar, 39
Logical records, 207-208
Logical vectors, 345
Los Angeles Times, 27
Lowe, Thomas C., 210
Lucas, Henry C., Jr, 221
Luhn, Hans Peter, 61, 247, 291, 294, 300, 301-304, 306, 308, 311, 315, 364
Luxenberg, H. R., 82, 85

Machine translation, 286, 289, 295, 310, 311, 316
Mack, James D., 172
MacQuarrie, Catherine, 163
Macro instruction, 231
Magnetic cores, 54, 64, 80, 82, **133-139**, 197
Magnetic disk, 40, 65, 78, **96-98**, 102, 141, 208, 210, 263, 264, 315
Magnetic drum, **93-94**, 98, 139, 199
Magnetic ink, 72
Magnetic media, 38, **89**
Magnetic strips, **98-99**
Magnetic tape, 13, 21, 23, 28, 40, 53, 62, 64, 65, 66, 72, 79, 89, **93-96**, 102, 107, 109, 208, 210, 263, 267
Maizell, R. E., 362
Man-machine interface, 220, 348
Man-machine text processing, 308
Management by Exception, 220
Management information systems (MIS), 219-221
Manual access, 37
Manual computation, 117
Manual indexing, 265, 266, 300, 343, 359
Manual/intellectual (as opposed to machine) methods, 247, 252, 255, 274
MARC (**Ma**chine **R**eadable **C**ataloging), 254
Market economy, 369-370, 384
Markuson, Barbara, 253
Maron, M. E., 265, 272, 311, 352

Marron, Harvey, 368
Martin, James, 3, 4
Martin, M. W., 379
Massachusetts Institute of Technology, 140, 263, 267, 278
Master (in duplication), 44, 45, 46
Matrix (linotype), 18
Matrix processing program, 276, 277
Maximum-depth indexing, 336
Maybury, Catherine, 163
McBee Key-Sort system, 179
McCarthy, George, 37
McGraw-Hill Book Company, 23
McMurtrie, Douglas C., 143
Meaning, 288, 294
Measure (relevance), 253-353
Medical knowledge, 11
Medical records, 76
MEDLARS (**Me**dical **L**iterature **A**nalysis and **R**etrieval **S**ystem), 278, 343, 349, 350, 357, 387
Meetham, Roger, 101
Memex, 385
Memorex, 107
Memory register, 120, 135
Menkus, Belden, 109
Merging, 228
Metcalfe, John, 179
Methodology (evaluation), 339, 350, 355-356, 362
Microbook Library, 45, 49, 258, 385
Microfiche, 38, 39, **40-45**, 61, 108, 241, 247, 261
Microfilm, 2, 12, 13, 27, 31, 32, 34, 53, 64, 107-109, 238, 239, 241, 247, 258, 269, 270, 280, 365, 384, 385
Microfilm, roll, **39-40**, 43, 61, 108
Microfolio, 50
Micrographics, **36-51**
Micrographics News and Views, 2, 31, 45, 48, 49, 270
Microjackets, 50
Micropublishing, 27, 48
Microseconds, 123, 139
Microvision, Inc., 49
Microwave communications, 5, 13, 59, 111, 112, 247
Miller, Edward F., 125
Mills, Peter D., 66
Mimeograph process, 30

Minicard, 268
Minicomputer controllers, 65, 66, 68
Minicomputer peripherals, 62
Minicomputer rationale, 267
Minicomputers (intelligent terminals), 89
Minimization of storage space, 202-204, 207
Miracode, 40, 270
Mohawk Data Sciences Corporation, 64
Monographs, 7
Monotype, 61
Montague, Barbara, 177, 342
Montgomery, C. A., 252, 286, 296
Mooers, Calvin, 177-179, 184, 262
Morgue (newspaper), 242, 257, 297
Moyer, S. R., 264
Multidimensional scaling, 363
Multifont readers, 74
Multiprogramming, 315, 318
Multiterms, 305-307
Mylar storage base, 101

Nanoseconds, 54
National Aeronautics and Space Administration (NASA), 8, 43, 101, 241, 246, 259, 280-281, 385
National Bureau of Standards, 315
National Cash Register Company, 46, 73
National Clearinghouse for Mental Health Information, 8
National Library of Medicine, 279, 349
National Oceanographic Data Center, 8
National Science Foundation, 146, 339
National Union Catalog, 254
NB Jackets Corporation, 50
Needham, R. M., 275, 277, 365
Negative (photographic), 19, 31
Nelson, Carl E., 28, 100
Network (communications), 5, 384
Neurochemistry, 294
New York Public Library, 2, 48
News information, 254
Newspapers, 27, 39, 241, 242, 244, 291, 297
Nobel prize, 392
Noise factor, 337
Nolan, J. J., 264
Nonimpact printers, 106
Nonprocedural languages, 222, 227, 228, 232

Nonprogrammer use of computers, 232-234
Nonvoice communications, 5
Norman, Adrian R. D., 3, 4
Normal scientist, 343
Nuclear physicists, 253
Nuclear physics, 311, 340
Number systems, 55
Numeric vector, 345

Octal numbers, 55, 103, 120, 229, 231
Office copying, 29, 30, 32, 35
Office of Science Information, 146
Offset printing, 13, **19-22**
O'Hara, F. M., 366
Ohlman, Herbert, 291, 294, 311
Olle, T. William, 223, 224
Olney, John, 2, 289
Omission factor, 337
On-line systems, 5, 62, 68, 76, **78-89**, 140, 234
Operand, 123
Operations research, 220, 377
Operator, keyboard, 60, 65, 77, 78, 87, 121
Opscan 288 character reader, 74
Optical character readers, 44, 60, **69-77**, 109
Optical copying, 31
Optical searching (microfilm), 38
Ordering, 43, 243-244
Osgood, C. E., 326, 352
Oswald, V. A., 305-308
Output, **103-109**
Overflow storage, 212
Ozalid process, 34

Pagination, 22, 26
Paisley, W. J., 389-392
Panizzi, Anthony, 16
Paperbacks, 29
Papyrus, 142
Paradigm, 343, 388-389
Parameters, 223
  evaluation, **337-339**, 358
Parametic user, 224
Parker, Edwin B., 379
Parker-Rhodes, A. F., 275
Parts catalog, 49, 194-195
Patents, 342

Index

Peek-a-boo cards, 175
Penney Co., J. C., 108
Pennsylvania statutes, 297
Performance, linguistic, 287
Periodicals, 39, 145
Peripheral equipment, 132, 133, 139
Permanence, 93
Permuted title index (See Keyword-in-context)
Perry, J. W., 179, 180, 181, 184, 268, 337
Personnel data, 167, 193, 204, 208, 217
Pertinancy, 337
Philips cassette, 67
Phosphor screen, 81, 83
Photocell, 40, 75, 87, 102
Photoclerk, 33
Photocomposition, 13, **21-27**, 53, 107, 290, 309
Photoconductivity, 31, 32
Photoelectric readers (See also Character recognition), 12
Photoelectric sensing, in microfilm search, 40, 269
Photography, 19, 32-33, 35, 36, 40, 43, 46, 107, 241
Photomultiplier, 70
Physical record, 207-208
Physics Review, 340
Pierce, John R., 13
Plotters, 103
Plugboard, 119, 229, 294
Pocket calculator, 83
Pointers, 213-219, 226
Polarization filtering, 102
Portable on-line terminal, 86
Post-editing, 295
Precision, 337-345, 349-350, **356-358,** 365, 366, 369
Precision devices, 273, 339
Precision Instruments, Inc., 101
Prepositional phrase method (automatic indexing), 308
Preservation, 260-261
President of the U. S., 12
Price, D. J., 7, 380, 386
Printers (See Line printers)
Printing, 16, **17-27,** 143, 196
Privacy, 204, 217
Probabilistic indexing, 265, 352
Procedural languages, 220, 228, 230-232

Processing, **16,** 207-219 (**See also** Data processing; Document processing)
Professions, 10, 391
Profiles, interest, 259, 361
Profiles, term, 272-273
Program card, 61
Program checkout, 78
Program debugging, 126
Program documentation, 126
Program maintenance, 125
Programmers, 55, 78, 103, 109, 117, 121, 125, 139, 204, 207, 211, 219-221, 224, 229-233, 262, 287, 288
Programming, 103, **117-132,** 318
Project MAC, 278
Projection printing, 31
Proofreading, 22, 60, 71, 290
Protosynthex, 323
Psychologists, 377-379
Public library, 192, 241, 245, 253, 335
Publishing, **17-27,** 28, 29, 57, 61, 242, 297
Pulsifer, Josephine, 113
Punched card, **57-61,** 64, 67, 69, 78, 118-120, 121, 197, 208, 229, 294
Punched paper tape, 21, **61-64,** 229
Putnam, Herbert, 158, 172

Question answering, 289, **323-324**
Questionnaire method (user studies), **378,** 386
Quillian, M. Ross, 329

Rabinow, Jacob, 76
Radar data, 87
Radiation, Inc., 106
Radio, 3, 59, 109
Radio Corporation of America, 70, 225
Ramac (disk), 210, 264
RAND tablet, 87, 88
Random access, 210
Random alarm (user studies), 379
Ranganathan, S. R., 184, 185, 186, 187
Rank (by relevance), 272-273, 344-345
Rapid Selector 39, 41
Rapidwrite, 230
Read/write heads,
  laser, 101-102
  magnetic, 65, 72, **90-99**
Reader (microfilm), 39, 43, 45, 46, 49
Ready reference, 149

Index 407

Reagan, Fonnie, 66
Recall, 273, 337-345, 340-350, **358-359,** 361-362, 265, 366, 369
Recall devices, 273, 339
Receiving, **244-245**
RECON (**R**emote **C**onsole) system, 281
Recordak, 37
Recording speed, 90, 92-93, 98-99, 102
Records (as data base units), 196, 198, 201-205, 207-219
Reduction ratio, 38, 45, 46, 49
Re-entry records, 69
Rees, Alan, 355
Reference, **148-149,** 165, 198, 200
Reflex method (duplication), 30, 34
Relative frequency, 308-310
Relative index, 156
Relevance, 249, 335, 341-344, **350-356,** 358, 362, 390
Relevance feedback, 346
Relevance judges, 311, 340, 344, 353-354, 356, 362, 363, 390
Remote-location computing, 5
Remote-location devices, 13, 227, 384
Report generation, 228
Reprography, 12, 19, **27-51,** 112, 261
Requester, 337, 343, 360-361
Resnick, A., 259, 354, 361-362
Resolution, 337
Resource sharing, 28, 245
Retrieval, advent of, 262
 and library methodology, 167
 and storage, 260
 and users, 375, 377
 as accident-prone process, 356-357
 as "provision of relevant responses," 351
 as selective, **16,** 286
 in data systems, 207
 in document systems, 240
 microfilm, 37, 40, 43
 with computers, **261-281**
Retrospective duplication, 27
Retrospective search, 240, 261, 365
Revere, Paul, 58
Revill, D. H., 34
Revision, 26
Revolutionary War, 58
Rhodium storage medium, 101
Richmond, Phyllis, 339

Ridenour, L. N., 165
Rider, Fremont, 145
Robertson, E. E., 357
Role indicators, 177, 180, 338, 339, 342, 349
Roman writing, 143
Rome Air Development Center, 313
Rosbury, A. H., 66
Rosen, Saul, 229
Rosetta Stone, 142
Rotary camera, 37, 43
Rotary press, 17
Royalties, 29
Russian language, 295

SAGE (Semi-**A**utomatic **G**round **E**nvironment), 87, 141, 199, 278
Salton, Gerard, 280, 307, 308, 313, 316, 343-348, 358, 362, 365, 368
Sammet, Jean, 212, 230, 232
Samuelson, Kjell, 5
Sanford, J. A., 175
Satellite, communications, 5, 111
Sawyer, Ted, 45
Schatz, V. L., 281
Schmedel, Scott R., 88
Schubert, Richard F., 216-217
Schultz, Claire, 171, 302
Schwartz, Jules, 232
Science, Government, and Information, 260
Science Newsletter, 266, 311
Scientific and Technical Aerospace Reports (STAR), 246
Scientific and technical documents, 43, 335
Scientific and technical information, **7-10,** 38, 241, 257, 367, 381
 international sharing, 5
 use of, **376-377**
Scientific management of libraries, 168
Scientific publication, growth of, 3
Scientific research library, 192
Scientist-user, as information processor, **386-392**
Scope notes, 152, 157
Search request, 343-346, 355
Search strategy, 342
Searcher (**See** requester)
Sears, Roebuck, and Company, 49

Index

Sedelow, Sally, 325
Sedgwick, Henry D., 26
Segre, Emilio, 6
Selection, 146, 222, 228, 242
Selective dissemination (SDI), 240, 259, 354, 361-362, 366-367
Selectric typewriter, 80, 107
Self-contained systems, 221-224
Semantic analysis, 316
Semantic factors, 180-184, 285
Semaphore, 58
Semiconductor memory, 133
Sentence analysis, 287
Sentence structure, 288, **316-324**
Sequential organization, 208
Sequential search, 209, 227
Serials records, 167
Shared processor (minicomputer), 65, 67
Sharp, John R., 315
Shatzkin, Leonard, 23
Shaw, Ralph R., 40
Shelf list, 153
Shell model, 253
Shera, Jesse H., 184, 255, 268
Silver halide process, 31, **32-33**, 34, 36
Simmons, Robert F., 322, 323
Simon, Newell, and Shaw, 212-213
Smart system, 313, 343-347, 368
Smart terminal, 88
Smoke signals, 58
Sobel, Alan, 86
Social effects of information growth, **10-12**
Social science, 387
Sophar, Gerald J., 29
Sorter, 60
Sorting, 57, 222, 223, 228
Source documents, 340, 341, 358
Space list, 213-215
Spaceband, 18
SPAN (System for Processing and Analysis), 225, 228
Sparck Jones, Karen, 266, 286, 289, 365
Special libraries, 145
Special purpose devices, 267-270, 273
Specifier user, 224, 227
Spelling errors, 290-291
Spirit duplication, 33
Spreitzer, F. F., 33

Stand-alone keyboarding, 64, 67
Standard Oil Company of California, 71
Standardization, 246
Stanford Research Institute, 72
Statistical phrases, 345
Stencil duplication, 30
Step-and-repeat camera, 44, 46
Stevens, Mary, 247, 275, 294
Stiles, H. Edmund, 271-273, 277, 352
Stone, D. C., 309
Stop list, 294, 300, 308
Storage, 16
  core memory, 138
  data, **207-219**
  laser, **99-102**
  magnetic, **89-99**, 102
Storage and preservation, 37, 41, 50, **260-261**
Storage capacity, 93, 98-99, 101-102
Storage density, 90, 92-93, 98-99, 101
Storage oscilloscope, 83
Storage overflow, 212
Storrer, R. L., 255
Strauss, Victor, 26
Stroke pattern character generation, 82
Stromberg Datagraphix, 107
Strong, Suzanne M., 364
Structure of information, 6, **197-206**
Structure of knowledge, 8, 156
Stursa, Mary Lou, 365
Subject catalog, 147, 185, 248
Subject classifiction (**See** classification)
Subject headings, 148, 150, 173, 185, 252, 340, 341
Subject indexing, 265, 340
Suboptimization, 360
Suffix splitting, 343, 345
Suffix variation, 306
Sumerian writing, 142
Superimposed coding, 177-179
Supreme Court, U. S., 29
Surrogates, 358, 361-363, 384 (See also Abstracts, Titles)
Swanson, D. R., 252, 311, 336, 340-341, 352, 362
Synonyms, 176, 252, 295, 301, 306, 339, 343, 345
Syntactic analysis, 289, 316, 317, 343
System analysis, 168, 172, 241
System approach, 37, 44, 220, 240

Index

System concept, 43, 189, 257
System consequences, 46, 108, 249, 261, 361, 381-383
System design, 260
System Development Corporation, 225, 230, 231, 232, 275, 276, 278, 279, 291, 311, 313, 323

TAB **(Technical Abstracts Bulletin)**, 246, 247
Tablet, RAND, 87
Tabula, 143
Tabulator, 60
Tanimoto, T. T., 275
Tape cartridge, 67, 102
Tape cassette, 67
Taube, Mortimer, 70, 171, 173, 177, 184, 268, 339, 352
Tauber, Maurice, 156
Taylor, Robert S., 172, 354
TDMS **(T**ime-Shared **D**ata **M**anagement System), 225, 226
Technological gatekeeper, 390
Telecommunications, 13, 28, 100, **109-113**, 245
Telegraph, 58, 109
Telegraphic abstract, **179-184**
Telephone, 13, 59
 use in data transmission, 5, 59, 112
 use in exchange of scientific information, 391
 use in on-line computer systems, 63, 79, 80, 110, 140, 384
Telephone books, production, 26
Teletype, 21, 26, 59, 62, 64, 78, **79**, 86, 104, 140, 141, 245
Television, 3, 5, 44, 381
Telpak communications, 111, 280
Termatrex, 175
Term diagram, 313, 363-364
Term profile, 272-273, 276
Text processing, 61
Theis, D. J., 83
Thermofax process, 31, 34
Thermography, **34**
Theory of clumps, 275
Thesaurus, 248, 255, 271, 273, 341, 343, 344, 345, 360
Thompson, Lawrence S., 175

Thompson Ramo-Wooldrdige Co. **(See also** Bunker-Ramo), 265, 311, 340-341
Thorndike, E. L., 310
3M Company, 31, 33, 35, 107
Threshold method, character recognition, 71
Tillitt, H. E., 263, 264
Time, 83, 287, 291
Time sharing, 78, **140-141,** 278, 291, 315
Titles, 291-301, 313, 345, 362, 364, 380, 384
Toffler, Alvin, 6
Topic sentence, 308, 364
Topical spectrum, 341
Transmission, future systems, 100, 110
Travis, Larry, 327
Treu, Siegfried, 313
Troller, Christina E., 356
Tungsten, 46
Turing test, 327, 328
Twohey, John C., 12
Typemetal, 17
Typesetting **(See also** Composition), **17-27,** 61
Typewriter, 19, 20, 61, 78, 79, 80, 87, 104, 107
Typography, 23, 104-108, 291

UL/1 (User Language 1), 225, 227
Ultramicrofiche, 38, **45-49**
Ultraviolet, 34
Unconditional branch, 125
Unconventional indexing systems, 340
Undertagging, 350
Unicon 190, 102
Unicon 690, 101-102
Union catalog, 144, 150, 254
United Kingdom **(See also** Great Britain, England), 279, 387
United Publishing Co., 250
United States, 3, 7, 12, 43, 279
Unitization, 38, 39, 40, 46
Univac DCT 500, 79
Universal Decimal Classification, **159-161,,** 185, 340
University libraries, 167, 258
University of Pennsylvania, 264
Updatable microfiche, **50-51**
Updating, 65, 96, 210, 222, 225, 227, 228

410 Index

User needs, 354-355
User studies, 356, **377-386**
User study reviews, 380-383

V-mail, 37, 41
Value of information, **366-370**
Van Dam, Andries, 88
Variable format, variable field file arrangement, 202
Variable length items, 202
Varian Associates, 31
Veaner, Allen, 32
Vehicle identification system, 209
Verification, 22, 23, **60**, 64, 78
Vickery, Brian C., 180, 184, 187, 387, 389
Video, 59, 90, 92, 111
Viewer (**See** Reader)
Vocabulary 342, 343, 361
Vulnerability (microfiche), 45

Ward, J. H., Jr, 276
Warheit, J. A., 176
Wattenberg, Ben J., 204
Webster's Seventh New Collegiate Dictionary, 289
Weights, 265, 341, 352
Weinberg, A. M., 253
Weisman, Herman M., 9
Weizebaum, Joseph, 328
Welles, Orson, 246
Westbrook, J. H., 380
Western Europe, 279
Western Reserve University, 179, 180, 181, 184, 187, 268, 285

Weston, Paul, 327
Whatmore, Geoffrey, 254, 257
Wheel printer, 105
Wheeler, Harvey, 11
Whirlwind I computer, 267
White light, 30
Wiener, Norbert, 152
Wilks, Yorick, 325
Williams & Wilkins vs the U. S. Government, 29
Wire services, 242, 244, 246
Wood, D. N., 378
Woods, Allen, 17
Wooster, Harold, 365
Word co-occurrence, 270-277
Word frequency, 266, **301-316**
Word pairs, 301
Word types, tokens, 301
Wyllys, Ronald E., 266, 308, 309

X-rays, 32, 241
Xerography, 32, **35**, 36
Xerox process, 30, 34, 35

Yellow light, 33
Youden, W. W., 296

Zaphiropoulos, Renn, 106
Zator Corp., 177, 179
Zientara, Peggy, 88
Zinc oxide, 31, 33
Zipf rank-frequency relation, 300, 301
Zunde, Pranas, 359

147983